Of Religion and Empire

Of Religion and Empire

Missions, Conversion, and Tolerance in Tsarist Russia

Edited by

ROBERT P. GERACI and
MICHAEL KHODARKOVSKY

CORNELL UNIVERSITY PRESS

Ithaca and London

First published 2001 by Cornell University Press
First printing, Cornell Paperbacks, 2001

Printed in the United States of America

Library of Congress Cataloging-in-Publication Data

Of religion and empire : missions, conversion, and tolerance in Tsarist Russia / edited by Robert P. Geraci and Michael Khodarkovsky.
    p. cm.
   Includes index.
    ISBN 0-8014-3327-4 (alk. paper)—ISBN 0-8014-8703-X (pbk. : alk. paper)
    1. Russia—Religion. 2. Russia—Church history. 3. Religion and state—Russia—History. 4. Church and state—Russia—History. 5. Russkaia pravoslavnaia tserkov'—History.   I. Geraci, Robert P.
II. Khodarkovsky, Michael, 1955–
   BL980.R8 O36 2001
   200'.947—dc21

                           00-010885

Cornell University Press strives to use environmentally responsible suppliers and materials to the fullest extent possible in the publishing of its books. Such materials include vegetable-based, low-VOC inks and acid-free papers that are recycled, totally chlorine-free, or partly composed of nonwood fibers. Books that bear the logo of the FSC (Forest Stewardship Council) use paper taken from forests that have been inspected and certified as meeting the highest standards for environmental and social responsibility. For further information, visit our website at www.cornellpress.cornell.edu.

Cloth printing   10   9 8 7 6 5 4 3 2 1
Paperback printing   10   9 8 7 6 5 4 3 2 1

Publication of this book was made possible, in part, by grants from Loyola University Chicago and the University of Virginia.

Contents

CONTENTS

Of Religion and Empire

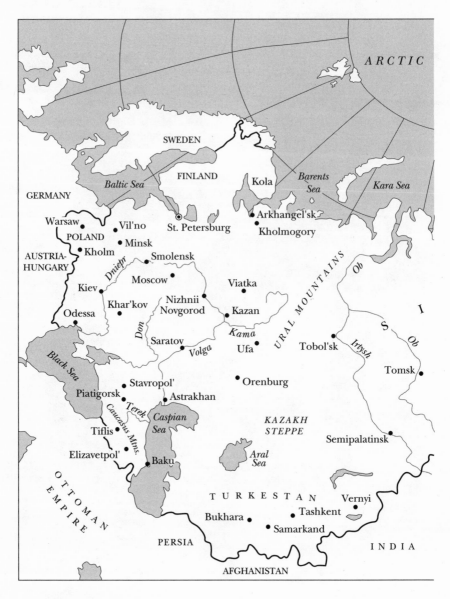

The Russian Empire in 1900

OCEAN

ALASKA

Bering
Sea

Kamchatka

S I B E R I A

Lena

Enisei

Sea
of
Okhotsk

Sakhalin

Krasnoiarsk

Lake
Baikal

Amur

Irkutsk

Nerchinsk

Chita

Kiakhta

MANCHURIA

Vladivostok

MONGOLIA

C H I N A

KOREA

0   500   1000 Miles

Introduction

Between the sixteenth and twentieth centuries the Russian state dramatically expanded its territory and its power in both Europe and Asia. In the process, it acquired not only one-sixth of the earth's land mass, but a multitude of peoples adhering to an enormous variety of languages, ways of life, and belief systems. Like any other state, Russia had rational grounds for desiring some greater measure of homogeneity among its subject peoples: to bring them under firmer and more efficient control, to prevent disorder, and to secure the polity and society from external forces and influences.

The pursuit of greater uniformity was a matter of ideology as much as pragmatism, however. Over these four centuries, at least four major ideological trends served to justify imperial domination and to inspire specific policies toward populations in the borderlands. All four envisioned certain changes in the lives of subject peoples, and can therefore be thought of as doctrines of social and cultural transformation. First was Christian evangelism or messianism, which was particularly visible in Moscow's policies toward newly conquered non-Christian peoples in the early modern period. During the eighteenth century there emerged the notion of Russia's civilizing mission; in the nineteenth century, nationalism (first articulated in Nicholas I's principle of "Official Nationality"); and finally, in the twentieth century, Marxism-Leninism. These ideologies, of course, were not always mutually exclusive and did not replace one another in discrete succession, but were overlaid each upon the previous one, producing a many-layered complex of motivations and programs for social and cultural change.

Of all the various axes of diversity in the Russian empire, this book seeks to explore the role and the fate of religions. Religions have been the carriers of basic values and identities for a longer time than any other human institutions. With respect to the most prominent and organized of the religions, Robert Hefner notes in *Conversion to Christianity*, "Political empires and economic systems have come and gone, but the world religions have survived. . . . Their genius lies in their curious ability to renounce this world and announce another, more compelling and true. They relocate the divisive solidarities of language, custom, and region within a broader community and higher Truth."[1]

In many multireligious societies, however, such traditions have acted as both centrifugal and centripetal forces. The Russian empire was home to variants of at least four of the great world religions—Christianity, Islam, Judaism, and Buddhism. And there, competing on the basis of claims to ultimate truth and visions of unity, these durable and potent religions themselves became sources of "divisive solidarities." Each became associated historically with a particular set of languages, customs, and regions. And all were challenged (though certainly in different ways and to vastly unequal degrees) to make profound institutional, social, and even doctrinal adaptations in the course of these encounters and rivalries. The more localized animist, polytheistic, or shamanistic belief systems of many of the empire's inhabitants often underwent the most dramatic changes of all because they became targets of proselytizing by the world religions.

There is to date no general study of religious diversity in the Russian empire and its ramifications. The few works that compare the treatment of various non-Orthodox religions are limited to superficial institutional accounts of missionary activities of the Russian Orthodox Church.[2] Such works are typically confined to church history and fail to discuss the broader political, social, and cultural contexts in which religious minori-

---

[1] Robert W. Hefner, "World Building and the Rationality of Conversion," in idem, ed., *Conversion to Christianity* (Berkeley, Calif., 1993), 34.

[2] The principal histories of Russian religious missions are Eugene Smirnoff, *A Short Account of the Historical Development and Present Position of Russian Orthodox Missions* (London, 1903); Serge Bolshakoff, *The Foreign Missions of the Russian Orthodox Church* (New York, 1943); Josef Glazik, *Die russisch-orthodoxe Heidenmission seit Peter dem Grossen* (Münster, 1954); idem, *Die Islammission der russisch-orthodoxen Kirche* (Münster, 1959); and Igor Smolitsch, *Geschichte der russischen Kirche*, vol. 2, ed. Gregory L. Freeze, Forschungen zur osteuropäischen Geschichte, vol. 45 (Wiesbaden, 1991).

A recent book that successfully draws religion into a general account of ethno-national diversity in the Russian empire is Andreas Kappeler, *Russland als Vielvölkerreich* (Munich, 1992).

Some other works address the treatment of specific religious groups at specific times. On Islam, see L. I. Klimovich, *Islam v tsarskoi Rossii* (Moscow, 1936). On sectarians, see A. I. Klibanov, *History of Religious Sectarianism in Russia, 1860s–1917* (Oxford, 1982). Considerable information on policies toward Old Believers can be found in John S. Curtiss, *Church and State in Russia, 1900–1917* (New York, 1965).

ties' experiences and identities were shaped. In our view, the historical study of religious communities must acknowledge from the outset that, especially in an imperial context, confessional identities intersect and intertwine with many other identities. Accordingly, research must be undertaken from several different angles at once.[3] The collapse of the Soviet empire has brought ethnic, national, and religious identities to the fore, led scholars to perceive new directions for research, and improved dramatically the accessibility of resources for future work.

The particular questions addressed in this volume include the following: What views of human identity prevailed in Russia, and where did religion fit into ideologies of social integration? How successful were attempts to convert subject peoples to Orthodoxy? How did the adherents of various religious communities experience subjecthood in the Russian empire and how did they react to it? How were the categories of Orthodoxy and Russianness themselves shaped or affected by the religious diversity of the empire? Since this book is the first attempt to pose these questions in a broad way, we by no means regard it as a comprehensive or definitive account. Rather, it is a reconnaissance mission into a new field that will grow in sophistication for years to come.

Historians of religious missions in the modern world have long perceived the involvement of the Russian state in spiritual matters as extraordinary compared with that of other governments. "It is characteristic of Russian missions, almost without exception," writes Stephen Neill, "that the connection between Church and state has been so close that it is almost impossible to separate the work [of missions] into its constituent elements."[4] Such a perception is largely justified. First, the Russians' field of religious activity was unique. Since there was no clear geographical demarcation between Russia's metropolis and its empire, the state frequently conflated the two, giving policies in the borderlands (including religious ones) a "domestic" importance not accorded to the administration of overseas colonies by other European powers. Revealingly, the Russian state was much less involved in the Orthodox Church's "foreign" missions in places such as Palestine, China, Japan, and Korea. Unlike Christian missions in so many other parts of the world, Russian missions typically followed military and political conquest; only in rare instances (such as that described in Sergei Kan's essay on Alaska in this volume) did they precede it. To an unusual extent the Russian church's outlook became saturated with the official ideologies promoted by the Russian au-

[3] Again, Kappeler adopts this approach in his monograph *Russlands erste Nationalitäten* (Münster, 1982); see also Gregory L. Bruess, *Religion, Identity, and Empire: A Greek Archbishop in the Russia of Catherine the Great* (Boulder, Colo., 1997). Each of these books provides a case study that integrates religious policies toward minorities into a sophisticated overall account.
[4] Stephen Neill, *A History of Christian Missions*, 2d ed. (London, 1986), 182.

3

tocracy. By the early twentieth century many missionaries were describing their work in terms of patriotism as well as piety, and the church was willing to use nationalistic arguments (and even alliances with radical nationalist movements) in defending its turf against the threat of new legislation on religious toleration between 1905 and 1917.

On the other hand, one must not submit to the traditional yet erroneous assumption that the Russian Orthodox Church was just one of many organs under state control, and had no autonomy or initiative. Gregory Freeze, for instance, has argued convincingly that the establishment of the Holy Synod, far from putting all church functions into the hands of the state, effected a strict separation between secular and spiritual spheres. The church was not "secularized" (as many scholars had maintained before Freeze) but rather became more intensely "spiritualized," while the state organs became significantly more secular. As a result of the reform, the Orthodox Church received an ecclesiastical domain parallel to the state's, which amounted to a "monopoly over the spiritual affairs of Orthodox citizens, a realm of activity that embraced liturgy, missions, education and religious thought" as well as the lives of Orthodox clergy, and which also had considerable importance in the marital and judicial affairs of lay Orthodox.[5] Neill's assertion notwithstanding, it is certainly possible to describe the distinct roles and activities of church and state with regard to the treatment of minority confessions as well.

As an established religion, Orthodoxy and its church enjoyed several key advantages (granted by the state) over other religions in the empire. In the Muscovite period and afterward, it was never questioned that the royal family must be Orthodox. Membership in the church, as a sign of political loyalty, was often a precondition for social mobility and financial exemptions and privileges. Most significantly, only Orthodox subjects and institutions could proselytize. Conversion away from the Orthodox Church to any other religion was illegal and severely punished. While marriages between Orthodox and non-Christian subjects were also illegal, those between Orthodox and non-Orthodox Christians were permitted from the time of Peter the Great, as long as the children from such marriages were raised as Orthodox. In principle, the church was represented in the tsar's closest circle of advisers by the Supreme Procurator of the Holy Synod, while no other religious institution had political influence at such a high level. Until 1905, clergy and other personnel of the Orthodox Church alone were granted exemption from military service. No attacks on the church (or on Christianity in general) were allowed in print, and the church had its own censorship organ to protect its public image.

[5] G. L. Freeze, "Handmaiden of the State? The Church in Imperial Russia Reconsidered," *Journal of Ecclesiastical History* 36, no. 1 (1985): 82–102; see esp. 89–90.

With regard to other religions, however, the Orthodox Church's prerogatives were quite limited; it held no spiritual monopoly over most of the non-Orthodox. Its formal and direct influence on religious minorities was confined principally to the proselytizing activities of its clergy. Beginning in the 1860s, the church could also form semi-independent church brotherhoods or missionary organizations to provide non-state financial and societal support for the propagation of Orthodoxy. Indirectly, the church could aim to limit the illicit spread of other faiths by educating and serving the needs of its own members so as to keep them in the church. It could and did also exercise indirect influence through the participation of the Supreme Procurator in high-level discussions of policies pertaining to the non-Orthodox.

But it was the state, as the guarantor of the Orthodox Church's privileged position, that determined in what ways other religions would be legally tolerated or persecuted. Even after the establishment of the Holy Synod in 1721, secular organs devised incentives for conversion and punishments for failure to convert. Beginning in the reign of Catherine II, the state created special administrative organs outside the Orthodox Church for the governance of several of the most prominent minority religions. The state stood at the apex of each one, appointing the clerics who ran them. These institutions, which in 1832 were transferred to the Ministry of Internal Affairs under the rubric of the Department of Spiritual Affairs of Foreign Confessions, functioned as Holy Synods for non-Orthodox religions. They set the formal parameters in which minority religions were professed, regulating the training and appointment of clergy, the confessional schooling of children and youth, the publication of religious texts, the building of sites of worship, and some specific religious practices such as pilgrimages. Such regulations were enforced by the state's secular judicial and police bureaucracies.

Not only did the Orthodox Church's proselytizing have to conform to a legal climate determined by the state; its success or failure might also depend on specific state interventions in the form of budget allocations, police reinforcement, or enabling legislation (for instance, the education ministry's approval of mission schools). Many of the formalities in the process of conversion itself, even if executed by the church and at its will, were also determined by civil law. These forms of dependence, which may sometimes have characterized the churches of Western Europe within the boundaries of particular countries but had less impact on their activities abroad, have led representatives of Protestant and Catholic missions to perceive the Orthodox missions as fully controlled by the state.

Thus, evaluating the experience of religious minorities in the Russian empire requires one to examine what Peter Waldron has called the "triangular" relationship between Orthodox Church, Russian state, and minority religions in the late imperial period (the period addressed by the majority of the essays in this volume).[6] What generalizations can be made about the dynamics within this triangle? Occasionally, state decrees forced the church to conform to state religious policy, usually by prohibiting missionary work. Such was the case in 1767, when Catherine II forbade the Orthodox Church from engaging in the conversion of non-Orthodox before instituting "enlightened" religious toleration in 1773. A century later, General K. P. von Kaufman persuaded Alexander II to bar the church's missionaries from newly conquered Central Asia for fear that Christian proselytizing would provoke the Muslims' intractable dissent. But decrees were not always necessary for the alignment of church and state policies. As Theodore Weeks shows in this volume, for example, in 1839 church and state collaborated (possibly with the church taking the lead) in outlawing the Uniate religion and converting its members en masse to Orthodoxy.

Frequently, however, state and church policies pulled in opposite directions. State bureaucrats might be permissive toward the forms of worship among a particular population while the church aggressively pursued conversion. For example, when the state broadened religious toleration in April 1905, it did not put a halt to all missions; in fact, the church's determination to convert became more pronounced to compensate for other religious groups' new right to proselytize and convert. Less often, bureaucrats might put limitations on a group's religious practices or expression at a time when the church was not pursuing conversion. Such was the case with regard to most of the empire's Muslims during the last several decades of tsarism: missions to Muslims were virtually extinct, yet the Ministries of Education and the Interior were zealously enforcing draconian restrictions on Islamic clergy and schools. Such differences in policy sometimes reflected important philosophical differences between church and state, just as different authorities within each bureaucracy might be able to follow somewhat contradictory aims without anybody intervening to enforce uniformity. As is evident in several of the essays here, state bureaucrats were far less likely than clerical authorities to favor the pursuit of religious conversion.

Yet a preference for tolerant policies, as Freeze has noted, was as likely to be motivated by pragmatism or realpolitik as by enlightened principles.[7] Even conservatives (lay or clerical) who embraced an ideology of far-reaching religious and cultural homogenization of the empire's peoples were often reluctant to pursue it at a given moment on the grounds

[6] Peter Waldron, "Religious Toleration in Late Imperial Russia," in *Civil Rights in Imperial Russia*, ed. Olga Crisp and Linda Edmondson (Oxford, 1989), 103–19.
[7] Freeze, "Handmaiden of the State?" 92–93.

that it would provoke widespread opposition, threatening law and order. Ambitions to convert the non-Orthodox were also thwarted by financial shortages and a dearth of well-educated and enthusiastic personnel. For such reasons—not because of widespread liberal attitudes or indifference to the challenge of other religions—missions never attained paramount significance or priority among Russian imperial strategies. Seemingly contradictory policies, therefore, might often be linked in perfectly logical ways: when a policy of conversion or repression in one sphere was deemed risky or impracticable, pressure might be exerted in another.

It is important at this point to emphasize that the Russian term *veroterpimost'* ("religious toleration" or "religious tolerance") was defined vaguely and ambiguously in tsarist Russia. Though it did have the connotation of a moral virtue, it rarely implied absolute freedom of worship or "freedom of conscience" (*svoboda sovesti*) and was not based on any notion of civil or human rights.[8] Freedom of conscience as such did emerge as both a demand and a topic of official discussion around 1905. After April 17, the law in theory allowed for conversion from Orthodoxy to other Christian denominations. But the church stalled on honoring the law fully or extending it to non-Christian faiths, and largely because of its opposition none of the Duma legislation using the term *svoboda sovesti* was ever passed between 1906 and the fall of tsarism in February 1917.[9]

Russian statesmen in the nineteenth century frequently used the word *veroterpimost'* to describe their policies. Yet the only common denominator in all such instances was the absence of a policy of forced conversion. Official tolerance of Judaism or Buddhism or Old Belief meant, for example, that the state would not punish a person simply for professing one of these religions. But if one had ever been a member of the Orthodox Church, it was still illegal for him or her to *become* a Jew or Buddhist or Old Believer; one's religion was not a matter of choice or preference. At most times, the practice of so-called "tolerated" religions was subject to various terms and conditions, sometimes including ones so strict that they might pressure people to violate core beliefs or abandon long-held religious traditions. The church might have missionaries proselytizing to discredit a "tolerated" religion and encourage conversion. It also bears mention that even without official consent, forced conversion could be practiced if local authorities or clergy were sufficiently determined. At all times, religious minorities were in effect second-class subjects of the empire.

Church and state personnel were aware of the ambiguity of the term, and sometimes invoked it hypocritically to fend off the complaints of sub-

[8] See Michael Walzer's description of multinational empires as an archetypal "regime of toleration" in *On Toleration* (New Haven, Conn., 1997), 14–19.
[9] Raymond Pearson, "Privileges, Rights, and Russification," in Crisp and Edmonson, *Civil Rights in Imperial Russia*, 85–102.

ject peoples or the criticisms of foreign commentators. They might also use it as a moral or principled disguise for hands-off policies they espoused only begrudgingly and regretfully. In a similar way, as some of the essays here suggest, officials often avoided inflammatory words such as "conversion" or "Christianization" by grasping at often dubious historical precedents in order to re-package missionary campaigns as acts of "reunion" or "re-Christianization." Such rhetoric, it appears, did not often succeed among the subject peoples; they too were usually aware of how various terms could be manipulated.

This brings us to the religious minorities themselves. What were the effects of Russian religious policies and attitudes on them? By all accounts, vastly more people were converted to Orthodoxy during the sixteenth, seventeenth, and eighteenth centuries than in the nineteenth or early twentieth. More were adherents of animist or polytheistic belief systems than of established world religions. Still, although church and government often boasted impressive numbers of converts in the earlier centuries, many of these conversions were merely nominal. Once Russian authorities in the early nineteenth century began to engage in serious discussions of method and self-consciously renounced tactics such as bribery and coercion in favor of a more exclusively spiritual approach to religious identity, their success was even more limited. Even when proselytizing was apparently successful, it remains questionable whether this was for the reasons intended by church and state. Thus, some of the essays here suggest that "voluntary" conversion was often achieved only among the weakest and most vulnerable individuals within subject populations: those extracted from their communities by force or circumstance, who resided among Russians, were economically dependent, and had already experienced significant extrareligious Russification. Some argue that most conversions were undertaken to overcome social discrimination or to enhance economic opportunities. Church and state officials were usually hard pressed to identify many cases of conversion in which religious conscience played a major role.

Despite the questionable efficacy of conversion efforts, Russian attempts to engineer the religious uniformity of the empire often had profound influences on subject populations. However, many of the most important consequences of church and state intervention were unintended and indirect. To understand better these consequences, one must examine the day-to-day implementation of policies on the local level, the minority communities' responses to these policies, and the sociocultural, economic, and geographical factors surrounding these peoples' religious traditions. Obviously, sources for this kind of analysis have usually been less accessible than those on central Russian institutions and perspectives. Using these sources requires extensive research in provincial and remote parts of the former Russian empire (which became possible for foreigners only in about 1991), and in many cases research in multiple languages. This collection may represent only the beginning phase of such research; we hope that it will provide tentative hypotheses on the subject while spurring others to further work.

Nonetheless, several of the essays here, including two written by cultural anthropologists, do focus considerable attention on subject ethnic and religious communities. These contributions describe several ways in which the targeted communities adapted to official restrictions so as to preserve their traditions and options, challenged or resisted efforts to undermine their cultures, or selectively absorbed Russian and Orthodox influences. Even when such resistance was successful and cultures survived, however, important social and cultural transformations often took place—emigration movements, changes in the authority or credibility of clergy or elites, the emergence and spread of alternative doctrines, violent social conflict within or between ethnic groups, changes in family life, the loss of economic or cultural opportunities, impoverishment.

One of the most important long-term consequences was growing political discontent in many borderland and minority regions. Increasingly throughout the nineteenth century, nationalism was espoused by these groups as an ideology of self-assertion and defense against Russian intervention. By the twentieth century, even some peoples whose faiths had traditionally been left alone—such as Estonians, Latvians, and Armenians—were newly subjected to religious pressures and regulations by the Russian state and church. In these and other cases, socialist as well as liberal movements benefited from such grievances. The persecution of Old Believers and sectarians backfired by alienating many ethnic Russians, bringing sympathy to these religions, and making them beacons for dissent and resistance. The grievances of all such groups, and their opposition to the Russian autocratic-imperial system as a whole, contributed to the rapid breakdown of state and empire in 1905 and 1917. With confessional differences having become so closely bound up with the formation of ethnic, national, and political identities, the Bolsheviks faced formidable obstacles in their attempt to isolate and destroy the religious affiliations of their subjects while preserving other forms of identity.

In the first essay of this volume, Georg Michels describes the establishment of Orthodox institutions in the northernmost part of European Russia by focusing on the life of the seventeenth-century archbishop Afanasii Liubimov. Central to this process was Afanasii's vigorous proselytizing of Old Believers in the region, and his often brutal persecution of those who would not conform to the reformed Nikonian church. Afanasii considered the religions of native peoples and Western European immigrants

much less threatening than Old Belief, and did not give priority to converting these people, except in cases where they had also been influenced
by Old Belief. Michels also draws attention to the close connection between the mission against Old Belief and Afanasii's measures for increasing the discipline of the mainstream Orthodox population.

Eugene Clay's essay shows that the struggle to define Orthodoxy continued long after the seventeenth century. In the last decades of the
imperial period, in fact, the church's efforts to combat old and new heresies became even more vigorous with the establishment of a special corps
of missionaries. The "Orthodox heresies" this article discusses did not reject the official church (as did the Old Believers and many sectarian
movements of the time); rather, they moved in charismatic, mystical, and
communal directions precisely at a time when official Orthodoxy was becoming more standardized and rationalized under the influence of the
theological academies. The missions Clay describes, therefore, resembled
Counter-Reformation campaigns against unauthorized popular piety. Yet
Orthodox missionaries and hierarchs could not always agree on which
groups were heretical and which were not.

In his analysis of the Russian assaults on the Uniate church in the nineteenth century, Theodore Weeks captures the complex interweaving of
ethnic, national, and religious categories in the Western Provinces of the
empire, as well as the way in which these categories were politicized by officialdom. Government and church authorities were loath to tolerate
even the mere existence of the Uniate faith, seeing it as a front for a cen-
turies-old Polish-Catholic campaign to take control of an essentially Orthodox population. They claimed that the Uniates were descendants of
Orthodox Russians who had been forced to practice Catholicism against
their will, and therefore that it was their inevitable "historical destiny" to
be spiritually "reunited" with the Russians. In his account of the forced
"reunions" of the Uniates with Orthodoxy in 1839 and 1875, Weeks argues that these events, though ultimately welcomed and supported by the
Russian state and church, were not the outcome of an overarching plan
originating in St. Petersburg; the chief orchestrators and players, in 1839
and 1875 respectively, were a zealous, supposedly Uniate cleric and a
provincial governor. But the exclusively nominal nature of these conversions became clear in the wake of the 1905 Edict of Toleration, when tens
of thousands of Uniate "persisters" returned to their faith en masse. In
the view of Russian officials, this was not only an abandonment of Orthodoxy, but also of Russian nationality.

The contribution of John Klier's essay on the conversion of Jews in the
Russian empire is to show that, notwithstanding the earlier claims of Jewish historians, the government's efforts to proselytize among Jews were
unsystematic and ambivalent. The most concerted effort at conversion

was the cantonist system of recruiting Jewish youths into the Russian army, which flourished during the reign of Nicholas I. Even here, religious conversion was not the original intention; it was pursued systematically only in the 1840s and 1850s, and was facilitated by the local Jewish communities' preference for sending underage boys into military service. Aside from the cantonists, Klier argues, the small number of Jewish converts to Orthodoxy in the tsarist period changed their religion not out of conviction or coercion but to escape legal discrimination in education or marriage.

Shifting our attention away from European Russia, Michael Khodarkovsky's essay traces the development of Russian missionary efforts in the southern and eastern parts of the Russian empire from medieval times through the eighteenth century. During this time, enormous numbers of animists and Muslims in the Volga, Ural, and Siberian regions were converted to Christianity. Khodarkovsky explores the rise of a key tension in Russian conversion practices that resonates throughout the other essays in the volume. This is the conflict between the temptation to use "carrot and stick" methods of conversion that were the most efficacious in the short run—material incentives, the pressure of laws, and outright coercion—and the occasional awareness that in the long run such means did not always lead to sustained Christian religiosity or loyalty to the Russian state. Khodarkovsky concludes that a high degree of government involvement was the single most striking feature of Russia's missionary activity.

Though Orthodox missions were generally successful among animist peoples, even some descendants of animists who had converted to Orthodoxy between the sixteenth and eighteenth centuries sought to revive their old beliefs and practices in the 19th century. Such an "animist reformation" among the Maris is the subject of Paul Werth's contribution to the volume. Despite the attempts of the Russian reformer N. I. Il'minskii to decouple Orthodoxy and Russianness in the popular mind, many people continued to view them as synonymous. To some Maris, to be both Orthodox and Mari (as Il'minskii taught many to identify themselves) seemed a grotesque contradiction. In this sense, the Mari animist revival was no less than a small nationalist movement seeking to reestablish a separate and "pure" Mari identity. Werth shows, however, that the reform movement was not simply a revival of old beliefs. Rather, its ideas and rhetoric represented a syncretic accomodation of Christian rationalizing influences into the Maris' worldview: in Werth's words, an "internal conversion."

In an essay on the Orthodox missions in Alaska before and after the territory's sale to the United States, Sergei Kan suggests that the colonial context in which the church operated was a key variable in its proselytizing activity. In contrast to continental Russia, Alaska was never fully taken under Russian governmental control. It was settled and governed by private companies chartered by the state to engage in fur trading. Before the arrival of church missionaries, merchants routinely baptized native inhabitants in order to use them as cheap labor. Eventually, at the request of the Russian American Company, the Holy Synod sent missionaries to Alaska. The missionaries pitched their approach to the conversion of Alaskans squarely against the exploitative practices of the company, playing a role that in Siberia might well have put them at odds with the Russian government.

The nineteenth-century missionary Ivan Veniaminov, seeing the Alaskan peoples as noble savages and reacting to the abuses of the merchants, used a particularly tolerant, voluntaristic approach to conversion. This stressed the use of native languages and education, and allowed for the accommodation of some native rituals to Christianity. The sale of Alaska to the United States in 1867 and the withdrawal of the Russian American Company, ironically, enhanced the influence of Orthodoxy among the native peoples. In part to compete with Protestantism, and in part because they had no other choice, the missions became even more tolerant of native customs. Ultimately, the Russian religion proved more appealing than the more heavy-handed approach of the American churches and government.

Dittmar Schorkowitz examines a century of Russian rule over two peoples practicing Tibetan Buddhism or Lamaism, the Kalmyks and the Buriats. Initially, the Russian government supported Buddhism (while trying to cut it off from influences outside the Russian borders) as a way of consolidating Russian control over shamanistic peoples of eastern Siberia and the shores of the Caspian. In the case of the Buriats, in the eighteenth century the state had established oversight over Buddhism by means of an imperial ecclesiastical hierarchy. Under Nicholas I, this liberal approach was opposed by officials working to diminish the lamas' influence. (The official framework of Lamaist organization remained in place until the end of the tsarist era, however, thanks to the resistance of the lamas at its head.) Simultaneously, the state began to counteract both Lamaism and shamanism by supporting Orthodox missions established among the Buriats. With the founding of the Orthodox Missionary Society, Schorkowitz argues, the Buriat mission became an integral part of state policy, and broadened its focus from proselytizing among a small elite to mass conversions.

By the middle of the nineteenth century a similar alliance of spiritual and secular powers had emerged in the Caspian region, where conversion was used to facilitate the settlement of Kalmyk nomads. There, however, the church's views frequently clashed with those of the Ministry of State

Domains, which supported conversion but insisted on its duty to preserve toleration and Lamaist interests. (As a result, fewer Kalmyks than Buriats were converted.) Both missions were officially abandoned in 1905. As with the Uniates (but despite the limited application of the toleration law to non-Christians), thousands of Buriat converts returned to Lamaism and shamanism. A controversy ensued between the Holy Synod and the state, in which the former opposed reconversion by calling it a nationalist movement and a political threat, whereas the latter stood by the policy of toleration. After 1917, a brief Lamaist revival incorporated revolutionary activism, but by the end of the 1920s the Bolsheviks had effectively crushed the practice of Lamaism.

Notwithstanding aggressive conversion campaigns and persecution of Muslims in the Volga region in the sixteenth to eighteenth centuries, in the nineteenth century Russian authorities approached Islam with far greater caution and hesitation than they did the religions of Orthodox heretics, Uniates, Jews, animists, or Buddhists. Three essays in this volume discuss Russian aspirations and attempts to Christianize Muslims in various parts of the empire, addressing the concerns and obstacles that account for the high degree of caution and low degree of success.

In the eighteenth- and nineteenth-century Caucasus Firouzeh Mostashari finds contrasting approaches taken in different subregions, depending on both historical and strategic considerations. In the western and central Caucasian highlands, where Byzantine Christianity had once been professed, the intensity of Islamic faith was thought to be very limited. The Holy Synod, optimistic that the region could be "re-Christianized," organized a commission in the mid-eighteenth century to pursue the conversion and education of the highlanders. It seems significant, though, that the commission employed Georgian Orthodox rather than Russian clergy. Interrupted by the emergence of the Muslim murid movement and the Russian war against Shamil and his guerrillas, missionary efforts did not reappear until 1860. In that year secular authorities founded a society aiming for the "resurrection" of Christianity in the Caucasus—this word (as in the use of "reunion" in the West, according to Weeks) being a rhetorical device to allay fears of conversion to an alien religion by force.

In eastern Caucasia and Transcaucasia, where Islam was more deeply entrenched and supported by proximity to the Persian and Ottoman empires, Russian policy was oriented toward preventing extremism and conflict by allowing wide autonomy to a subset of "official" Muslim clergy (*ulema*) in their traditional activities. After Shamil's capture in 1859, however, officials were able to pursue the actual integration of the *ulema* into Russian bureaucracy and the close control of all religious activities by a muftiate. Mostashari shows why this policy backfired and created tensions between different types of clergy. Many lower clerics invited help in from beyond the borders, whereas the Russian-salaried clergy became discredited in the eyes of Caucasian Muslims.

Agnès Kefeli's essay, like Werth's, brings to the forefront the reactions of imperial subjects to religious change imposed by the Russian state. Focusing on the Volga region in the nineteenth century, Kefeli describes forms of passive and active resistance practiced by Tatars and Kriashens attempting to preserve their communal ways. Though there was no large-scale uprising in the Volga after Pugachev, Kefeli helps to explain why the Russians were unable to stop mass defections of the Kriashens, much less effect conversions to Orthodoxy. She does so by invoking two factors traditionally neglected in studies of Muslim peoples: women and Sufi religious traditions. Women, Kefeli argues, exercised considerable influence in religious matters by virtue of their roles outside of the family. By analyzing popular Sufi literature and the ways in which it influenced women's worldview, Kefeli suggests that Tatar women played an important role in preserving Islamic teachings and customs among fellow Muslims and in spreading them to Christianized Tatars.

The subject of Robert Geraci's essay is the belated and short-lived attempt by the Russian Orthodox Church to spread Christianity among the Muslims of the Kazakh steppe. As in the Caucasus, the church justified these missionary efforts by claiming that Islam among the Kazakhs was established only superficially. Unlike the Caucasus, however, the steppe became an area of heavy Russian settlement while the missionaries worked there. For Geraci, then, the Kazakh mission provides an opportunity to investigate Russians' own identities. Using the missionaries' writings, he shows that the church's attention to the Kazakhs was overshadowed by its preoccupation with the spiritual condition of the settlers. Geraci also portrays the identity of the missionaries themselves as problematic: though in principle they were spreading Russian culture and civilization along with religion, many were ill-disposed to this role because they were themselves members of ethnic minorities. Their training under the influence of Il'minskii had bolstered their non-Russian consciousness and pride at the expense of a Russian identity. When local Russian communities proved uncooperative or actively hostile toward the Kazakhs' conversion and Russification, some missionaries grew to doubt the feasibility of their own work. Like others in the volume, Geraci also finds evidence of church-state conflicts over missions; as elsewhere, missionaries struggled with state bureaucrats for the support they needed.

The last chapter in the volume, by Shoshana Keller, ventures beyond the tsarist period to explore the ways in which the Soviet atheism campaign resembled a mission of religious conversion. In Central Asia, the campaign was far more than a challenge to the precepts of Islam, as it had also to divorce the previous rituals, customs, holidays, and festivals from Islamic tradition. The government also sought to replace Islam with Marxism-Leninism, itself a quasi-religion in Keller's view. Keller describes the debates over what kind of propaganda should be used against Islam. Particularly interesting in the context of this volume is the view put forth by Sultan Galiev that a positive, constructive approach was needed: blunt attacks on Islam might seem to Muslims a continuation of imperial missions against their faith.

Despite this warning, the aggressive anti-Islamic campaign undertaken by the Soviet state in the later half of the 1920s stressed negative themes—the Muslim clergy's legacy of oppressing and exploiting the people, and its oppression of women in particular—in addition to positive emphasis on the replacement of religion by scientific knowledge. Keller describes how the campaign was tailored to fit the economic initiatives of collectivization and industrialization, and how it coexisted with early policies of nurturing national identities. Eventually, although antireligion activists turned to violent and coercive means, the campaign failed to replace Islam with Marxism-Leninism; rather, it often led to a strange hybrid of the two. A new breed of local Party members syncretically reconciled their political views with their Islamic heritage, calling themselves "Muslim Communists" or even "Muslim atheists."

Collectively, the essays in this volume represent a point of departure for studies of religious identities in Russian imperial history, not a completed set of conclusions. Clearly, only a limited subset of the many regions, religions, and peoples of the Russian empire have been included here. It is our hope, still, that the volume will provide readers with a new awareness of the complexities of the Russian imperial experience.

I

THE WESTERN REGIONS: CHRISTIANS AND JEWS

CHAPTER ONE

Rescuing the Orthodox: The Church Policies of Archbishop Afanasii of Kholmogory, 1682–1702

GEORG MICHELS

Archbishop Afanasii Liubimov was one of the most powerful bishops of the late Muscovite period to promote the cause of Orthodox Christianity among his contemporaries. For twenty years after late 1682, when he became the first leader of the new diocese of Kholmogory in northern Russia, Afanasii confronted several formidable challenges to the authority of the Muscovite church. First, his diocese had more Old Believers, that is opponents of the liturgical revisions of Patriarch Nikon (1652–66), than any other region of Muscovy with the possible exception of Siberia.[1] Second, the population of the Kholmogory region included a large percentage of non-Russians and non-Christians: native peoples such as the Karelians, Lapps, and Samoyeds. Finally, unknown numbers of Russians went to the Catholic and Protestant churches (*kirki*) established by foreign merchants in major White Sea ports.[2]

The policies that Afanasii adopted to address these challenges were not just of local significance. They were of extraordinary interest to Russia's spiritual as well as secular leadership. Patriarch Ioakim (1674–90) himself had handpicked Afanasii for the assignment to Kholmogory and the assembled hierarchs of all Russia had endorsed this decision at the 1682

---

[1] On Nikon's reforms, see N. F. Kapterev, *Patriarkh Nikon i ego protivniki v dele ispravleniia tserkovnykh obriadov* (Moscow, 1887). I use the terms "Old Believer" and "Old Belief" in their broadest possible meaning, that is, to signify all individuals who in some form or other failed to assimilate the principal symbols of Nikon's reforms, such as the three-fingered sign of the cross, the four-ended cross, and the new liturgical books.

[2] V. Veriuzhskii, *Afanasii Arkhiepiskop kholmogorskii: Ego zhizn' i trudy s sviazi s istoriei Kholmogorskoi eparkhii* (St. Petersburg, 1908), 60, 72, 100 (hereafter *AK*). This remarkable book presents a unique collection of documents from a variety of northern church archives.

church council. The records of this little-studied council also indicate that Afanasii's policies at Kholmogory were to serve as a model for the foundation of other bishoprics. Indeed, there were plans to establish at least twenty-two new eparchies (dioceses) in other parts of Muscovy; if ever realized, these plans would have more than doubled the number of Russian bishoprics. Given the great importance attached to Afanasii's appointment it is not suprising that he also had the full support of the Kremlin. Not only did he receive a substantial endowment, but Tsar Peter I himself repeatedly came to Kholmogory and seriously considered making Afanasii the new patriarch.[3]

There were at least three reasons why Afanasii was chosen over other candidates. First, church leaders were impressed by his fifteen years of successful service in Siberia—another vast territory where the presence of the Orthodox church was only weakly developed. Afanasii had been the abbot of the remote Dalmatov Monastery in southern Perm province. The monastery, which was then the last Russian outpost before the steppe, had at least twice been burnt down by Kalmyk and Nogay raiding parties. A third documented destruction occurred during the 1660s at the hands of Bashkirs. Afanasii, unintimidated by these raids, continued his work as abbot despite the dangers of renewed attacks. This heroism brought him to the attention of the archbishop of Tobol'sk who wrote about him to the Patriarch.[4]

Another important reason for Afanasii's election was his intimate familiarity with Old Belief. Indeed, there is evidence that he had once been an Old Believer himself. For example, an apocalyptic treatise condemning Patriarch Nikon originated during Afanasii's early years at the Dalmatov Monastery. It was addressed to men and women in his hometown of Tiumen' and shows distinctive stylistic features that are also found in other manuscripts produced by Afanasii.[5] Later Afanasii drew on this Old Believer learning to fight Old Belief. For example, he engaged the Old Believer intellectual Nikita Dobrynin in public debate at the Kremlin.

[3] Before the 1682 council Russia had only seventeen bishoprics. Other plans which also were never realized during subsequent centuries called for the creation of thirty one and even sixty-nine additional eparchies. Rossiiskii gosudarstvennyi arkhiv drevnikh aktov, Moscow (hereafter RGADA), f. 153, Rossiiskie dukhovnye dela, op. 1, d. 61, Kontsept 15 predlozhenii . . . o ustroenii eparkhii (1682); I. M. Pokrovskii, *Russkie eparkhii v XVI-XIX vv., ikh otkrytie, sostav i predely*, vol. 1 (Kazan, 1897), 314–41, 370–72; N. Vinogradskii, *Tserkovnyi sobor v Moskve 1682 goda: Opyt istoriko-kriticheskogo issledovaniia* (Smolensk, 1899), 6–9, 38–78; *AK*, 26, 31–33.

[4] *Opisanie muzhskogo Uspenskogo monastyria i byvshogo pripisnym k nemu zhenskogo Vvedenskogo monastyria* (Ekaterinburg, 1891), 10–14; *AK*, 10–11, 14, 22; G. Plotnikov, "Nastoiateli Dalmatova monastyria," *Permskie eparkhial'nye vedomosti*, 1869, nos. 19:253–54, 26:319–20; I. Gorskii, *Patriarkh vserossiiskii Ioakim v bor'be s raskolom* (St. Petersburg, 1864), passim.

[5] Unfortunately, the autograph has not survived and a comparison with other documents in Afanasii's hand is therefore not possible. See S. Smirnov, *Vnutrennie voprosy v raskole v XVII veke* (St. Petersburg, 1898), lxxxv–lxxxvi, 20–30; *AK*, 11, 13.

While the patriarch and other hierarchs were too ignorant to argue with the highly learned Nikita, Afanasii refuted one by one most of Nikita's arguments. After the debate he wrote a long polemical treatise against Nikita and his followers. This text, the so-called *Spiritual Exhortation* (*Uvet dukhovnyi*), became the single most important weapon against Old Belief during the remainder of the seventeenth century.[6]

Finally, Afanasii owed his position to the fact that he was much better educated than the average Muscovite hierarch. He not only had a thorough grounding in church patristics and Greek Orthodox theology, but also was familiar with Latin and German texts. Much of this erudition was probably acquired in later years. Still, upon his arrival in Moscow in 1679 Afanasii was already sufficiently learned to become a student of the Chudov monk Evfimii who was probably the most learned Russian churchman of the seventeenth century. Afanasii also immersed himself in the work of the eminent Ukrainian scholar Epifanii Slavinetskii. There is evidence that Patriarch Ioakim was seriously considering making Afanasii the head of the prestigious Greek-Slavonic Academy.[7]

Afanasii was very pleased about his rapid promotion from obscurity to the limelight of Muscovite church politics. He saw his assignment to Kholmogory as an important rescue mission on behalf of the church. In a letter to the abbot of a northern monastery he wrote that he was eager to leave the comforts of Moscow and looking forward to "seeing him face to face." The time for decisive action had come because the Russian Orthodox were now being "pressured from all sides and great misfortunes were about to come." He would arrive soon, but in the meantime the abbot and his flock should pray that the "Holy Orthodox Church would remain firmly grounded for all time on the rock of faith against the onslaughts of the apostates."[8]

Afanasii finally arrived at Kholmogory, after more than a month of travel, in October 1682.[9] He had ventured into a region that had for cen-

---

[6] *Uvet dukhovnyi, vo utverzheniia blagochestivykh liudei, vo uverenie-zhe i obrashchenie k pokaianiiu ot prelesti raskol'nikov sviatoi tserkvi* (1682; reprint, Moscow, 1753), fols. 42v–53v; S. Romanov, "Istoriia o vere i chelobitnoi o strel'tsakh," in *Letopisi russkoi literatury i drevnosti*, ed. N. S. Tikhonravov, vol. 5 (Moscow, 1863), 111–30; "Vozglashenie uveshchatel'noe vsemu rossiiskomu narodu velikogo gosudaria sviateishogo Ioakima patriarkha," fols. 30r–31v. Library of the Siberian Academy Sciences, Novosibirsk, Sobranie M. N. Tikhomirova, no. 348; I. I. Rumiantsev, *Nikita Konstantinov Dobrynin ("Pusto-sviat"): Istoriko-kriticheskii ocherk (K istorii bor'by pravoslaviia s staroobriadchestvom v XVII veke)*, vol. 2 (Sergiev Posad, 1917), 152.

[7] A. Golubtsov, *Chinovniki kholmogorskogo Preobrazhenskogo sobora* (Moscow, 1903), xxvii; M. Smentsovskii, *Brat'ia Likhudy: Opyt issledovaniia iz istorii tserkovnogo prosveshcheniia i tserkovnoi zhizni kontsa XVII i nachala XVIII vekov* (St. Petersburg, 1899), 22–25; *AK*, 8, 14–15, 28–30; A. V. Florovsky, "Chudovskii inok Evfimii," *Slavia* 19 (1949–50): 100–152. Afanasii's amazing erudition and its origins have not yet been explored. On Afanasii's comprehensive library at Kholmogory, see *AK*, 575–91.

[8] *AK*, 46 n. 170. See also Afanasii's letters to the tsars, ibid., 46–47 n. 172.

[9] Ibid., 46–47.

turies been terra incognita for the Russian church. Even though the lands along the Dvina, Vaga, and Pechora rivers were by the end of the fifteenth century formally subject to hierarchs in Novgorod and Moscow, these authorities probably had no local influence. There were almost no parishes to speak of and even the few in existence were often without priests and most certainly without regular supervision. Only occasionally did church agents descend upon the few *pogosty*, or villages that actually had a church building. Other, more isolated villages may never have seen any churchmen, though they probably paid some form of church tithe since tithe collectors were notorious in the north for their use of violence. If the centers of Muscovite religion ever had any influence in the area during the fifteenth and sixteenth centuries it was through large monastic foundations. Still, these monasteries hardly could agree on a coordinated religious policy. Each monastic territory existed in its own socio-religious cosmos and had its own special relations with Moscow. In short, if there were any ecclesiastical ambitions to integrate the northern regions into the church—as suggested for example by plans to found a Karelian bishopric—they had not been very successful.[10]

Change came only after the Time of Troubles (1598–1613) when one of the most important monasteries of the Dvina region, the Antonievo-Siiskii Monastery, began to cooperate closely with Moscow. The reason was that the monks had developed good relations with the exiled head of the Romanov clan, Fedor Nikitich, who—after his confinement to the monastery by Boris Godunov—became known as the monk Filaret.[11] After his triumphant return to the Kremlin as the Patriarch of All Russia (1619–33), Filaret immediately initiated the construction of new churches and submitted some older churches directly to patriarchal authority in Moscow. Under his successor, Patriarch Iosif (1642–52), locally elected candidates for the priesthood had to travel more than twelve hundred kilometers to Moscow to receive ordination papers. Under Patriarch Nikon such candidates had to obtain letters of recommendation from local church agents before they could even think of embarking on the time-consuming journey.[12] In short, by the time of Afanasii's arrival in Kholmogory the Muscovite church had made some strides towards connecting this remote region to its nerve centers in the Kremlin.

---

[10] Archimandrite Makarii, "Khristianstvo v predelakh Arkhangel'skoi eparkhii," *Chteniia v Obshchestve istorii i drevnostei rossiiskikh pri Moskovskom universitete* (hereafter *Chteniia*), 1878, bk. 3, pp. 7–8; *AK*, 52–55; I. Smolitsch, *Das russische Mönchtum: Entstehung, Entwicklung und Wesen. 988–1917* (Würzburg, 1953), 184–86, 291–93.

[11] On Filaret's captivity in the Siiskii Monastery, see S. Platonov, *The Time of Troubles* (Lawrence, Kansas, 1985), 68–69.

[12] P. F. Nikolaevskii, "Patriarshaia oblast' i russkie eparkhii v XVII veke," *Khristianskoe chtenie*, 1888, nos. 1–2:161–63; *Istoricheskoe opisanie prikhodov i tserkvei Arkhangel'skoi eparkhii*, vol. 1 (Arkhangel'sk, 1894), 72–74.

Still, Afanasii had many remaining obstacles to surmount. By far the greatest obstacle was, of course, the proliferation of Old Believers on a scale that was so alarming that Patiarch Ioakim had initially considered founding five new bishoprics in the area. The two other greatly visible symptoms of crisis were—as indicated above—the substantial presence of non-Christian ethnic groups and a tendency among town dwellers to abandon Orthodoxy altogether for Western Christianity. Before turning toward Afanasii's efforts to eradicate Old Belief which became the center of his reform policies let us take a brief look at how he handled these other challenges to his authority.

Non-Christians and Foreigners

Afanasii did not use violence to convert the so-called "pagans" (*iazytsy*). Instead, he attempted to draw them into the church with the help of sermons and material incentives. For example, a document which decribes Afanasii's policy towards the Lapps on the Kola Peninsula states that officials were to treat them "with love and welcome, with good care and unfailing zeal [*neoploshnym radeniem*], but not with coercion." Priests and abbots were to refrain from the use of force at any cost, "to avoid inciting rebellion among the people of other faith [*liudi inovernye*] and chasing them from Kola Island." If any Lapp wanted to became Orthodox he was to be given two rubles as a reward and hopefully this would offer an incentive "for other adherents of a different faith [*inye inovertsy*] to come to the Orthodox Christian faith."[13]

All native converts had to be registered. For example, the converted Lapps on the Kola Peninsula were listed by name in special manuscript books. Such official lists were then given to Orthodox parish priests and church emissaries who had to report at regular intervals on whether the converts were actually obedient to the Orthodox church. Afanasii's suspicions about native conversions became apparent when he blamed converted Lapps for leaving out the names of their deceased parents and ancestors in church prayers. He suspected them of worshiping their kin at pagan community shrines and gave orders to enter the names of all the dead members of converted Lapp families into church necrologies (*sinodiki*). Only by obeying this order would the Lapps "gain great benefit from God Almighty and liberate the souls of the dead from suffering and help them to gain eternal life."[14]

There is good evidence that Afanasii never pursued a systematic con-

---

[13] "Tsarskaia gramota k kol'skomu voevode Vasiliu Averlakovu," *Chteniia*, 1887, bk. 1, smes', 152–153.
[14] *AK*, 177–79.

version policy targeting the pagan non-Russians of his diocese. Most importantly, the archive of the Kholmogory bishopric remains almost completely silent about efforts to convert the indigenous population.[15] Also, there are indications that Afanasii did not mind at all when the natives remained loyal to their own religion. Non-Orthodox Lapps who lived on episcopal lands of the Kola peninsula enjoyed his protection against over-taxation by the regional military governor (*voevoda*).[16] On occasion Afanasii would even hold up the example of the local pagans to the Orthodox. In a widely disseminated circular to his Russian Orthodox flock, for example, he insisted that Christians could learn from the "nonbelieving pagans [who] hate, shame, and greatly punish wine drinkers and tobacco smokers."[17] In short, Afanasii did not devote much of his energy and power to converting the natives.

It is interesting, however, that Afanasii used threats and force against those natives who converted to Old Belief. For example, he angrily denounced a few Lapps from Kola peninsula who had been baptized by wandering Old Belief missionaries. He also had some Samoyed shepherds arrested for being the followers of an Old Believer peasant. Such measures did not break the hold that preachers of the pre-Nikonian faith had on non-Russians. One of the most successful of these dissidents, the monk Pimen, was converting numerous Lapps and Karelians to the old Orthodox religion. Not suprisingly, the leaders of established Old Believer communities such as Elder Semën Denisov of Vyg considered newly converted non-Russians to be among the most fervent supporters of their cause.[18] Archbishop Afanasii was so angered by the connections between ethnic paganism and the old Muscovite rites that he overreacted on some occasions. Once, for example, he launched a brutal investigation into the appearance of gypsies in a remote area, fully convinced that these gypsies were really "schismatic" Old Believers.[19] Such actions demonstrate that Afanasii saw the presence of non-Christian minorities in his diocese only as a serious threat to church authority when there was real—or potential—contact with Old Believers.

Afanasii treated the presence of large numbers of foreigners in his diocese in a similar fashion. He was aware that the prosperous ports of Arkhangel'sk and Kholmogory attracted thousands of Westerners every

---

[15] *AK*, 61.

[16] "Akty i materialy sobrannye v kholmogorskom Spaso-Preobrazhenskom sobore," *Trudy Arkhangel'skogo statisticheskogo komiteta za 1865*, 62–63 (hereafter *Trudy*).

[17] *AK*, 131 (excerpt from *nastavlenie*).

[18] *AK*, 76, 88; R. B. Miuller, ed., *Kareliia v XVII veke. Sbornik dokumentov* (Petrozavodsk, 1948), 308–9; I. F. Filipov, *Istoriia Vygovskoi staroobriadcheskoi pustyni* (St. Petersburg, 1862), 30–34; S. Denisov, *Vinograd rossiiskii ili opisanie postradavshikh v Rossii za drevletserkovnoe blagochestie* (Moscow, 1906), fol. 62r–v.

[19] *Trudy*, 74–81.

year. He also knew that many Russian urban dwellers had daily contact with Catholics and Protestants from Spain, Holland, and other countries. Indeed, he learned that many Russians lived as domestic servants in foreign homes. Moreover, unknown numbers of Orthodox went to the houses of prayer that merchants and sea captains had built for the members of their national communities.[20]

True, Afanasii warned his Orthodox flock repeatedly against the dangers of social and sexual contacts with Western Christians, and at least once called angrily for the forced conversion of all foreigners who wanted to have any regular relations with the Russian Orthodox. However, he did not do much to prevent such contacts. Only foreigners who wanted to convert to Russian Orthodoxy of their own volition came under official scrutiny. They were separated from their communities and confined to monasteries to learn about the basic teachings of Orthodoxy. Some of the "newly baptized" were accused of being "crypto-Catholics" (*podlinno katoliki*).[21] By contrast, foreigners who had no intention to convert to Orthodoxy were welcome guests at Kholmogory. They were even invited to Afanasii's palace as long as they brought him lavish gifts such as parrots, telescopes, or wine. The learned Afanasii was especially eager to receive books in foreign languages and eventually assembled a large library featuring Latin, Greek and German volumes on topics such as medicine, geography, cosmography and military strategy. The main reception hall of the episcopal palace featured the offering of a Dutch merchant: a large map of Amsterdam.[22] Clearly, there was a discrepancy between the bishop's anti-foreign rhetoric and his enjoyment in socializing with Westerners.

There was only one major investigation into foreign religious influences. This was the spectacular case of the Russian deacon Peter Artem'ev, who was actively advocating the Catholic faith. The reason for Afanasii's unusual zeal was probably that this deacon defended not only Catholicism but also views held by the Old Believers.[23]

Peter had studied under the well-known Likhud brothers, teachers at the Greek-Slavonic Academy in Moscow. During the late 1680s he had accompanied one of the brothers on a journey to Venice, where he stayed for three years. After returning home, he became friendly with two Fran-

---

[20] "vo vremia mol'by vsegda k ikh kirkam prikhodiat i peniia ikh slushaiut" (D. Tsvetaev, ed., "Otniatie u inozemtsev russkoi prislugi v gorodakh Arkhangel'ske i Kholmogorakh. 1686 god," *Chteniia*, 1883, bk. 3, p. 89).

[21] Ibid., 89–91; *AK*, 103–9.

[22] *AK*, 470, 476. On Western books in Afanasii's library, see especially S. Luppov, *Kniga v Rossii v XVII veke* (Leningrad, 1970), 140–46.

[23] Information about Peter Artem'ev is found in Gosudarstvennyi istoricheskii muzei, Moscow, "Sinodal'noe sobranie svitkov," no. 393 (to which I unfortunately have had no access). I have relied here primarily on M. Nikol'skii, "Russkie vykhodtsy iz zagranichnykh shkol v XVII. Petr Artem'ev," *Pravoslavnoe obozrenie*, 1863, no. 10:246–69.

sciscan friars who were hiding in the capital after the expulsion of the Jesuits in 1689. Peter soon began to preach against the official church, and a quickly assembled church council had him arrested and exiled to Kholmogory. Bishop Afanasii was given the task of "looking over his [writings] and bringing the defrocked deacon to a genuine conversion."[24]

Afanasii was greatly intrigued by this case. For several months he and Peter met regularly in the episcopal palace for religious debates. Peter rejected the Photian Schism which had led to the split of the Orthodox and Catholic churches in 1054, and regretted that the Council of Florence (1438–39) had failed to reunite the churches. But Peter was particularly outraged about the Russian schism of the seventeenth century. He denounced the Muscovite patriarchs because they "had changed all apostolic dogmas in Russia forty years ago and introduced the three-fingered sign of the cross." In mystical poems that recall the writings of the Old Belief heresiarch Avvakum, Peter glorified the heroism of "the elect" (*izbrannye*), that is, the Old Believers whom he saw as the only genuine Christians left in Russia. Failing to convert Peter to Orthodoxy, Afanasii had him "locked into a windowless dungeon to die" at the Solovki Monastery.[25]

There is a curious parallel in Afanasii's treatment of pagans and foreigners. Despite occasional threats and warnings he practiced toleration and left both groups to their own devices. Only when natives and foreigners came into contact with Old Believers and began to support the old church rites did Afanasii strike out against them with brutal force. Clearly, the Old Believers were the main targets of Afanasii's church policies.

Old Believers

During the 1680s and 1690s, Old Believers could be found virtually everywhere in Afanasii's diocese. The most important centers of Old Belief activity were the town of Pustoozero and the Vyg Monastery. The missionary efforts of the Vyg leadership under Semën Denisov have been well studied. Much less is known about the community at Pustoozero which was recruited mostly from disciples of Old Belief's principal hero, Avvakum. After Avvakum's execution in April 1682 the community continued to exist for at least another ten years, attracting numerous followers

---

[24] D. Tsvetaev, *Iz istorii inostrannykh ispovedanii v Rossii v XVI i XVII vv.* (Moscow, 1886), 368–76, 389–99; Nikol'skii, "Russkie vykhodtsy," 254–55; letter from Patriarch Adrian to Archbishop Afanasii, Arkhangel'sk seminary archives, *AK*, 520.

[25] Nikol'skii, "Russkie vykhodsty," 257–64, 269.

thanks to the open encouragement of the local *voevoda*. Missionaries of these two communities persistently spread the influence of Old Belief in Afanasii's diocese.[26]

In addition, there were a large number of isolated clerics and peasants who acted independently of these established congregations. Typical was, for example, the "unemployed priest" Samson who roamed the forests with a gang of peasant bandits. He would rebaptize the children of local peasants according to the old rites. If peasants refused to allow this his supporters intimidated them with fierce-looking dogs and guns. Other important preachers against the Nikonian reforms had been expelled from established monastic institutions and roamed the forests of the north as itinerant monks. One of them was Efrosin, whom Afanasii singled out as a dangerous "bandit and rebel" because he led "ignorant simple people" into perdition.[27] Finally, there were self-declared peasant prophets who used apocalyptical sermons and—on occasion—violence to lure local peasants into self-immolation. The most notorious among them was one Ivan Kozel who was suspected of abducting and burning several peasant women.[28]

Afanasii took action to fight the disseminators of Old Belief immediately after his arrival at Kholmogory. Copies of his polemical work *Uvet dukhovnyi* and other "pamphlets telling the truth about the church schismatics" (*tetradi oblichitel'nye*) were distributed to all parish priests of his diocese. The priests were to read the texts to their parishioners "many times in front of all the people."[29] Next he implemented brutal persecutionary measures. Military detachments were sent into the forests to hunt down some of the most notorious preachers of Old Belief. Afanasii's servitors (*deti boiarskie*) conducted interrogations on the spot with the help of whips so that suspects would provide information about their identity and places of origin. Then, the culprits were put in chains and taken to Kholmogory under guard. At Kholmogory they were given several opportunities to recant their beliefs. Those who refused to recant were tortured and thrown into dungeons, and if they still did not recant after a few weeks they were burned at the stake as heretics. Any property and other assets

[26] Smirnov, *Vnutrennie voprosy*, x–xi, ciii; *AK*, 89. It is likely that a similar center of Old Belief actively existed at Mezen' where surviving members of Avvakum's family lived during the last decades of the seventeenth century, see *AK*, 86 (archives of the Arkhangel'sk eparchy).

[27] *AK*, 79, 84; G. Michels, "The Violent Old Belief: An Examination of Religious Dissent on the Karelian Frontier," *Russian History* 19, nos. 1–4, (1992): 203–29, esp. 219–22.

[28] *AK*, 82–83. There was also the runaway peasant Ivan Emel'ianov who enjoyed a similar notoriety in the Russian north; E. Barsov, "Sudnye protsessy XVII–XVIII vekov po delam tserkvi," *Chteniia*, 1883, bk. 3, pt. 5, pp. 40–41.

[29] *Trudy*, 26.

belonging to such unrepenting dissenters were to be confiscated, and their houses were to be burnt to the ground.[30]

The Old Believer historian Semën Denisov wrote panegyrical biographies of some of these victims of Afanasii's persecutions. Still, most Old Believers captured by Afanasii recanted their beliefs as soon as they were arrested or when confronted with torture and possible execution.[31] Afanasii was very concerned about making sure that such recantations were genuine. He had converts to the "true Orthodox faith" sent to monasteries for instruction and then resettled in regions where they had no family ties. There were, of course, still numerous cases where former Old Believers converted back to the old rites, but Afanasii responded by forcing local communities to vouch collectively for the loyalty of converts to the church. Another method was to send converts into the homes of reliable Orthodox laymen in the town of Kholmogory or to keep them indefinitely "under strict supervision" in monasteries.[32]

Not all monasteries could be entrusted with such tasks. For example, Afanasii continued to be very much concerned about the loyalty of the Solovki Monastery. The Solovki monks had been in open revolt against Nikon's reforms for about two decades. Only in 1676 had military detachments been able to subdue the monks and enforce the new rites. The leaders of the revolt had been killed in the ensuing bloodbath. However, the defiance of the Solovki monks had not yet been broken completely. Afanasii knew, for example, that the monks were secretly supporting some dangerous "schismatics," that is, escaped participants in the revolt who were still hiding nearby. Also, he blamed the monks for doing nothing to eradicate the old rites in the surrounding districts. Determined to break the power of the rebellious Solovki Monastery, Afanasii went there on several visitations to discipline the monks in person.[33]

At least one other monastery was given similar attention. Since the late 1670s the isolated Pertominskii Monastery on the White Sea littoral had been a thorn in the side of church leaders in Moscow. Despite repeated

---

[30] When dissenters were caught as a result of a denunciation their assets and homes were spared, but only in order to be handed over to the denouncers. See *AK*, 90–92; *Trudy*, 77–80; RGADA, f. 163, Raskol'nicheskie dela, d. 29, Ukaz 7193 goda.

[31] *Vinograd Rossiiskii*, chaps. 42, 52–53, 58, 61, etc. A typical case of mass recantation is found in RGADA, fond 163, delo 7a, fols. 39–46, O raskol'nich'ikh zhenakh i detekh zakliuchennykh na ovine vo trapeze sobornoi tserkvi (Feb. 1684). Of particular interest is the statement by the investigating official, Archpriest Peter, "that all of these schismatics with the exception of the monk Andronnik demonstrated their complete obedience to the Holy Church" (fol. 40).

[32] *AK*, 92–94 (various documents from the archives of the Siiskii Monastery).

[33] Ibid., 85–86, 270–77; Archimandrite Dosifei, *Geograficheskoe, istoricheskoe i statisticheskoe opisanie Stavropigial'nogo pervoklassnogo Solovetskogo monastyria*, 3 vols. (Moscow, 1853), 3:241–50; "Gramoty arkhiepiskopa Afanasiia k patriarkhu Adrianu," *Pamiatniki drevnei pis'mennosti*, 1879, no. 3:12–38.

warnings, Superior Mikhail Kharzeev had refused to have a spiritual director, go to confession, or take communion. Kharzeev was determined to defend himself with violence. When the archpriest of Arkhangel'sk and another episcopal official came to inspect the monastery's church "with all of its liturgical utensils," they were threatened by hostile monks and had to leave. In fact, Archbishop Afanasii's agents were lucky to escape with their lives since Kharzeev was known as a brutal tyrant and torturer. Among his victims were a former mistress and her husband who were found dead on the road, as well as a pregnant woman whom he beat so badly that she lost her child. Monks who dared to disobey Kharzeev were also severely beaten or tortured to death.[34] When Afanasii finally demanded that the monks elect a new superior, Kharzeev's supporters dug pits and threatened to bury alive anybody obeying the bishop.[35] Under the circumstances it was lucky for Afanasii that Kharzeev was arrested while visiting Moscow in 1689. Only then was Afanasii in a position to enforce the new rites at the monastery.[36]

Most of Afanasii's measures against Old Belief were much less spectacular. They were aimed at peasants who had not yet given up the two-fingered sign of the cross or continued to hold on to old liturgical books out of ignorance. In December 1682, for example, one of Afanasii's most trusted officials, the monk Tikhon, inspected the liturgical books in various village churches. He saw to it that only "new books" were used and forced parishioners to buy them from the episcopal treasury. Tikhon also confiscated the old liturgical books as well as old eight-ended crosses. Finally, he wrote down the names of all priests in whose parishes old liturgical books and crosses had been found.[37]

Old books were also confiscated from all parishes of the town of Arkhangel'sk. Parishes in and around Kholmogory were personally inspected by the bishop or members of his entourage. Also, there were orders providing for the distribution of new liturgical books in isolated areas such as the Solovki parishes on the White Sea littoral. Finally, Afanasii introduced the practice of giving copies of the *Chinovnik*, a book describing the officially accepted Church rituals, to all newly appointed parish priests.[38]

[34] *AK*, 277–79; 321–22.
[35] "napisano, chto nam promezh sebia iz bratii vybrat' stroitel'ia, no ashche-by i po dve golovy na plechakh imeli, no sego i pomyslit' ne smeli, potomy chto, Gosudar', zhivym grob izgotovili, da khoteli i polozhit' " (ibid., 321–22).
[36] Gosudarstvennyi istoricheskii muzei, Sinodal'noe sobranie svitkov, no. 110, Delo o Mikhaile Kharzeeve. The unruly monk was exiled to Siberia and instructions were given to keep him from writing secret letters to his supporters—a topos that is frequently found in papers ordering the exile of dissenters. See *AK*, 279, 305, 531; "Istoriko-statisticheskoe opisanie Pertominskogo monastyria," *Arkhangel'skie eparkhial'nye vedomosti*, 1894, nos. 17:469, 18:503–6.
[37] *Trudy*, 22, 25.
[38] *AK*, 84, 96, 370–74; Golubtsov, *Chinovniki*, 172.

Afanasii did everything in his power to undermine the status of Old Believers in local parish life. Parish priests were ordered to denounce all adherents of the old rites to Kholmogory. They also had to compile lists of all men and women who failed to attend church services or take communion. This made it possible to identify the names of potential Old Believers. Afanasii also insisted that the priests of his diocese should learn more about the Orthodox faith so that they could defend themselves against the Old Believers. In the meantime, however, he demanded that they obey their bishop and pray every Sunday for the conversion of these dissenters.[39] Afanasii's efforts to introduce the new liturgies have left substantial traces in church documents. The torture chambers and prisons of Kholmogory became notorious among Old Believers, and executions by fire were a quite regular sight. Not surprisingly, the head of the Vyg community, Semën Denisov, spoke of the devastating impact of Afanasii's persecutionary measures on Old Belief. He repeatedly referred to the archbishop as the most dangerous enemy that Old Belief had ever had.[40]

The Orthodox Population

Afanasii did not rely on punitive measures alone. He saw that there was only one real hope for victory in his struggle with Old Believers: he had to increase church controls over ordinary Russian believers and make the exercise of Orthodoxy more attractive to them.[41] One might say that he followed the basic logic of the Western Counter-Reformation, that is, to consolidate the Church's hold over the rank-and-file population and thereby curb the proliferation of religious dissent.[42]

Before he embarked on this enormous task, Afanasii first built stronger church institutions. Most importantly, he set up two central bureaus, that is, the so-called Office of the Treasury (*Kazennyi prikaz*) and Office of Legal Affairs (*Sudnyi prikaz*) which dealt respectively with church taxation and the religious supervision of the Orthodox population. The offices were headed by experienced and learned secretaries (*d'iaki*) whose activities have left a substantial paper trail. They were assisted by Afanasii's personal retainers

[39] "Chelobitnaia i doprosnye rechi popov Permogorskoi volosti o kapitonskoi eresi v ikh prikhodakh," in *Akty Kholmogorskoi i Ustiuzhskoi eparkii*, pts. 1–3, Russkaia istoricheskaia biblioteka, vols. 12, 14, 25 (St. Petersburg, 1890–1908), pt. 1, 12:687 (hereafter *Akty*); AK, 129–30 (excerpts from *nastavlenie*).

[40] See, for example, *Vinograd Rossiiskii*, chaps. 70–71, 74.

[41] See, for example, Rossiiskaia natsional'naia biblioteka, St. Petersburg, f. 717, d. 665/723, Okruzhnoe pouchitel'noe poslanie po eparkhii Afanasiia Arkhiepiskopa v 12 polozheniia protivu raskol'nikov (1696).

[42] See, for example, L. Chatellier, *The Europe of the Devout: The Catholic Reformation and the Formation of a New Society* (New York, 1989).

who often acted as tax collectors and special emissaries to the provinces. Afanasii ensured the loyalty of these and other lower-ranking officials by the regular distribution of gifts as well as by sometimes brutal purges. Also, he tightened his hold on his officials by giving some of the most influential positions to family members such as his brother and his nephews.[43]

In short, Afanasii made sure that he had at his disposal a group of dedicated and able men willing to execute episcopal wishes. With their help he launched a systematic campaign to change the religious affairs of the Russian north. One of the first measures was to confront locals with constant reminders of the arrival of a new bishop at Kholmogory. For example, papers were sent out to parishes ordering all to pray for the health of Archbishop Afanasii and the patriarch.[44] Also, parish priests received regular pastoral letters to be read during church services. These letters painted a very pessimistic picture of Christian religion in the hinterlands. A good example is a letter sent to all priests of the Kholmogory district on March 10, 1683:

> Deplorable and greatly lamentable news [*glas*] has reached us. . . . We have heard about you, the members of my flock, that many who call themselves Christians have been carried away by the vanity of this age. They do not go to church and prevent others from going. Many have not seen spiritual fathers [priests] for thirty, forty, and fifty years. Others even have not had any contact with priests from the time of their birth to the time of their death.[45]

To fight such widespread religious indifference toward official Orthodoxy Afanasii gave orders that every Christian was to attend church services on Sundays and go to regular confession. Every Orthodox person also had to take communion at least once a year during Lent. Those negligent in their Christian duties were regularly fined.[46]

One of the principal tasks of the new bureaucracy was to investigate so-called "sexual crimes." The tax books of the bishopric list regular fines for illegimate pregnancies and births, fornication with nuns, the rape of girls, and other "evil beginnings and lawless acts."[47] Fees were now also regularly assessed for the performance of marriages. Episcopal officials had to make sure that certain rules were implemented. For example, no marriage could be performed without the presence of a priest, and the names of the newlyweds had to be entered into marriage registers. Secret marriages were to be investigated and severely fined. Also, boys and girls could no longer be married off to widows and widowers who had been

[43] *AK*, 9, 402–7, 417, 419, 446.
[44] *AK*, 34.
[45] *Akty*, pt. 2, 14:462.
[46] Ibid., 463–67; *AK*, 120–123.
[47] *Trudy*, 23; *AK*, 134 n. 134 (excerpts from the episcopal archive).

married twice or more in the past.[48] Other examples of measures against age-old popular customs could be cited, but suffice it to conclude that such measures were important precisely because they led to a more regular contact between ordinary believers and episcopal officials.

Some officials traveled regularly to the villages and hamlets of the diocese and saw with their own eyes how little peasants knew about the Orthodox faith. They reported that peasants did not know basic prayers such as the Lord's Prayer, the Hail Mary, and the Creed.[49] Also, village and family icons were "the most disgusting pictures" and had "a corrupt influence [*soblazn*] on Orthodox Christians." Well-qualified icon painters from Kholmogory should be sent to the provinces to make lists of "good, mediocre and evil" icons. Samples of such icons were to be taken to Archbishop Afanasii for inspection. First, however, all icons that had been painted without official permission were simply confiscated on the spot.[50]

Archbishop Afanasii faced a very difficult task. His officials constantly discovered new problems. In 1692, for example, they began a detailed description of more than 430 votive chapels (*chasovni*) that had been built by peasants without official authorization. Peasants were convinced that the chapels would protect them against foreign invasion, animal disease, violent death, the plague, famine, and drought. They were used as family shrines and—in some cases—as burial sites.[51]

Afanasii put the chapels under the control of the nearest parish churches, and forbade peasants to make any donations to them in the future. Money that in the past had been earmarked for candles or family icons should now be paid to the local parish church or directly into the coffers of the Treasury Office. In fact, Afanasii's agents plundered the so-called "chapel treasure chests" (*chasovennye kazny*), some of which contained large sums of money from past donations as well as artifacts highly valued by local peasants such as buckets for brewing beer. There are signs that peasants were not very happy with these changes, but the pressure exerted by Kholmogory officials was unrelenting. Troublemakers were punished and church agents continued to explore the hinterlands for yet unknown chapels. By the end of the century every chapel in the diocese had been described and assessed. In fact, so much money was flowing into the coffers of the church that Afanasii began to embark on the construction of new churches everywhere.[52]

---

[48] *Trudy*, 19–21; *AK*, 123–24, 456–57 (data from tax registers in the episcopal archive).

[49] *AK*, 122; *Akty*, pt. 2, 14:475–77.

[50] *AK*, 366–69.

[51] "Perepisnye knigi chasoven' v Vazhskom uezde i v Ust'ianskikh sokhakh," *Akty*, pt. 2, 14:347–762, esp. 410, 415, 446, 451, etc.

[52] *AK*, 246–53; *Akty*, pt. 3, 25:391–93, 407, 423, 432, 438, 664–65. By 1696 church agents had registered an additional 160 chapels, see *AK* 337 n. 36 (diocesan tax income register).

The new churches—many of them made of stone—were the most visible sign of Afanasii's determination to establish the permanent presence of the church among the Orthodox of the Russian north. Most of these churches stood on the sites of former chapels and eventually became the centers of new parishes. Afanasii himself took a lively interest in this construction activity and travelled from parish to parish giving meticulous instructions to the craftsmen regarding form and design. He also personally consecrated some of these new churches and expressed his conviction that they were going to be holy spaces and no longer gathering places for secular community business. As he once put it, "human beings should no longer trample [the altar area] with their feet."[53]

Most importantly, however, the new churches were to be reliable outposts of the new Nikonian religion. Afanasii saw to it that they were generously endowed with new liturgical books and that the new four-ended crosses were visibly displayed not only on the altar but also on the church domes. Thus, Afanasii signaled agressively to the defenders of the old liturgies that he would no longer tolerate their presence. In fact, it is rather revealing that detected Old Believers had to contribute to Afanasii's church-building campaign by financing the cathedral at Kholmogory. They did so only too gladly, hoping that they might appease the archbishop and escape punishment, but in the end they helped Afanasii to consolidate his grip over the Orthodox.[54]

The cathedral built with the money of Old Believers became the center of an officially engineered religious revival that eventually spread to all outlying parishes.[55] One feature of this revival was the vigorous promotion of a Marian cult that centered around the veneration of a miracle-working icon from Georgia. Archbishop Afanasii personally headed the ceremonial processions that carried the icon through the streets "in order to bless the town and all Christ-loving people who ask mercy from God and the Mother of God." The cult was eventually also introduced in Arkhangel'sk, and its yearly celebration became an important religious event. Large crowds of pilgrims from all parts of the north would follow the icon and numerous miracles were attested.[56]

It is likely that the initiative for the Marian cult came from Afanasii's mother, Abbess Praskovia, who had moved from Siberia to Kholmogory during the late 1680s. Soon after her arrival she became the abbess of the

[53] *AK*, 328–29, 339, 355; *Akty*, pt. 1, 12:115; "Materialy dlia istorii Arkhangel'skoi eparkhii," *Chteniia*, 1880, bk. 2, pp. 5–6; I. Sibirtsev, *Istoricheskie svedeniia o tserkovno-religioznom byte v Arkhangel'skoi eparkhii* (Arkhangel'sk, 1890), 51–52; "Russkaia tserkov' v severnom Pomor'e v XV-XVII vv.," *Pravoslavnyi sobesednik*, 1860, no. 2:273–79.

[54] *AK*, 342 n. 55, 354 n. 105, 357.

[55] Ibid., 347–48, 376–80.

[56] "Istoricheskoe opisanie Krasnogorskogo monastyria," *Chteniia*, 1880, bk. 3, pt. 1, 12–13, 34–35, 38–42; *Akty istoricheskie*, 5:502–3; *AK*, 383.

newly built Assumption Convent which was—if we discount two remote hermitages in the forests—the first convent of any significance in the Russian north. The convent was "richly beautified with books and bells" and the nuns received regular endowments from the episcopal palace.[57] The Assumption Convent became the home for numerous itinerant nuns and homeless widows who until then had been roaming the towns and hinterlands of the north. Afanasii was convinced that unless they were given a permanent abode, many of these unaffiliated women would be recruited by the Old Believers. "The schismatics," he stated in a letter to another hierarch, "are luring peasant women, their children and their daughters, that is, girls of adult age, into the forests. After bewitching them they lead them away to their blasphemous hideouts [*bogomerzkie zhilishcha*] and live with them in fornication."[58]

That the preponderance of women among Old Believers was not just a figment of Afanasii's imagination is confirmed by surviving lists of captured dissenters. There is also evidence that many homeless and dislocated women flocked to the Old Believer community of Vyg.[59] In response Afanasii also organized a poor relief program. Numerous widows and wandering nuns flocked to the Assumption Convent and another convent that was built shortly afterward. Large crowds of the poor women waiting for help in front of the cathedral and Afanasii's episcopal palace also became an important feature of church life in Kholmogory.[60]

Clearly, Archbishop Afanasii took such measures in order to create alternatives to Old Belief. The same purpose is also visible in his policies toward local miracle cults. Afanasii's initial impulse was simply to abolish Old Believer cults. During his first year in office, for example, a cult of the relics of Evfimii, the legendary sixteenth-century abbot of an Archangel'sk monastery, was closed forever. Both Evfimii's *vita* and icons depicting him were forbidden and his gravesite was sealed.[61] During the late 1680s, however, Afanasii changed his mind. From now on Old Believer cults were no longer eliminated but officially coopted. For example, a popular cult of the miracle-working relics of German of Solovki was temporarily closed, and reopened after a commission had carefully investigated all information about reported miracles. Worshipers were, however, obliged to use

[57] *AK*, 8, 383; *Trudy*, 87–89.

[58] *AK*, 80 n. 41.

[59] See, for example, V. S. Rumiantseva, ed., *Narodnoe antitserkovnoe dvizhenie v Rossii XVII: Dokumenty prikaza tainykh del o raskol'nikakh* (Moscow, 1986), nos. 114–15; Filipov, *Istoriia Vygovskoi staroobriadcheskoi pustyni*, 345–66.

[60] *AK*, 405–7, 445–46.

[61] I. Sibirtsev, *K istorii Mikhailo-Arkhangel'skoi tserkvi v gorode Arkhangel'ske* (Arkhangel'sk, 1896), 3–7; Episkop Makarii, "Istoricheskie svedeniia ob Antonievo-Siiskom monastyre," *Chteniia*, 1878, bk. 3, p. 69.

only the new "liturgical services and canons" that had been "compiled with the blessing of the Orthodox monarchs."[62] Another example of this cooptation is the canonization of the Saints Vassian and Iona at the Pertominskii Monastery which—as indicated above—had been an outpost of Old Belief. Afanasii arrived at the monastery in June 1694 accompanied by none other than Peter I. Both witnessed the exhumation of the remains and after a thorough examination "recognized them as holy."[63]

Among the many other measures taken by Archbishop Afanasii was a reform of the parish clergy. Afanasii knew that his initiatives could not be implemented without the cooperation of local priests. Indeed, without the presence of priests the population would be left to its own devices. As one peasant informed the new archbishop, "infants remain without baptism and even worse, many die without repentance and reception of the Holy Sacraments."[64] For Afanasii it was not sufficient, however, to increase the number of parishes; he wanted to make sure that the priests obeyed his orders. He therefore established basic rules for their appointment. All existing parish priests had to register their sons who were to be the only candidates for the priesthood. In exceptional cases a parish priest was allowed to register close relatives. Under no circumstances, however, were peasant elders to elect priests randomly from the ranks of the peasantry. Runaway serfs who posed as priests to avoid taxation were severely punished. The archbishop made it absolutely clear that all candidates for the priesthood were to be approved by the episcopal palace.[65]

By the end of the seventeenth century every priest in the diocese of Kholmogory had to pass two examinations in order to procure official ordination papers. One examination tested the candidate's familiarity with the Nikonian liturgies, the other his ability to read and write. Prospective priests also had to pass certain moral standards. Violent behavior and sexual debauchery, for example, were reasons for debarment from the priesthood. Peasants who resisted the appointment of officially sanctioned priests were excommunicated or punished in other ways. Episcopal agents also disciplined priests who had been appointed by peasant communes without obtaining ordination papers.[66]

Despite occasional resistance to the appointment of his priests, Afanasii had clearly established the presence of the church among both clergy and laity of the Russian north. As we have seen, parish priests conveyed the

---

[62] V. O. Kliuchevskii, *Drevnerusskie zhitiia sviatykh, kak istoricheskii istochnik* (Moscow, 1871), 424; Dosifei, *Opisanie Solovetskogo monastyria*, 1:66.

[63] Episkop Makarii, "Istoriko-statisticheskoe opisanie Pertominskogo muzheskogo monastyria," *Chtenia*, 1881, bk.4:8–10.

[64] *Akty*, pt. 1, 12:112; *AK*, 339–40 n. 48.

[65] *AK*, 142–49, 202–4, 209–11, 329–30.

[66] Emissaries were sent out to punish peasants who had expelled priests, calling them "Germans and foreigners." See ibid., 188–204, 212–14, 218–22.

bishop's reform message to the peasantry and kept the bishop informed about the religious behavior of their flock.

Conclusion

Undoubtedly, Archbishop Afanasii's church policies left a strong imprint on the religious affairs of the Russian north. Most importantly, he created enormous obstacles to the proliferation of Old Belief. It is interesting to note (and it is probably unique during the late seventeenth century) that Afanasii did not blame Old Believer propaganda alone for the persistence of the old pre-Nikonian religious order, that is, the so-called "schism" in the Russian north. Rather, he saw the presence of many opponents of the new Nikonian religion as a symptom of a much deeper cause. Most importantly, he pointed to great structural weaknesses within the church, which had not done enough to control the population of the north and had left it essentially to its own devices in religious matters. To Afanasii, the gulf that had always separated the local population from the Orthodox Church was responsible for the persistence of the old Muscovite religion in the Russian north.

Afanasii's response to this crisis was to embark on a major reform work that has no known parallel in the history of Muscovite bishoprics, but resembles the "confessionalization" campaigns of the Counter-Reformation Catholic church in the West.[67] In a sense, he continued the previous efforts of Patriarch Filaret and other patriarchs to bring the church into closer contact with the Russian north. However, as one of the first modern Russian church reformers and administrators, Afanasii established policies that were much more comprehensive and systematic. This probably explains why he became a favorite of Peter I.

The success of Afanasii's policies can be gauged by the significant reduction of Old Belief activities in the Kholmogory eparchy. We know, for example, that itinerant preachers of Old Belief had more and more difficulty gaining support among local parishioners after 1700.[68] Afanasii also managed to weaken and eventually destroy the influence of the important community of Pustoozersk which had been organized by surviving supporters of Avvakum. As a result, Old Belief became increasingly an affair of a few isolated congregations, most notably that of Vyg which became the center of Old Belief culture during the eighteenth century. Interestingly enough, even the famous Vyg elders found it difficult to spread the

[67] H. Schilling, ed., *Die Katholische Konfessionalisierung*, Religionsgeschichtliche Studien und Texte, vol. 135 (Münster, 1995).

[68] P. S. Smirnov, *Spory i razdeleniia v russkom raskole v pervoi chetverti XVIII veka* (St. Petersburg, 1909), 6–31.

message of Old Belief inside the diocese of Kholmogory after Afanasii's reform work had taken full effect. In fact, we know that they had to draw many of their followers from other areas of Russia.[69]

Why did Afanasii focus on Orthodox dissenters instead of targeting pagans and foreigners? One possible answer is certainly that Afanasii himself had converted from Old Belief and therefore was very zealous to demonstrate his loyalty to the church. At the very least he had been shaped by this conversion experience and was much more familiar with Old Belief than with paganism and Western Christianity. More importantly, however, Afanasii perceived the great success of Old Belief in the Russian north as a direct reflection of the church's institutional underdevelopment. Not surprisingly, he wrote several polemical works against Old Believers but none against foreigners or pagans.[70] The Old Believers were the Church's archenemies, or as he put it, "the apostates" who were undermining "the rock of faith." This conviction explains why he did not do much to keep ordinary Russians from attending Western churches. Only when a Catholic convert began to advocate Old Believer views did he take drastic disciplinary action. Similarly, Afanasii left Lapps and Samoyeds alone as long as they did not convert to Old Belief.

Thus, Afanasii clearly focused on one goal: to Christianize the Russian Orthodox population of the north and thereby eliminate the threat of dissent, that is, Old Belief. If Afanasii did not succeed completely in his purpose he still stands out in the history of the Russian church. Long before the Holy Synod began a systematic Christianization campaign in the Russian empire during late eighteenth century, Afanasii had done so in his diocese.[71]

---

[69] The reasons for the Vyg community's success cannot be investigated here. Suffice it to say that factors beyond the control of any church reformer played a crucial role, such as the war with Sweden, economic success, official toleration, and a more rigorous leadership after 1702. See Smirnov, *Spory i razdeleniia*, 7–15; R. Crummey, *The Old Believers and the World of Antichrist* (Madison, Wis., 1970), 126–28

[70] For another example, see RNB, Osnovnoe sobranie, O. I., no. 209, Kniga glagolemaia Brozda dukhovnaia ... v nei zhe oblichitel'nye otvety na miatezhnikov i na tserkovnykh razvratnikov.

[71] See, for example, I. Smolitsch, "Die Ausbildung des 'geistlichen Standes,'" in idem, *Geschichte der Russischen Kirche 1700–1917*, vol. 1 (Leiden, 1964), 428–58.

CHAPTER TWO

Orthodox Missionaries and "Orthodox Heretics" in Russia, 1886–1917

J. EUGENE CLAY

From 1886 to 1917, in an effort to purify the Russian Orthodox Church of what they regarded as superstitious and false religious practices, a new class of professional missionaries began to identify certain Orthodox groups that engaged in these practices, and exclude them from the fellowship of the church. Missionaries faced three major types of Christian dissenters: (1) the Old Believers (*staroobriadtsy*) who claimed the Orthodox tradition as their own, but who rejected the official church as heretical or schismatic; (2) the free-church Christians (including the Molokans, Dukhobors, Baptists, and Evangelical Christians) who rejected Eastern Orthodoxy and the official Russian church, yet did not belong to one of the legally recognized Christian confessions; and (3) the "Orthodox heretics," who regarded themselves as part of the official church, but were rejected and even excommunicated by the leaders of that church.[1] This article deals exclusively with the last category, which includes religious groups such as the *besedchiki* of Samara province, the Podgornites

The research for this article was supported in part by the International Research and Exchanges Board, a Faculty Grant in Aid of Arizona State University, and a Pew Evangelical Scholarship.

[1] On religious dissent at the end of the empire, see P. S. Smirnov, *Istoriia russkogo raskola staroobriadstva* (St. Petersburg, 1895); Roy R. Robson, *Old Believers in Modern Russia* (DeKalb, Ill., 1995); Sergii Margaritov, *Istoriia russkikh misticheskikh i ratsionalisticheskikh sekt*, 4th ed. (Simferopol', 1914); T. I. Butkevich, *Obzor russkikh sekt i ikh tolkov* (Khar'kov, 1910); A. S. Prugavin, comp., *Raskol-sektantstvo: materialy dlia izucheniia religiozno-bytovykh dvizhenii russkogo naroda*, no. 1: *Bibliografiia staroobriadchestva i ego razvetvlenii* (Moscow, 1887); F. K. Sakharov, comp., *Literatura istorii i oblicheniia russkogo raskola: Sistematicheskii ukazatel' knig, broshiur i statei o raskolie, nakodiashchikhsia v dukhovnykh i svetskikh periodicheskikh izdaniiakh*, 3 vols. (Tambov–

(*podgornovtsy* or *stefanovtsy*, the adherents of the Khar'kov peasant Vasilii Karpovich Podgornyi), the Serafimites of Pskov, the Ioannites (*ioannity*, the followers of Father Ioann of Kronstadt), the teetotalers (*trezvenniki*, the disciples of the Samara peasant Ivan Churikov), and the name-glorifiers (*imiaslavtsy*) among the monks of Mount Athos.[2]

The conflict between these "Orthodox heretics" and the Orthodox missionaries highlighted many of the problems and choices that the church faced at the end of the Old Regime. Both groups were trying to define what it meant to be Orthodox in the rapidly changing social and economic conditions of the late nineteenth and early twentieth centuries. Both the missionaries and the popular collegia that they condemned represented new forms of Orthodoxy and competing religious visions that tried to formulate an Orthodox praxis for the modern world.

For their part, the missionaries represented a radical belief in reason as the principal means to truth. Committed to the proposition that logical debate was primarily what was necessary to win converts and protect the Orthodox faithful from Protestantism and other heterodox errors, professional missionaries appeared at the apogee of a long period of rationalization of church doctrines and institutions that had begun in the seventeenth century.

Orthodox heretics, on the other hand, embraced charismatic forms of spirituality, including miraculous healings, prophetic denunciations of secret sins, visions of the saints, visitations of the Holy Spirit, and private revelations to ascetic athletes. They generally followed a simple but strict morality often based on a monastic ideal. Sharply opposed to the rapidly growing Protestant movements, such as Baptism, that enjoyed surprising success in Russia after the Emancipation of 1861, these Orthodox collegia enthusiastically fulfilled their obligations to the church, venerated icons, observed the fasts, and performed pilgrimages to holy sites. Some, like the Ioannites and the teetotalers, grew up among peasant migrants to the city. Others, such as the Podgornites and the *besedchiki*, enjoyed their greatest strength in the villages where they developed traditional local forms of spirituality.

These pietistic groups presented a serious dilemma for the missionaries. On the one hand, their members at least appeared to be devoted Orthodox Christians who faithfully performed their duties to the church; on

---

St. Petersburg, 1887–1900); Frederick Cornwallis Conybeare, *Russian Dissenters*, Harvard Theological Studies, vol. 10 (Cambridge, Mass., 1921).

[2] Evgenii Kesarev, *Besednichestvo kak sekta: Besedchiki Samarskoi eparkhii* (Samara, 1905); Konstantinos K. Papoulides, *Hoi rosoi Onomatolatrai tou Hagiou Orous*, Ekdoseis, vol. 173 (Salonica, 1977). I am grateful to my colleague Stephen Batalden for pointing out Papoulides' work.

the other hand, their emphasis on charismatic revelation threatened to undermine the authority of the hierarchy and its agents. These groups sometimes questioned the legitimacy of the Holy Synod (the ruling council of the Orthodox church which had replaced the Patriarchate in 1721), the value of theological education, the worthiness of the clergy, and the Russian missionary effort. For these reasons, most missionaries regarded these pietistic believers as "mystical sectarians"—people who needed to be converted in spite of themselves. Yet because they raised issues that also were being debated among the bishops, clergy, and church intellectuals, these collegia sometimes found defenders even within the hierarchy and the clergy.

The creation of the professional antisectarian missionary represented a radical innovation for the Orthodox Church—an innovation that did not go unopposed. The clash between the missionaries and these other Orthodox believers revealed some of the deep fissures inside the church on the eve of the Revolution.

The Rationalization of Orthodoxy and the Creation of a Professional Missionary Corps

The missionary represented the culmination of the rationalization of Russian Orthodoxy. In an insightful article, the anthropologist Robert W. Hefner has argued that religious rationalization includes (1) the creation and clarification of doctrine by intellectual systematizers; (2) the canonization and institutionalization of these doctrines by certain social carriers, and (3) the effective socialization of these cultural principles into the ideas and actions of believers.[3]

Over two centuries during the imperial period, the Orthodox Church became increasingly rationalized in all three ways. First of all, by 1850 Russian Orthodox theologians had begun to clarify and systematize the doctrines of their church in new ecclesiastical textbooks which were widely used in theological academies and seminaries. While before the 1840s the main theological textbooks in Russian seminaries were the translated works of German Protestant scholars (such as F. C. Baumeister, J. F. Buddeus, and J. J. Rambach), by 1847 these began to be replaced by the works of Russian Orthodox scholars. In that year, the prolific monk Makarii (Bulgakov, 1816–82) published his *Introduction to Orthodox Theology* which went through seven editions before World War I

---

[3] Robert Hefner, "World Building and the Rationality of Conversion," in *Conversion to Christianity: Historical and Anthropological Perspectives on a Great Transformation* (Berkeley, Calif., 1993), 18.

and became a standard textbook in the ecclesiastical educational system. Deeply influenced by Counter-Reformation theology, Makarii's textbook emphasized the power of reason and systematization and provided its readers with precise definitions of the sacraments and of God's essential characteristics.[4]

This same period witnessed the flourishing of the theological educational system designed to transmit this rationalized vision of the church and its theology to the ecclesiastical cadres of priests and monks, who canonized and institutionalized the emerging doctrinal synthesis. In order to counteract the rapid growth of free-church Christianity, a bishops' council in 1886 established a new set of agents—the antisectarian and antischismatic missionaries—to inculcate Orthodoxy (as defined in the theological academies) into the minds and hearts of ordinary believers.[5] Trained in the elite theological academies, the missionaries (who were often not ordained) traveled from place to place to educate the Orthodox laity and to engage (and subdue) the growing numbers of Old Believers and free-church Protestants in polemical debate. They believed strongly in the power of education. Their standard textbooks, such as Petr Smirnov's *The Russian Schism of Old Ritualism*, posited ignorance as the source of heresy and reasoned discourse as the means to battle doctrinal error. Smirnov approvingly noted the development of libraries and schools, and encouraged his readers to follow the example of the Abbot Isaakii (I. F. Kuchin, 1645–1736) of the Sarov hermitage who successfully converted an Old Believer through gentle and gracious argument.[6] Most missionaries agreed with Vasilii Mikhailovich Skvortsov (1859–1932), publisher of the journal *Missionerskoe obozrenie* (The Missionary Review), who insisted that "polemics is the art that brings unbelievers into submission to the church."[7] When the Petersburg diocesan missionary Dmitrii Ivanovich Bogoliubov (1869–1953) tried to suggest at the 1908 Kiev missionary congress that public debates were but a small part of the duties of

---

[4] Gregory Lee Freeze, *The Parish Clergy in Nineteenth-Century Russia: Crisis, Reform, Counter-Reform* (Princeton, N.J., 1983), 121; Makarii (Bulgakov), *Vvedenie v pravoslavnoe bogoslovie* (St. Petersburg, 1847; 7th ed., St. Petersburg, 1913); Georges Florovsky, *The Collected Works of Georges Florovsky*, vols. 5–6: *The Ways of Russian Theology*, ed. Richard S. Haugh, trans. Robert L. Nichols (Belmont, Mass., 1979–87).

[5] In 1867, Nikita Isaevich Voronin (1840–1905) became the first ethnic Russian to convert to Baptism; by 1912, the Department of Spiritual Affairs of the Ministry of Internal Affairs numbered Baptists and Evangelical Christians (a closely related denomination) from traditionally Orthodox populations at 96,776. *Istoriia evangel'skikh khristian-baptistov v SSSR* (Moscow, 1989), 74–75; Hans Brandenburg, *The Meek and the Mighty : The Emergence of the Evangelical Movement in Russia* (New York, 1977); *Statisticheskie svedeniia o sektantakh (k 1 ianvaria 1912 g.)* (St. Petersburg, 1912), 14–23. On the bishops' councils leading up to the formation of the professional missionaries, see Freeze, *Parish Clergy*, 446–47.

[6] Smirnov, *Istoriia russkogo raskola*, 189–92, 256–58.

[7] *Missionerskii s"ezd v gorode Kazani 13–26 iiunia 1910 goda* (Kazan, 1910), 60.

the missionary, who needed primarily to organize and equip the Orthodox laity, he was outvoted by the delegates.[8]

The missionary acted to spread the systematized, rationalized theology of the academies into the countryside. The rules for missionaries adopted in 1888 specified a preference for academy graduates. Like the Jesuits of the sixteenth century, the antisectarian and antischismatic missionaries sought not only to convert heretics but to educate and protect the faithful—both priests and parishes—from doctrinal error. In many respects, the missionary was a traveling seminary professor—and in fact many professors served as missionaries.

Rural Heretics on the Volga:
The *Besedchiki* of Samara Province

Traditional rural Orthodoxy in Samara province differed markedly from the Orthodoxy of the theological academies. First of all, Old Belief had greatly influenced local piety. From the 1760s until 1837, five Old Believer monasteries on the Irgiz River provided a sacramental and institutional center for adherents of Orthodoxy as it had been practiced before the liturgical reforms of Patriarch Nikon (r. 1652–66).[9] Under Tsar Nicholas I (r. 1825–55) and Bishop Iakov (Iosif Vecherkov, 1792–1850) of Saratov (r. 1832–47), a campaign of repression forced all five monasteries to join *edinoverie*, the uniate movement of the official Orthodox Church. Created in 1800 as an effort to end the schism in the church, the uniate movement allowed its members to use the pre-Nikonian liturgy as long as it recognized the canonical authority and complete validity of the Holy Synod and the official Orthodox Church.[10] (This movement is not to be confused with the Uniate Church of the Western Provinces discussed by Theodore Weeks in this volume.) Despite the repression, Samara remained a significant center of Old Belief; and the uniate move-

[8] Andrei Gavriilovich Kuliashev, "Chetvertyi Vserossiiskii Kievskii missionerskii s"ezd," *Permskie eparkhial'nye vedomosti* 42, no. 28 (1 October 1908): 579.

[9] Iakov (Vecherkov), "Raskol beglopopovskoi sekty po Saratovskoi eparkhii," Arkhiv Russkogo geograficheskogo obshchestva, St. Petersburg, razdel 36, op. 1, no. 42. Before 1851, these monasteries were located in Saratov province; the new boundaries placed them in Samara.

[10] K. A. Papmehl, *Metropolitan Platon of Moscow (Petr Levshin, 1737–1812): The Enlightened Prelate, Scholar and Educator*, Russian Biography Series, vol. 16 (Newtonville, Mass., 1983) 60, 76; Pia G. Pera, "Edinoverie: storia di un tentativo di integrazione dei Vecchi Credenti all'interno dell'ortodossia," *Rivista di storia e letteratura religiosa* 30 (1984): 290–351; L. K. Brodskii, "K voprosu ob edinovercheskom episkope," *Khristianskoe chtenie*, 1906, 909–30; E. E. Lebedev, *Edinoverie v protivodeistvii russkomu obriadovomu raskolu: Ocherk po istorii i statistike edinoveriia s obzorom sushchestvuiushchikh o nem mnenii i prilozheniiam* (Novgorod, 1904); *Vtoroi Vserossiiskii s''ezd pravoslavnykh staroobriadtsev (edinovertsev) v N.-Novogorode 23–28 iiulia 1917 goda* (Petrograd, 1917).

ment, as often as not, helped to introduce Old Believer ideas into the Orthodox population.[11]

In the late 1830s, even as the leaders of the official church sought to repress Old Belief, the peasant Vasilii Shcheglov founded a movement that obscured the distinctions between the state church and the dissenters. Born in the village of Prislonikha in Simbirsk province, on the pilgrimage routes from Samara to Moscow and Kiev, Shcheglov built upon the common monastic ideal that the Samara Orthodox and Old Believers shared. This ideal had been embodied in the cloisters on the Irgiz. Both Old Believers and Orthodox honored the ascetic athlete who gained otherworldly wisdom by spending his or her life in prayer and fasting.

Shcheglov created communities in four districts of Samara province: Samara, Stavropol', Buguruslan, and Nikolaevsk. From the late 1830s through the 1850s, he traveled within the province, organized prayer meetings, and spread his simple moral teaching and ascetic doctrine. In his prayer meetings, his followers crossed themselves with three fingers (as did the Orthodox) or with two fingers (as did the Old Believers). Despite this indifference to the schism, Shcheglov was no Old Believer, and read and honored Tikhon (Sokolov) of Zadonsk, the eighteenth-century spiritual writer and bishop of Voronezh. Unlike the Old Believers, Shcheglov also devoutly fulfilled his ritual obligations as an Orthodox Christian, and regularly confessed to the priests and attended the liturgy. So seriously did he regard the sacrament that he fasted for a week before partaking of it.[12]

Shcheglov's openness to Old Belief was not the only characteristic that distinguished his faith from the Orthodoxy that was being developed and taught in the academies. He also had a radically different understanding of truth (*pravda*) and how to attain it. For the academic theologians and the missionaries that they later trained, truth could be contained in books and rational arguments; it could be appropriated by study and transmitted through educational institutions. Truth, like reason, was impersonal.[13] None of this was correct for Shcheglov. For him, truth was intensely personal, a spirit sent from God that dwelt only in righteous people; it could be obtained only through a personal relationship with such people. Only through the righteous was it possible to learn righteousness, for, as Christ had said, the disciple could never be greater than

[11] N. S. Sokolov, *Raskol v Saratovskom krae: Opyt issledovaniia po neizdannym materialam: Popovshchina do piatidesiatykh godov nastoiashchago stoletia* (Saratov, 1888); Samson Bystrov, "Cheremshan: Staroobriadcheskie skity na Volge," Rukopisnyi otdel Muzeia istorii religii, St. Petersburg, kollektsiia I, f. 22, no. 22.

[12] Kesarev, *Besednichestvo*, 3–12.

[13] For example, see P. S. Smirnov, *Istoriia russkogo raskola staroobriadstva* (St. Petersburg, 1895) 228–37; "Pravila uchrezhdaemoi Donskoi eparkhial'noi missionerskoi shkoly," *Donskie eparkhial'nye vedomosti* 27, no. 19 (1 October 1895): offitsial'nyi otdel, 439–53.

his teacher. Obtaining righteousness was entirely a matter of God's mysterious grace; but to obtain it, one had to submit to the spiritual direction of a superior guide. The spirit of truth crowned the righteous person with supernatural gifts, including healing, prophecy, spiritual insight (*prozorlivost'*), and the ability to unmask secret sins. The mysterious power of righteousness was evident immediately to all. When a righteous man entered a home, families ceased to quarrel and disobedient children obeyed their parents meekly. When a righteous person entered a church, everyone felt that someone greater than the books and the icons had arrived. In death, the righteous entered the Kingdom, and on their graves, the faithful built cathedrals and churches.[14]

No program of individual ascetic discipline, church attendance, or participation in the sacraments could ensure that an adept would achieve righteousness, as Shcheglov illustrated with a variety of anecdotes. In one, a monk argued with a demon:

> MONK: I fast.
> DEMON: I have never eaten.
> MONK: I stay awake to pray to God.
> DEMON: And I have never slept.
> MONK: I fear God.
> DEMON: And I tremble before him.
> MONK: I read the Scriptures.
> DEMON: And I know them by heart.[15]

Like the Old Believers, Shcheglov valued asceticism highly and imposed a severe regime on himself and his followers. A vegetarian, he usually ate once a day, and twice only during the summer harvest. He denounced the revels and debaucheries that accompanied weddings and baptisms. He condemned not only the eating of meat—which, he said, inflamed the passions—but the consumption of alcohol and tea as well. He equated the samovar with the golden calf that the Israelites had worshiped before entering the Promised Land. These attitudes—especially the prohibition of tea—betray the influence of an Old Believer morality.[16]

Like many other Orthodox Christians, Shcheglov was highly critical of the parish clergy, who were, in his view, both unworthy and incapable of fulfilling their true vocation as spiritual guides. The priests were mercenaries, serving "not for Jesus' sake, but for a piece of bread."[17] Unlike the righteous man, priests became drunk, quarreled with their families and sacristans, and clearly did not have the spirit of truth necessary for salva-

---

[14] Kesarev, *Besednichestvo*, 6–7.
[15] Ibid., 7.
[16] Ibid., 6–11; Robson, *Old Believers*, 106–8.
[17] Kesarev, *Besednichestvo*, 8.

tion. At the same time, Shcheglov never rejected the priesthood as an institution; priests, who had the power to bind and loose sins, possessed a rank higher than the angels.

After Shcheglov's death, the peasant woman Anastasiia Kerova proved to be the most capable of his successors. Kerova's followers regarded her as one of the righteous folk of whom Shcheglov had spoken, and they placed her portrait—painted with a nimbus—beside the icons on their icon shelves. For them, she possessed both spiritual insight and the power to heal. For example, she gained the undying support of Dmitrii Semēnovich Bakhmutov, a peasant from the neighboring village of Malaia Kamenka, when she healed him of a nervous disease from which he had suffered all his life. A formidable organizer, she successfully petitioned in 1859 to have her religious group officially recognized as a women's community, the first step to becoming an official convent.[18] Although a mere novice, Kerova attracted many pilgrims who came to seek her advice. She also traveled to neighboring districts to dispense advice, organize prayer meetings, and preach against vices such as alcohol and tea.

Beleaguered by the large numbers of Old Believers in the province, the church apparently made no effort to suppress the *besedchiki*—who, after all, zealously performed all their obligations as Orthodox Christians—until the 1880s, long after Shcheglov himself had died. This was partly because of the inadequacy of the church administration; both the diocese and the province of Samara were created only in 1850 and 1851 respectively.[19] But the expansion of the missionary bureaucracy in the 1860s and 70s, and the creation of full-time professional missionaries in 1886, improved the church leaders' ability to impose their views of Orthodoxy on the laity.

In 1880, Kerova was denounced for the first time to the local police, which turned the case over to the diocesan consistory. The resulting investigation accused the novice of spreading doctrines opposed to the faith and morals of the state church. Allegedly, she had declared that only the *besedchiki* could be saved; that marriage destroyed the soul; and that theft to support the *besedchiki* was morally acceptable. She mocked priests for being "big-bellied fathers" instead of "spiritual fathers" (*"ottsy briukhovnye, a ne ottsy dukhovnye"*), and encouraged mothers of illegitimate children to

---

[18] Most of the convents established during the long monastic revival of the nineteenth century started out as women's communities. Brenda Meehan, "Popular Piety, Local Initiative, and the Founding of Women's Religious Communities in Russia, 1764–1907," in *Seeking God: The Recovery of Religious Identity in Orthodox Russia, Ukraine, and Georgia*, ed. Stephen Kalmar Batalden (DeKalb, Ill., 1993), 83–105; idem, *Holy Women of Russia: The Lives of Five Orthodox Women Offer Spiritual Guidance for Today* (San Francicsco, 1993), 11–15.

[19] Pavel Mikhailovich Stroev, comp., *Spiski ierarkhov i nastoiatelei monastyrei rossiiskiia tserkvi* (St. Petersburg, 1877), cols. 1027–28; Georgii Mikhailovich Lappo, ed., *Goroda Rossii: Entsiklopediia* (Moscow, 1994) s.v. "Samara."

murder their infants. She was also charged with shamelessly exploiting her admirers by collecting money from them. In 1881, the consistory handed over its findings to the civil authorities, who began their own preliminary criminal investigation in preparation for a trial on the basis of article 196 of the criminal code. The evidence, however, was so weak that the case never came to trial. One expert witness, a Father Arkhangel'skii, even supported Kerova, and testified that, although the *besedchiki* might eventually develop into a sect, currently they were Orthodox Christians. On 16 February 1883, the Kazan Judicial Chamber closed the investigation for lack of evidence.

The *besedchiki* themselves complained that tavernkeepers had falsely denounced them and paid off some of the priests who had testified against them. Their accusations carried enough weight that several of the accused priests were later removed from their posts. Like many of the founders of women's religious communities, Kerova also faced serious local lay opposition from the *bol'shaki*, the peasant heads of households.[20] Kerova's movement, which encouraged eligible single women to remain celibate, worked against the economic interests of the peasant paterfamilias who wanted to obtain a high bride-price for his nubile daughters. The economy of the peasant commune favored early marriage and large families, while Kerova discouraged young women from marrying altogether.[21] As the missionary Evgenii Kesarev observed, many of these would-be nuns regarded a celibate monastic life as preferable to marriage, which would tear them from their families and place them under the (often tyrannical) authority of husband and mother-in-law.[22]

These *bol'shaki* initiated a new case against Kerova and her disciples in 1889 when the village assemblies of Tul'skoe and Kul'manovka, Samara district, denounced Kerova as a heretic and claimed that her followers deified her.[23] Most revealing is the elders' complaint that Kerova was undermining their authority over their children. The Tul'skoe assembly declared, "Even some of our commune members' young children who wish to enter the sect abandon their parents and threaten us with unjustified complaints."[24] The peasants of Kul'manovka voiced a similar grievance: "This teaching has seduced many of our fellow villagers—very elderly

---

[20] For other examples of opposition to the development of new monasteries, see Meehan, "Popular Piety," 90.

[21] Christine D. Worobec, *Peasant Russia: Family and Community in the Post-Emancipation Period* (Princeton, N.J., 1991), 116–17, 151–216.

[22] Kesarev, *Besednichestvo*, 1–2. Such would-be nuns existed in several provinces, including Nizhnii Novgorod and Tambov as well as Samara. M. M. Gromyko, *Mir russkoi derevni* (Moscow, 1991), 120–23; Meehan, *Holy Women*, 43.

[23] I. G. Aivazov, comp., *Materialy dlia issledovaniia russkikh misticheskikh sekt. Khristovshchina*, 3 vols. (St. Petersburg, 1915–16), 1:336–38.

[24] Aivazov, *Materialy*, 1:337.

people and especially our thoughtless and gullible children who have unwaveringly started to attend these meetings."[25] A second ecclesiastical investigation again found enough evidence to refer the case to the civil authorities, but again the latter found the case so weak that they refused to bring it to trial.

On 24 October 1892, Bishop Gurii (Sergii Burtasovskii, 1845–1907), who was fiercely devoted to the missionary enterprise, ascended the episcopal throne of Samara, where he reigned until 1904. A graduate of the Kazan Theological Academy, upon his tonsure, Burtasovskii had chosen the name of the first bishop of Kazan in the middle of the sixteenth-century, known for his devotion to spreading Christianity among the Tatars. As bishop of Kamchatka (1885–92), Gurii had forced the indigenous population to send their children to a large two-year boarding school located in Khabarovsk. Quite willing to use force when necessary, Gurii (nicknamed "Gurii the Tempest [*Gurii s burei*]" for his sharp temper) showed the same diligence in his efforts to make the *besedchiki* conform to his understanding of Orthodoxy.

Disappointed by the secular authorities' unwillingness to imprison heretics without convincing evidence against them, Gurii took his own measures. On 16 August 1893, he traveled to Rakovka, Kerova's home village, and after celebrating the liturgy, formally pronounced an anathema against Kerova and her followers. When Kerova came to receive a blessing from her bishop, according to Gurii, "not only did I not bless her, but, within the hearing of all present, I excommunicated her from the Church and forbade the local priest to admit her to confession or communion because she had spread the Montanist heresy to almost all the districts of Samara diocese." (As was typical, Gurii identified Kerova's group with a well-known heresy—in this case, Montanism, an apocalyptic group led by charismatic prophets in the second century—that church councils had already thoroughly condemned.) The excommunication had the desired effect; Kerova repented and requested that she be allowed to enter the monastery to pay for her sins. But, although she repented of her audacity in teaching others, she insisted that she had never been part of any heretical movement. Gurii was not satisfied, and in subsequent correspondence with Kerova, he demanded that she repent of having taught at all: "Your great guilt lies not only in that you taught the people without authorization, but primarily in that you . . . attributed greater significance for salvation to these assemblies than to the divinely established sacred authority of the church and the divinely established sacraments of the church."[26] Finally, Kerova produced a statement that Gurii could accept. In 1894, he permitted her to be ton-

[25] Ibid.
[26] Ibid., 343, 354–55.

sured as the nun Mariia in Samara's Iverskii Convent. This was to no avail; Kerova's disciples continued to flock to her. After only three years, Gurii had her sent to the monastery prison of the Pokrovskii Convent in Suzdal'.

Surrounded by heterodoxy, Gurii wanted to ensure that all teaching would be in the hands of competent, seminary-trained professionals. But the shortage of resources to support parish priests, their lack of charismatic authority, and the social distance between cleric and peasant virtually assured the persistence of cults such as Kerova's. By the end of his reign in Samara, even Gurii was uncertain about his treatment of the *besedchiki*. In February 1902, he declared: "Whenever the question of the *besedchiki* arises, I feel deeply conscience-stricken; it seems to me more and more that we have incorrectly understood them and we ourselves have alienated them from the life of God by suspecting them of sectarianism."[27] Gurii appointed a commission to study the question, but its report was inconclusive. Some of the members, such as the missionary Evgenii Kesarev, were convinced that the *besedchiki* had largely left Orthodoxy behind in their spiritual yearnings. But many priests regarded them as model parishioners. For example, in 1911, Father Vasilii Krylov wrote:

> One cannot say anything bad about our *besedchiki*. Their relations with the clergy and the Orthodox are completely peaceful. Clearly, the *besedchiki* express nothing contrary to Orthodoxy; according to outward signs, the material situation of the *besedchiki* is better than that of the Orthodox and their religio-moral situation is also better. They are attached to the local Orthodox church; they are interested in the salvation of their souls; and they are sober.[28]

Despite Gurii's efforts, the *besedchiki* continued to maintain their religious communities and practices in the four districts where Shcheglov had spread his message. The controversy over their activities testified to a serious dilemma for the church leaders like Gurii, who, on the one hand, sincerely wanted to reach his flock with the Orthodox message, but, on the other, deeply distrusted the charismatic religion of peasant holy men and women, however attached they might be to the church.

The Podgornovtsy: Orthodox Heretics in Ukraine

Bishops on the outskirts of the empire confronted the same dilemma. Because Moscow perceived religious pluralism as a serious threat in polit-

---

[27] Kesarev, *Besednichestvo*, 114.

[28] Cited in Mikhail Alekseev, "Otchet o sostoianii sektantstva i staroobriadchestva i protivosektantskoi i protivostaroobriadcheskoi missii v Samarskoi eparkhii v 1911 g." *Samarskie eparkhial'nye vedomosti* 46, no. 1 (1 January 1912): 39.

ically sensitive Ukraine, Orthodox collegia there faced more stringent scrutiny than in other parts of the empire. Missionaries in the Western Provinces received special state subsidies. The repressed Byzantine Catholic (Uniate) Church (forcibly united to the Russian Orthodox Church in the nineteenth century) was deemed dangerous enough that the Holy Synod took special measures to ensure liturgical conformity in its Ukrainian dioceses. And Catholicism was not the only menace; after the 1860s, Baptism enjoyed its greatest success in Ukraine and the Caucasus. With an episcopate wary of pietism, the Orthodox Church leaders regarded even zealously Orthodox movements, if they were popular and charismatic, with concern.

Vasilii Karpovich Podgornyi, a peasant from Trostianets, a village in the Akhtyrsk district of Khar'kov province, led one such movement. From an early age, he had demonstrated a deep and conscientious Orthodox piety. While still a young man, he opened a school in his own home, and on Sundays he read saints' lives and other edifying works to adults. In the 1870s, he obtained a small brick factory and used his money to support pilgrims who stayed with him for considerable periods of time. Podgornyi himself made several pilgrimages to Mount Athos, the world center of Orthodox monasticism, and to other holy places.[29]

Podgornyi sponsored the formation of several unofficial monastic communities. One of these, which he had helped to found on land he owned near the town of Bogodukhov, was formally registered in 1889 as a women's community.[30] Distinguished by his extraordinary piety, Podgornyi never missed the liturgy and often traveled to Khar'kov to attend episcopal services.

Podgornyi attracted primarily unmarried women into his communities, where he imposed a strict cenobitic rule. He also introduced a rigorous devotional life; on the eves of Sundays and feast days, his followers met for all-night prayer meetings, which included the singing of popular spiritual hymns. He and his followers held to a strict moral code, which condemned alcohol, tobacco, and swearing.

Much to his misfortune, Podgornyi came to the attention of Archbishop Amvrosii (Aleksei Ivanovich Kliucharev, 1820–1901) of Khar'kov (r. 1882–1901). A native Muscovite, Amvrosii had been sent to Khar'kov to impose liturgical conformity on the Ukrainians. Far more conservative

---

[29] Butkevich, *Obzor*, 166–70.

[30] V. V. Zverinskii, comp., *Material dlia istoriko-topograficheskogo issledovaniia o pravoslavnykh monastyriakh v Rossiiskoi imperii, s bibliograficheskim ukazatelem*, 3 vols. (St. Petersburg, 1890–97), 1:262, no. 498; Leonid Ivanovich Denisov, comp., *Pravoslavnye monastyri Rossiiskoi imperii: Polnyi spisok vsekh 1105 nyne sushchestvuiushchikh v 75 guberniiakh i obliastiakh Rossii (i 2 inostrannykh gosudarstvakh) muzhskikh i zhenskikh monastyrei, arkhiereiskikh domov i zhenskikh obshchin* (Moscow, 1908), 897.

than his episcopal peers, Amvrosii was suspicious of the liturgical innovation and charismatic spirituality represented by Podgornyi and his followers. Amvrosii permitted one of Podgornyi's communities to become a full-fledged convent, but when choosing an abbess for the community in 1889, Amvrosii deliberately passed over Podgornyi's daughter and picked an outsider, a nun from Kursk, to lead the community. He permitted the community to become an official monastery only in 1893, after the Holy Synod had imprisoned Podgornyi.[31]

Podgornyi faced the same opposition from the local village patriarchs as did Kerova. Eventually, he was accused of organizing orgies, and one peasant woman complained that her underage daughter had been raped in a Podgornite meeting. Amvrosii's investigation of these charges led the synod to decree on 17 October 1892 that Podgornyi's continued freedom was a danger to the morals of the community. Significantly, Podgornyi was never tried in a secular court and never charged with any specific crime. Two weeks later, on 31 October, Podgornyi was taken to Suzdal' and imprisoned in the Spaso-Evfimiev monastery. His wife and two daughters followed him there where they lived in an apartment in the nearby Pokrovskii convent.

The imprisonment only augmented Podgornyi's reputation among his followers who now regarded him as a martyr, unjustly punished for his faith. He did not repent and maintained a vigorous correspondence with his followers who supported him with their offerings. While Podgornyi was in prison, the numbers of his adherents actually grew.

The Khar'kov heresiologist Timofei Ivanovich Butkevich accused Podgornyi's followers of sexual depravity. He claimed that the *podgornovtsy* encouraged—and even demanded—promiscuity to rid virgins of their pride. But the veracity of these charges seems very unlikely in light of the support that Podgornyi enjoyed from some of the local clergy, including the diocesan missionary of Kursk, Father Ioann Petrovich Riabukhin, who regarded him as a genuine "spiritual elder" (*starets*).[32] Another priest of Kursk diocese, Aleksandr Nedrigailov, publicly defended the *podgornovtsy* in print.[33] And even Butkevich had to admit that Podgornyi's disciples scrupulously attended church, observed the Orthodox fasts, invited priests to their homes, and made pilgrimages to traditional Orthodox holy sites.[34]

After Amvrosii died in 1901, a new investigation began on 25 October

---

[31] Manuil (Lemeshevskii), Metropolitan of Kuibyshev, *Die Russischen Orthodoxen Bischöfe von 1893–1965: Bio-Bibliografie*, ed. Coelestin Patock, 6 vols. (Erlangen, 1979–89), 1:178–87; Freeze, *Parish Clergy*, 418–21; Butkevich, *Obzor*, 166–70.

[32] F. K——v, "Stefanovtsy," *Missionerskoe obozrenie* 20, no. 4 (April 1915): 655–56.

[33] L. Z. Kuntsevich, "Pravda o podgornovtsakh" *Revnitel'* 2, no. 6–7 (June–July 1912): 36.

[34] Butkevich, *Obzor*, 166–70.

that ultimately cleared Podgornyi of the vague accusations against him.[35] On 17 January 1903, Abbot Serafim (Leonid Mikhailovich Chichagov, 1856–1938) declared him to be perfectly Orthodox and offered him his freedom. By this time, Podgornyi's wife had died; rather than return home, Podgornyi preferred to remain in the monastery as the monk Stefan. Even Butkevich gives no indication that the monk ever admitted to or repented of the charges of promoting sexual depravity that had led to his imprisonment. Clearly, as the journalist Aleksandr Prugavin concluded, these charges were baseless fabrications.[36]

But why, then, did hierarchs such as Amvrosii and heresiologists like Butkevich so quickly condemn Podgornyi and his disciples? Their reaction demonstrated a profound distrust of charismatic spirituality that possessed a power independent of the church hierarchy. Spontaneous night-long prayer meetings in private homes led by peasants in informal monastic communities seemed too close to sectarianism for Amvrosii, an academy-trained Muscovite member of the clerical estate. When peasant families, disturbed by their daughters' embrace of the celibate life, attacked the movement, it was easy for Amvrosii to believe the worst.

Abbot Serafim (Chichagov), who ultimately freed Podgornyi, had a much more sympathetic view of charismatic Orthodoxy. An aristocrat who had graduated from the elite Corps of Pages, Chichagov had had a successful military career, and became a priest in 1893 only after retiring from the army as a colonel. He adopted his religious vocation under the influence of Father Ioann Sergiev of Kronstadt, the charismatic, miracle-working priest famous for his passionate celebrations of the liturgy and his public healing services. Chichagov devoutly venerated another charismatic thaumaturge, Serafim of Sarov (1754–1833),[37] and chose the name Serafim for himself when he was tonsured in 1898 after his wife's death. Both Amvrosii and Serafim were conservative Orthodox monks, but Chichagov's lay background and his natural sympathy toward the solitary ascetic made him far more supportive of Podgornyi. Even after he had left the Spaso-Evfimev Monastery to take the episcopal see of Orel, Serafim kept in contact with the Podgornites.[38] The 1912 census of the Department of Spiritual Affairs found only thirty-five Podgornites, all in Khar'kov

[35] Kuntsevich, "Pravda o podgornovtsakh," 38–39.

[36] *Polnyi pravoslavnyi bogoslovskii entsiklopedicheskii slovar'*, 2 vols. (St. Petersburg, 1913), s.v. "Kishinevskaia eparkhiia" and "Serafim (Chichagov)"; Butkevich, *Obzor*, 170; A. S. Prugavin, *Monastyrskie tiur'my v bor'be s sektantstvom: K voprosu o veroterpimosti*, Izdanie "Posrednika" dlia intelligentnykh chitatelei (St. Petersburg, 1904), 119–21.

[37] Serafim was born in 1754–not 1759, as commonly stated. F. S. Sokolov, "Prepodobnyi Serafim, Sarovskii chudotvorets: Novye dannyia dlia zhizneopisaniia ego," *Izvestiia Tambovskoi uchenoi arkhivnoi kommissii* 51 (1906): 9.

[38] *Revnitel'* 2, no. 6–7 (June–July 1912): 38–39.

province.[39] By 1913, Podgornyi's followers seem to have been reintegrating into the church.

Urban Heretics on the Right: The Ioannites

The urbanization of Russia in the last decades of the empire also resulted in new forms of urban Orthodoxy, not all of which found acceptance in the church. Filled with recent peasant migrants working in menial jobs, the city presented the church with serious challenges at the end of the Old Regime. To retain the allegiance of this new urban class was no easy task. However rude life was in the village, at least the church and agrarian calendars were tied closely together; peasants remembered St. George when they drove the cattle to pasture, and observed church fasts in part because they made some sense in terms of the annual food production schedule.[40]

In factories, run by the clock, saints' days passed unnoticed.[41] Moreover, many urban immigrants worked long hours and had little time to attend the liturgy. In addition, vices such as alcoholism and prostitution, though present in the countryside, were more obvious in the city.[42] As a body, the Orthodox Church tried to confront these vices and minister to the proletarians in various ways, in part by establishing temperance societies.[43] But the most dramatic developments in urban missions were led by individual religious innovators, such as Father Ioann Sergiev (1829–1908), the pastor of St. Andrew's Cathedral in the port city of Kronstadt.

By the 1880s, Ioann had gained a nationwide following for the reputed power of his prayers. An ascetic who lived a celibate life with his wife, Ioann had devoted his life to reaching the urban poor and to combatting alchoholism. To accomplish his mission, he had introduced innovations into the liturgy, including public (as opposed to the traditional private)

---

[39] *Statisticheskie svedeniia o sektantakh (k 1 ianvaria 1912 g.)*, 39. This was undoubtedly an undercount.

[40] Robert E. Smith, F. and David Christian, *Bread and Salt : A Social and Economic History of Food and Drink in Russia* (New York, 1984).

[41] Semen Kanatchikov, *A Radical Worker in Tsarist Russia: The Autobiography of Semen Ivanovich Kanatchikov*, ed. and trans. Reginald E. Zelnik, (Stanford, Calif., 1986).

[42] On the history of prostitution, legalized in 1843, see *Sbornik pravitel'stvennykh rasporiazhenii kasaiushchikhsia mer preduprezhdeniia rasprostraneniia liubostrastnoi bolezni*, Izdanie Knizhnago magazina iuridicheskoi literatury D. V. Chichinadze (St. Petersburg, 1886); Laurie Bernstein, *Sonia's Daughters: Prostitutes and Their Regulation in Imperial Russia* (Berkeley, Calif., 1995); Laura Engelstein, *The Keys to Happiness: Sex and the Search for Modernity in Fin-de-Siècle Russia* (Ithaca, N.Y., 1992), 86–93.

[43] Patricia Herlihy, *Strategies of Sobriety : Temperance Movements in Russia, 1880–1914*, Occasional paper (Kennan Institute for Advanced Russian Studies), vol. 238 (Washington, D.C., 1990).

Father Ioann of Kronstadt in the 1880s. Tsentral'nyi Gosudarstvennyi Arkhiv Kinofotofon-odokumentov, St. Petersburg.

confession; ad hoc and impromptu prayers; and—most dramatic of all—healing services.[44]

Ioann was remarkably successful. By the early 1880s, his reputation as a miracle-worker was attracting pilgrims from all over the empire. Some of these followers bought homes and established in them informal monastic communities that observed a strict discipline. These communities also rented space to pilgrims who came to see Father Ioann.[45]

The most important of these communities was founded by Porfiriia Ivanovna Kiseleva, who would later be accused of styling herself as Father Ioann's "Theotokos" (*bogoroditsa*). In 1895, Kiseleva moved to Kronstadt from Oranienbaum and formed a community of women who lived under monastic discipline and worshiped at St. Andrew's Cathedral. She also attracted male followers from Kronstadt's lower classes, such as Vasilii Fedorovich Pustoshkin, a former bailiff, and Nikolai Ivanovich Bol'shakov, who had once worked in a bathhouse.[46] Never a formally structured denomination, the Ioannites grew by sending out colporteurs who sold literature and religious artifacts, such as portraits of Father Ioann, at inflated prices. These colporteurs were often women who had lived for a time in the semimonastic communities of Kronstadt and St. Petersburg. According to reports from several dioceses, they had the most success with other pious Orthodox women, who bought the portraits, placed them with their icons, and prayed to Father Ioann as to a saint.[47] They never regarded themselves as anything but true Orthodox believers.

The most active and visible publicists for the admirers of Father Ioann were Pustoshkin and Bol'shakov. Convinced that Father Ioann represented true Orthodoxy, which was being betrayed by less devoted and more educated priests, Pustoshkin and Bol'shakov formed the Brotherhood of Ioann of Kronstadt after the 1905 revolution. In 1906, Bol'shakov started the weekly *Kronshtadtskii maiak* (The Kronstadt Beacon), the chief Ioannite publication.[48] At the same time, Pustoshkin organized dormitories, orphanages, and workshops which produced the literature, photographs, and religious items that the independent Ioannite colporteurs

---

[44] Nadieszda Kizenko, *A Prodigal Saint: Ioann of Kronstadt and the Russian People* (University Park, Pa., 2000).

[45] Feodosii Kirika, "Ioannity," in *Russkie sektanty: Ikh uchenie, kul't i sposoby propagandy: bratskii trud chlenov IV Vserossiiskogo missionerskogo s″ezda (s portretami sektantov i kartinami sektantskikh radenii)*, ed. M. A. Kal'nev (Odessa, 1911), 288.

[46] I. A. Alekseev, *Razgrom ioannitov* (St. Petersburg, 1909), 17.

[47] Ioann Efimov, priest, "Besedy s sektantami v stanitse Tikhoretskoi," *Missionerskie izvestiia po Stavropol'skoi eparkhii. Ezhenedel'nyi listok: Prilozhenie k Stavropol'skim eparkhial'nym vedomostiam* 6, no. 21 (2 October 1916): 153; M. Alekseev, "Sostoianie sektantstva za 1910," *Samarskie eparkhial'nye vedomosti*, 1911, 41–42.

[48] Butkevich, *Obzor*, p. 160; L. N. Beliaeva, M. K. Zinov'eva and M. M. Nikiforov, comps., *Bibliografiia periodicheskikh izdanii Rossii 1901–1916*, ed. V. M. Barashenkova, O. D. Golubeva and N. Ia Morachevskii, 4 vols. (Leningrad, 1958–61), 3:216, no. 4200.

sold throughout the empire.[49] In 1909, Nikolai Nikolaevich Zhedenov, a member of the Brotherhood of Ioann of Kronstadt, began publishing a daily newspaper, *Groza* (The Storm).[50]

Extreme devotion to Father Ioann troubled some members of the Orthodox hierarchy, who had never been terribly comfortable with his innovations. In 1892, the aged Metropolitan Isidor (Nikol'skii, 1799–1892) of St. Petersburg (r. 1860–92) ordered the popular priest to travel to Lugov hamlet in Gdov district, to exhort the peasant Vasilii Kondratov, who stood accused of regarding Father Ioann as Christ himself. Such public denials became routine; in 1895, Ioann published a letter disavowing the claim of a Samara peasant that he was a second incarnation of Christ.[51] And in 1902, the synod directed the priest to Kostroma to exhort another misguided group of peasants. In his report for 1901, the synodal Supreme Procurator Konstantin Pobedeonostsev announced the existence of a new sect, the *ioannity* or Ioannites, who paid too much veneration to the pastor of the Kronstadt cathedral.[52] In 1904, the police in St. Petersburg arrested the peasant Prokhor Skorobagatchenkov of Karpovka sloboda in the Don region, for spreading the Ioannite heresy.[53] Finally, in 1908 the Fourth All-Russian Missionary Congress in Kiev formally condemned the Ioannites as outside the pale of Orthodoxy; the synod confirmed this censure with its own resolution of December 1908.

Father Ioann, who was extremely adept at self-promotion—he had his signed photographs sent out to subscribers of *Russkii Palomnik* (The Russian Pilgrim)—initially did little to discourage the veneration of his adoring public; writing in 1911 after Ioann's death, the missionary priest Feodosii Kirika tried to absolve the popular priest of any responsibility for the rise of the Ioannites by blaming Kiseleva's "diabolical cunning" in taking advantage of Ioann's "childlike trust."[54] Yet as late as 1905, Father Ioann was actually publicly defending Kiseleva and Bol'shakov—although hardly in the most flattering way. In a carefully worded letter to the newspaper *Kotlin*, Ioann wrote: "the woman [Kiseleva] who is blasphemously called a Theotokos is not guilty at all of this nickname, as I know positively [*dostoverno*]; she is sick, and sits at home all day in her corner. . . . Believe me,

---

[49] Alekseev, *Razgrom*, 1–32.

[50] *Padenie tsarskogo rezhima: Stenograficheskie otchety doprosov i pokazanii, dannykh v 1917 g. v Chrezvychainoi sledstvennoi komissii Vremennogo pravitel'stva*, ed. P. E. Shchegolev, 7 vols. (Moscow, 1924–27), 6:193, 7:339.

[51] "Novoe lzheuchenie," *Strannik* 36, no. 3 (March 1895): 629; Ioann Sergiev, "Pis'mo prot. Ioanna Sergieva oblichaiushchee lzheverie krest'ianki Klipikovoi," *Samarskie eparkhial'nye vedomosti* 29, no. 6 (15 March 1895): offitsial'naia chast', 60.

[52] Kirika, "Ioannity," 289–91.

[53] M. Lisitsyn, "Khronika: Missionerstvo, sekty i raskol. Sostoianie raskolo-sektantstva v istekshem godu," *Missionerskoe obozrenie*, 1904, 232–39.

[54] Kirika, "Ioannity," 291.

reader, as a priest. I am the confessor of the unhappy and sick Porfiriia. . . ."[55] But by 1907, Father Ioann had realized the danger that these
admirers posed for his own position within the church. Ever more syco-
phantic toward his ecclesiastical superiors, Ioann obligingly issued denunciation after denunciation to distance himself from the Ioannites.[56]

What was so dangerous about the Ioannites that led to their excommunication? The most sensational charge—that they regarded Ioann of Kronstadt as God Incarnate—was probably false and was bitterly denied by
prominent members of the Brotherhood of Ioann of Kronstadt, such as
Il'ia Alekseev, who became editor of *Kronshtadtskii maiak* after Bol'shakov's
death.[57] Moreover, two distinguished missionaries defended the Ioannites
against these charges. Dmitrii Ivanovich Bogoliubov, the diocesan missionary of St. Petersburg, and Father Arsenii (Minin, 1841–1914), an
Athonite monk and former synodal missionary, both affirmed the fully
Orthodox character of Ioannite devotion.[58]

Certainly, the Ioannites considered Ioann to be a saint. They treated his
photograph as an icon, placed it on their icon shelves, venerated it, and
(after Ioann's death) prayed to the priest for help and healing. Missionaries criticized such behavior, but the cult simply anticipated a future canonization and is hardly evidence that Ioann's devotees regarded him as
Christ himself.[59] Indeed, many official church publications supported the
cult of Ioann and publicized his posthumous miracles. In September
1911, for example, the official church journal *Revnitel'* (The Zealot), published in Khar'kov, reported that Father Ioann had posthumously healed
a merchant's daughter through the prayers of her teacher, to whom the
dead priest had miraculously appeared.[60]

The condemnation of the Ioannites is especially surprising given the

[55] Alekseev, *Razgrom*, 30.
[56] A. G. Kuliashev, "Beseda Permskogo eparkhial'nogo missionera s ioannitom—Vasiliem
Chernakovym," *Permskie eparkhial'nye vedomosti* 42, no. 2 (11 January 1908): 22–23.
[57] Alekseev, *Razgrom*, 1–32.
[58] N. M. Griniakin, "Advokaty ioannitstva kak svideteli ego eretichestva," *Missionerskoe
obozrenie*, no. 11 (November 1909): 1789–1800; no. 12 (December 1909): 1969–86; *Soiuz
russkogo naroda: Po materialam chrezvychainoi sledstvennoi kommissii vremennogo pravitel'stva 1917
g.*, ed. A. Chernovskii and V. P. Viktorova (Moscow, 1929), 32–35; S. P——lin, "Sobese-
dovaniia missionera ieromonakha Arseniia v Voronezhskoi dukhovnoi seminarii," *Voronezh-
skie eparkhial'nye vedomosti*, 1889, 18–33.
[59] A. G. Kuliashev, "Beseda Permskogo eparkhial'nogo missionera s ioannitom—Vasiliem
Chernakovym," *Permskie eparkhial'nye vedomosti* 42, no. 2 (11 January 1908):21–25; no. 3 (21
January 1908): 61–65; "Protokol doznaniia pristava Usmanskogo uezda o propagande sredi
krest'ian sela Zaval'nogo ucheniia ioannitov," *Sovremennoe sektantstvo i ego preodelenie: Po materialam ekspeditsii v Tambovskuiu oblast' v 1959 g.*, Voprosy istorii religii i ateizma, vol. 9
(Moscow, 1961) 110.
[60] A. I. Khmelevskaia, "Molitva ottsa Ioanna Kronshtadtskogo," *Revnitel'* 1, no. 5–6 (Sept.
1911):40.

many characteristics they shared with the professional missionaries. Both groups staunchly supported the monarchy.[61] Both groups believed that Orthodoxy faced a serious threat from Western religious movements, such as Baptism, and from freethinking intellectuals, such as Lev Nikolaevich Tolstoy.[62] Professional missionaries and Ioannites voiced similar reproaches of the parish priests, whom they held responsible for a perceived decline of faith in the empire.[63]

Both groups also promoted anti-Semitism. At the Third All-Russian Missionary Congress of 1897, Bishop Meletii (Mikhail Koz'mich Iakimov, 1835–1900) of Riazan' (r. 1896–1900) compared religious dissenters with the Jews:

> In Russia there is no small number of Jews, another force that is destroying our Russian communities. . . . [T]heir passion for lucre is known to the whole world. Wherever Jews appear, they squeeze the property of honest citizens and lead them to poverty and a hopeless situation. Obviously, it is no longer possible to take away this evil, so that [the government] has begun to limit the rights of the Jews to live where they wish. The same thing must be said of the harm of the schism and sects. Here is the same system of exploitation for the support of the lifestyles that schismatics and sectarians have chosen for themselves.[64]

During the infamous 1913 Beilis case (in which the Jew Mendel Beilis [1874–1934] was falsely accused of a ritual murder of a Christian child) the most important journal of the official missionary movement, *Missionerskoe obozrenie*, ran a long article accusing Jews of practicing ritual infanticide. And one of the most prominent missionaries, Father Ioann Vostorgov (1866–1918), served as president of the Moscow chapter of the anti-Semitic Union of Russian People.[65]

As crude as this anti-Semitism was, the anti-Semitism of the Ioannites was far cruder. *Groza*, one of the Ioannite journals, peppered its pages with limericks about the "Yids" (*zhidy*). A typical poem, appropriately entitled "The Yids," blamed the Jews for all of Russia's problems and called for their expulsion:

[61] *Groza*, 11 January 1912, 2.

[62] "Sviateishii Sinod i pravoslavnye liudi," ibid., 3 January 1912, 1–2.

[63] "Vnimaniiu g. Skvortsova," ibid., 4 October 1909, 4; *Deianiia 3-go Vserossiiskogo missionerskogo s''ezda v Kazani po voprosam vnutrennei missii i raskolosektantstva*, ed. Vasilii Mikhailovich Skvortsov (Kiev, 1897), 43–44; N., "Neskol'ko slov ob uchastii prikhodskogo dukhovenstva v missionerstve," *Permskie eparkhial'nye vedomosti* 38, no. 1 (1 January 1904): 37–39; "Missioner," *Permskie eparkhial'nye vedomosti* 42, no. 9 (21 March 1908): 160–64.

[64] *Deianiia 3-go Vserossiiskogo missionerskogo s''ezda*, 35.

[65] *Missionerskoe obozrenie* 18, no. 12 (December 1913): 559–97; *Soiuz russkogo naroda*, 21, 31, 103–106, 143–44, 147, 201–4.

> From the beginning of the world
> To our time
> There has never been anything more malicious
> Than the Yid tribe.
> They enserfed
> All our Russian people
> They themselves live like gods
> Without needs.
>
> Will we soon drive out
> All the arrogant Yids
> And start to live anew
> Without heavy chains?[66]

But anti-Semitism, instead of bringing these two representatives of right-wing politics together, simply underscored the subtle but important differences between them. Missionaries, who were more refined and educated than most Ioannites, rarely used the rude epithet *zhid* and preferred the more neutral term "Jew" (*evrei*)—even when defending anti-Semitic absurdities like the myth of Jewish ritual infanticide. The Ioannites, on the other hand, attacked all their enemies, including the missionary establishment and the Baptists, as "Yids."[67] In an improbable exchange, the two sides accused each other of philo-Semitism: the editor of *Kronshtadt-skii maiak* complained of "Yid-like" missionaries, while the official church journal *Kolokol* (The Bell) responded that Jewish merchants published and bound Ioannite literature.[68]

Other points of apparent similarity also masked underlying differences. Both the Ioannite and the missionary presses wrote of the grave threat that Protestant and freethinking heresy presented to Orthodoxy, but the Ioannites wrote in a desperate, apocalyptic tone. Nikolai Bol'shakov's 1906 pamphlet *The Twentieth Century* predicted the imminent end of the world. In a 1907 sermon, the Ioannite Vasilii Chernakov declared that death was preferable to living in these times.[69] In 1910, a group of Ioannite women claimed that Halley's Comet was a harbinger of the final judgment.[70]

The Ioannites differed from the missionaries in their rejection of the *rationalized* Orthodoxy that the latter represented. They stood instead for

---

[66] Russkii palomnik, "Zhidy," *Groza*, 21 January 1912, 2.

[67] Alekseev, *Razgrom*; "Zhidy kak osnovateli Baptizma," *Groza* 4 October 1909, 3.

[68] "Novyi udar glavnomu shtabu ioannitsko-kiselevskoi sekty," *Kolokol*, 16 February 1912, 3.

[69] A. G. Kuliashev, "Beseda Permskogo eparkhial'nogo missionera s ioannitom—Vasiliem Chernakovym," *Permskie eparkhial'nye vedomosti* 42, no. 2 (11 January 1908):20, no. 3 (21 January 1908): 64–65.

[70] Alekseev, "Sostoianie sektantstva za 1910," 41–42.

a popular anti-intellectual spirituality that was suspicious of the theological training provided in the academies—theological training that missionaries were required to undergo. In one typical article in *Groza*, a Ioannite attacked a list of "unbelieving" academy graduates whose atheism was supposedly driving away the faithful. In place of education—so highly revered by the missionary establishment—the Ioannites honored the charismatic power of ascetic athletes, exemplified by Father Ioann.[71] In his pamphlet *A Confession to Metropolitan Antonii*, addressed to the liberal Metropolitan Antonii (Vadkovskii) of St. Petersburg (already under pressure for his protection of liberal clerics), Pustoshkin attacked the Orthodox clergy for being too deeply influenced by Tolstoyanism.[72]

The Ioannites also rejected the authority of the synod and its bureaucracy. During the last years of the Old Regime, they bitterly condemned the synod for its cozy relations with Grigorii Efimovich Rasputin (1870–1916), the Siberian faith healer who had gained the confidence of the imperial family. They especially castigated Vasilii Skvortsov, the chief antisectarian missionary attached to the synod, for his failure to censure Rasputin.[73]

Perhaps most importantly, the Ioannites differed sociologically from the missionaries. The professional missionaries came primarily from the clerical estate and had been educated in elite theological institutions. The leading Ioannites, like Bol'shakov and Pustoshkin, were peasant migrants to the city with little formal education. According to the 1912 census of sectarian movements, the Ioannites numbered 1,079 and were concentrated primarily in St. Petersburg and Tavrida provinces, where the Black Sea and Baltic Sea fleets were located (see table 1). Drawn from an urban proletariat, suspicious of theological education and the church bureaucracy, the Ioannites naturally clashed with the missionaries, despite their many similarities.

Urban Heretics on the Left: The Teetotalers

The Orthodox Church and its missionaries also had difficulty understanding what to do with the *trezvenniki*, the pietistic, teetotaling followers of the Samara peasant Ivan Alekseevich Churikov (1862–1929?). Like the Ioannites, Churikov and his followers began as a popular urban move-

---

[71] Boris Vasil'ev, "Dukhovnye mstiteli," *Groza*, 29 October 1909, 2–3; "Ioannovskoe bratstvo," ibid., 8 November 1909, 2.

[72] Kuliashev, "Beseda Permskogo eparkhial'nogo missionera," 23.

[73] "Khlysty i Skvortsov," *Groza*, 2 March 1912, 2. The former head of the Department of Police, Stepan Beletskii, testified in 1917 that Skvortsov had enjoyed close and friendly ties to Rasputin (*Padenie tsarskogo rezhima*, 4:166–69).

Table 1. Ioannites in the Russian
Empire, by province, 1912

St. Petersburg	519
Tavrida	227
Ekaterinoslav	116
Ufa	114
Minsk	60
Khar'kov	13
Mogilev	10
Tomsk	11
Saratov	7
Kostroma	2
Total	1079

Source: MVD census of 1912, in *Statisticheskie svedeniia o sektantakh (k 1 ianvaria
1912 g.),* Izdanie Departamenta dukhovnykh del, Ministerstva vnutrennikh
del (St. Petersburg, 1912), 40.

ment that sought to renew Orthodoxy in the context of the city. But unlike the Ioannites, who regarded Tolstoy as evil, Churikov and his followers, over time, came increasingly under the influence of the great writer
and the religious movement that he founded.

A prosperous trader in the village of Aleksandrov-Gai in Novouzensk
district of Samara province, Churikov fell into a deep depression after the
deaths of his daughter and wife. Turning to Father Ioann of Kronstadt for
comfort, in 1894 Churikov left Samara for St. Petersburg, where he settled in a worker's neighborhood on the Vasil'evskii Island. There, in apparent imitation of his spiritual mentor, Churikov began to preach
against the evils of alcohol, swearing, and debauchery.[74] Like Father
Ioann, Churikov preached the gospel, healed the sick through prayer,
and encouraged public confession.

In 1897, the St. Petersburg police informed church authorities of
Churikov's unusual ministry, and he was forced to return to his village.
Accused of claiming supernatural power, Churikov was placed in an in-
sane asylum in 1898, but was released after three months. In 1900 the
strict Bishop Gurii of Samara (who regarded Churikov as a dangerous
charlatan) had him imprisoned in the Suzdal' Spaso-Evfimev Monastery—
the same monastery where Podgornyi spent ten years of his life. But again,
thanks to his connections in the capital, Churikov remained in prison for
a mere five days; a special synodal resolution liberated him, and he re-

[74] I. M. Gromoglasov, "Rech' prof. I. M. Gromoglasov," in *Sbornik rechei o trezvennicheskom
dvizhenii, proiznesennykh v sobraniiakh Tsentral'nogo komiteta Soiuza 17-go oktiabria v Moskve i Pe-
terburge 5, 6, 13 i 14 maia 1913 g.,* ed. K. E. Lindeman (Moscow, 1913), 12.

turned to St. Petersburg. From 1903, he began holding weekly public meetings on Petrovskii Island. Known as the "little brother" (*bratets*), Churikov enjoyed increasing popularity among the urban poor.[75]

A follower of Tolstoy, Ivan Mikhailovich Tregubov (1853–1938), befriended Churikov and published transcripts of his meetings. These documents provide a dramatic picture of Churikov's oratorical abilities. Wearing a large pectoral cross (usually reserved for priests), Churikov exhorted his adoring public with admonitions to abstain from meat and alcohol and to study the Word of God. As he expounded on the scriptures or the lives of the saints, Churikov's audience responded vocally to his preaching. For example, as he read the prayers for 14 January 1912, the day of the Georgians' Saint Nina, the crowd equated their preacher with the Orthodox saint. "Praise the God of Nina," Churikov read. "The God of the little brother," responded the crowd.[76]

Typically, Churikov provided simple ethical interpretations of religious texts. He criticized those who performed pilgrimages to holy places, while failing "to live for others." On 22 January 1912, while expounding on the Creed, he took the resurrection of the body as a metaphor for overcoming alcoholism: "Besides the bodily resurrection . . . there is also a spiritual resurrection, and therefore I hope for a resurrection from drunkenness to sobriety."[77]

These personal interpretations, delivered with evident authority, provided ammunition for Churikov's critics, who accused him of denying basic Orthodox truths (such as the resurrection of the body). These critics included the most prominent members of the missionary movement, including Ivan Georgievich Aivazov (Professor of the History and Unmasking of Sectarianism at the Moscow Theological Academy) and Vasilii Skvortsov, the editor of *Missionerskoe obozrenie.*

Nevertheless, Churikov's deep piety, his commitment to rehabilitating alcoholics, and his success in reaching urban workers appealed to Metropolitan Antonii (Aleksandr Vasil'evich Vadkovskii, 1846–1912) of St. Petersburg (r. 1898–1912), who protected him while he was alive. The St. Petersburg diocesan missionary Dmitrii Bogoliubov also initially supported Churikov's movement; an investigation by the diocesan missionary council in 1910 concluded that Churikov and his followers were neither heretics nor sectarians. *Missionerskoe obozrenie* reported this finding with evident bewilderment, and, indeed, in the very same year, Bishop Vasilii (Preobrazhenskii) of Mozhaisk (r. 1908–14) excommunicated two of

---

[75] Rossiiskii gosudarstvennyi istoricheskii arkhiv, St. Petersburg, f. 821, op. 150, d. 460, ll. 1–8ob.

[76] *Besedy brattsa Ioanna Churikova* 2, no. 15 (15 January 1912): 1–2.

[77] Ibid. 2, no. 16 (22 January 1912): 1.

Churikov's followers, Dmitrii Grigor'ev and Ivan N. Koloskov, who had begun a similar ministry in Moscow.[78]

Increasingly influenced by Tregubov and the Tolstoyans, Churikov publicly renounced the consumption of meat in 1910.[79] Such connections did not help him with church authorities, especially after 1912 when Metropolitan Antonii died and Metropolitan Vladimir (Vasilii Bogoiavlenskii, 1848–1918) of Moscow (r. 1898–1912) succeeded him. In 1901, Vladimir had been one of the bishops signing the decree excommunicating the author of *War and Peace*. Moreover, Vladimir had also anathematized Churikov's followers Ivan Koloskov and Dmitrii Grigor'ev in 1910. Immediately upon Vladimir's accession in 1912, the Petersburg missionary committee reversed itself and forbade Churikov's preaching. It was only a matter of time before Churikov himself would face excommunication—and, indeed, on 13 August 1914 Vladimir banned the Samara peasant from the communion table.[80]

Despite the church's curse, the Ministry of Internal Affairs continued to allow Churikov to hold his meetings. Pushed outside of the church, Churikov became the leader of a sectarian religious movement. He had gained supporters among the Octobrists, a moderately conservative political group that included wealthy Old Believer industrialists and their descendants and sympathized with religious dissenters, and who organized a conference devoted to the movement in 1913.[81] In December 1922, Churikov briefly joined the modernist reformers of the "Living Church" movement led by Aleksandr Vvedenskii (1889–1946), who sought to make Orthodoxy compatible with socialism. But disappointed by the factional fighting among the Renovationists, Churikov and his followers soon left.[82]

Like the Ioannites, Churikov did not found an organized denomination but a spiritual movement that quickly became a national one. By 1913, Professor K. E. Lindeman estimated the number of *trezvenniki* at one hundred thousand in St. Petersburg and Moscow alone. Within five years, imitators of Churikov, who carried his message of sobriety and applied his method of conducting public "conversations," arose not only in Moscow, but in Omsk, Kostroma, Iaroslavl', Novgorod, and Ukraine.[83]

---

[78] Aleksandr Prugavin, *Brattsy i trezvenniki: Iz oblasti religioznykh iskanii* (Moscow, 1912), 90–119.

[79] *Otrechenie ot miasa trezvennikov brattsa Ioanna Churikova* (Petrograd, 1917).

[80] I. Ia. Eliashevich, *Pravda o Churikove i churikovtsakh* (Leningrad, 1928), 21; Gav. Petrov, *Sekta "Vyritskogo proroka": Trezvenniki-churikovtsy* (Kostroma, 1929), 6.

[81] The prominent Octobrist leader A. I. Guchkov, although Orthodox, was descended from Old Believers. On the 1913 conference on the *trezvenniki*, see *Sbornik rechei*.

[82] Anatolii Levitin and Vadim Shavrov, *Ocherki po istorii russkoi tserkovnoi smuty*, 3 vols. (Kusnacht, Switzerland, 1977), 1:206–9.

[83] *Sbornik rechei*, 4; Petrov, *Sekta "Vyritskogo proroka"*, 28.

Heretics in the Monastery: The Name-Glorifiers

In 1913, a new Orthodox heresy appeared, this time on the Holy Mountain, the monastic republic of Mount Athos in Greece. Mount Athos, which included monasteries from a variety of Orthodox nations, contained seventy-one Russian monastic communities. The most important Russian community on Athos was St. Panteleimon, founded in the eleventh century and with buildings capable of housing about a thousand monks.[84] In 1913, 833 monks on the Mountain were accused of following a new heresy of "onomatolatry" (name-glorification, *imiaslavie*), the practice of deifying the name of God (*imiabozhie*).[85]

Imiaslavie represented a development of hesychasm, the monastic movement of constant prayer which the Orthodox Church had embraced in local councils held at Constantinople in 1341, 1347, and 1351. Hesychasm had always been closely associated with the Holy Mountain. St. Gregory Palamas (1296–1359), the chief theologian and defender of the hesychasts, had argued that through the ascetic discipline of ceaseless prayer monks could apprehend the "energies" (as opposed to the unknowable essence) of God. To this end, the fourteenth-century hesychasts constantly repeated short prayers, especially the Jesus prayer ("Lord Jesus Christ, Son of God, have mercy on me, a sinner"). They tried to find ways of attaching these words to physiological processes, such as breathing or the beating of their hearts, so that they might truly pray without ceasing even while asleep.[86]

The twentieth-century *imiaslavtsy* went one step further and argued that the very divine energies of which St Gregory had spoken were somehow mysteriously contained in the name of God, which was constantly on their lips. A Russian monk Ilarion, who belonged to the neo-Athonite Her-

[84] *Polnyi pravoslavnyi bogoslovskii entsiklopedicheskii slovar'*, s.v. "Afon."
[85] The controversy produced a vigorous debate in the ecclesiastical press. The best recent account of the controversy is Papoulides, *Hoi rosoi Onomatolatrai*. See also *V uteshenie skorbiashchim po povodu afonskikh religioznykh smut* (Odessa, 1913), 1–4; S. V. Troitskii, *Uchenie afonskikh imiabozhnikov i ego razbor* (St. Petersburg, 1914); Aleksii, Bishop of Saratov and Tsaritsyn, *Razbor "Ispovedaniia very v Boga i vo imia bozhie" predstavlennogo v Sviateishii sinod afonskimi izgnannikami* (Chernigov, 1914), 1–28; S. V. Troitskii, *Ob imenakh bozhiikh i imiabozhnikakh* (St. Petersburg: Sinodal'naia tip., 1914); *Po povodu zaprosov po Afonskomu delu* (Odessa, 1914); Pakhomii, *Istoriia Afonskoi smuty ili imiabozheskoi eresi* (St. Petersburg, 1914); Nikon (Nikolai Ivanovich Rozhdestvenskii), Archbishop of Vologda and Tot'ma, *Imiabozhniki: Velikoe iskushenie okolo sviateishego imeni bozhiia i plody ego* (Sergiev posad, 1914); Mikhail Dushenkevich, *Golos mirianina* (Kiev, 1914); Sergei Viktorovich Troitskii, *K istorii bor'by s Afonskoi smutoi: Otvet V. M. Skvortsovu* (Petrograd, 1916); *Sviatoe pravoslavie i imenobozhnicheskaia eres'* (Kharkov, 1916); *Sbornik dokumentov, otnosiashchikhsia k Afonskoi imiabozhnicheskoi smute* (Petrograd, 1916); *V poiskakh pravdy: Po delu afonskikh imiabozhnikov* (Petrograd, 1916).
[86] On hesychasm, see Irenée Hausherr, *The Names of Jesus*, trans. Charles Cummings (Kalamazoo, Mich., 1978); John Meyendorff, *St. Gregory Palamas and Orthodox Spirituality*, trans. Adele Fiske (Crestwood, N.Y., 1974); Gregory Palamas, *The Triads*, ed. John Meyendorff, trans. Nicholas Gendle (New York, 1983).

mitage of Simon the Canaanite in the Kuban', advanced this theory in his book *In the Mountains of the Caucasus* which ran through three separate editions from 1907 to 1912.[87] Citing the Bible and the church fathers to support their point of view, the *imiaslavtsy* noted the power that the names of God and Christ possessed to heal and to exorcise demons. This doctrine also lent psychological and moral support to their extremely demanding hesychastic practice of ceaselessly repeating the Jesus prayer. If the name of God was God himself, then repeating that name brought the monk into direct contact with the Almighty. Moreover, the name-glorifiers held that Father Ioann of Kronstadt had himself supported their position. As their most prolific champion, the hieromonk Antonii (Aleksandr Ksaver'evich Bulatovich, 1870–1919) argued, the scriptures and the holy tradition of the church fully supported the position of the name-glorifiers; far from being heretics, the *imiaslavtsy* were defending true Orthodoxy against those who would defile the name of God, the *imiabortsy*.[88]

But in the eyes of its critics, this doctrine was a dangerous heresy. The learned reactionary Archbishop Antonii (Khrapovitskii) of Volhynia

[87] Ilarion, *Na gorakh Kavkaza: beseda dvukh startsev pustynnikov o vnutrennem edinenii s Gospodom nashikh serdets cherez molitvu Iisus Khristovu, ili dukhovnoi deiatel'nost' sovremennykh pustynnikov* (Baltapashinsk, 1907; 2d ed., Baltapashinsk, 1910; 3d ed., Kiev, 1912); Constantin Papoulidis, "Aleksandr Ksaver'evic Bulatovic; sa participation parmi les onomatolâtres du Mont-Athos," *Balkan Studies* 16, no. 1 (1975): 126; N. Bolkhovetskii, "Otkliki: zhivye teni srednevekovykh 'erese-iskatelei' (k bogoslovskomu sporu ob imenakh Bozhiikh)," *Missionerskoe obozrenie* 21, no. 3 (March 1916): 450.

[88] Bulatovich was a remarkable figure. As an officer in the Life Guards, he had conducted three important military and diplomatic missions to Ethiopia, which was threatened by Russia's imperial rival, Great Britain. His 1899 report on Ethiopia to the Russian Geographical Society earned him the society's silver medal. In 1900, he helped to suppress the Boxer Rebellion in Manchuria. After a distinguished military career, he was tonsured as the monk Antonii in 1906 and was ordained four years later. While a monk in the Russian skete (hermitage) of St. Andrew on Mount Athos, Antonii rose to become a member of the monastery's administrative council. His military training proved very useful during the controversy; in January 1913, he helped to overthrow the canonical abbot Ieronim and replace him with a name-glorifier, the monk David. On 13 February 1913, Bulatovich returned to Russia to undergo an operation on his eyes, and thus missed the major confrontation between the monks and the Russian navy in July 1913. His skill as a diplomat also served him well, for, without ever formally repenting, he succeeded in having the doctrines of the onomatolators placed on the agenda of the impending Russian Church Local Council, which was finally opened in 1917. Interrupted by the Revolution, the council never resolved these issues. After serving as a chaplain in World War I, Bulatovich was murdered on the night of 5–6 December 1919 on his family's estate where he had established his own private cell. A. K. Bulatovich, *Tret'e puteshestvie po Efiopii,* ed. A.B. Davidson and I. S. Katsnelson (Moscow, 1987), 120; Papoulidis, "Aleksandr Ksaver'evic Bulatovic," 126–29; Papoulides, *Hoi rosoi Onomatolatrai,* 22–23; Antonii (Bulatovich), *Istina o istine k predotvrashcheniiu imiaborstva* (Mount Athos, 1913?), 1–54; idem, *Proshenie v Pravitel'stvuiushchii sinod* (St. Petersburg, 1913); idem, "Drevnie i novye uchiteli Tserkvi o Imeni Gospodnem," *Missionerskoe obozrenie* 21, no. 9–10 (September–October 1916): 462–97; idem, "Uchenie noveishikh uchitelei i pastyrei Tserkvi o Imeni Gospodnem i molitve Iisusovoi," ibid., no. 11 (November 1916): 613–40; idem, *Afonskii razgrom (5 iiuliia 1913 g.): Tserkovnoe bessilie* (St. Petersburg, 1913); idem, *Moia bor'ba s imiabortsami na sviatoi gore* (n.p., 1917).

opened the controversy by publicly criticizing Ilarion's book.[89] Other bishops and clerics joined the attack. If the name of God were God himself, then what of the Antichrist? Since he bore the name of Christ, was he God as well? Since the name of God could be formed only by perishable elements, such as sounds or ink, did this mean that God too would perish with the end of the world?[90]

On 30 May 1913, the supreme procurator of the Holy Synod, Vladimir Karlovich Sabler (1845–1926) sent Archbishop Nikon (Nikolai Ivanovich Rozhdestvenskii, 1851–1918) of Vologda (r. 1906–1916) to Athos to investigate the heresy. The choice of Nikon, who had never attended a theological academy and was more of a publicist than a theologian, made it apparent that the synod and its supreme procurator were not interested in exploring the theological implications of *imiaslavie*. It did show that the power of both the church and the state would be brought against the rebellious monks, for Nikon was a member of both the State Council (the upper house of the Russian legislature) and the Holy Synod.[91] Nikon also had a reputation for freely using the weapon of excommunication in dramatic ways; in 1910 when the peasant Manefa Shirokova converted to Islam, Nikon excommunicated her, published his anathema, and sent an archdeacon from his cathedral church to inform her village.[92]

Nikon's negotiations with the monks, who felt that they were being called upon to abandon the essence of Orthodoxy, was fruitless. Determined to crush forcibly what he considered a dangerous error, Nikon called for a military detachment from the naval vessels *Donets* and *Kherson* to force the monks to return to Russia. On 4/17 July, several hundred monks barricaded themselves inside the St. Panteleimon Monastery and succeeded in convincing the commander of the detachment to allow them to pray before boarding the vessels. The commander's patience grew thin, however, when the service had gone on for three hours, and he ordered his fire brigade to spray the monks with cold water. His men then forced the recalcitrant monks onto the waiting vessels and back to Russia. In all, 833 monks were arrested on Athos and brought back to Odessa.[93]

This harsh treatment is partially explained by the tense international sit-

[89] "Heresy at Mount Athos: A Soldier Monk and the Holy Synod," *The Times* (London), 19 June 1913, 7.

[90] O. L. Epifanovich, "Imiaslavie i ego nepravda," *Donskie eparkhial'nye vedomosti*, 1914, 100–106, 144–48; Bolkhovetskii, "Otkliki," 446–56.

[91] Manuil, *Die Russischen Orthodoxen Bischöfe*, 5:250–52.

[92] Prugavin, *Brattsy*, 84.

[93] Papoulides, *Hoi rosoi Onomatolatrai*, 40–42; Papoulidis, "Aleksandr Ksaver'evic Bulatovic," 126–29; "Na Afone," *Sektantskii vestnik* 1, no. 2 (July 1913): 12; "Heresy at Mount Athos: The Recalcitrant Monks Deported," *The Times* (London), 24 July 1913, 7; "Heresy at Mount Athos: A Soldier Monk and the Holy Synod," 7; John Shelton Curtiss, *Church and State in Russia: The Last Years of the Empire, 1900–1917*, reprint ed. (New York, 1965), 356–57.

uation in the Balkans where the Balkan League, a delicate alliance of Serbia, Greece, Montenegro, and Bulgaria, which Russia had instigated in 1912 to drive the Ottomans from Europe, was unraveling. Dissatisfied with the division of conquests at the Treaty of London (signed on 17/30 May 1913) which had ended the first Balkan War, King Ferdinand of Bulgaria attacked Serbian and Greek troops in Macedonia on the night of 16/29 June, at the very time when Nikon was negotiating with the monks. The Russian show of force against the recalcitrant monks was a useful display designed to discourage the Turkish troops advancing on Bulgaria and to underscore Moscow's role as a protector of true Orthodoxy in the Balkans.[94]

Even after their return to Russia, the monks were treated extraordinarily harshly. Kept in police and monastery prisons for an average of two months, those who did not repent had their beards shaved, were stripped of their monastic garb, and were forced to wear civilian clothes. Many of the name-glorifiers were Russian peasants who had never had any formal theological training and could hardly be expected to hold their own in a serious theological debate. Moreover, many were already elderly and had spent decades on the Holy Mountain. Some had already taken the Greater Schema, a more ascetic form of the monastic life that Orthodox monks sometimes adopt at the end of their days. Yet the Synod regarded none of these facts as extenuating. The monks who failed to renounce the heresy of *imiaslavie* were returned to their home villages which they had left many decades before. The head of the Department of Police at the time, Stepan Petrovich Beletskii (1873–1918) later recalled the sad impression made on him by the sight of "these monks of advanced age (many of them had taken the Schema) with their shaved beards and civilian clothes."[95]

Not surprisingly, the Brotherhood of Ioann of Kronstadt supported the name-glorifiers; *Groza* ran a series of articles that supported their position.[96] The *imiaslavtsy* enjoyed support from other quarters as well. Although apparently unaware of the theological implications of the heresy, Empress Alexandra in a letter to her husband dated in 1916 requested that the unrepentant Athonite monks be allowed to take communion. Her confidant, the faith-healer Grigorii Rasputin, an erstwhile resident of the Holy Mountain, also sympathized with the monks and encouraged the downfall of Sabler (forced to resign in 1915), the man responsible for their punishment.[97]

[94] On the First Balkan War as a religious war of Orthodox Christians against Muslims, see "Pravoslavnyi grecheskii Vostok v 1912 godu" *Tserkovnyi vestnik* 39, no. 1 (3 January 1913): 15–24.
[95] *Padenie tsarskogo rezhima*, 4:165.
[96] Epifanovich, "Imiaslavie," 100–106, 144–48.
[97] *Padenie tsarskogo rezhima*, 4:165.

But far more surprising was the support offered to the onomatolators from missionaries, who were closely connected to the synod. The controversy surrounding the *imiaslavtsy* and the harsh manner in which the Athonite monks had been treated split the missionary community. In 1916, *Missionerskoe obozrenie* printed several articles sympathetic to the name-glorifiers, including at least two written by their leading defender, Bulatovich.[98] Even articles which criticized the so-called heretics did so reluctantly. N. Bolkhovetskii argued that the name-glorifiers were not heretics at all; and although he criticized their theological formulations, he lauded their devotional praxis.[99]

The same ambivalence can be found among missionaries working in the provinces. While remaining circumspect in its 1914 report, the missionary committee of Samara diocese clearly sympathized with the exiled monks. One of the exiles, Ivan Nikolaev Bashykov, a sixty-year-old former peasant of Sorochinskoe village of Buzuluk district, had spent twenty years on Mount Athos. Claiming that his faith had not changed in any way, he refused to sign any abjuration of *imiaslavie*, which he regarded as Orthodoxy itself. His principled stand gained him the sympathy of many of his friends and family who were shocked at the harshness of his punishment. Timofei Evdokimov, who had spent thirty years on Athos before returning to his home village of Bartenevka in Nikolaevsk district, was clearly bewildered by the church's reaction to *imiaslavie*; he claimed that the authorities had forbidden the monks to pronounce the name of Jesus and that soon a synodal bishop would force everyone to sign a paper denying the divinity of Christ.[100]

Conclusion: The Missionary Movement as an Attempt to Transform the Religious Field

The pietistic groups discussed in this essay represented a major difficulty faced by missionaries in late tsarist Russia.[101] Even as they tried to encourage lay zeal for Orthodoxy, the missionaries also had to ensure the primacy of the systematized theology that they embodied. Yet their own arguments and rhetoric against the rationalistic positivism of an increas-

---

[98] Antonii, "Drevnie i novye uchiteli," 216–97; idem, "Uchenie noveishikh uchitelei," 613–40.

[99] Bolkhovetskii, "Otkliki," 446–56.

[100] Mikhail Alekseev, "Otchet o sostoianii sektantstva i deistviiakh protivosektantskoi missii v Samarskoi eparkhii za 1913 god," *Samarskie eparkhial'nye vedomosti*, 1914, separate pagination, 30.

[101] On the concept of the "religious field," see Pierre Bourdieu, "Genesis and Structure of the Religious Field," trans. Jenny B. Burnside, Craig Calhoun, and Leah Florence, *Comparative Social Research* 13 (1991): 1–44.

ingly secular intelligentsia could also be used against their own rationalized theology. Deprived of the "cultural capital" of a seminary education, zealous Orthodox believers such as the Ioannites and *trezvenniki* chose to emphasize the "religious capital" of ascetic feats and pious devotion to holy men—capital that was, for them, more easily attainable. Eventually, this difference in emphasis led to an irreconcilable gulf between the Orthodoxy of the missionaries and the Orthodoxy of these pietistic collegia. The missionaries had to walk the narrow ground between the charismatic enthusiasm of lay Orthodox leaders, such as Podgornyi and Churikov, and the atheistic rationalism of the leftist intelligentsia.

The rules of 1888 which created the missionary establishment made the missionary the tool of the bishop. Armed with his academy education, the missionary extended the urbane, systematized Christianity of the bishops and the seminary into the countryside and the parish church. Faced with an increasingly literate and independent laity who were attracted to charismatic religious entrepreneurs, the bishops sought to use the missionary to impose a normative Orthodoxy upon their flock. As the laws against religious dissent were liberalized in 1874, 1883, and especially 1905, the missionary discourse became ever more central, for the new tolerance deprived the church of much of its judicial arsenal.

At the same time, the "Orthodox heretics" developed traditions of charismatic spirituality that for most missionaries was suspect, the product of ignorance. Rural movements, such as the Podgornites or the *besedchiki*, remained localized in a few districts. But once peasants such as Churikov and Pustoshkin came to the city, they brought their charismatic conceptions with them—and they used their access to the mass media to spread their gospels through newspapers and books. And before 1913, Athonite monasteries and the neo-Athonite monasteries of the Caucasus also provided a place for peasant monks to develop charismatic practices and a theology to defend them.

Although the missionaries ultimately failed to stem the tide of religious dissent and atheistic socialism, their greatest victories were primarily in the discursive realm. Our understanding of popular religion and sectarian movements in Russia has been shaped largely by the missionary heresiologists, such as Ivan Georgievich Aivazov, Tikhon Semënovich Rozhdestvenskii, and Timofei Ivanovich Butkevich, who studied and catalogued them. Even today, the language that cultural historians such as James Billington use to describe Russian religion owes much to these men.[102]

---

[102] James Billington, *The Icon and the Axe: An Interpretive History of Russian Culture* (New York, 1966); T. S. Rozhdestvenskii, *Pamiatniki staroobriadcheskoi poezii*, Zapiski Imperatorskago Moskovskago arkheologicheskago instituta, vol. 6 (Moscow, 1910); *Pesni russkikh sektantov mistikov*, ed. T. S. Rozhdestvenskii and M. I. Uspenskii, Zapiski Imperatorskogo Russkogo geograficheskogo obshchestva po otdeleniiu etnografiiu, vol. 35 (St. Petersburg, 1912).

Recent studies of the Counter-Reformation suggest that the Catholic Church was most successful where it built upon local religious piety rather than where it tried to impose entirely new religious forms upon lay populations.[103] But the Russian missionaries and the episcopate that they served were far less willing and less able to build on popular piety, as had Tridentine-minded bishops in France and Spain.[104] Certainly, Dmitrii Bogoliubov's dialogue with the Ioannites and Bolkhovetskii's defense of the *imiaslavtsy* suggest an effort to work with popular forms of Orthodoxy; but they were in the minority. Ultimately, the gulf between the urban Christianity of the missionary and the varieties of Orthodoxies in the village proved too great to bridge. The missionaries, who sometimes even disagreed among themselves as to what was Orthodox and what was not, revealed the fractures within the church, fractures that later would also prevent a common Orthodox response to the Bolshevik Revolution.

[103] Philip T. Hoffman, *Church and Community in the Diocese of Lyon, 1500–1789*, Yale Historical Publications, Miscellany, vol. 132 (New Haven, Conn., 1984); Sara T. Nalle, *God in La Mancha: Religious Reform and the People of Cuenca, 1500–1650*, The Johns Hopkins University Studies in Historical and Political Science, 110th ser., vol. 2 (Baltimore, 1992).

[104] As Gregory Freeze argues, even the few canonizations which took place at the end of the empire served to undermine the church's authority. "Subversive Piety: Religion and the Political Crisis in Late Imperial Russia," *Journal of Modern History* 68, no. 2 (June 1996): 308.

CHAPTER THREE

Between Rome and Tsargrad:
The Uniate Church in Imperial Russia

THEODORE R. WEEKS

The Uniate Church, or *Unia*, arose out of a desire to bridge the gap between the Eastern and Western rites. In the late 1430s, faced by the impending Ottoman threat, representatives of the Eastern Orthodox and Roman churches agreed to a union at Florence. The Ottoman conquest of 1453, however, as well as the dissatisfaction of most Orthodox bishops, made this union largely moot. Real church union had to wait until the end of the following century when the pope and Orthodox bishops of the Polish-Lithuanian Commonwealth (*Rzeczpospolita*) signed the Union of Brest (1569), creating the Uniate Church.[1] Though the Uniates established their own hierarchy, they on the one hand continued to follow the Eastern rites (including use of the vernacular in services, along with married parish priests), and on the other acknowledged the supremacy of the pope.

From the start, many Orthodox churchmen, bishops, and secular clergy opposed the new church and feared that the rapprochement with Rome would soon lead to a complete engulfing and total assimilation of the ex-Orthodox—in effect, a "conversion" of Uniate faithful to the Roman Catholic Church. Such fears were not entirely groundless. The Uniate

The research and writing of this essay benefited from support by the International Research and Exchanges Board (IREX) and East European Studies at the Woodrow Wilson International Center for Scholars, Washington, D.C. The author alone is responsible for any opinions stated here.

[1] Oscar Halecki, *From Florence to Brest (1439–1596)*, 2d ed. (Hamden, Conn., 1968). A major recent collection of essays on the Union of Brest and its consequences is Ryszard Łużny, Franciszek Ziejka, and Andrzej Kępiński, eds., *Unia brzeska: Geneza, dzieje i konsekwencje w kulturze narodów słowiańskich* (Cracow, 1994).

70

Church, after all, had been pushed through under the aegis of the Polish Commonwealth, as a measure to better unite the Commonwealth's eastern (Orthodox) lands with the western (Catholic) regions.

Ethnicity and politics were always inseparable from the religious aspects of the Uniate question. While one cannot discount the importance of language even at an early stage, in the prenational era religion was a far more binding and tangible aspect of identity than any nebulous "national feeling." This was certainly the case in the Western Provinces of the Russian empire, where various mutually comprehensible Slavic dialects were spoken by the peasant masses (the Lithuanian question does not concern us in this essay). Particularly in the borderlands between "Poland" (however defined) and "Russia," where Catholicism implied "Polish" and Orthodoxy "Russian," it was inevitable that the Uniates would find themselves in an uncomfortable position between the two dominant cultures. Poles often viewed the Uniates, including the Uniate hierarchy, as second-class citizens, and constant pressure was placed on Uniates—despite specific papal prohibitions—to adopt Catholic rituals or, indeed, to convert entirely to the Catholic rite. The Russian authorities and the Orthodox Church hierarchy, on the other hand, viewing the Uniate Church as no more than a cynical maneuver to pry faithful away from Orthodoxy and (not incidentally) from Moscow, did everything they could to encourage the Uniates to "remain faithful" and retain their separateness. Of course, ostensible "protection" of the Orthodox and Uniate population of the Commonwealth figured large in the arsenal of Russian propaganda from Ivan the Terrible on, as the Muscovite-Russian state extended its western borders at the Commonwealth's expense. While some measure of genuine religious belief doubtless entered the equation, Poles and Russians alike excelled in using the Uniate Church as a tool for extending political and cultural hegemony in the centuries between the Union of Brest and the partitions of Poland in the late eighteenth century.

During the three partitions, Russia seized territories approximately equivalent to the present-day Belarus, Lithuania, and western Ukraine. In the Russian empire, this region would be known as the "Western Provinces" (*Zapadnyi Krai*).[2] It was inhabited mainly by Polish landlords, Jewish townspeople, and Belarusian, Ukrainian, and Lithuanian peasants. What according to today's categories seems a complex ethnographic situation, however, was forced into a somewhat simpler mold by many tsarist officials of the nineteenth century. Just as the state did not recognize either Belarusians or Ukrainians as peoples or nations fundamentally separate from the Russians (nor did Slavic peasants themselves necessarily

[2] For the record, these nine provinces were: Kiev, Podolia, Volhynia (western Ukraine); Vitebsk, Minsk, Mogilev, Grodno (Belarus); and Vil'na and Kovno (Lithuania). The modern equivalents given in parentheses are only approximate.

have a high degree of national consciousness), it looked askance at the Uniate affiliation of many residents of the western lands as well.

Catholicism occupied a prominent position in the Russian mind (both official and popular) insofar as it was inevitably and inextricably linked with Polish national identity and class-economic influence. For centuries Polish landowners had played important political, social, cultural, and economic roles in the western borderlands. In fact the region's ruling elite was nearly exclusively Polish and Catholic. Besides its awareness of Catholics' power over Orthodox peasants, the Russian church, with its roots in Constantinople (in Russian, "Tsargrad"), never felt comfortable with the Roman church. From the partitions of Poland until the demise of Imperial Russia in 1917, the Catholic and Polish questions plagued and complicated Russian administration of the eastern lands of the former Polish-Lithuanian Commonwealth. With the notable exception of the Jews, who were of course seen as a uniquely troublesome ethnic and religious category (see John Klier's article in this volume), the rivalry between Russian-Orthodox and Polish-Catholics overshadowed all other ethnic and religious identities. (Catholic Lithuanians, for instance, were generally seen as potential allies or a subset of the Polish camp, though they will not be discussed in this essay.)

The very existence of the Uniates, a "third" Christian faith in the confessional and geographical interstices between Orthodoxy to the East and Catholicism to the West, confused and violated the Russian state's conception of the western border region.[3] Consisting principally of Belarusians and Ukrainians in today's terms, the Uniates were a great irritant to the Russian government. Accordingly, they were made the pawns of a broad national-confessional struggle between Orthodox Russians and Catholic Poles in the region. Though the Russian state and church never made serious attempts to convert Catholics, they not only forcibly converted Uniates en masse but strove to eliminate that church entirely from the empire.

In this essay we will use a variety of sources to evaluate the Russian attack on the Uniate Church in the tsarist era. The historical accounts of P. N. Batiushkov and E. M. Kryzhanovskii, both active Russian educators in the southwest provinces, exemplify the patriotic Russian approach. The circumstances and outcomes of the mass conversions of Uniates in 1839 and 1875 also reveal much about the Russian government and its conception of "legitimacy" in the religious sphere. Finally, we will consider Rus-

[3] After 1905, I stress, the Ukrainian national movement rapidly picked up momentum, both among educated and peasant sectors of society. On this question, see Olga Andriewsky, "The Politics of National Identity: The Ukrainian Question in Russia, 1904–1912" (Ph.D. diss., Harvard University, 1991); and Bohdan Krawchenko, *Social Change and National Consciousness in Twentieth-Century Ukraine* (New York, 1985).

sian governors' reports from the turn of the century and official reactions to events (including mass conversions to Catholicism) after the granting of religious freedom in April 1905. Throughout, the emphasis will be on the "official mind" of Russia, partly due to available source materials, and partly due to the intrinsic difficulty of gauging popular attitudes on such intangible subjects as religion and nationality. One can assume, however, that the religious and national attitudes held by Russian officials did not differ in any fundamental way from those of certain segments of Russian society, and indeed, might well have been shared by significant numbers of educated Russians of the day.

In the aftermath of the partitions, the Russian government faced for the first time the problem of administering a region where Polish culture and Catholicism predominated. Although Catherine the Great was in most respects reluctant to embark on any reform of local administration that would replace Polish and Catholic authorities, as a German Protestant princess turned Russian Orthodox empress, she carried a great deal of anti-Catholic baggage. Her "enlightened" policies were also aimed in great measure against the Catholic Church as an institution. In any case, Catherine was vitally interested in strengthening the power of the state over churches, including the Orthodox Church. She strove to limit the secular authority of the Catholic hierarchy and in 1774 reorganized the administration of the Belorussian diocese without consulting the pope. She also made an effort to oversee and restrict the activities of the Jesuits in these provinces. As for the Uniates, the "official line" taken by the government was that "the majority of the population in the Western Provinces annexed to Russia [by the first Polish partition] did not belong to the Roman Catholic religion, but to the United Greek Confession [i.e. the Uniates]. Catholicism had been violently imposed on them . . ."[4]

Though Catherine's son Paul is known for having overturned many of his mother's projects, he did not pursue any major change in policy with respect to the Catholic Church. Although he apparently liked and respected the local Catholic archbishop (of Mogilev), Stanisław Siestrzencewicz, seeing in him a loyal subject as well as a devout Catholic, the idea of *Unia* itself irritated Paul because it represented a blurring of categories. In an oft-cited remark, he complained, "I don't like it [*Unia*]. It is neither one thing nor the other, neither fish nor fowl."[5] But during Paul's few years in power, and even more during the first half of his son Alexander's reign, the Russian emperors were faced with threats far more immediately

---

[4] Count Dmitry Tolstoy, *Romanism in Russia: An Historical Study*, trans. Mrs. M'Kibbin, 2 vols. (London, 1874), 1:389. While Tolstoy's words were written much later, the inability to make a clear distinction between "Roman Catholic" and "Uniate" is present in Russian thought even in Catherine's period.

[5] Paul I, quoted ibid., 1:47.

menacing than the Catholics or the Uniate Church. The French Revolution and fears of its spreading ideas caused the Russian authorities to look rather more benevolently on the Catholic Church and even on the Jesuits. After the defeat of Napoleon and the Congress of Vienna, Alexander I's increasing mysticism and his desire to "recompense" the Poles for the historical injustice caused by the partitions meant that the Russian authorities generally left Catholics and Uniates to their own devices until after Alexander's death.[6] It was left to Nicholas I to embark on a new policy toward the Roman Christians.

The reigns of Nicholas I and Alexander II (1825–81) marked a significant break with the preceding decades. Indeed, this period of just over fifty years witnessed two major Polish revolts; increased restrictions and punishments meted out to Catholic priests, monks and bishops; and the formal dissolution of the Uniate Church within the boundaries of the Russian empire. Count Sergei Uvarov, minister of education under Nicholas I, formulated the ideological project known as "Official Nationality," usually summed up in the "trinity" of Orthodoxy, Autocracy, and Nationality (*narodnost'*).[7] As the link between Orthodoxy and Russian nationality (and even with political reliability) gained in strength, it became increasingly difficult to be both a loyal subject of the Russian tsar and a non-Orthodox believer.

It comes as no surprise that the first major assault on the Uniate Church, the mass conversion of 1839, occurred during the reign of Nicholas I. It grew out of the official reaction to the November 1830 political insurrection in Poland against Nicholas. Though the uprising was centered in Warsaw and the Kingdom of Poland, it also swept through the Western Provinces, particularly the northwestern (Belarusian and Lithuanian) region.[8] Once the uprising had been suppressed, Russian authorities carried out harsh measures to prevent any future manifestations of Polish "separatism." Many Catholic monasteries were shut down and clergy placed under strict surveillance, and thousands of Polish landowners were exiled and had their property confiscated (particularly in the Western Provinces). Since, in many cases, local Uniate priests and monasteries had assisted the Polish rebels, the government took steps to "purify"

[6] To be sure, this summary is somewhat simplified. For more detail, see ibid., 2:82–173; and Eduard Winter, *Russland und das Papsttum*, vol. 2 (Berlin, 1961), 105–207.

[7] On Uvarov and Official Nationality, see Nicholas Riasanovsky, *Nicholas I and Official Nationality in Russia, 1825–1855* (Berkeley, Calif., 1967), esp. pp. 70–183; and, more broadly on the man and his times, Cynthia H. Whittaker, *The Origins of Modern Russian Education: An Intellectual Biography of Count Sergei Uvarov, 1786–1855* (DeKalb, Ill., 1984).

[8] The standard treatment of the 1830 uprising in English is Robert Leslie, *Polish Politics and the Insurrection of November 1830* (London, 1956). The Kingdom of Poland was set up at the Congress of Vienna with the Russian tsar as its king. This mainly ethnic Polish territory contrasts with the ethnically mainly Lithuanian, Belorusian, and Ukrainian Western Provinces.

the Uniate Church of Catholic influences by closing down Basilian monasteries, forbidding interchange between Catholic and Uniate clergy, removing organs from Uniate Churches, and introducing iconostases. This
process led inexorably to the official "reunion" (*vozsoedinenie*) of the Uniate Church with the Orthodox Church in March 1839. The Holy Synod
prepared a report recommending the reunion, and Nicholas, giving
thanks to God, endorsed it.[9] Officially speaking, no Uniates remained in
the Western Provinces after 1839.

The official interpretation of the *vozsoedinenie* was expressed in a long
article published in late 1839 in the journal *Khristianskoe chtenie* (Christian
Reading). The article begins: "In the present year the Orthodox Church
has inscribed on the tablet of her History one of its most joyous and important events. Together with our beloved Fatherland [the Orthodox
Church] celebrates the return to its embrace of children [*chada*] who had
been pulled away from her during the time of domination by an alien
faith." Thus the "conversion" of the Uniates to Orthodoxy was presented
merely as a righting of historical wrongs. The Uniate Church was described as fundamentally illegitimate: "[it] never truly prospered: like a
bough severed from the native tree and forcibly grafted onto an alien
growth, it [the Uniate Church] lived a kind of half-life or, more properly
speaking, lived out the remains of its life, and faced by the Latin church,
was fated gradually to disappear."[10] The article described the church's entire history as the reign of Polish-Latin violence against Orthodox faithful.
When the Catholic authorities had realized that no amount of physical
pressure could wrench the Orthodox away from their faith, they introduced *Unia* as a way of reaching the same goal by a different means. The
Uniate Church had never been anything more than "*a bridge* from piety
[*blagochestie*] to Latinism [*Latinstvo*]."[11]

The article treated the categories "Orthodox" and "Russian" as equivalent. The fact that the Uniates had always considered themselves "*russkie*"
was taken to mean that at heart they were already Orthodox. Describing
joyful reactions to the "purifying" measures taken after 1831 to bring Uniate Churches more in line with Orthodox ritual, the article exulted, "the
Uniate people . . . hearing the word of God in their native tongue, could
no longer see any difference between their own and Orthodox temples. . . . Despite all the ill turns of fortune, even earlier [i.e. before the
purifying measures] they had never ceased to call themselves and their
faith—Russian." Thus, following this account, the post-1830 reforms set

---

[9] A copy of this report (*Vsepoddaneishii doklad Sinoda*, dated 23 March 1839) may be found
ibid., 407–10.

[10] "O vozsoedinenii uniatov s Pravoslavnoiu Tserkov'iu v Rossiiskoi Imperii," *Khristianskoe
chtenie*, no. 4 (1839): 351, 354.

[11] Ibid., 368.

off a natural process culminating in the Uniate clergy petitioning en masse to be allowed back into "their ancestral Church."[12] The conclusion of the article brought together the themes of faith, nationality, and history: "From today one may truly say that, excepting only the so-called Lithuanians and Samogitians, all the rest of the population of the western districts of the empire is not only Russian, but Orthodox; and in vain will our enemies attempt to claim the opposite, contrary to historical truth and the actual essence of things."[13]

The actual train of events leading to the 1839 *vozsoedinenie* was neither as simple nor as uniformly glorious as the above account suggested. The *vozsoedinenie* came about through the interaction of militant local forces and mainly passive but acquiescent central authorities. This is not to say, of course, that anyone in St. Petersburg was unhappy to see the Uniate Church "disappear." On the contrary, it is clear that the tsar, the supreme procurator of the Holy Synod, and other high officials were delighted that this thorny problem had ceased to exist, but nobody in 1830 had either planned or predicted such a speedy end to the problem. How, then, did it happen?

All sources agree on the importance of one man: the Uniate bishop and later Orthodox archbishop, Iosif Semashko, who had given St. Petersburg the cue for the wholesale conversion by calling for a mass "return" of Uniate flocks in the Western Provinces to the Orthodox Church. Polish accounts tend to describe Semashko as a staunch Russian patriot and ambitious individual who harbored antagonistic feelings toward the Poles and the Catholic hierarchy.[14] From the Russian perspective, Semashko was motivated mainly by sincere religious outrage at the decay of the Uniate Church and its subordinate position in relation to the Roman Catholic hierarchy. In any case, there can be no denying the central position played by Semashko first in urging forward the "purifying measures" to rid Uniate Churches of Catholic influences and then, very rapidly, to eliminate all difference between Uniate and Orthodox by merging the two.[15] Popular resistance to the elimination of *Unia* appears to have been muted, possibly because of the repressive measures that had already been taken against Poles and Catholics since the crushing of the

[12] Ibid., 373, 374.

[13] Ibid., 383. At that time, Russians tended to distinguish between "Zhmud' " ("Samogitians") and Lithuanians. Both groups are now considered as Lithuanians.

[14] See, for example, E. Likowski, *Dzieje Kościoła Unickiego na Litwie i Rusi w XVIII i XIX wieku uważane głównie ze względu na przyczyny jego upadku*, 2d ed., vol. 2 (Warsaw, 1906), 48ff.

[15] The most detailed account of the *vozsoedinenie* is M. Ia. Moroshkin, "Vozsoedinenie Uniatov: istoricheskii ocherk," *Vestnik Evropy*, April 1872, 606–43; June 1872, 588–648; July 1872, 60–111; August 1872, 524–93; September 1872, 35–73. Moroshkin's sympathies are overwhelmingly on the Russian/Orthodox side, and it is perhaps not without interest to note that he was also the author of *Iezuity v Rossii, s tsarstvovaniia Ekateriny II-i do nashego vremeni*, 2 vols. (St. Petersburg, 1867–70).

1830 uprising, and perhaps also because the government allowed for the "reunited" ex-Uniate parishes to retain temporarily certain non-Orthodox prayers and rites. The feared peasant disturbances failed to materialize and by the end of 1839 both civil and religious authorities could heave a sigh of relief that another great step in the struggle against "Polonism" in the western territories had been taken without significant opposition.

It appears that St. Petersburg considered the Uniate question closed after 1839, but one small remaining Uniate diocese continued to function. This was the Kholm (Polish: Chełm) diocese along the western bank of the Bug River, in the Kingdom of Poland. Some have suggested that these Uniates would have been included in the 1839 mass conversion but for the fact that St. Petersburg simply did not know of their existence. According to the leading Russian historian of the 1839 *vozsoedinenie*, the Catholic clergy rushed to convert Uniates in this region to Catholicism: "In order not to give our government the possibility to realize the idea of 'reunion' of the Kholm Uniates, the Polish-Jesuit party particularly deployed their mystic [sic] activities with the effect that of 400,000 Uniates more than 150,000 converted to Catholicism [*priniali latinstvo*]."[16] There still remained, however, a large number of Uniate faithful in this region who were allowed to follow their religion relatively undisturbed, until after the next Polish uprising in 1863.

The 1863 insurrection was to a great extent supported and abetted by Catholics and Uniates, particularly the Basilian monks. After quelling the uprising, the Russian government once again embarked on a series of repressive measures aimed at Polish culture, Polish landholding (particularly in the Western Provinces), and, needless to say, the Catholic Church. St. Petersburg once again took up the cause of "cleansing" local Uniate Churches from Catholic rites and influences. As in 1839, the program of rapprochement between the Uniate and Orthodox Churches rapidly accelerated into a process that ended by eliminating the Uniate Church entirely. Given the Russian position that the Uniate Church was never more than a "bridge" or "false front" to convert Orthodox peasants to Catholicism, it was only natural that this "bridge" be disassembled after the reestablishment of Russian authority in the region.

Some have seen in the 1875 "reunion" the culmination of a sinister Russian plan to "denationalize" the local peasants. This argument is unconvincing from two points of view. First of all, the events leading up to 1875 hardly show a carefully thought-out plan to eliminate the Uniate Church entirely. Secondly, as mentioned above, the Kholm Uniates were considered "Russians" by St. Petersburg in the first place and the mea-

---

[16] Moroshkin, "Vozsoedinenie," September 1872, 73.

sures taken were aimed more against Polish Catholicism as an "anti-Russian force" than against the Uniate Church per se. In a sense, the Kholm Uniates were forced historically to choose between Russian-Orthodox or Polish-Catholic influences. In 1875 the Russian government put an end to this choice, at least for another three decades.[17]

The strength of Catholic influences in Kholm diocese was clear for all to see. In Uniate Churches one could find such Catholic features as organs, pews, and even clean-shaven priests. Catholic practices were so widespread that the Russian government found itself obliged to bring in Uniate clergy—even at the highest levels—from neighboring Austrian Galicia in order to carry out its "purifying" measures. The irony of the "Russifying" imperial government calling in foreign subjects to carry out this "Russian deed" seems to have been lost both on contemporaries and on subsequent historians. Here there was no Semashko to encourage a coming together of Uniate and Orthodox Churches; the chief advocate of the ultimately successful *vozsoedinenie* was not a religious figure, but the governor of Siedlce province, Stepan Gromeka. While religious authorities and St. Petersburg, fearful of peasant unrest, vacillated and hesitantly urged the cautious implementation of measures introducing "purified" (i.e., Orthodox) rites, Gromeka rushed ahead with a campaign to gather signatures from local Uniate bishops and congregations begging the tsar to allow the Uniates to be accepted into the Orthodox fold. It is clear, however, that the government exerted very considerable force in persuading Uniates to accept Orthodox rituals and, finally, to acquiesce to the church union. The brutality of government measures against recalcitrant peasants, including the use of Cossacks and exile to Siberia, is only too well documented.[18]

The use of force was accompanied by caution so as to prevent further peasant disturbances. The "administrator" of Kholm diocese, Markell Popiel (who could not be called "bishop" because he lacked papal confirmation), wrote in the spring of 1874 that Uniate priests should not be forced to allow their hair and beards to grow (like Orthodox priests) unless that could be done without causing "an unpleasant impression." In general the "cleansing of rites" (*ochishchenie obriada*) should be carried out "with extreme prudence in order not to excite the displeasure of the

[17] I have elaborated on the events leading up to 1875 in T. Weeks, "The 'End' of the Uniate Church in Russia: The *Vozsoedinenie* of 1875," *Jahrbücher für Geschichte Osteuropas* 44, no. 1 (1995): 1–13.

[18] See, for example, "Prześladowanie Unii na Podlasiu," *Przegląd Polski* 10 (April 1875), 47–81; V. Svatkovskii, "Vozsoedinenie Uniatov," in *Materialy k voprosu ob obrazovaniiu Kholmskoi gubernii* (Warsaw, 1908), 75–84; and Evhen Paternak, *Narys istorii Kholmchshyny i Pidliashshia (Novishi chasy)* (Winnipeg, 1968), 68–92.

parishioners." "Above all," he wrote, "A strict consistency and unbending perseverance must be maintained."[19] From these words it would appear that Popiel, at least, foresaw a relatively extended period of "cleansing of ritual" to bring Uniates in line with Orthodox practice.

Similarly cautious was a report issued by the Conference on Uniate Affairs (*Soveshchanie po uniatskomu delu*) in St. Petersburg at the end of 1874. While stressing the need for rites in Uniate Churches to follow Orthodox models, the conference did not wish to encourage conversions of Uniates to Orthodoxy. While such conversions, the report stated, could not be refused, it was necessary to act "with particular circumspection" to assure that the requests were sincere and not forced. "Any initiative whatsoever on the part of the administration in the matter of conversions of Uniates to Orthodoxy . . . must be eliminated."[20] The highest administrators of the Uniate Church also viewed an immediate unification with the Orthodox Church with misgivings. To quote a report from the Ministry of Internal Affairs, "The [Uniate] Consistory regards the present movement among Uniates toward a final reunion [*vozsoedinenie*] with Orthodox premature as not all members of the clergy are without exception imbued with the spirit of Orthodoxy. . . ."[21] To be sure, the final outcome of these measures bringing Uniate rites closer to Orthodoxy would probably be the dissolution of the Uniate Church, but this was a future goal, not an immediate target.

Such was not the opinion of Gromeka. He insisted that now was the time to strike and eliminate this outdated and superfluous institution once and for all. Writing in November 1874, Gromeka emphasized the need for the government to take strong, even extreme measures now before the political situation changed. At present, he wrote, the local Catholics were still cowed after post-1863 punishments, but the election of a new pope or "the return of Napoleonids to the French throne" could "stimulate the activities of Polono-Latin influence." Nor should the government shy away from using severe, even violent methods: "At present, when any Uniate can refute [government claims that the cleansing of rituals is simply a return to old ways] by the simple reference to an encyclical in which the holy and infallible pope claims that he never desired and could in no way desire the purifying of Greek Catholic rites, the government is left with no choice but to use physical force in order to maintain order and tranquility [*tishina*] among the Uniates." Because the Uniate

---

[19] Russian State Historical Archive, St. Petersburg, f. 821, op. 4, 1874, d. 1582, ll. 9–10, April 25, 1874 (hereafter RGIA).

[20] RGIA, f. 821, op. 4, 1874, d. 1594, ll. 32–33, December 8, 1874.

[21] Ibid., l. 47, December 18, 1874.

Father Markell Popiel, administrator of Kholm (Chełm) diocese. *Khol'mskaia Rus'* (St. Petersburg, 1887).

clergy and hierarchy were discredited in the people's eyes, Gromeka argued, the government should take the lead in ushering the Uniates into the Orthodox Church. An activist, unswerving policy would eliminate this problem once and for all, and "without doubt, at the very moment of *voz-*

soedinenie [there will appear] an immediate and profound breach" between former Uniates and the "Latin-Polish element."[22] Gromeka's advo-
cacy of energetic measures carried the day. The Kholm Uniate diocese
was officially "reunited" with the Orthodox Church in early 1875, and
thereafter, officially speaking, no Greek Catholics resided within the
boundaries of the Russian Empire.

It is remarkable, given the relatively small number of faithful involved
(particularly when compared with the 1839 conversions), that the 1875
vozsoedinenie has received such extensive attention in the literature, both
at the time and later.[23] One may attribute this interest to several factors,
including a heightened sense of national identity toward the end of the
century and the abundant evidence that in this case, far more than in
1839 and contrary to contemporary Russian claims, the Uniate masses of
Ukrainian ethnicity did not wish to be absorbed into the Orthodox
Church. Indeed, the mass conversions of ex-Uniates to Catholicism in
1905 suggest that here the Catholic-Uniate nexus was far stronger than
Uniate links to Russia and Orthodoxy. From the Russian point of view, of
course, the feelings of solidarity between Roman Catholics and ex-Uniates
could be blamed on the strong Polish influences in this region, where
Catholicism and Polish culture were far more dominant than in the Western Provinces. The 1875 "reunion," to a much greater extent than the
events of 1839, may be justifiably described as "Russification," that is, an
effort by the Russian government to extend and strengthen Russian culture on the western borderlands. But because Russian officials regarded
the Uniate faithful in the Kholm region as "Russians" from the outset,
they termed the process a "defense" against "militant Polonism." To put it
another way, as far as the Russian government was concerned, only its assistance could "save" these "Russians" from the fate of total Polonization.

In the second half of the nineteenth century, particularly after the Polish insurrection of 1863, the assumed and largely unconscious fusing of
Russian nationality and Orthodox faith pervaded both official Russian discourse and government-sponsored histories of the Western Provinces.[24]
One of the best-known practitioners of the latter genre of historical writing was E. M. Kryzhanovskii, a longtime administrator and educational expert in the Western Provinces and Russian Poland who penned a number

---

[22] RGIA, f. 821, op. 4, 1874, d. 1594, ll. 2–11.

[23] For some contemporary examples, see Józef Bojarski, *Czasy Nerona w XIX w., czyli ostatnie chwile Unii* (Lwów, 1878); Nikolai N. Livchak, *K istorii vozsoedineniia Uniatov Kholmskoi eparkhii. Zapiski i vospominanii* (Vil'na, 1910); and the works of E. Kryzhanovskii cited below, notes 25–28. Among more recent works are Luigi Glinka, *Diocesi ucraino-cattolica di Cholm (Liquidazione ed incorporazione alla Chiesa russo-ortodossa)* (Rome, 1975); and Edmund Przekop, "Verlauf der Auflösung der kirchlichen Union in der Diözese Chełm (1875)," *Ost-kirchliche Studien* 31, no. 2 (August 1982): 160–75.

[24] On 1863, see Leslie, *Reform and Insurrection in Russian Poland.*

of historical works on this region, particularly in the 1860s and 1870s.[25] As an employee of the Ministry of Education in the western region, Kryzhanovskii was particularly interested in the history of education there, both under the Poles and in the postpartition period.

Kryzhanovskii's interpretation of the Uniate Church took as its starting point the official view put forth in 1839. In his view, the Catholic Church was purely a tool of denationalization used by the Poles in their efforts to exterminate the Russian nationality in the region. The Uniate Church served as the antechamber to Catholicism and complete Polonization. Thus Kryzhanovskii portrayed Russian restrictions on Catholic and Uniate activities after the partitions as nothing more than defensive measures to protect the helpless "Russian" peasants from denationalization.

Kryzhanovskii's fundamental conception of the history of the region may be summarized as follows: this land had been Russian "from ancient times"; the Poles, taking advantage of Russian weakness, had established themselves as the political and economic masters of the region from the fourteenth to the eighteenth centuries. This historical injustice was undone by the Polish partitions of the late eighteenth century; now Russia's task was to strip away the foreign Polish and Catholic influences that had been imposed by force on the area's Russian and Orthodox inhabitants.

In "Letters from Podlias'e" (1867), Kryzhanovskii wrote of the deplorable effects of centuries-long Catholic domination.[26] This essay begins with a reference to the bitter effects of "Polono-Jesuit tutelage." Catholic Churches are large and imposing, while Uniate Churches are small and in poor repair. The rituals of the Uniate Churches are full of Catholic practices; the gospel and sermons are pronounced in Polish, Orthodox feasts are ignored or celebrated in the Catholic manner, and Uniate priests go so far as to tell their congregations that St. Vladimir was a Uniate. Uniate priests, unlike their Orthodox counterparts, hold themselves apart from the Uniate faithful, considering them "cattle" (*bydło*—the Polish word is invariably used in such contexts). Most terrible of all, the Uniate peasants themselves, far from longing for "their own" Russian language and "pure Slavic ritual," instead have internalized the Polish hatred for the Russian "schismatics" (an offense Polish term referring to all Russian Orthodox believers, suggesting that they had "split off" from the true,

---

[25] Kryzhanovskii preferred the essay form, but published widely on topics ranging from Catholic influences on Orthodox ritual in the southwest before the introduction of *Unia* to the life of rural Orthodox clergy in the region in the eighteenth century to the Czechs in Volhynia. His essays are collected in three bulky tomes: E. M. Kryzhanovskii, *Sobranie sochinenii* (Kiev, 1890).

[26] E. Kryzhanovskii, "Pis'ma iz Podlias'ia" (1867) in *Russkoe Zabuzh'e (Kholmshchina i Podlias'e): Sbornik statei* (St. Petersburg, 1911). This volume's title refers to "Russia beyond the Bug," that is, the region to the west of the Bug river populated (before 1945) mainly by ethnic Ukrainians.

Roman faith). Obviously the Russian government could not allow such a situation to continue, particularly in places bearing names like "Savishche *russkoe*" and "Iablonna *russkaia.*"

In another essay, "Uniate Disturbances in Podlias'e" (1868), Kryzhanovskii described peasant resistance to the "purification of Uniate ritual" after 1863.[27] While acknowledging the existence of peasant discontent over these "innovations," Kryzhanovskii argued that in fact by removing organs from Uniate Churches, putting in iconostases, and bringing in Orthodox liturgy, the Russian authorities were not "innovating" but on the contrary were undoing the innovations introduced by the Catholics over the centuries. Peasants, egged on by their Polonized Uniate priests and encouraged by Polish landowners, could not understand the government's benevolent motives and attacked officials and even military units, forcing the government to protect itself. Kryzhanovskii insisted that the government was doing all it could to avoid violence, but that the dogged resistance of local Polish and Catholic forces, combined with their propaganda among the Uniate peasants, obliged the local Russian authorities to take defensive measures.

The injustices and baleful Polono-Catholic influences of several centuries, Kryzhanovskii implied, could only be stripped away by forceful, decisive action. The final act, the 1875 "reunion" of the last Uniates in the Russian Empire with the Orthodox Church, then, was to Kryzhanovskii not only the logical culmination of this process, but indeed the only possible outcome of this epic struggle between Pole and Russian: "[In 1875 the government] took advantage of the most critical moment in the [Uniate] people's mood, [took heed of] the anguished cry of the masses and decided a great matter, cut through the Gordian knot!"[28] After 1875, with the elimination of the Uniate Church in the Russian empire, the "normal" process of strengthening Russian nationality and Orthodox faith and weakening Polono-Catholic influences could follow its historical course, unhindered by the confusing and ambiguous presence of the "neither-fish-nor-fowl" Uniates. This rhetorical model of Russian vs. Pole with the Uniates somewhere in between, either "quasi-Russians" or "masked Poles," crops up again and again in official Russian representations of the events of 1839 and 1875.

P. N. Batiushkov, writing about a generation later than Kryzhanovskii, dealt with similar topics and themes, though at greater length. Let us take, almost at random, two of his many works: *Belorussia and Lithuania* (1890), treating the northwest region, and *Volhynia* (1888), which con-

---

[27] E. Kryzhanovskii, "Volneniia uniatov na Podlias'e" (1868) in *Russkoe Zabuzh'e*, 155–202.
[28] E. Kryzhanovskii, "Zapiska ob uniatskom dele v privislianskom krae," in *Sobranie sochinenii*, 3:388.

cerns one southwestern province.[29] The subtitles of both of these works refer to the *"istoricheskie sud'by"*—"historical destinies"—of these territories. Such phrasing is more than an empty rhetorical device; the story told by Batiushkov is truly one of "historical destiny" unfolding through the centuries. In both works (and, indeed, in all of Batiushkov's historical endeavors) a clear historical teleology is at work: the local, "rooted" Russian Orthodox faith/people is challenged by pernicious Polono-Catholic intruders, an epic battle between Russians (or: "Orthodox") and Poles (or: "Catholics") rages over several centuries and ends with the triumph of the long-suffering but morally pure Russian/Orthodox party. Terms that we would differentiate as either "national" or "religious" are used by Batiushkov (and, indeed, by practically everyone in the region at this time) as complete synonyms. Though the struggle sometimes takes on political form, as when the Polish-Lithuanian state comes to blows with Muscovy, religious distinctions are always paramount.

In *Belorussia and Lithuania*, Batiushkov traces the history of the northwestern provinces (the title page bears the coats of arms of Minsk, Kovno, Vil'na, Mogilev, Grodno, and Vitebsk provinces) from the earliest times when "Belorussians . . . were known as Krivichi" through the period of the "Lithuanian-Russian state," the era of increasingly oppressive Polish rule culminating in the Union of Brest, and the ensuing two centuries of efforts from the Polish side to transform the local "Orthodox Russian people" into good Catholics. These Polish intrigues had, however, the opposite effect of strengthening Russian national self-consciousness and solidifying the position of the Orthodox Church. The final episode of this "historical destiny" is played out under the benevolent aegis of the Russian state in the decades after the first Polish partition of 1772. The book concludes with a chapter entitled "The Reunion [*vozsoedinenie*] of the Uniates and the Reestablishment [*vosstanovlenie*] of Orthodoxy and the Russian Nationality." It is important to understand Batiushkov's logic and his interpretation of the conversion of Uniates. For him, this was no conversion at all but a mere "return" of originally Russian people to the religion of their forefathers. Batiushkov specifically establishes that these people (for us, Belarusians and Ukrainians) were originally baptized into the Eastern Church and only after the sixteenth century came to be Uniates or, in some cases, even Catholics. Thus when in 1839 (and in 1875) these people were "reunited" with the Orthodox Church, no *conversion* took place, but a mere "righting of historical wrongs." In this way Batiushkov and the archconservative Russian empire sidestepped the touchy issue of conversion.

[29] P. N. Batiushkov, *Belorussiia i Litva* (St. Petersburg, 1890); idem, *Volyn': Istoricheskie sud'by Iugo-zapadnogo kraia* (St. Petersburg, 1888).

Here, as throughout Batiushkov's works, the fates of Orthodoxy and of the Russian nation are inextricably intertwined. Indeed, it is emblematic that Batiushkov's history of Belarus and Lithuania ends with the absorption of the region's Uniates into the Orthodox Church in 1839. With this act, the "historical destiny" of the region has played itself out; henceforth it has no history separate from that of the great Russian state and nation. The 1863 Polish rebellion, mentioned in the book's last pages, is portrayed as the Poles' final, futile attempt to oppose this historical destiny.

For Batiushkov, the Uniate Church assumed a peculiar and ambivalent position between Poles and Russians. His discussion of the Union of Lublin (1569) emphasizes the growth of Polish *state* power but hardly mentions the creation of the Uniate Church. The Uniates appear somewhat later, in a discussion about Jesuit efforts to spread Catholicism in the 1570s. At this time arose, to quote Batiushkov, "the idea of an ecclesiastical union [*unia*] of the Eastern Church with the Western and of attracting to this union not only the Orthodox population of Lithuania, but also that of the northeastern, Muscovite Russia [*Rus'*]."[30] Thus from the start the *Unia* not only presented a threat to the Orthodox population in the western region, but even to Moscow itself. The linking of *Unia* with the Jesuits may in the Russian context be termed "guilt by association," given the Jesuits' unsavory reputation in that culture.

The "end" of the story, when the Uniates were ushered back into the Orthodox fold in 1839, follows similar rhetorical paths. The measures undertaken by Tsar Nicholas I in the first years of his reign to "protect" Uniates from Catholic influences and to "reestablish" the purity of Orthodox rituals in Uniate Churches helped spark the Polish uprising of November 1830 which, in turn, gave impetus to further measures to reduce Catholic influences on the Uniates. "There is no doubt that the Polish uprising of 1831 [sic] itself, was if not precipitated, then at least strengthened, by elements discontented by the incipient transformation of the Uniate Church; but this very uprising was the unwitting instrument of further rapprochement of the Uniate Church with the Orthodox."[31] And the final unification of the Uniates with the Orthodox Church followed spontaneously and naturally from the defeat of the Polish uprising. This natural process was helped along, to be sure, by the Russian government and the Orthodox hierarchy, but the impetus for change came, in Batiushkov's portrayal, from the Uniates themselves. While he does not deny that some Uniate clergy opposed the "reunification" (*vozsoedinenie*) of 1839, he attributes this resistance to Catholic influences (particularly of the Uniate Basilian monastic order with its strong links to Rome) and

---

[30] Batiushkov, *Belorussiia i Litva*, 188.
[31] Ibid., 356.

to ignorance. In all, he claims, some one and a half million Uniates transferred their allegiance to the Orthodox Church in 1839, and only fifteen stubborn and disobedient Uniate clergymen had to be exiled to central Russia.[32]

In Batiushkov's tome on Volhynia one encounters similar figures, processes, and rhetoric. Under the Poles, Orthodox faithful are oppressed and encouraged to convert, while the Uniate clergy itself lives in miserable poverty and all efforts concentrate on bringing Uniate rituals, church architecture, and liturgy in line with Catholic norms. Here also the Basilian monasteries play an important and insidious role in spreading Latin ritual and strengthening Polish culture. The return of Volhynia to Russia "after four and a half centuries of foreign [i.e., Polish] rule" was cause for great rejoicing, but the harmful effects of the long Polish domination could not be so easily effaced. "The long centuries under the foreign yoke exhausted [Volhynia's] strength and left on her deep wounds [*iazvy*]. For that reason it was necessary to reinforce her strength and heal her wounds—and this task which fell to Russia's lot is being fulfilled and carried out by her in the fourth and final period of the life of Volhynia, from 1793 even to the present time."[33] Thus as in the case of the northwestern region, the process of eliminating Polish and Catholic influences in Volhynia in the nineteenth century was a case of historical justice, whereby the "Russian" people of the province regained its faith and nationality. Similar rhetorical devices are at work in nearly all official descriptions of the events of 1839 and 1875.

After 1875, in spite of the government's claims, thousands of ex-Uniates continued secretly to follow their old religion, helped and encouraged by Catholic priests. Before 1905 the Russian government did not allow conversions from Orthodoxy even to other Christian denominations; hence once the Uniates were officially inscribed in government records as "Orthodox," they could not change their religion. Unable to convert legally, they took their religion underground, having their children baptized secretly by Catholic priests and journeying across the border to Austrian Galicia to celebrate their marriages (a custom so widespread that locals spoke of "Cracow weddings").[34] The numbers of ex-Uniates who resisted the elimination of their church and refused to worship in Orthodox Churches was large enough to merit government attention and, in fact, a word was coined to describe this stubbornly faithful group: they were known as the "resisters" or "the stubborn" (in Russian, *uporstvuiushchie*, in Polish *uporni*). They continued to vex the Russian adminis

---

[32] Ibid., 358–62.

[33] Batiushkov, *Volyn'*, 230.

[34] For a highly emotional literary source, allegedly based on personal observation in the Kholm region, see W. Reymont, *Z ziemi chełmskiej: Wyrażenia i notatki* (Warsaw, 1911).

trators in this area into the twentieth century, as is attested by the frequent mention of "resisters" in official documents.

Nearly a decade after the 1875 *vozsoedinenie,* the governor general of Warsaw, the redoubtable I. Gurko, had a detailed memorandum drawn up on the overall situation in the "Vistula Country" which also mentioned the ex-Uniates living in the eastern districts of Siedlce and Lublin provinces. The situation there was, to quote the memorandum, "hardly comforting." Nearly a third of the officially Orthodox population there refused to attend Orthodox Churches and avoided all contact with the Russian authorities and Orthodox clergy. Gurko suggested that measures be taken to strengthen the position of Orthodoxy in these districts, including a complete ban on hiring non-Orthodox workers for government jobs there and replacing any non-Orthodox employees in the course of two years. Gurko also suggested that local Orthodox clergy exhibit more energy in their dealings with the local peasantry, that Catholic and Uniate propaganda be more strictly and effectively punished, and that elementary education in the area be improved. Gurko's suggestions were, with some minor changes, approved by the Ministry of Internal Affairs.[35] The problem, however, remained.

In the next decade, Gurko's successor in Warsaw, the milder and less polonophobic Prince A. Imeretinskii, admitted that the *vozsoedinenie* of 1875 had been rushed, poorly planned, and ineffective.

Unfortunately this "reunion" [in 1875] which bore a primarily formal character and encountered frenzied resistance from Polish-Catholic propaganda, was unsuccessful in penetrating the depths of popular consciousness to a sufficient extent as to efface the profound vestiges which the *Unia* has left behind. For this reason, even to the present day the population of the Kholm region [*Kholmskaia Rus'*] continues to present a peculiar picture of significant confessional instability.[36]

Imeretinskii's bureaucratic phrase, "significant confessional instability" (*znachitel'naia veroispovednaia neustoichivost'*), meant very simply that the officially Orthodox population of these districts was not, by any real measure, Orthodox at all. But it is interesting to note that even this relatively pro-Polish official placed the blame for this regrettable situation mainly on the "frenzied resistance" of Catholic propaganda. His phrasing suggests that had the local population been left alone, it would have "naturally" found its way back to the bosom of the Orthodox Church.[37] This

[35] RGIA, f. 1284, op. 190, 1886, d. 420, ll. 2–16.

[36] RGIA, f. 797, op. 68, I otd. 1 stol, 1898, d. 4, l. 6. The quotation is from the governor-general's 1897 report.

[37] This is not to suggest, of course, that Catholic propaganda played no role in strengthening the Uniate "resistance." Examples of this propaganda in the form of flyers seized by

view of the "Russian" population as basically passive and reactive, and thus at great risk from Catholic propaganda, permeates the official discourse of the time.

Between 1900 and 1905, official reports continued to bewail the baleful activities of Catholic propagandists among the "persisters." "Orthodox" faithful were buried in Catholic cemeteries with a Catholic priest administering the final blessing; brochures to "Brother Uniates" (*"Bracia Uniaci"*—significantly, in Polish) were distributed that excoriated the "Muscovites" as "hangmen" and the worst enemies of the faith; local peasant community (*gmina*) officials conspired with the "persisters" to look the other way when Orthodox rites were flouted, and in certain cases even "corrected" some individuals' religious affiliation in official registers from "Orthodox" to "Roman Catholic." Perhaps most alarming were rumors of a collective petition sent to the pope by peasants of Radlinskii district, Siedlce province, complaining of Russian oppression.[38] In all of these cases, Russian officials recognized that the local peasantry went to great lengths to avoid Orthodox clergymen and Russian officialdom, but they did not blame these "wayward Russians" (for us, of course, Ukrainians). Instead, the onus of guilt was placed firmly on the shoulders of that stock figure of Russian anti-Polonism: the energetic, fanatical and sly Catholic priest or *ksendz.*[39] This symbol of "militant Catholicism" was also to play an important role in official discussions of Catholicism and Orthodoxy after 1905.

In religious matters, as in so many others, 1905 was a pivotal date in Russian history. In the spring of that year, precisely on 17 April 1905, the government issued an *ukaz* of religious toleration.[40] Of course, various religions had been previously tolerated within the Russian Empire, but this new law took religious freedom one step further: from this point on, it was permissible for those officially registered as Orthodox to change their religion to another (Christian) denomination. The law should not have

---

Russian authorities and sent to St. Petersburg are found in RGIA, f. 797, op. 75–1905, II otd. 3 stol, d. 161, ll. 19–20. Another source is the memoirs of a veteran "propagandist" from Galicia who participated in secret meetings and ceremonies in the Kholm area: Jan Urban, T.J. (Society of Jesus), *Wśród Uniatów na Podlasiu: Pamiętniki wycieczek misyjnych* (Cracow, 1925).

[38] All of these instances, and more, are to be found in Archiwum Głównie Akt Dawnych, Warsaw, PomGGW 330 and 412.

[39] The word is, of course, a Russian transliteration of the Polish *ksiądz,* "priest." The Russian language not only distinguishes Catholic from Orthodox clergyman (*ksendz* vs. *pop*) but also uses different words for Orthodox and Catholic Churches (*tserkov'* vs. *kostel*).

[40] The best work on the revolution of 1905 is Abraham Ascher, *The Revolution of 1905,* 2 vols. (Stanford, Calif., 1988–92). In general on religious toleration both before and after 1905, see Peter Waldron, "Religious Toleration in Late Imperial Russia," in *Civil Rights in Imperial Russia,* ed. Olga Crisp and Linda Edmondson (Oxford, 1989), 103–19. For the text of the toleration law, see *Polnoe sobranie zakonov Rossiiskoi Imperii: Sobranie tret'e,* vol. 25 (1905), no. 26125, pp. 257–58.

taken anyone by surprise as religious toleration had been discussed widely in the press since the *ukaz* of 12 December 1904 which had promised a review of restrictions on non-Russians. Indeed, in the spring of 1905 the deliberations within the Ministry of Internal Affairs on this issue were widely reported in the press.[41] Still, the Orthodox clergy in many areas was unprepared for the new situation, and in the areas where former Uniates resided many thousands of conversions took place in the months after the promulgation of the new law.

Shortly after word of the new law had reached his diocese, the Orthodox bishop of Kholm, Evlogii, wrote in apocalyptic terms to the supreme procurator of the Holy Synod, K. Pobedonostsev: "With feelings of inexpressible depression I consider it my duty to report to Your Excellency on the extremely alarming and sad position of the Orthodox-Russian cause in Lublin and Siedlce provinces. . . . The promulgation of the *ukaz* of religious freedom has called forth terrible ferment and disorder [*brozhenie i smutu*] among the ex-Uniate population."[42] Evlogii blamed this situation partly on the failure of St. Petersburg to prepare local Orthodox authorities by informing them in advance of the law, but mostly on the activities of the Catholic clergy in the area. "Bands of fanatics have begun to roam the streets singing Polish songs—not only religious ones, but outright revolutionary ones as well—and subjecting to terrible insults all things Orthodox or Russian [*vse pravoslavnoe, russkoe*]." The Poles, Evlogii continued, were spreading rumors that all Orthodox Churches in the area would be given over to the Catholics and even that the tsar himself had converted to Catholicism. Under these circumstances, "our poor, ignorant people" could not resist the pressure and went over to the Catholic faith in droves.[43] In all, over one hundred thousand ex-Uniates converted.

Evlogii's words—and he was but the most energetic and articulate spokesmen for traditional and official Russia—once again clearly equated "Russian" and "Orthodox" (and "ours") on the one hand, and lumped together "Poles," "Catholics," and "sedition" on the other. The "poor, ignorant" Russian people was seemingly devoid of will, the passive object of Catholic machinations. And again Evlogii called on St. Petersburg to "protect" the weak, uneducated, passive "Russians" from the activist, educated, well-organized Poles. The fact that even government sources admitted the inadequacy of the 1875 conversions and the presence of thousands of "resisters" in the area did not enter Evlogii's consciousness, or at least not his written reactions to the post-April 1905 conversions.

[41] For the protocols and stenographic reports of the deliberations concerning the Poles (both in the Kingdom of Poland and in the Western Provinces), see RGIA, f. 1276, op. 1, 1905, dd. 105–6.

[42] RGIA, f. 797, op. 75-1905, II otd. 3 stol, d. 161, l. 12, May 6, 1905.

[43] Ibid., l. 12v.

The Uniate cathedral in Kholm (Chełm). *Khol'mskaia Rus'* (St. Petersburg, 1887)

To be sure, Evlogii's was not the only official voice. The governor general of Warsaw, Konstantin Maksimovich, wrote to Pobedonostsev that the complaints of Catholic violence and pressure placed on ex-Uniates to convert were in many cases exaggerated or simply invented. Maksimovich admitted that the "persisters" had been and were continuing to convert en masse to Catholicism and that this presented an "infectious example" for other ex-Uniates. He went on, "But such conversions should not be seen as in any way surprising." According to Maksimovich, when the central authorities had discussed the ramifications of religious freedom, they expected some 100,000 to 150,000 conversions from Orthodoxy in this area, a figure rather close to subsequent statistics on the conversions.[44] "Of course, the cutting off [*ottorzhenie*] of such a large group [*massa*] from the Orthodox Church and consequently from the Russian nationality . . . causes great pain in the hearts of Russian patriots and particularly of Orthodox pastors."[45] Thus Maksimovich, too, while denying in part Evlogii's charges, accepted the fundamental paradigm that a loss to the Orthodox Church represented ipso facto a blow to the Russian nation.[46]

Official Russia's concern for the Orthodox Church as a central element of Russian nationality only increased after 1905. The process of conversion from Orthodoxy was made more difficult, ostensibly to reduce the effectiveness of Catholic pressure on wavering peasants. The Ministry of Internal Affairs asked governors to supply annual figures on the number of converts from Orthodoxy in their provinces.[47] Most importantly, increasing attention was paid to Belarusians (both Orthodox and Catholic) in an effort to reduce Polish pressures on them and perhaps in the long run, bring them back to the Orthodox Church.[48] The Belarusian example, where at least some officials hesitatingly accepted the idea that a "Russian" could in principle be of Catholic faith, indicates that by the early twentieth century modern conceptions of nationality were beginning to filter into the Russian bureaucracy. And yet in most respects, at least in the Western borderlands, Russian nationality continued to be identified with the Orthodox religion, and the idea of a "Catholic Russian" remained a radical, almost incredible novelty. The Uniate Church in the Russian empire was but one casualty of this narrow conception of nationality.

[44] See, for example, Stefan Dziewulski, "Statystyka ludności guberni Lubelskiej i Siedleckiej wobec projektu utworzenia gubernii Chełmskiej," *Ekonomista*, 1909, 157–93.

[45] RGIA, f. 797, op. 75-1905, II otd. 3 stol., d. 161 ll. 76–77, June 7, 1905. This letter responds to Evlogii's complaints.

[46] For more details on the conversions in the Kholm/Podlas'e region, see Robert Blobaum, "Toleration and Ethno-Religious Strife: The Struggle between Catholics and Orthodox Christians in the Chełm Region of Russian Poland, 1904–1906," *Polish Review* 35, no. 2 (1990): 111–24; and Theodore R. Weeks, *Nation and State in Late Imperial Russia: Nationalism and Russification on the Western Frontier, 1863–1914* (DeKalb, Ill., 1996), chap. 9: "The Dubious Triumph of Russian Nationalism: Formation of the Kholm Province."

[47] For some of these statistics on converts from Orthodoxy—the expressive Russian term is *otpavshie* ("those who have fallen away"), see RGIA, f. 821, op. 10, 1910, d. 263; and ibid., 1905–1916, d. 287.

[48] See, for example, RGIA, f. 821, op. 128, 1912, d. 697; and ibid., op. 150, 1912, d. 167.

CHAPTER FOUR

State Policies and the Conversion of Jews in Imperial Russia

JOHN D. KLIER

"All Jews are to leave Our Empire . . . save those who embrace
the Greek faith."
—Empress Elizabeth Petrovna (1742)

"A third [of Russia's Jews] will be converted, a third will
emigrate, and a third will die of hunger."
—Attributed to Konstantin P. Pobedeonostsev

The assumption that religious factors, usually reduced to the formula
of "traditional Russian religious Antisemitism," were the essential determinant of Russian treatment of the Jews carried an obvious corollary: that
state policy aimed at the conversion of Jews to Christianity. A number of
factors buttressed this view, including the legal principle that any Jew who
formally converted to Christianity immediately ceased to be a Jew in the
eyes of the Russian law. Moreover, a number of overt and covert efforts
were made throughout the nineteenth century to promote conversion.
Numerous statements attest to the scorn with which Christian statesmen
viewed Judaism, and the law continued to characterize it as a "false" religion almost to the end of the empire.[1]

I have argued elsewhere that religious intolerance was not, in fact, the
linchpin of Russian policy toward the Jews after 1772.[2] What are the implications of this assertion for the attitude of the Russian state to conver-

[1] *Obzor nyne deistvuiushchikh iskliuchitel'nykh zakonov o evreiakh* (St. Petersburg, 1883), 1; M.
I. Mysh, *Rukovodstvo k russkim zakonam o evreiakh*, 4th rev. ed. (St. Petersburg, 1914), 2–5.
[2] See John D. Klier, "Muscovite Faces and Petersburg Masks: the Problem of Religious
Judeophobia in Eighteenth Century Russia," in *Russia and the World of the Eighteenth Century*,
ed. R. P. Bartlett (Columbus, Ohio, 1988), 125–40, and throughout *Russia Gathers Her Jews:
The Origins of the Jewish Question in Russia, 1772–1825* (DeKalb, Ill., 1986). I argue that official Russian attitudes toward the Jews were shaped by European emancipationist models, especially as filtered through the late Polish-Lithuanian Commonwealth.

sion? I seek to demonstrate below that the Russian state did not have a continuous, consistent policy of conversion directed at the Jews. In fact, as the nineteenth century waned, Russian statesmen became more and more jaundiced about the desirability of large numbers of Jewish con- verts. The Russian Orthodox Church, the vehicle through which conver- sion was supposed to proceed, was likewise very ambivalent about the con- versionary process, especially its practical applications.

It is nonetheless easy to understand why many contemporary Jews were convinced of the state's conversionary intent. Conversion remained the surest means to escape all legal disabilities. Talented Jews were thus con- tinually faced with the temptation of conversion in order to gain a profes- sorial post, a position in the civil service, or enrollment in the university.[3] They were surrounded by a society that made a great external show of Christian belief, and in which the institutional church was deeply involved in public life. Increasingly in the late nineteenth century Russian nation- alists equated Orthodoxy with "Russianness." Civic rituals were permeated with Christian imagery. A number of other confessions, most notably Is- lam, the Eastern Rite Catholic Church (the so-called Uniates), the Evan- gelical Christian Church and even Orthodox sectarians, were targets of sporadic Orthodox Christian conversionary campaigns.

Small wonder, then, that the pioneers of Russian-Jewish history empha- sized the conversionary element in Russian state policy. For scholars such as Simon Dubnow, it was all a seamless web, stretching from Ivan the Ter- rible who, upon capturing the Polish city of Polotsk, ordered the death of all Jews who refused to convert; to the intolerant decree of Empress Eliza- beth offering either conversion or expulsion; and on through the prose- lytizing efforts of Alexander I's Society of Israelite Christians, to the ruth- less conversion of the Jewish cantonists, and finally to the activities of the "Russian Grand Inquisitor," Konstantin Pobedonostsev, the supreme procurator or lay head of the Russian Orthodox Church. Two of the most important initiatives toward the Jews of the reign of Nicholas I, the imple- mentation of military service for Jewish townspeople (*meshchane*) in 1827, and the creation of a state Jewish school system (after 1844) have repeat- edly been interpreted as conversionary initiatives.[4]

Let us consider the "usual suspects" allegedly pursuing conversionary goals, beginning with the Russian Orthodox Church itself. Both its Byzan- tine inheritance and its own experience with alleged "Judaizing" made

---

[3] This is a major theme of Sholom Aleichem's late novel *The Bloody Hoax* (1912–13). See also S. M. Ginsburg, *Meshumodim in tsarishn rusland* [Apostates in tsarist Russia] (New York, 1946).

[4] S. M. Dubnow, *History of the Jews in Russia and Poland*, 3 vols. (Philadelphia, 1916–1920), 1:243, 255, 396–401; 2:44–45, 51; 3:9–10. See also I. G. Orshanskii, *Russkoe zakonodatel'stvo o evreiakh* (St. Petersburg, 1877), 15–60.

the Russian church more concerned with protecting the faithful from Jewish influence than with converting them.[5] Individual priests and bishops did take an interest in conversionary activity, and an Orthodox association, the St. Vladimir Brotherhood in Kiev, was active in the Ukraine in the second half of the century. Refuges for converted Jews—who allegedly required protection from the vengeance of their former coreligionists—were opened in St. Petersburg and Warsaw, the former under imperial patronage.[6] Nonetheless, a case can be made that the attitude of the church as a whole was "eto ne nashe delo": it's not our business. Russian church publications were usually inclined to view the conversion of the Jews in one of two distinct ways. Occasionally conversion was viewed in eschatological terms, as a herald of "the end of days," but not necessarily as a realistic field of practical endeavor.[7] Alternatively, individual conversions were human interest stories, employed to liven the pages of diocesan newspapers.[8] The typical Christian missionary, and the most active and dedicated, was most likely to be a converted Jew who sought to "enlighten his people."[9] It took no great clerical sophistication to realize that many converts were moved by practical considerations, rather than any modicum of piety, and this made the church doubly distrustful of converts. Thus, the church approved of restrictive legislation at the end of the nineteenth century which included Jews "and those of Jewish birth." This was not racism in the modern sense, but fear of contemporary Marranos.[10]

The Russian state rested on Eastern Christianity as an established religion, tied to a spiritual concept of the sacred Russian land and the "Orthodox Tsar." To admit that the desiderata of Russia's rulers was that all their subjects be devout and obedient Orthodox Christians, however, is

---

[5] The canon law of the Byzantine Greek Church sought to prevent the interaction of Christians and Jews for fear of the influence of the latter on the former. The Russian Orthodox Church was especially fearful of sectarianism after the great church schism in the seventeenth century. A particular variety of sectarian development was "Judaizing," the incorporation of concepts associated with the Old Testament, such as celebration of the Jewish Sabbath rather than the Christian Sunday. The appearance of "Judaizing" was often blamed on contemporary Jewish influences. A law dating to the reign of Alexander I ordered the expulsion of all Jews from areas where peasant Judaizing sectarians were discovered.

[6] Mikhail Agursky, "Conversions of Jews to Christianity in Russia," *Soviet Jewish Affairs* 20, no. 2–3 (1990): 69.

[7] For a mixture of eschatological confidence in the ultimate conversion of the Jews, mixed with complaints about their "stubborn opposition to the generosity of God," see Ivan Vasil'evskii, "O imeiushchem posledovat' obrashchenii iudeev," *Strannik* 2 (February 1860): 69–94.

[8] Ibid., 71–75.

[9] Ibid., 76–79. In this I differ with Mikhail Agursky who argues that "few Jewish converts were moved to convert their former co-religionists with missionary zeal." See the examples of the convert-missionaries Aleksandr Alekseev and Iakov Brafman below.

[10] Hans Rogger, in his classic essay on "The Jewish Policy of Late Tsarism: A Reappraisal," reprinted in *Jewish Policies and Right-Wing Politics in Imperial Russia* (Basingstoke, UK, 1986), first drew attention to this phenomenon (35–36). Marranos were Spanish crypto-Jews.

not to say that they ever envisioned this as a practical reality. As Russia evolved into a modern state, conversionary activity became less common. Even such episodes of state proselytizing as took place were products of a very specific set of historical circumstances.

Catherine II (1762–96), who inherited from her predecessor Elizabeth an empire stripped of legally resident Jews, initially opposed the readmission of Jews, and added the formula "except Jews" to decrees that extended toleration to religiously heterodox peoples. However, this was done for entirely pragmatic reasons: part of Catherine's claim to the throne she usurped was that of "defender of the faith," and she feared to arouse the faithful by taking toleration too far.[11] Once significant numbers of Jews entered the empire in the first partition of Poland, however, Catherine willingly extended toleration to them. Her agent supervising the annexation of the new provinces of Vitebsk and Mogilev, Count Zakhar Chernyshev, issued a specific decree that guaranteed religious toleration to the Jews.[12] Under Catherine's mercantilist economic policies, exemplified by the Charter for the Towns of 1785 (under whose rubric the Jews were specifically included), Jews enjoyed civil rights unique in Europe or the American colonies, at least in theory.[13]

Under Emperor Alexander I (1801–25) the first comprehensive law code for Russian Jewry, the Statute of 1804, was enacted. It permitted Jewish children to enroll in any Russian state educational institution, with the guarantee that their religious beliefs would be respected.[14] But Alexander's reign also saw the first state-supported activity involving Jewish conversion, the foundation of the Society of Israelite Christians (*Obshchestvo izrail'skikh khristian*) in 1817. Dubnow characteristically sees in this "a vast undertaking, that of encouraging baptism among the Jewish population, and organizing the converted masses into separate, privileged communes, to serve as a bait for the Jews still languishing in their old beliefs."[15] The society was, in fact, far removed from most of these considerations. It was not even conversionary in the strict sense. The motive of its foundation was to provide support and sustenance for Jews who had converted or were intending to convert, and who had thus lost the sympathy of Jews while not yet winning the respect of Christians. The society conducted no overt propaganda beyond announcing its existence. The "bait . . . of a rather substantial nature" was in the form of free land for agricultural colonization and the remission of state taxes for twenty years. Such privileges

---

[11] Klier, *Russia Gathers Her Jews*, 35–36.
[12] *Polnoe sobranie zakonov Rossiiskoi imperii: Sobranie pervoe*, 19, 13,865 (13 September 1772) (hereafter *PPSZ*).
[13] Klier, *Russia Gathers Her Jews*, 71–5.
[14] *PPSZ*, 28, 21,547 (9 December 1804).
[15] Dubnow, *History of the Jews*, 1:397.

were broadly similar to the inducements that the government offered in the Jewish Statute of 1804 to non-converted Jews to encourage them to re-settle in the south and pursue agriculture. While the tsar, the creator of the society, may well have envisioned the mass conversion of the Jews, he set high standards for its putative members. Eligibility was extended not to just any convert, but to those "who by their life and qualities show themselves worthy of the name of Christian which they have taken on themselves, and who can justify the all-gracious benefits granted to them." Significantly, Israelite Christians were forbidden to engage in tavernkeeping, the disreputable occupation from which the Russian government was attempting to wean the unconverted Jewish population. Nor was this even a Russian Orthodox initiative: the enabling legislation mentioned in several places that eligible recruits to the society might be drawn from any Christian confession.[16]

This latter consideration provides the key to the understanding of the Society of Israelite Christians. Rather than a unique initiative, it was a product of the emperor's post-1812 religious preoccupations. These in turn were linked to European pietism, exemplified by movements like the English Quakers and the English and Foreign Bible Society. Significantly, the head of the Russian Bible Society, Prince Aleksandr Golitsyn, was also deeply involved in the administration of the Society of Israelite Christians. The mysticism and millenarianism of this period produced efforts to convert the Jews, most notably by Pastor Lewis Way, who championed amelioration of the legal position of European Jewry as a means of expediting conversion. British missionaries, not Russian, were the most vigorous agents of conversion, and they were permitted to operate in the Kingdom of Poland only with great reluctance on the part of the Russian government.[17] The ultimate testimony to the lack of conversionary impetus in the society was its complete failure to attract candidates of the high standards envisioned by the emperor. By 1824 Prince Golitsyn was advising the emperor that the entire enterprise should be abandoned, but the personal prestige of the emperor worked against abolition. It existed until 1833 when it was disbanded by Nicholas I.[18] At first glance it might seem ironic that Nicholas, universally reviled by the first generation of Russian-Jewish historians as the "Russian Haman," whose entire Jewish politics was said to be dominated by conversionary intent, should be the ruler to abol-

[16] *PPSZ*, 34, 26,752 (25 March 1817).

[17] The largely unsuccessful activities of the London Society for Promoting Christianity among the Jews may be followed in the documents contained in the "Papers of the Church's Ministry among the Jews" in the Bodleian Library in Oxford, England. For the efforts of the Russian Bible Society among the Jews, see William Canton, *A History of the British and Foreign Bible Society*, vol. 1 (London, 1904), 414.

[18] *Polnoe sobranie zakonov Rossiiskoi imperii: Sobranie vtoroe* 8, 6,085 (30 March 1833) (hereafter *VPSZ*).

ish a body designed for Jewish converts. But according to Dubnow, this was no anomaly: "the new ruler had in the meantime discovered entirely different and by no means fantastic contrivances for driving the Jews into the fold of the Orthodox Church. These contrivances were the military barracks and the institution of Cantonists."[19]

Dubnow and others are correct to characterize the cantonist regiments—military units for underage boys—as conversionary in intent. Saul Ginsburg, who more than any other scholar elucidated this dark corner of Russian-Jewish relations, even located a memorandum to the emperor, supposedly written by a member of the political police, the "Third Section," that suggested the drafting of underage recruits as an effective means of proselytizing them.[20] Thus, the military recruitment that Nicholas I introduced in 1827 was all of a piece: from the very first, the tsar envisioned military service as an attack upon the religious beliefs of the Jews. Having begun in this fashion, it has been argued, the tsar proceeded along the same path to create a state-sponsored Jewish school system which had as its goal the attraction of Jews to "the religion of the cross." A careful rereading of the evidence, however, brings into question the reality of a single-mindedly conversionary policy during much of the reign of Nicholas I.

Nicholas held no sympathy whatsoever for the Jewish population of his empire. He considered them backward, superstitious, isolated, dirty, parasitic, and unproductive. At their worst, they were capable of ritual murder.[21] In a realm whose symbolic motto was "Orthodoxy, Autocracy and Nationality," the Jews were found wanting in at least two of these categories. Nicholas did sponsor conversionary efforts among the sectarians and Old Believers, as well as among the Jews, and he would have been well satisfied if all Jews had converted. But Nicholas never believed that this was realistically possible, and was even mistrustful of converts—insisting, for example, that they be baptized with maximum publicity in order to differentiate them from the Jewish community, and moving to isolate Jewish converts in the army from other Jews.[22] In 1850, the law even required

---

[19] Dubnow, *History of the Jews*, 401.

[20] S. M. Ginsburg, *Historishe werk*, vol. 2 (New York, 1937), 7–8. I have located this memorandum in the Moscow archives. It appears to be a contribution to the contemporary debate about drafting Jews at double the rate of Christians, an issue that arose in the Third Jewish Committee appointed under Alexander I. There is no indication that it was actually seen by the tsar. Gosudarstvennyi Arkhiv Rossiiskoi Federatsii, Moscow, f. 109, op. 3, ed. kh. 2317 (1820–30 gg.) 5 ll.

[21] Ginsburg, *Werk*, vol. 3 (New York, 1937), 370.

[22] *VPSZ* 2, 1,360 (6 September 1827). This same edict expedited conversion, however, by permitting Jews in St. Petersburg to convert to Catholicism or the Evangelical church. Likewise, a decree of 1828 relaxed penalties for Jewish criminals exiled to Siberia if they converted, Ibid., 3, 1,924 (6 April 1828).

that Jewish converts not drop their original, Jewish surnames.[23] All these measures were apparently designed to make such individuals easily identifiable so that their adherence to the Christian faith could be more easily monitored.

During Nicholas's reign, the common disdain for Jews expressed by Russian officials acquired an ideological and scholarly underpinning that it had heretofore lacked. The chief event in this process was the Russian discovery of the rich legacy of Western Talmudophobia. Russian officials had become convinced that the negative features of the Jews could be reduced to "religious fanaticism" which had the effect of leading the Jews to "exploit" their non-Jewish neighbors without qualms. Under Nicholas, the fountainhead of Jewish fanaticism was specifically located in the pernicious teachings of the Talmud. Nicholas sponsored publication of a work by Abbé Luigi Chiarini, a scholar of oriental languages at the University of Warsaw, which "revealed" to the reader the evils of the Talmud.[24]

Yet Nicholas differentiated among types of Jews, specifically between the Jews of the empire and those of France or England, whom he met in the person of visitors like Sir Moses Montefiore. He patiently explained to those who voiced concern about his "persecution" of Russian Jews that, given their backward condition, they could not be treated on equal terms with progressive foreign Jews.[25] Such reforms as the state Jewish school system were based on foreign models, and were an attempt to bring something approaching the German Reform movement to Eastern Europe. As Michael Stanislawski has shown, the main thrust of Nicholaevan reforms was to reduce Jewish "fanaticism" and make Jews economically productive.[26]

This still leaves the issue of the military recruitment. Stanislawski has adequately demonstrated that there was nothing anomalous about the decision to draft Jews of the *meshchanstvo* estate. The exceptional law regu-

---

[23] Ibid., 25, 23,905 (6 February 1850). Pointing to this law, Michael Stanislawski observes that "in Russia alone in Christendom, the state required that the descendants of Jews bear their Jewish surnames as a mark of their tainted origin forever," *Tsar Nicholas I and the Jews* (Philadelphia, 1983), 148. In point of fact, the Prussian state made a number of unsuccessful attempts to require Jews to bear "Jewish" names. See Dietz Bering, *The Stigma of Names* (Cambridge, UK, 1992). The common occurrence of Jews in Russia carrying "Russian" names suggests that Russian efforts were no more successful than Prussian efforts. As noted in the body of the text, I differ with Stanislwski in my interpretation of the intent of Russian law.

[24] See Abbé L. A. Chiarini, *Théorie du Judaïsme appliquée a la réforme des Israélites*, 2 vols. (Paris, 1830).

[25] To the assurances of Moses Montefiore that the Jews were "faithful, loyal subjects, industrious and honorable citizens," Nicholas replied "S'ils vous ressemblent" ("If they are like you"). L. Loewe, ed., *Diaries of Sir Moses and Lady Montefiore*, vol. 1 (London, 1890), 334.

[26] Stanislawski, *Tsar Nicholas I*, 49–101. For the curricula of these schools, which still contained a talmudic element, see John D. Klier, *Imperial Russia's Jewish Question, 1855–1881* (Cambridge, 1995), 224.

lating the Jews was the statute of 1794 which exempted all Jewish *meshchane* from military service upon payment of a set tax. This anomalous law apparently derived from the fear of the military that the Jews could never be trained to become adequate soldiers. The Jews thus exercised a special privilege as compared with non-Jews, a point alluded to by the stated rationale for the recruitment of Jews: "considering it just . . . that the recruit obligation should be equal for all those estates which bear it . . ." The recruitment law of 1827 can thus be viewed as an effort to regularize the legal position of the Jews with Christians of the corresponding social estate (even if this produced, as I have argued elsewhere, "equality in inequality").[27] There was an element of social engineering present as well, reflecting Nicholas's persistent concern that the Jews were an unproductive, parasitic element of the population. The recruitment edict expressed the hope that "the education and skills to which they will become accustomed in military service, after their return home . . . will be passed on to their families for the general good [*dlia viashchei pol'zy*] and success in their general and domestic economy." An 1828 supplement to the recruitment statute stipulated that officials, in identifying those liable for recruitment, differentiate between families engaged in productive labor, and those, such as tavernkeepers or middlemen, who were not. The latter were expected to bear the full measure of recruitment.[28]

There is no question that recruitment of Jewish minors into the army became the focus for a concerted effort to convert Jews to Christianity. It must be asked, however, whether this was the original intent or a policy into which the government unthinkingly wandered. There is evidence to support the former view. The memorandum on the drafting of underage children that was mentioned earlier suggested that the recruitment of such children at a double rate would produce conversion, rapprochement of Jews and Christians, and the eventual mixing up (*smeshenie*) of Jews with the general population.[29] On the other hand, all evidence suggests that Nicholas, irrespective of conversionary aims, was very eager to bring the recruitment of the Jews into line with that of Christian townspeople (*meshchane*). The Jews were one of a number of groups—including Finnish gypsies and Polish noble rebels—who were newly subjected to the draft.[30]

Military recruitment regulations for the Russian empire were always ad

[27] "The Concept of 'Jewish Emancipation' in a Russian Context," in *Civil Rights in Imperial Russia*, ed. Olga Crisp and Linda Edmondson (Oxford, 1989), 121–44. By this expression I suggest that Jews were saddled with all the liabilities and responsibility of the specific social classes of which they were members, while not being allowed to benefit fully from the corresponding estate prerogatives.

[28] *VPSZ*, 3, 2,045 (22 May 1828), art. 4.

[29] See note 20 above.

[30] Stanislawski, *Tsar Nicholas I*, 15.

hoc, devised each time for a specific levy of recruits.[31] The recruitment statute of 1827 was thus specifically devised for the Jews, so it should reflect the government's thinking at that precise moment. Interestingly enough, on the surface the enabling legislation that interpreted the recruitment law displayed few of the conversionary features which were later to mar the treatment of Jewish recruits. The legislation specifically declared that the faith of the Jews was to be respected while they were in service, and that Jews were permitted to fulfill any of their religious rites, to observe their holidays collectively with leaders of their choice, and to attend local synagogues, should they exist. The state even committed itself to providing military chaplains for groups of at least three hundred Jewish soldiers. The statute, in a brief mention, also permitted Jewish communities to provide recruits between the ages of twelve and seventeen for the cantonist system.[32]

The drafting of underage recruits became the most reprehensible aspect of the Jewish recruitment, so it is worth examining in detail. The Russian state had long established that children born to men in the ranks while on active service were "state property." Additional categories, such as orphans or illegitimate children of soldiers' wives, were later included as so-called "military cantonists." At an early age these young boys were sent for military training, with the assumption that they would learn practical skills that could be put to good use when they were inducted into active service as adults. Reality soured these optimistic plans. The cantonist schools became notorious as "stick academies," where the most brutal military discipline was imposed upon children as young as seven years of age. The schools had shockingly high mortality rates: in the 1820s, one recruit died for every two who graduated from the schools. According to all contemporary accounts, the system was little more than well-organized child abuse on a horrifying scale.[33] The recruitment regulations for 1827 did no more than authorize individual Jewish communities to send young boys ages twelve to seventeen to cantonist schools in lieu of adult recruits, who entered active service at eighteen. No particular encouragement was offered to supply underage recruits (as had been demanded by the Third Section memorandum). An elaborate system was also mandated to insure that the assessment of recruits was fairly shared across the Jewish community, the so-called *kahal,* including the keeping of "queue books" which

[31] For the complex system of recruitment, see John L. H. Keep, *Soldiers of the Tsar: Army and Society in Russia, 1462–1874* (Oxford, 1985), esp. 143–74.

[32] *VPSZ,* 2, 1,330 (26 August 1827).

[33] Nor is this an anachronistic reading back of modern values. Numerous memoirs of former cantonists paint a frightening picture of terror and suffering, and the brutality of the system was recognized by contemporaries. See the descriptions in Emmanuil Flishfish, *Kantonisty* (Tel-Aviv, n.d.) and the Ginsburg article cited in note 37.

listed each family in order of eligibility for recruitment. Ultimate responsibility was left to the communal leadership (the *kahalniki*) to produce candidates for inspection by the draft boards. Practice quickly demonstrated that production of the requisite number of recruits took precedence over strict legality.

The *kahalniki* faced a daunting task in supplying this "blood tax." Beside their own selfish if understandable determination to protect themselves and their families from recruitment, they were guided by social pressures inherent in communal life. They were also obliged by the traditional conception of their duty to protect the integrity and prestige of the community, in both a physical and a religious sense. These considerations deterred them from recruiting either young men with families (the marriage age for Jewish males was very young) or young scholars of the religious academies, *yeshivot*. In short, Jewish communities pursued the same goals as their Christian neighbors: to protect the most useful and influential members of society while disposing of those on the margins. A famous Jewish folk lament from this period complains of the drafting of the widow's only son in preference to the many sons of the communal elite; this may have been reprehensible, but it was also understandable. Under the system of collective responsibility (*krugovaia poruka*), the communal elite were responsible for the taxes of the communal poor. Now the poor were expected to contribute in their own way. The temptation to present the young sons of the communal poor—unmarried and uneducated— was too great for the *kahalniki* to resist.[34] There is ample documentation showing that the rules the Russian government established for recruitment were routinely violated, and that recruitment within the Jewish community was based on favoritism, coercion and bribery.[35] This situation reached its nadir when some *kahalniki* actually employed Jewish kidnappers (the notorious *knappers*) to abduct Jewish children for the draft. The *kahal* system of Jewish autonomous government, which the Russian state had retained from the years of Polish rule, was already being torn apart by centrifugal forces in the early nineteenth century. There were tensions between rival social elements, a growing burden of communal debt, and religious disputes between the Hasidim and Mitnagdim. Added to this were the growing constraints imposed by the Russian state, anxious to leave no area of Jewish life outside its control. The recruitment statute of 1827 proved the last nail in the coffin of the *kahal*. The moral authority of

[34] Stanislawski, *Tsar Nicholas I*, 28–34.

[35] The archives of centers in the Pale of Settlement are filled with complaints to the authorities against illegal recruitments. A particularly poignant case is found in Kiev where two underage orphans petitioned, with the "help" of the *kahal*, to be taken as recruits to satisfy debts allegedly owed to the community by their deceased parents. See Tsentral'nyi Gosudarstvennyi Istoricheskii Arkhiv Ukrainy, Kiev, f. 442, op. 65, d. 402 (1833), ll. 1–8 (hereafter TsGIA-Ukrainy).

the *kahal* was totally shattered, and complaints and denunciations flooded into the Russian authorities in the capital and in the periphery.[36] Russian commissions routinely denounced the *kahal* system. It is possible that this final crisis encouraged the authorities to embark finally upon the formal abolition of the *kahal*, which was ordered in 1844.

The employment of the cantonist system as a missionary enterprise can be sharply divided into two phases, before and after 1843. Military officials could not anticipate the possibilities that Jewish cantonist recruitment presented for missionary activity because they had no way of knowing that the Jewish community would provide substantial numbers of cantonists in lieu of adults, for the reasons discussed above. They soon seized the initiative, however, acting to encourage and increase Jewish cantonists even as the general trend was to reduce the total number of non-Jewish cantonists and to allow them to reside with their parents for as long as possible before active service. Jewish cantonists, selected at the earlier age of twelve, were immediately separated from their parents and, preferably, stationed far from home and from Jewish communities. Most significantly, a secret regulation was circulated in 1829 that permitted individual priests, counter to past practice, to baptize underage recruits without the prior authorization of their superiors.[37] Despite Nicholas I's hypocritical insistence that no coercion should be used (he stated this overtly in 1849), the military decorations and bonuses given to military commanders who presided over successful conversionary campaigns amply demonstrated the monarch's will. In an institution like the Russian army, which insisted upon total, unquestioning obedience, religious belief counted for no more than any other autonomous desire of the hapless recruit. Results, nonetheless, were random, depending upon the enthusiasm of individual commanders and priests. For example, between 1827 and 1842, all the Jews in the Smolensk Cantonist Battalion were baptized, while only three were converted in the Tomsk Battalion. Even Ginsburg, who characterizes the conversion of cantonists as "a well-delineated and thought-out system, dictated from above and implemented extremely consistently and methodically," concedes that before 1843 the campaign proceeded unsystematically, without a concerted plan or unified direction.[38]

This laxity ended in 1843, through the intervention of the tsar himself. On 29 April 1843, the War Ministry advised the supreme procurator of

---

[36] For a random selection, see TsGIA-Ukrainy, f. 533, op. 3, d. 488 (1830–1), ll. 1–19; f. 1252, op. 1, d. 21 (1843), ll. 1–7; f. 442, op. 151, d. 703 (1842), ll. 1–8; f. 422, op. 153, d. 515 (1844), ll. 1–11.

[37] S. M. Gintsburg [Ginsburg], "Mucheniki-deti. Iz istorii kantonistov-evreev," *Evreiskaia starina* 13 (1930): 54–55.

[38] Ibid., 55, 50.

the Holy Synod that a special regulation should be devised to promote the conversion of Jewish cantonists, albeit with "absolute caution, mildness, and without the slightest coercion." A senior military chaplain, V. Kutnevich, drafted an elaborate memorandum on missionary activity that was approved by the tsar in January 1844 and sent to all cantonist institutions. Father Kutnevich carefully explained which techniques and arguments were most likely to prove successful with young Jewish recruits.[39] Lest there be any doubt in the matter, the Chief Chaplain of the Army and the Fleet informed his priests in 1844 that "the conversion of Jews to Orthodoxy, which attracts the special attention of the higher government, should constitute one of the most important objects of their care, and success in this matter will be taken as the basis for the evaluation of their abilities and zeal for the carrying out of their responsibilities."[40] Nicholas closely followed this campaign. He demanded monthly status reports and covered them with his comments. Against this background, all the promises made by the government in the first recruitment statute proved hollow. Efforts were made to isolate cantonists from other Jews, including their own families. A ban was placed on the reception of letters from home in Yiddish, and all outgoing correspondence had to be in Russian. Jews were discouraged from attending synagogue and from participating in religious services conducted by Jewish soldiers: the authorities sought any pretext to transfer a sailor-rabbi, for example, from his unit in Astrakhan. (There is evidence that older Jews in service exhorted young cantonists not to abandon their faith. There were also a number of embarrassing relapses into Judaism in the last years of the system.[41]) Conversely, cantonists were required to attend Christian religious services and religious education in the hopes that it would show them the "falsity of the Jewish faith" and detach them from "the general superstition of the Jewish people."[42]

In 1868 Aleksandr Alekseev (Vul'f Nakhlas), a former cantonist who had converted, published his autobiography in *Novgorodskie gubernskie vedomosti*. Alekseev had become a missionary among the Jews both during and after his military service, and his memoirs were designed to demonstrate the most effective techniques for converting Jews to Christianity. They are also a graphic and unsettling portrait of the combination of subtle and brutal measures to which the cantonists were exposed, including intense personal activity by the bishop of Saratov himself. The most effective measures were carried out by an Orthodox priest, Father Peter, who

[39] The complete memorandum can be found in Ginsburg, *Werk*, 3:369–57.

[40] Ginsburg, "Mucheniki," 62.

[41] For episodes of attempted apostasy between 1855 and 1857, see Rossiiskii Voenno-Istoricheskii Arkhiv, Moscow, f. 405, op. 9, d. 3143, 36 ll., and op. 9 (1856–57), d. 3354, 22 ll.

[42] Ginsburg, "Mucheniki," 59–75.

ultimately effected Alekseev's conversion. The techniques he employed could have come directly from the handbook of Father Kutnevich, discussed above. Ultimately it was the solicitude and warmth that the hapless, brutalized recruit received from this religious father figure, rather than the superiority of Christianity over Judaism, that brought him to the baptismal font. Alekseev's effusive gratitude to Father Peter makes embarrassing reading to a modern reader attuned to the conversionary techniques of contemporary cults. In any event, Alekseev devoted the rest of his life to Christian proselytizing among Jews, during which he wrote an entire shelf of books on popular theology.[43]

What was the total effect of these measures? Michael Stanislawski, on the basis of the published recruitment records of the Russian army and archival material analyzed by Saul Ginsburg, estimates that approximately seventy thousand Jews served in the army during the reign of Nicholas I. Of these, approximately fifty thousand were under the age of eighteen, and would therefore have served in cantonist battalions. About twenty-five thousand of these recruits converted to Christianity. Stanislawski posits that these Jews constituted a distinct social grouping within the army and, upon release, in Russian society at large.[44] Certainly, the unconverted *nikolaevskii soldat* enjoyed a legal position superior to that of the majority of Jews, eventually receiving the right of residence outside the Pale, but Stanislawski's broader thesis remains to be tested.

One of the first symbols of the new spirit in Russia which was to lead to the Reform Era was the abolition of the cantonist battalions by Alexander II in 1856. This was a boon to the system's Christian victims as well, but the empire's Jewish subjects saw it as a particularly welcome and reassuring sign. Nor was this a completely misguided response. While Tsar Alexander II was never as sympathetic to the Jews as acculturated Jews would have liked to believe, the reformist atmosphere of his reign ensured that the crude conversionary tactics of his father were completely abandoned. Indeed, Alexander's ministers were surprisingly ambivalent about even the legality of state-sponsored missionary activity among the Jews. In 1858 a teacher in the Russian Orthodox seminary in Minsk, the converted Jew Iakov Brafman (not a cantonist), submitted a memorandum to the local authorities proposing establishment of a Christian mission to work among the Jews of the western provinces. The missionaries were to be under the protection of the local administration, and to carry

---

[43] Interestingly enough, Alekseev performed yeoman service for his former coreligionists by actively rebutting the blood libel made against Jews in the course of the so-called Saratov Affair in 1854. For a biography of Alekseev, see *Evreiskaia entsiklopediia*, vol. 1 (St Petersburg, n.d.), 839–40. For his autobiography, see nos. 7–24 of *Novgorodskie gubernskie vedomosti* for 1868.

[44] Michael Stanislawski, "Jewish Apostasy in Russia: A Tentative Typology," in *Jewish Apostasy in the Modern World*, ed. Todd M. Endelman (New York, 1987), 193–94.

on their activities in Yiddish. The memorandum was passed on to the capital to the Department of Foreign Confessions of the Ministry of the Interior. This Department forwarded the memorandum to the supreme procurator of the Holy Synod, with the curious observation—as though there were some doubt in the matter—that Brafman's proposal could be considered because the law specifically permitted the Orthodox Church in Russia to propagate its teachings to nonbelievers.[45] (Brafman achieved notoriety not as a successful missionary, but as the exposer of the *kahal*, which he claimed was a malevolent "secret Talmudic republic.")[46] A similar loss of faith in the ethics of agressive conversion could be seen in a series of criminal trials that took place throughout the Reform Era of former baptized cantonists who had abandoned their Christian faith and reverted to Judaism. In Russia with its established church, this was the criminal offense of apostasy. In virtually all cases, defendants admitted their apostasy but justified it with reference to conversion as a cantonist. In response, juries found the accused innocent of wrongdoing, thus implicitly faulting the Nicholaevan conversion program.[47]

A mood of defensiveness towards Judaism—perhaps born of a guilty conscience—is indicated by a curious role reversal adopted by some Christian polemicists in the Reform Era. Rather than being a persecuted minority, the prominent Judeophobe Ivan Aksakov complained, "the Jews in our western and southern provinces undoubtedly are one of the most privileged races in Russia." In support of this extraordinary claim, Aksakov pointed to a letter from an Orthodox priest in the Pale, who complained of the difficulties encountered in baptizing would-be converts. Faced with the active hostility of the Jewish community, who actually assaulted a monastery where one proselyte had sheltered, local clergy were reluctant to baptize Jews.[48] The Russian press took up this theme in a campaign against "Jewish fanaticism" which portrayed Christianity as the beleaguered minority religion in the western borderlands.[49] It was partially in response to such episodes that refuges were opened for proselytes, although Jews tended to view these institutions as overt missionary activity.[50] Such feelings of persecution conveniently ignored the active Christian conversionary efforts of the St. Vladimir Brotherhood in Kiev.

While a climate of toleration may have developed in the third quarter of the nineteenth century, it quickly passed with the onset of the reign of

---

[45] Rossiiskii Gosudartvennyi Istoricheskii Arkhiv, St. Petersburg, f. 821, op. 8, ed. khr. 184 (1858), ll. 1–5.

[46] Klier, *Imperial Russia's Jewish Question*, 263–83.

[47] For representative cases, see *Den'* (Moscow), 12 February 1871; *Kievlianin*, 3 September 1877; *Golos* (St. Petersburg), 18 January 1880.

[48] *Moskva*, 15 July 1867.

[49] See *Vilenskii vestnik*, 20 July 1867; *Kievlianin*, 6 September 1869.

[50] Klier, *Imperial Russia's Jewish Question*, 437.

Jews massacred in the 1905 pogrom in Odessa. Gerard Silvain and Henri Minczeles, *Yiddishland* (Corte Madera, Ca., 1999).

Alexander III, with its generalized attack on many of the accomplishments of the Reform Era. The consensus that had developed within Russian society and the state bureaucracy that while the Jews were in need of reform they were ultimately reformable was shattered by the outbreak of pogroms in 1881. The resultant crisis made the Jewish question a matter of immediate official concern. The minister of the interior, N. P. Ignat'ev, attributed the pogroms to popular rage against "Jewish exploitation," and demanded that Christians and Jews be kept apart, in contrast to past policies that promoted acculturation and "merger." Ignat'ev's assumptions led to the genesis of the notorious May Laws of 1882, which restricted Jewish residence outside the urban centers of the Pale.[51] Critics of the authorities attributed the popular pogroms as well as what Dubnow called the "legal pogroms" (i.e., the May Laws) to the government. A frequent corollary was the belief that persecution was placed in the service of conversion. That was certainly the implication of the remark attributed to Pobedonostsev by a foreign Jewish publicist that appears as an epigraph to this essay. Unfortunately, this famous quotation, which has so often been said to perfectly encapsulate Russian policy on the Jews, is of very dubious

[51] See John D. Klier, " 'Popular Politics' and the Jewish Question in the Russian Empire, 1881–1882," *Jewish Historical Studies* 33 (1992–94): 175–85.

provenance.[52] The chief argument against its authenticity (except possibly as a bon mot) is the fact that it manifestly conflicts with Pobedonostsev's oft-stated views on the Jews. He was never an advocate of—or a believer in the possibility of—the conversion of the Jews. In his very first annual report as supreme procurator of the Holy Synod he expressed his skepticism at the prospects for Jewish conversion. The Jews, he lamented, were bound by their conception of themselves as a chosen people, the power of family ties, and a long tradition of holding fast to their religion. Moreover, Jews made unreliable converts.[53]

Given such sentiments, it comes as no surprise that the Holy Synod under Pobedonostsev's aegis made no real effort to carry on missionary activity among Jews. More than that: Pobedonostev rejected promising initiatives that might have brought more converts into the state church. The period following the crisis of 1881 was marked by a number of reform movements by individuals at the margins of Jewish society. The best known were the Spiritual Biblical Brotherhood of Iakov Gordin, the New Israel of Iakov Priluker, and the movement of the New Testament Israelites, founded by Joseph Rabinowich. The movements sought to synthesize Judaism and Christianity, in part by recognizing Jesus Christ as the "Jewish Messiah." (In present-day terms, they were "messianic Jews," or "Jews for Jesus.")[54] The movements offered an opportunity for imaginative evangelism among Russian Jews. The Holy Synod not only refused to support these endeavors, but actively thwarted them. Pobedonostsev, while viewing with approval the disintegration of Jewry, viewed the movement as an "artificial creation." At his suggestion, the Ministry of the Interior habitually harassed the various sects of messianic Jews.[55]

---

[52] Michael Aronson, "The Attitudes of Russian Officials in the 1880s toward Jewish Assimilation and Emigration," *Slavic Review* 34, no. 1 (March 1975): 1–2, is one of the first scholars to question the authenticity of the remark. The earliest version I have found in print is Leo Errera, *Les Juifs Russes: Extermination ou Emancipation?* (Brussels, 1893). The version found in A. S. Rappoport, "Pobiedonostzev, The Apostle of Absolutism and Orthodoxy," *Fortnightly Review*, 1 May 1907, 871, attributes the original quotation to the Russian-Jewish publicist Aleksandr Tsederbaum, the editor of the Hebrew-language *Hamelits* (St. Petersburg). This version resembles that given by Dubnow, *History of the Jews*, 3:10. Neither speaks directly of conversion: Rappoport indicates that "they will become assimilated with the Orthodox population," while Dubnow's quote (in English translation) refers to being "completely dissolved in the surrounding population." The terms here appear to refer to the Russian words *sliianie* and *sblizhenie* for which see Klier, *Imperial Russia's Jewish Question*, 66–83.

[53] Robert F. Byrnes, *Pobedonostsev: His Life and Thought* (Bloomington, Ind., 1968), 207.

[54] For a contemporary description of these movements, see V. Portugalov, *Znamenatel'nyie dvizheniia v Evreistve* (St. Petersburg, 1884). For other treatments, see Ginsburg, *Meshumodim*; Kai Kjaer-Hansen, *Joseph Rabinowitz and the Messianic Movement* (Eidenburgh, Mich., 1995); Steven J. Zipperstein, "Heresy, Apostasy and the Transformation of Joseph Rabinovich," in Endelman, *Jewish Apostasy in the Modern World*, 206–31.

[55] N. A. Bukhbinder, "K istorii sektanskogo dvizheniia sredi evreev v Rossii v 80–kh gorodakh," *Evreiskaia starina* 13 (1930): 129.

Pobedonostev's suspicion of Jewish converts was seemingly confirmed at the end of the 1880s. In response to legal restraints on admission to secondary and higher education (the notorious *numerus clausus*, first imposed by the Ministry of Education in 1887), acculturated Jews threatened with nonadmission converted to Christianity, albeit with obvious insincerity. (There is the famous anecdote told of the Jewish-Russian scholar Daniel Khvolson: "Did you convert out of conviction?" he was asked. "Yes, out of the conviction that it is better to be a professor in Petersburg than a *melamed* [Jewish primary school teacher] in Shipishok."[56]) During the very first university admissions period held after the introduction of norms for Jewish admissions, in the summer of 1887, young Jews who were denied admission promptly reappeared with baptismal certificates.[57] This provoked a polemic in the Russian press on the issue of whether "bad Christians" (converted Jews) were to be preferred to "good Jews." Conservative papers editorialized against this "mockery of the faith," while the church press voiced fears that Jewish wolves were now to be loosed upon the unwary Russian Orthodox flock.[58] It was this epidemic of insincere conversion, more than the influence of western racialism, I would hypothesize, that led the Russian state occasionally to introduce restrictions not just against Jews, but against persons "of Jewish origin" (*iz evreiskogo proiskhozhdeniia*), although this never became an essential legal principle.[59] Consequently, while the Russian state did not formally abolish the privileges offered to Jewish converts, concerted efforts were made neither by the Orthodox Church nor by the state to encourage conversion until 1905, when the state, wracked by revolutionary unrest, issued an edict of religious toleration, ending the legal foundation of officially sanctioned proselytizing and permitting the return of converts to Judaism.[60] According to I. Cherikover, as many as four hundred persons made use of this concession to return to Judaism in 1905.[61]

The most eloquent illustration of the failure of conversionary efforts (or lack thereof) of the Russian state are the statistics of formal religious

---

[56] Khvolson's biography is found in Ginsburg, *Meshumodim*, 119–56.

[57] See *Nedel'naia khronika Voskhoda* (St. Petersburg), no. 37–39 (September 1887): 13–27. See Stanislawski's discussion of the sincerity of converts in "Jewish Apostasy," 196–203.

[58] *Russkoe delo* (Moscow), 13 February 1888; *Pravoslavnoe obozrenie* (Moscow), reprinted in *Novoe vremia* (St. Petersburg), 11 March 1884.

[59] See Rogger, *Jewish Policies and Right-Wing Politics in Imperial Russia*, 35–36.

[60] The edict was dated 17 April 1905, and was followed by the departure from Orthodoxy of a large number of converts from various faiths. See Peter Waldron, "Religious Toleration in Late Imperial Russia," in Crisp and Edmondson, *Civil Rigths in Imperial Russia*, 111–12.

[61] I. Cherikover, "Obrashchenie v khristianstvo," *Evreiskaia entsiklopediia*, vol. 12 (St. Petersburg, 1906–13), 894. By contrast, between 1864 and 1874, when the Russian state permitted Estonian and Latvian peasants, who had been coerced into conversion to Orthodoxy, to return to Lutheranism, almost thirty-five thousand left the church. Waldron, "Religious Toleration," 111. Much of the conversionary activity of the Orthodox Church in the Baltic provinces had a political objective, as part of the state's Russification policies for the region.

conversion. Although there are many gaps and contradictions—the reports of the Holy Synod do not tally with the annual reports of the governors—the overwhelming message is clear: very few Jews converted to Christianity in the Russian Empire.[62] In no single year, for example, did the St. Vladimir Brotherhood convert more than 81 Jews, and its yearly average for the period 1870–89 was a paltry 31.[63] According to governors' reports, and excluding cantonist conversions, in thirteen provinces of the Pale between 1842 and 1869, fewer than 300 Jews were baptized in any given year, save for the anomalous year of 1854, when 1,080 approached the font. Only two provinces totaled more than 500 conversions for the entire twenty-eight-year period, the exceptions being Podolia, with a total of 1,080, and Chernigov, with a total of 760.[64] Between 1825 and 1855, excluding cantonists, the Orthodox Church in Lithuania could record only 83 conversions.[65] German researchers tabulated a total of only 30,000 converts for the second half of the nineteenth century.[66]

More disquieting than mere numbers for the leadership of the church were the underlying causes of this failure. Neither bribery, coercion, nor the patient "hands-on" evangelism of English missionaries showed positive results. Many of those who converted did so in order to escape legal disabilities. Others, like the hapless cantonists, were the victims of a combination of brute force and psychological pressures. The venal sought the twenty-five rubles offered to all converts. (There were even undocu-

[62] The major primary sources for statistics on conversion are the annual reports of the supreme procurator of the Holy Synod; the yearly summary reports on their regions submitted by the governors of the provinces of the Pale; the archival records of the Lithuanian Consistory of the Russian Orthodox Church held at the YIVO Institute in New York City; the published reports of the St. Vladimir Brotherhood in Kiev, and the records of the English missionary society in Russian Poland housed in the Bodleian Library at Oxford. The Synod reports were used for two works devoted to the second half of the nineteenth century: J. F. A. de la Roi, *Judentaufen im 19. Jahrhundert* (Leipzig, 1899), and N. Samter, *Judentaufen im 19en Jahrhundert* (Berlin, 1906). These records have also been usefully tabulated by Agursky in "Conversions," 69–84. Michael Stanislawski discusses the Lithuanian records in *Tsar Nicholas I*, 141–44, and "Jewish Apostasy," 193–203. The reports of the governors are conveniently collected in Genrich M. Deych, *Putevoditel': Arkhivnye dokumenty po istorii evreev v Rossii v XIX–nachale XX vv.*, ed. Benjamin Nathans (Moscow, 1994), 41–86. There are no central statistics for the conversion of Jews to Roman Catholicism, a phenomenon that would have had importance for Russian Poland, or to the various branches of Protestantism, which would have had the greatest impact in the Baltic region.

[63] Agursky, "Conversions," 77. Significantly, the peak year for conversions was 1887 (with eighty-one), which may be ascribed to the introduction of norms for Jewish admissions in that year.

[64] Deych, *Putevoditel'*. Statistics in the reports of the governors exist for 279 of the 364 years surveyed (13 provinces times a 28 year period equals 364 years).

[65] Stanislawski, *Tsar Nicholas I*, 142. However, to illustrate the reliability of the statistics expressed above, note that the conversion reports of the governor of Vilna province, which would have comprised part of the Lithuanian Consistory, recorded 203 cases for the years 1842–55 alone. Given the alleged conversionary pressures, this is not an impressive total. Deych, *Putevoditel'*, 45.

[66] Deych, *Putevoditel'*, 213 n. 67.

mented rumors in the Jewish community of professional converts, traveling from place to place in order to receive baptism—and the corresponding stipend.) Hardly ever did Jews convert out of religious conviction, still less out of respect for the moral superiority of Russian Orthodoxy, however much the Orthodox clergy occasionally pretended that this was the case.[67]

The convert was most likely to come from the margins of Jewish society. Mikhail Agursky has made an important hypothesis about the role of women in the phenomenon of conversion. He points to statistics that reveal a disproportionate imbalance between female and male converts,[68] and argues that conversion was often an escape for women who had been marginalized by Jewish society: "older" girls who had failed to find a husband by their early twenties; divorcees, who had been rejected by their husbands for adultery or barrenness, "chained women" (the *agudot*), who had broken with or lost their husbands but who had not been given a *get*, or bill of divorcement. The conversion of such women, Agursky argues, was part of the "disintegration of the traditional Jewish community."[69] Stanislawski, who noted the growing percentage of female converts at the end of the century, concurs: "as Russian-Jewish society underwent the dramatic revolutions of the nineteenth century, its female members were less able to adjust to the new social, economic, political, and cultural conditions than their brothers, husbands, and sons; therefore, more women than men made their way to the baptismal font."[70] Stanislawski, unlike Agursky, does not attempt to explain why women should have been less able to cope with the stresses of social and economic change than men.

These hypotheses raise a number of questions. The traditional Jewish community was indeed under strain from a wide variety of economic, political, ideological, and religious factors in the last half-century of tsarist rule. Religious conversion, however, is not necessarily the most effective marker of this crisis. If one can speak of trends when the statistical base is so low (approximately thirty thousand conversions out of a total Jewish population of more than five million),[71] then the rate of conversion was down, not up, in the years chronicled by Agursky. Affairs of the heart were

[67] Stanislawski examines a total of 244 cases reported by the Lithuanian Consistory of the Russian Orthodox Church of Jews who requested baptism between 1819 and 1911. Only 5 of these cases—all women—appeared to be motivated by sincere religious feeling, "Jewish Apostasy," 197–98.

[68] This ratio does not appear in one case, the statistics of the Lithuanian Consistory between 1825 and 1855. Of a total of eighty-three converts, sixty-two were male and only sixteen female (and there were also five children whose sex was not given). Stanislawski, *Tsar Nicholas I*, 142.

[69] Agursky, "Conversions," 69.

[70] Stanislawski, "Jewish Apostasy," 200.

[71] Mordechai Altshuler, *Soviet Jewry since the Second World War: Population and Structure* (Westport, Conn., 1987), 239 n. 1.

a factor in many conversions, since Russian law did not admit marriage between Orthodox Christians and unconverted Jews. This was a demonstration of acculturation in action, since the couple had to have a common medium of communication. It also suggests that knowledge by Jews of non-Jewish, even "peasant" languages, has been underestimated. The most common pattern was that of the Jewish girl running off with the peasant lad. This was hardly a new phenomenon, since Polish and Russian literature were filled with such romances, invariably centering on the stereotype of the exotic, sensual, dark-haired Jewess.[72] Whereas originally the Gentile lover was usually a Polish nobleman, at the end of the century he was replaced by the Ukrainian peasant—as illustrated by the village clerk Fedka, who elopes with Tevye's daughter Chava in Sholom Aleichem's cycle of stories about Tevye the Dairyman. In this connection one might also note the Russian revolutionary movement, where liaisons were often without benefit of clergy, and where Jewish-Gentile pairings were so common as to be entirely unremarkable.[73]

Another noteworthy phenomenon was the low rate of conversion of Jews who had attained a career and status in Russian society. For such highly educated individuals, nonobservance rather than conversion was often the norm. In contrast to assumptions in the secondary literature, legal restrictions may actually have served to retard conversions of convenience among those for whom "Paris was well worth a mass." The persecution rained down on the Jewish masses by the imperial government made conversion a disreputable option, an abandonment of the defenseless people. This was a phenomenon that had often been noted by contemporaries, some of whom praised those whose consciences prevented them from "renouncing the oppressed, abandoning the weak, and siding with the victorious."[74] Even the celebrated Judeophobe Ivan Aksakov recognized the phenomenon, though he characterized Jews who had completely acculturated but refused to convert as "moral and intellectual amphibians."[75] It is noteworthy how reluctant even the religious reformers mentioned above were to convert formally to Christianity except on terms that allowed them to retain a Jewish identity, while their Jewish critics consistently accused them of trying to abandon the Jewish people for personal gain.

What was at work here was not so much the disintegration of the traditional Jewish community as its transformation. New varieties of Jewish

---

[72] For the Polish tradition, see Magdalena Opalski and Israel Bartal, *Poles and Jews: A Failed Brotherhood* (Hanover, 1992); for the Russian tradition, J. Kaunitz, *Russian Literature and the Jew* (New York, 1929).

[73] See Erich E. Haberer, *Jews and Revolution in Nineteenth-Century Russia* (Cambridge, 1995).

[74] *Nashe vremia* (Moscow), 4 March 1862.

[75] *Den'*, 8 February 1864.

identity—pioneered by nationalists, both Zionist and non-Zionist, and by various forms of Jewish socialism—were emerging to challenge the old definitional criteria of religion and culture. The weakness of a conversionary movement among Russian Jews from 1772 to 1917 was eloquent testimony to the enduring strength of Jewish communal institutions, as well as to their potential for evolution and growth.

The low rate of conversion also suggests that the enthusiasm of the Russian state for conversionary policies in the case of the Jews has been much exaggerated. This is not to deny that a low level of conversionary pressure existed: the state did keep statistics of converts, offered various monetary and legal bribes, and permitted English missionary activity in the Kingdom of Poland. Nonetheless, except for the cantonist interlude, especially the years between 1843 and 1855, the Russian state tended to respect the promise of religious toleration that it had made to the empire's new Jewish subjects in 1772. Few of the first native historians of Russian Jewry, themselves victimized by the growing intolerance of late imperial Russia, were willing to concede this point. But the raw statistics present another, more eloquent message.

II

CONVERTING ANIMISTS AND BUDDHISTS

CHAPTER FIVE

The Conversion of Non-Christians in Early Modern Russia

MICHAEL KHODARKOVSKY

In 1742, a certain English merchant traveling through Central Asia on behalf of the Russian government submitted a detailed report about his journey. With his eye on the potential for commerce in the region, he did not fail to observe other things that could be of interest to the Russian officials. He reported that one of the khans among the Karakalpaks was a certain Murat, about fifty years of age and literate in Tatar. Upon further inquiry, Murat khan turned out to be a fugitive Bashkir from the Ufa region, who had previously been baptized and married to a Russian.[1] While not every former convert was able to escape and assume such authority among his former coreligionists, the story, nonetheless, was symptomatic of the Russian government's continuous, even though sporadic, efforts to integrate its non-Christian subjects into the Russian empire through their conversion to Orthodox Christianity. It was also no less symptomatic of the Russian government's limited success in pursuing this policy, the non-Christians' resistance to it, and their persistent backsliding.

This article discusses the policies of religious conversion pursued by the Russian Orthodox Church and government toward non-Christians in the newly acquired southern and eastern territories before 1800. In contrast to the abundant literature on conversion and missions of the Catholic and Protestant churches in the New World and elsewhere, it is remark-

This essay is an expanded version of my article "Not by Word Alone: Missionary Policies and Religious Conversion in Early Modern Russia," *Comparative Studies in Society and History* 38, no. 2 (1996): 267–93.
[1] *Kazakhsko-russkie otnosheniia v 16–18 vekakh (Sbornik dokumentov i materialov)* (Alma-Ata, 1961), no. 88, 209.

able how little has been written about religious conversion in Russia. The elusiveness of the subject, the paucity of sources, and the ideological preferences of Soviet historiography have all conspired to make historians abandon the subject to the dilettantish exercises of nineteenth-century church writers, leaving it in relative obscurity in the twentieth century.[2]

Before the sixteenth century, conversion to Christianity resulted from the work of the most zealous missionaries and took place only sporadically. Thereafter, however, the process was an integral part of the government's policies toward the empire's new subjects. The intensity of state and church efforts to convert non-Christians varied from brutal campaigns under Ivan IV to benign neglect in the seventeenth century, from unambiguous discrimination under Peter I to systematic coercion during the middle of the eighteenth century, and finally, to toleration under Catherine II. At all times, however, religious conversion remained one of the most important tools of Russia's imperial policies.

Conversion in Russia was spiritual least of all; it generally involved only a nominal transfer of religious identity. For non-Christians of the Russian empire, conversion promised tangible economic benefits and a hope of social and economic mobility. As in other premodern societies, where religion defined not only forms of worship, but also the cultural, social, and political norms of the society, conversion in Russia was a process of cultural transformation and assimilation of the Other.

Religious conversion was also a process of exchange, as a Russian Orthodox sense of identity was itself further crystallized in the encounter

---

[2] Articles published in nineteenth-century Russian church journals, such as *Pravoslavnyi sobesednik*, *Pravoslavnyi vestnik*, and *Pravoslavnoe obozrenie*, had a specific agenda and were intended for church officials. See a bibliographical essay by Alexandre Bennigsen and Chantal Lemercier-Quelquejay, "Musulmans et missions orthodoxes en Russie orientale avant 1917: Essai de bibliographie critique," *Cahiers du monde russe et soviétique* 13, no. 1 (1972): 57–113. The most comprehensive study of the subject in pre-1917 Russia was done by Apollon Mozharovskii, "Izlozhenie khoda missionerskago dela po prosveshcheniiu inorodtsev s 1552 po 1867 goda," in *Chteniia v Imperatorskom obshchestve istorii i drevnostei rossiiskikh pri Moskovskom universitete*, bk. 1 (1880): 1–237 (hereafter *Chteniia*). A more recent article based on the works of prerevolutionary Russian writers is Chantal Lemercier-Quelquejay, "Les missions orthodoxes en pays musulmans de Moyenne et Basse-Volga, 1552–1865," *Cahiers du monde russe et soviétique* 8, no. 3 (1967): 369–403. One of the few typical works of the Soviet era is by A. N. Grigor'ev, "Khristianizatsiia nerusskikh narodnostei, kak odin iz metodov natsional'no-kolonial'noi politiki tsarizma v Tatarii (s poloviny 16 v. do fevralia 1917 g.)," in *Materialy po istorii Tatarii*, vol. 1 (Kazan, 1948), 226–85. The best work on the subject has been done by the German historians in the 1950s and 1960s: Joseph Glazik, *Die russisch-orthodoxe Heidenmission seit Peter dem Grossen* (Münster, 1954), and *Die Islammission der russisch-orthodoxen Kirche: Eine missionsgeschichtliche Untersuchung nach russischen Quellen und Darstellungen* (Münster, 1959); Michael Klimenko, *Ausbreitung des Christentums in Russland seit Vladimir dem Heiligen bis zum 17. Jahrhundert* (Berlin, 1969). More recently, the issue of conversion has been discussed by Igor Smolitsch, *Geschichte der russischen Kirche*, ed. Gregory L. Freeze, vol. 2, Forschungen zur Osteuropäischen Geschichte, vol. 45, (Wiesbaden, 1991), 246–346; and by Andreas Kappeler, *Russlands erste Nationalitäten: Das Zarenreich und die Völker der Mittleren Wolga vom 16. bis 19. Jahrhundert* (Cologne, 1982), 350–77.

with non-Christians. Yet this was an exchange with different expectations on both sides. As such, conversion in Russia implied an area of confrontation, for the goals and expectations of those who did the converting and of those who chose to convert were different. If the missionaries sought to bring salvation and enlightenment to the natives and hoped for their eventual acculturation, non-Christians expected to receive the benefits and privileges entailed in conversion without assimilation.

Historical sources on early modern Russia do not provide any significant discussion of such important issues as religious syncretism among the natives and their interpretations of the Orthodox rituals and beliefs.[3] Only later, in the nineteenth century, would these issues be of great concern, to be described and discussed by Russian officials and churchmen. In this sense, the period under discussion could be considered the initial phase of government and church policies toward the non-Christians. During this time the Russian government pursued policies that encouraged the non-Christians' conversion to Orthodox Christianity as a way of consolidating the society into a single political and religious identity under one tsar and one God. We shall see below whether the government and the church were successful in achieving this goal.

Classifying the Other

By the late eighteenth century, nearly 250 years after Moscow established its presence in the Volga River region, Russia had emerged as one of the largest empires in the world. The numerous vanquished peoples included Orthodox, Catholic, and Protestant Christians along with Jews in the west and Muslims, Buddhists, and pagans in the south and east. All the non-Christian peoples were referred to by the generic term *inorodtsy* (the non-Russian or the non-Christian subjects of the empire).[4] As the number and significance of non-Russians within the Russian empire grew, it became increasingly important to describe and classify them, to ensure their loyalty, and to develop a set of uniform policies in order to incorporate the new territories and peoples into the empire.

The first attempt at a comprehensive classification of Russia's subjects was made by the late eighteenth-century Russian writer and historian

---

[3] For example, in the late nineteenth century, the Caucasus highlanders of the Khevsur region of Georgia were described as observing the Muslim Friday, the Jewish Sabbath, and the Christian Sunday.

[4] Usually, both terms are used interchangeably. The term "non-Russian," however, may also include numerous Christians in Russia's western borderlands, who were not Russian Orthodox. I chose to use the term "non-Christian", as it appears to be more precise and embraces only the pagan, Muslim, and Buddhist subjects of the Russian empire.

Prince Mikhail Shcherbatov. In his 1776 treatise, Prince Shcherbatov suggested that the peoples of the empire could be divided into six categories in accordance with their lifestyle, taxation, military service, and religious affiliation:

1. Russians and all non-Christians who pay the soul tax and provide recruits,
2. Russians and non-Christians who pay taxes but do not provide recruits,
3. Christians other than Russian Orthodox,
4. All kinds of Cossacks and other military settlers,
5. Bashkirs and other savage peoples who practice Islam, and
6. Kalmyks and other nomadic idol worshipers.[5]

It is not surprising that Prince Shcherbatov drew no clear distinction between religious, ethnic, and social identities. The overlapping of these categories typical of premodern societies was also quite common in Russia. For example, the word *krest'ianin* in Russian parlance meant not just any peasant but specifically a peasant of the Russian Orthodox faith. Likewise, the non-Russian pagan peoples considered Christianity a Russian faith and Islam a Tatar one.[6] Russian official correspondence referred to non-Christian peoples by their specific names, such as Chuvash, Bashkir, or Tatar. "Chuvash" implied not only ethnicity but the fact that a person was a taxpaying peasant and a pagan. Bashkir or Tatar meant that a person was a tax-paying subject and a Muslim. Those Tatars who performed a military service were known as "military service [*sluzhilye*] Tatars."

There were also more general terms used to refer to the non-Christians in the south and east of the empire. Of the original terms *inozemets* (literally, a person of a different land), *inorodets* (of a different kin) and *inoverets* (of a different faith), the latter two were applied more systematically in the eighteenth century. Redefining the status of the non-Christians clearly reflected a change in the self-perception of the Russian state and its evolution into an empire. The newly vanquished peoples were first attributed an extra-territorial identity (*inozemets*) and considered foreigners (compare the etymology of the German *Ausländer* or the English *foreigner*). As the non-Christians became further integrated into the Russian empire, they were referred to by the terms *inorodets* or *inoverets*, that is, they became non-Christian subjects of the Russian empire.

---

[5] M. M. Shcherbatov, "Statistika v razsuzhdenii Rossii," in *Chteniia*, 1859, bk. 3, pt. 11:46.

[6] S. V. Chicherina, *O privolzhskikh inorodtsakh i sovremennom znachenii sistemy N. I. Il'minskogo* (St. Petersburg, 1906), 4. For a discussion of the Russians' and Siberian natives' perceptions of each other, see Yuri Slezkine, "Savage Christians or Unorthodox Russians? The Missionary Dilemma in Siberia," in *Between Heaven and Hell: The Myth of Siberia in Russian Culture*, ed. Galya Diment and Yuri Slezkine (New York, 1993), 15–31.

The First Missions

Little is known about the efforts of the Orthodox Church to win converts among pagans before the sixteenth century. Most likely, few such efforts were made, as the priority of the church was to unite Russian lands under one religion and one ruler and to solidify its hold on the Russian population. The story of St. Stefan's life in the Perm region of the 1380s is the best known case of early attempts to proselytize non-Christians. The story is of significant interest not only because it is one of the few available accounts of early missionary activity by the Russian Orthodox Church but also because St. Stefan's approach stands in sharp contrast to the missionary work of the church after the 1550s.

A didactic story of St. Stefan's life in Perm is related by Epifanii the Wise, a Russian monk of the late fifteenth century. According to Epifanii, St. Stefan arrived in the Perm region, in the foothills of the Ural Mountains, by his own will in order to spread Christianity.[7] The local inhabitants coming to admire the beauty of the church built by St. Stefan were converted to Christianity. Soon thereafter, the people of Perm divided into two rival groups: the converts (*novokreshchennye*) and the infidel idol worshippers (*kumirosluzhiteli nevernye*).[8] St. Stefan destroyed pagan temples and burned idols but remained unaffected by the vengeance of the local gods. He burned the fur treasures that adorned the temples but did not take any for himself. He refused to punish a shaman who was captured and handed over to him by converts, saying he was sent to save souls, not punish them. Impressed by such devotion and generosity, the natives flocked to St. Stefan to be baptized.[9]

In 1383, St. Stefan arrived in Moscow to convince the authorities that it was time to "harvest the planted crop"; Perm, in other words, was in need of a bishop. The metropolitan of Moscow and the grand prince agreed to appoint St. Stefan the first bishop of Perm. Until his death, St. Stefan continued his efforts to convert the natives of the region, where he created a native alphabet, translated the Scriptures from the Russian language, and conducted services in the vernacular.[10]

Such an approach to winning converts was quite common. After all, the Rus' themselves received an alphabet from a Greek monk in the tenth century and adopted Christianity shortly thereafter. As long as the pagan peoples were outside of Moscow's direct control, missionaries continued to be the true pioneers, residing among the pagans without government

---

[7] Epifanii, *Zhitie Sviatogo Stefana, episkopa Permskogo* (St. Petersburg, 1897), 24.
[8] Ibid., 30.
[9] Ibid., 34, 35, 38, 55, 56.
[10] Ibid., 61, 63, 69, 72, 74.

protection and winning converts by accommodating their needs. This changed, however, when Moscow acquired Kazan and Astrakhan and the numerous non-Christian peoples who resided there. After the mid-sixteenth century, the missionaries took a back seat to the interests of the government, as they were to preach in lands that had already been conquered by Moscow.

The Conquest of Kazan and the World of Islam

Before Moscow's spectacular expansion in the 1550s, a religious conversion of non-Christians took place only occasionally. Renegade Tatar princes from the south and Lithuanian and Polish nobles from the west came to offer their services to the Russian ruler and, in time, became Orthodox Christians. In the north and northeast, the numerous Finnic peoples, after having come into contact with the advancing Russian merchants and monks, were attracted by the benefits and favors entailed in becoming a Christian and chose to convert.[11]

Moscow's continuous expansion was not immediately articulated in terms of a religious struggle with Roman Christianity and Islam. By the early sixteenth century, however, the expansion was slowly acquiring the features of political theology as a result of a gradual rise of Moscow's self-consciousness as the only sovereign Orthodox Christian state. The confrontation between Muscovy and various Muslim peoples began increasingly to be seen on both sides as a religious war. In 1521, the Muscovite grand prince, Vasilii III, had to explain to the Ottoman sultan, Suleyman, that contrary to Crimean claims, he had not given orders to destroy mosques and build churches in Kazan.[12]

Yet it was not until the middle of the sixteenth century that the idea of religious conversion began to enjoy the all-embracing support of a government imbued with an overpowering sense of manifest religious destiny, Moscow's own version of *non plus ultra*. Thus, Moscow's conquests of Kazan in 1552 and Astrakhan in 1556 were not mere military victories. These conquests were first and foremost a manifestation of the political and ideological supremacy of Orthodox Muscovy over its former Muslim overlords. A new missionary spirit was forcefully expressed by the triumphant Russian tsar, Ivan IV. In his 1556 letter to Archbishop Gurii of

[11] One finds converts to Christianity among the Karelians and Lapps in the fifteenth and early sixteenth centuries. *Ocherki istorii Karelii*, vol. 1 (Petrozavodsk, 1957), 76; *Prodolzhenie drevnei rossiiskoi vivliofiki*, 11 vols. (St. Petersburg, 1786–1801; reprint ed., ed. C. H. van Schooneveld, Slavic Printings and Reprintings, vol. 251, (The Hague, 1970), 5:192–95, no. 172.

[12] *Sbornik Imperatorskogo russkogo istoricheskogo obshchestva*, 148 vols. (St. Petersburg, 1867–1916), 95:696.

the newly founded Kazan diocese, Ivan IV suggested that converting pagans was a divine duty, adding that missionaries "should teach the pagans [*mladentsy,* literally "children"] not only to read and write, but to make them understand truly what they read, and [they], then, will be able to teach others, including the Muslims."[13]

After it conquered Kazan in 1552, Moscow acquired large numbers of new subjects who were neither Christian nor Russian-speaking. The six major languages of the Kazan region were Tatar, Bashkir, Mordvin, Chuvash, Cheremis (Mari), and Votiak (Udmurt).[14] While the Tatars and Bashkirs practiced Islam, the other peoples were predominantly pagan. The Tatars constituted a ruling elite, and their language was the lingua franca of the region. Now, the Muscovites decided, the Russian language and administration had to replace those of their Tatar predecessors and Christianity had to replace Islam. Ivan IV banned the construction of new mosques and ordered the mosques of Kazan demolished and churches built in their stead.[15]

Moscow's rapid expansion along the Volga, its conquest of Astrakhan in 1556, and the construction of the Tersk fortress in the north Caucasus in 1567 were both a surprise and a matter of great concern for the Crimea and the Ottoman Porte. Ivan IV's explanations that he meant no harm to Muslims and their faith and that he had conquered the Volga cities merely to ensure their loyalty were a poor excuse. In what looked more like a pattern rather than single occurrences, Muscovite priests were sent to convert the Kabardinian chiefs, many Kazan Muslims were converted and resettled, and Muslim captives were converted by force.[16]

Unsatisfied with Moscow's explanations, the Ottoman sultan, Selim II, stated that the regions of Astrakhan and Kabarda in the Caucasus were traditional Ottoman domains with Muslim residents and demanded that pilgrims and merchants from Bukhara and elsewhere be allowed to proceed through Astrakhan en route to Mecca. In 1571 Ivan IV informed the sultan that the Tersk fortress was being demolished and the Astrakhan route reopened.[17] Propelled almost instantly into the forefront of a struggle with Islam, Moscow was as yet unprepared for such a confrontation. For the time being, the government refrained from missionary or any other activity that could provoke the Ottomans.

---

[13] *Prodolzhenie drevnei rossiiskoi vivliofiki* (PDRV), 5: 242.

[14] Andrei Kurbskii, "Istoriia o velikom kniaze Moskovskom," in *Russkaia istoricheskaia biblioteka,* 39 vols. (St. Petersburg-Leningrad, 1872–1927), 31:205–6.

[15] Efim Malov, "O tatarskikh mechetiakh v Rossii," in *Pravoslavnyi sobesednik* (December 1867): 288; Mozharovskii, "Izlozhenie," 25.

[16] *PDRV* 11:24, 221; *Nikonovskaia letopis'* (Moscow, 1965), 13: 281, 313, 324.

[17] *Puteshestviia russkikh poslov 16–17 vv.: Stateinye spiski* (Moscow, 1954), 76; *Kabardino-russkie otnosheniia v 16–18 vv.: Dokumenty i materialy,* 2 vols. (Moscow, 1957), 1: 20, no. 10; 26, no. 13; 27–29, no. 16.

Conversion and Punishment

In the last half of the sixteenth century, the policy of conversion was spelled out in the tsar's instructions to the Kazan archbishop Gurii, who was directed to baptize those who came of their own will or fled justice. Gurii was advised to threaten the latter with capital punishment—even if they had committed a minor crime—then forgive them and thus bring them to Christ through love.[18] Still, few conversions occurred during this period, as the Ottoman threat, a series of uprisings in the Kazan region, and the corruption of local military governors (*voevodas*) served to restrain the zeal of the Russian government and church to spread the gospel among the natives.[19]

The issue was raised again in earnest in the early 1590s by Kazan metropolitan Germogen, who complained in a letter to the tsar that due to the neglect of the local governors, new converts did not observe Christian laws and continued to live among their non-Christian kin, while the Tatars flouted earlier prohibitions and built new mosques. A decree of the tsar in 1593 addressed Germogen's concerns by stipulating that converts should be resettled in a separate compound near Kazan, be given farmland, and live among the Russians. The Russian officials were to ensure that converts observed Christian law and did not intermarry with Tatars or foreign prisoners of war. Furthermore, children of mixed marriages and the slaves of the converts were to be baptized. Those converts who did not follow Christian ways were to be put in chains and thrown in jail to make them forget the Tatar faith and become firm believers in Christ. All mosques were to be destroyed.[20]

The combination of intimidation, force, and the revocation of traditional privileges was only part of the government's missionary policy. Coercion could be applied only in territories already under the firm control of the Russian military and bureaucracy, such as the middle Volga region. In addition to a stick, a carrot was no less important in Russia's initial ap-

---

[18] *Akty, sobrannye v bibliotekakh i arkhivakh Rossiiskoi Imperii Arkheograficheskoi ekspeditsieiu Imp. Akademii Nauk.* 4 vols. (St. Petersburg, 1836), 1: 259–61, no. 241.

[19] In the late 1560s, population registers of the city of Kazan listed twenty-four converts. *Materialy po istorii Tatarskoi ASSR: Pistsovye knigi goroda Kazani , 1565–68 gg. i 1646g* (Leningrad, 1932), 179. Even fewer converts could be found in Kazan province. K. I. Nevostruev, *Spisok s pistsovykh knig po g. Kazani s uezdom* (Kazan, 1877), 67, 75. I have found no evidence to support Mozharovskii's claim that initially conversions were numerous and that, in contrast to those of the eighteenth century, the converts were inspired by true belief (Mozharovskii, "Izlozhenie," 22–23). In response to Russian colonization of the Kazan region, powerful anti-Russian uprisings led by local nobles took place in 1556, 1572, and 1582. V. D. Dmitriev, "Krest'ianskaia voina nachala 17 veka na territorii Chuvashii," in *Trudy Nauchno-issledovatel'skogo institututa iazyka, literatury, istorii i ekonomiki Chuvashskoi ASSR* 93 (1979): 46–48.

[20] *Akty . . . Arkheograficheskoi expeditsieiu*, 1:436–39, no. 358.

peal to the non-Christians. This was particularly true in the frontier areas, where the government's hold over the new territory remained tenuous and the need to gain the natives' cooperation was acute. Here, church officials were instructed to win the converts not by force but by love. Each convert was rewarded with woolen clothing, a shirt, a pair of boots, and cash. Converts were also enlisted as musketeers, assigned to one of the frontier garrisons, and given compensation in cash and flour.[21]

More generous rewards awaited non-Christian nobles who came to the Russian court from the sixteenth century onward in increasing numbers seeking protection and privileges. Most of these nobles came from the south and southeast, where the expanding Russian state offered new opportunities to local elites. Upon the 1552 conquest of Kazan, various members of the Chinggisid dynasty from Astrakhan, Crimea, Kazan, Siberia, and Kasimov converted to Christianity.[22] One of the more celebrated examples was the conversion of the Kasimov khan, Sayin-Bulat, in 1573. Better known as Simeon Bekbulatovich, he was put on the Muscovite throne by Ivan IV to rule Russia for almost a year.[23]

Chinggisid princes from Siberia to the Crimea, non-Chinggisid Tatar nobles of the Kazan region, Kabardinian nobles and the Imeretian ruling dynasty from the Caucasus, Nogay and Kalmyk chiefs from the Volga steppes—all at different times and for different reasons chose to convert to Christianity. Some hoped to obtain Moscow's support against their rivals; others sought refuge from their enemies. Yet most found themselves increasingly attracted to the benefits that conversion offered. Upon their baptism, non-Christian nobles were granted a Russian title of nobility and in exchange for military service, they were given generous annual compensation in land and cash.[24]

---

[21] Such were the instructions of Tsar Boris concerning the Vogul converts in Siberia in 1603. *Akty istoricheskie, sobrannye i izdannye Arkheograficheskoi komissiei*, 5 vols. (St. Petersburg, 1841–43). 2:56–57, no. 43. Archbishop Makarii of Siberia and Tobolsk was similarly instructed in 1625. P. I. Ivanov, comp., *Opisanie gosudarstvennogo arkhiva starykh del* (Moscow, 1850), 253–66.

[22] The last khan of Kazan, Ediger, converted in 1553 and took the Christian name of Simeon. Utemish Giray, taken from Kazan to Moscow as a child, was given the name of Aleksandr upon his conversion. *Rodoslovnaia kniga kniazei i dvorian Rossiiskikh i vyezzhikh*. 2 vols. (Moscow, 1787), 24–27; "Pravlenie tsaria Ivana Vasil'evicha," in *Drevniaia rossiiskaia vivliofika*, 2d ed., 22 vols. (Moscow, 1788–91); reprint ed., C. H. van Schooneveld, Slavic Printings and Reprintings, vol. 250–51 (The Hague, 1970), 17:173. In 1591, Abul-Khayir, the son of the Siberian Kuchum Khan, converted and was baptized as Andrei. V. V. Vel'iaminov-Zernov, *Issledovanie o kasimovskikh tsariakh i tsarevichakh*, 4 vols. (St. Petersburg, 1863–87), 3:54–55.

[23] M. G. Khudiakov, *Ocherki po istorii Kazanskogo khanstva* (Kazan, 1923; reprint ed., Kazan, 1990), 174–75. By the middle of the seventeenth century, the descendents of the Kasimov khans were all converted to Christianity and found themselves under Moscow's complete control (Vel'iaminov-Zernov, *Issledovanie*, 2:24; 3:200–202, 333).

[24] A list of prominent converts and their land grants can be found in *Russkaia istoricheskaia biblioteka* 8: 278–84, no. 39, and in *Chteniia*, 1899, bk. 191, no. 4, pt. 5:5–8. A long list of valu-

Ultimately, conversion was the only means by which the government could ensure the non-Christians' loyalty and their acceptance into Russian society. Apparently, their racial characteristics mattered less than their religious affliliation. For non-Christian nobles, conversion meant a fast track to assimilation. The converted nobles intermarried with the Russian nobility, held high military positions, and often served in the frontier regions as Russia's trusted intermediaries.[25] Within two generations their names often no longer betrayed their non-Russian and non-Christian origin.[26] Assimilation was complete when a dynasty entered the Genealogical Book of the Russian nobility.[27]

The plight of those non-Christians who did not belong to noble families often differed from that of their noble brethren; ordinary converts were designated as "new converts" and considered a separate social group.[28] Their privileges, such as exemption from taxes or military service, were only temporary, and after three or five years they had to resume their onerous obligations.[29] Moreover, they found themselves victims of frequent abuse by local Russian officials, who took advantage of the converts' ignorance of the Russian language, laws, and customs.[30]

Although certain Russian governors refused to baptize those who re-

---

able items granted to the Kabardinian princes upon their conversion included golden crosses, sable furs and hats, caftans, silks, and numerous other items (*Kabardino-russkie otnosheniia*, 1:75, no. 46; 173–75, no. 120).

[25] A daughter of Tsar Aleksei was promised in marriage to Kasimov prince Seyid-Burkhan upon his conversion (Vel'iaminov-Zernov, *Issledovanie*, 3:200). Cf. the names of the commanders in Tsar Boris's campaign against the Crimea in 1598. M. M. Shcherbatov, *Istoriia Rossiiskaia*, 11 vols. (St. Petersburg, n.d.), 7, pt. 1:23. From the early seventeenth century, the Kabardinian dynasty of Cherkasskii princes were extremely important in implementing Russian policies in the North Caucasus (*Kabardino-russkie otnosheniia*, 1:73–75, no. 46).

[26] The Tatar Prince Abul-Khayir of Siberia was the first of his dynasty to convert in 1591. Although his son was known as Vasilii Abulgairovich, his grandson's name, Roman Vasil'e-vich, could no longer be distinguished from a native Russian name (Vel'iaminov-Zernov, *Issledovanie*, 3: 54–55).

[27] In 1686 the tsar decreed that the dynasties of the ruler of Imeretia in the Caucasus and the princes of Siberia and Kasimov were to be entered into the Geneological Book of the Russian nobility (Vel'iaminov-Zernov, *Issledovanie*, 4:144).

[28] "Vypiski iz razriadnykh arkhivov," in *Drevnaia rossiiskaia vivliofika*, 16:339–45; *Drevnie gosudarstvennye gramoty, nakaznye pamiati i chelobitnye sobrannye v Permskoi gubernii* (St. Petersburg, 1821), 79. In her thorough study of several generations of new converts in the Novgorod area in the sixteenth century, Janet Martin convincingly showed that the economic profile of their estates remained different from their Russian counterparts and instead resembled that of the estates of Muslims. "The Novokshcheny of Novgorod: Assimilation in the 16th Century," *Central Asian Survey* 9, no. 2 (1990): 13–38.

[29] *Polnoe sobranie zakonov Rossiiskoi imperii: Sobranie pervoe.* 45 vols. (St. Petersburg, 1830), vol. 2, no. 867, pp. 312–13 (hereafter *PPSZ*); *Polnoe sobranie postanovlenii i rasporiazhenii po vedomstvu pravoslavnogo ispovedaniia Rossiiskoi imperii*, 10 vols. (St. Petersburg, 1869–1916), 2, 1722 g.: no. 888, p. 578 (hereafter *PSPR*).

[30] *Opisanie dokumentov i del, khraniashchikhsia v arkhive sviateishego sinoda*, vol. 1 (St. Petersburg, 1868), 144, no. 157; *PSPR*, vol. 2, 1744–45 g. (St. Petersburg, 1907), no. 608, pp. 83–89. I will discuss this issue in detail below.

quested conversion, others simply ordered natives to convert and used force to ensure that they did. When reports that Russian officials had used excessive force reached Moscow, the government instructed the overzealous provincial governors to desist, to convert only those who came of their own free will, and to attract others by promising compensation and presents.[31] Moscow's main concern remained, however, not the use of force per se but its ability to control officials in the provinces and to ensure that excessive force did not result in social unrest. When deemed necessary, government orders directed these officials to ignore the complaints of non-Christians or authorized the forceful resettlement of those who complained.[32]

Throughout the seventeenth century, government policies directed toward winning more converts became more systematic and penal. As Russia continued to consolidate its control over the Kazan region, non-Christians increasingly found themselves subjected to Russian laws, some of which were clearly intended to encourage conversion. Moscow could no longer tolerate the fact that some Orthodox Christians remained slaves of Muslim Tatars. Indeed, Russia's first comprehensive legal code of 1649 barred Russians from serving Tatars and decreed punishment for those Russians who attempted to sell themselves into slavery to non-Christians. Furthermore, the government assumed responsibility for those contract slaves in the service of the non-Christians who wanted to convert, and was prepared to free them by paying slave owners fifteen rubles per slave. But for many in Russia, slavery was a preferred way of life, and the government was forced to resort to penal measures to forbid converts from seeking new owners and to prevent Russians from serving non-Christians.[33]

In the latter part of the seventeenth century, numerous government decrees continued to address the issue of the converts' landed estates. Non-Christian military service people were provided with a clear incentive to convert, as the government used every opportunity to confiscate the lands of non-Christians and redistribute them among Russians and converts.

---

[31] "Akty, otnosiashchiesia k istorii Sibiri, 1625–30 g." in *Russkaia istoricheskaia biblioteka*, 8:469–70, no. 33. In 1647 the governor of the town of Romanov ordered the Muslim Tatars to convert. When they refused he put them in chains and threw them in jail. *Dopolneniia k aktam istoricheskim, sobrannye i izdannye Arkheograficheskoi komissiei*, 12 vols. (St. Petersburg, 1846–75), no. 35, 3:118–19.

[32] *Dokumenty i materialy po istorii Mordovskoi ASSR*, vol. 1, pt. 2 (Saransk, 1950), no. 10, 264. In 1669, 150 musketeers were sent on the tsar's orders to expel the non-Christian Mordvins from the village of Bol'shoi Vad and resettle them in the district of Teriushevsk. "Dela Tainogo Prikaza: Zapisnye knigi," in *Russkaia istoricheskaia biblioteka*, 21:1482–3.

[33] *The Muscovite Law Code (Ulozhenie) of 1649*, trans. Richard Hellie, pt. 1 (Irvine, Calif., 1988), 182, ch. 20, art. 70–71. This law was based on the previous decree of Tsar Aleksei in 1628. N. V. Nikol'skii, "Khristianizatsiia sredi chuvashei srednego Povolzh'ia v 16–18 vv.," in *Izvestiia Obshchestva Arkheologii i Etnografii pri Kazanskom universitete* 28. no. 1–3 (1912): 43–44. *PPSZ*, vol. 2, no. 1099, p. 644.

Those who converted before such a confiscation were allowed to retain their service or hereditary estates, while those who converted after confiscation were allotted new ones. Over time, however, the government tended to limit the initial privileges of converts.[34]

Some converts elected to rejoin their non-Christian kin, but for most the road back was closed, and they were punished in accordance with the Russian law for "taking off the cross." The most severe punishment was reserved for Muslims who attempted to convert Christians to Islam: such a person was to be burned.[35] Later the law was expanded to include proselytizing Jews as well. In Smolensk in 1738, when a retired Russian captain named Voznitsyn confessed under torture that he had been circumcised and converted to Judaism by a Jew named Barukh, both were burned at the stake under the same 1649 law.[36]

There are no reliable data allowing for a precise estimate of converts in the sixteenth and seventeenth centuries. Enactment of laws favoring those who converted to Christianity, complaints from Russian priests about new-Christians who were Christian in name alone, and scattered available records of converts' names may serve as indications, however, that the number of proselytes grew slowly.[37]

Conversion under Peter I

The importance and duty of converting non-Christians was reiterated by Ivan Pososhkov, a contemporary of Peter the Great often referred to as "the Russian Adam Smith." In a treatise written in 1719, Pososhkov con-

---

[34] *The Muscovite Law Code*, 112, ch. 16, art. 44; *PPSZ*, vol. 1, no. 616, p. 1029. In 1681 the Tatars of the Kurmysh district of the Kazan region were confronted with an ultimatum to convert or lose their lands to those who did. *Dopolneniia k aktam istorichsekim*, 8:311–12, no. 89; "Novoukaznye stat'i o pomest'iakh" in *PPSZ*, vol. 2, no. 633, art. 25, pp. 24–25; ibid., vol. 2, no. 1287, 916–17. A brief discussion of the issue is in James Cracraft, *The Church Reform of Peter the Great* (Bristol, 1971), 64–70.

[35] *PPSZ*, vol. 2, no. 1009, 521–22; *Dokumenty i materialy po istorii Mordovskoi*, vol. 1, pt. 2, no. 30, pp. 293–39. Capital punishment for Muslims who proselytized among the Christians is first found in the legal code of 1649 and was later upheld in 1669 criminal law (*PPSZ*, vol. 1, ch. 22, art. 24, p. 156,; no. 431, p. 774).

[36] *PPSZ*, vol. 10, no. 7612, pp. 556–60; John Doyle Klier, *Russia Gathers Her Jews: The Origins of the "Jewish Question" in Russia, 1772–1825* (Dekalb, Ill., 1986), 28.

[37] In one of the more successful examples of missionary work, 530 men, women, and children were reported to have been baptized between 1675 and 1680 in the entire Kazan region. N. Pisarev, "K istorii pravoslavnoi missii v Rossii v 17 veke," in *Pravoslavnyi sobesednik*, September 1902, 420–21. The number does not seem impressive, given the fact that the total non-Christian population of the region was over two hundred thousand, according to the 1678 census. Ia. I. Vodarskii, *Naselenie Rossii v kontse 17–nachale 18 veka* (Moscow, 1977), 109–10. In 1678, among 674 Mordvin households in Temnikov district, 34 belonged to converts. M. P. Soldatkin, *Politika russkogo tsarizma po khristianizatsii mordvy* (Avtoreferat kandidatskoi dissertatsii, Moscow, 1974), 15.

trasted the feeble missionary efforts of the Russians with those of the Roman Catholic Church and chastised the Russian government and the Orthodox Church for their inability to attract non-Christians to Christianity:

> And these peoples have been the subjects of the Russian empire for two hundred years, but they did not become Christians and their souls have perished because of our negligence. The Catholics are sending their missionaries to China, India, and America. [Despite] the fact that our faith is the right one— and what could be easier than converting the Mordvins, the Cheremis, and the Chuvash?—yet we cannot do this. And our pagans are like children, without a written language, without a law, and they do not live far away, but within the Russian empire, along the Volga and the Kama rivers; and they are not sovereign, but the subjects of Russia.[38]

Inspired by the missionary work of the Catholic Church and particularly by the Jesuit order, Pososhkov was primarily concerned with saving the souls of non-Christians and making them good Christians. His crusading spirit was shared by the government, albeit for different reasons. Increasingly defined by Russia's new missionary sense of struggle with Islam, government policies on religious conversion acquired further importance as a policy tool aimed at securing the political loyalty of Moscow's non-Christian subjects.

Russia had long been defined as a crusading state and a depository of the only true religion. By the late seventeenth century, the idea of Russia's destiny as a Christian state at the forefront of the struggle with the Islamic world had further crystallized, as the government prepared to confront the Ottoman empire. In 1696 Peter I conquered the Ottoman fortress of Azov and was nurturing plans of a broad anti-Ottoman coalition of the European states. Such plans had to be shelved, however, because European powers had other priorities. In 1699, at Carlowitz, Russia became a reluctant signatory to a peace treaty with the Ottoman Porte.

Moscow's militant stance against the Ottoman empire was accompanied by more aggressive policies toward Muslims inside Russia. In 1654, these Russian policies compelled the Crimean khan, Mehmet Giray IV, to complain of Moscow's treatment of its Muslim subjects. He noted that many Christians lived under the protection of the Ottoman sultan and were free to worship, whereas the Muscovite tsar burned the Quran, destroyed mosques, tortured Muslims, and forced them to convert.[39]

Under Peter I, Russia's conversion policies in the east became more vig-

[38] I. T. Pososhkov, *Zaveshchanie otecheskoe*, ed. E. M. Prilezhaev (St. Petersburg, 1893), 323. Pososhkov further urged the government to send missionaries to the Kamchatka Peninsula in the Far East, "for if the Catholics find out, they will send their mission" (ibid., 327).

[39] V. D. Smirnov, *Krymskoe khanstvo pod verkhovenstvom Ottomanskoi porty do nachala 18 veka* (St. Petersburg, 1887), 565.

orous and comprehensive than in the past. The major means of winning neophytes remained a combination of fiscal incentives and draconian laws; the latter discriminated against non-Christians and were rigorously applied. The relentless attitude of the government toward Muslims was particularly striking when compared to its diminishing hostility toward non-Orthodox Christians.[40]

New efforts to convert non-Christians were prompted in part by Russia's strategic interests; the government feared that an Islamic axis—a united front of the various Muslim peoples under the Ottoman umbrella—might emerge against Russia. At various times the Ottomans and the Crimeans attempted to unite the Muslim Kazakhs, Karakalpaks, Bashkirs, and Nogays in a broad anti-Russian coalition. Being a Muslim, however, was not a requirement for joining this motley alliance, and renegade Cossacks and Buddhist Kalmyks were often invited to participate in the common campaigns against Russia.[41]

No less important, however, were disturbing reports of a growing number of non-Russian converts to Islam. The news that some non-Christians were lured by the "disgusting faith of Muhammad" prompted Peter I to order that missionaries be taught native languages and sent to preach among non-Christians.[42] Not relying on preaching alone, the Russian government also resorted to discriminatory legislation to induce the conversion of its Muslim subjects. Thus, in 1681, under the pretext that some Tatars had tried to convert Russian peasants to Islam, the government decreed that the tsar's treasury was to confiscate the service and hereditary lands of those Tatars who failed to convert and to compensate them with lands in districts where non-Christians lived. On one occasion, in 1713, when impatient authorities tried to expedite the conversions, the Muslim landowners of the Kazan and Azov provinces were presented with an ultimatum to convert within six months or face the confiscation of their estates.[43] In contrast, converts were not only allowed to retain their lands

---

[40] By the early eighteenth century, the Russian Orthodox Church no longer demanded the baptism of those Catholics and Protestants who turned to Orthodoxy and in 1721, it permitted Orthodox marriages to non-Orthodox Christians as long as their children became Orthodox. *Opisanie dokumentov . . . v arkhive sviateishego synoda*, 1: cxxxii–cxxxiv, appendix, no. 18; S. M. Solov'ev, *Istoriia Rossii s drevneishikh vremen*, 29 vols. (Moscow, 1959–66), bk. 8, vol. 16, p. 587.

[41] Michael Khodarkovsky, *Where Two Worlds Met: The Russian State and the Kalmyk Nomads, 1600–1771* (Ithaca, N.Y., 1992), 98, 113, 145–46.

[42] *Pis'ma i bumagi imperatora Petra Velikogo*, 12 vols. (St. Petersburg, 1887–1977), vol. 1, note to no. 227, pp. 694–95.

[43] The ultimatum was not issued in vain, and two years later one of the Muslim landowners from the Azov region arrived in St. Petersburg to petition that his lands, which had been confiscated for his refusal to become a Christian, be returned to him. *Rossiiskii gosudarstvennyi arkhiv drevnikh aktov*, f. 248, op. 3, kn. 96, Kantseliariia Senata, Dela po Azovskoi gubernii, 1713–18gg, ll. 808–9 (hereafter *RGADA*).

and promised the lands confiscated from those choosing to remain Muslim but also received a remuneration upon conversion: ten rubles per Tatar noble, five rubles for his wife, and one and a quarter rubles for each child.[44]

The government's legislation clearly discriminated against Muslim landowners, who either lost their property outright or were compensated with inadequate lands in other districts. Moreover, these anti-Muslim laws also allowed the government to redistribute the confiscated lands among the Russian nobles. Such policies continued a process of Russian colonization of the middle Volga region by changing both its economic and ethnic landscape.

The issue of conversion emerged as one of the most important concerns of the imperial government not only in the regions well within its control but also along Russia's expanding frontiers. Since the 1670s, numerous treaties with the Kalmyk nomads in the south included a clause concerning those Kalmyks who fled to Russian towns and converted from Tibetan Buddhism to Christianity. While some fled to avoid prosecution, others left to escape poverty and to find military service with the Cossacks or jobs at the Russian fisheries. The Kalmyk chiefs, concerned with the loss of their people, demanded that these fugitives be returned unbaptized. The government initially rejected such demands but often, in exchange for the Kalmyks' cooperation, placated the chiefs and instructed the governors in the Volga towns to return Kalmyk fugitives or pay the Kalmyk chiefs a thirty-ruble fine for each Kalmyk converted by force. By the 1720s, with the dramatic improvement in Russia's security along the southern frontier, the government's attitude became less compromising; and it launched the first missions among its nomadic neighbors.[45]

During the first quarter of the eighteenth century, the reformed and modernized Russian empire was in firmer control of its non-Christian subjects, and the government intensified its efforts to convert non-Christians. In part, the modernization of the Russian state was subsidized by increased taxation, corvée, and military service, which were now extended to include non-Christians. As the Muslim and pagan subjects of the Rus-

[44] The ordinary Tatars were to be paid on a similar scale, but only half as much. *PPSZ,* vol. 2, no. 867, 312–13; ibid., vol. 5, no. 2734, pp 66–67; ibid., no. 2990, p. 163; *Dokumenty i materialy po istorii MordovskoiASSR,* vol. 1, pt. 2, no. 79, 398–99.

[45] *RGADA,* f. 248, op. 126, no. 90, Dela i prigovory Pravitel'stvuishchego Senata po Astrakhanskoi gubernii, 1716–1722 gg., l. 10; Khodarkovsky, *Where Two Worlds Met,* 106, 107, 112, 132, 180–2, 203, 205–6. On Christianity among the Kalmyks, see K. Kostenkov, "O rasprostranenii khristianstva u kalmykov in *Zhurnal Ministerstva Narodnogo Prosveshcheniia* 144 (August 1869): 103–59. In the 1750s the government issued orders to baptize uncompromisingly the fugitives from among the nomadic Kazakhs (*RGADA* F. 248, op. 113, no. 1412, l. 6).

sian empire found themselves carrying these rapidly increasing burdens, converts were offered exemption from corvée, military service, and tax exemptions of three to six years.[46]

The intensification of conversion efforts was made all the more important by the Russian emperor's personal interest in the issue. In 1724, when the Kalmyk chief, Baksaday-Dorji, was baptized, Peter I ordered a mobile church specifically built for the occasion, and a priest sent to the new convert. Baksaday-Dorji later became known by his Christian name of Petr Taishin, given to him in honor of his godfather, the Russian Emperor Peter I.[47]

The New Dimension of the Mission

In the 1720s, the missionary effort of the Russian state began to take on another dimension. Although the number of converts had continued to grow on paper, reports from the field lamented the fact that the conversions were only nominal and that the converts remained ignorant of Christianity and did not observe any of its precepts. It was becoming more apparent that reliance on sheer force or legislative discrimination to effect conversions was not sufficient.[48]

The government and the church responded by focusing missionary activity less on reporting large numbers of converts and more on spreading the Gospel among them and ensuring their understanding of and attachment to Christianity. The language of church officials reflected a change of attitude, as they began to refer to non-Christian converts as the "newly enlightened" (*novoprosveshchennye*). The new approach was further spelled out in 1721 in the Synod's instructions to the bishop of the Viatka region. The bishop was cautioned to teach potential converts the Gospel before their baptism and to find out whether they wanted to become Christian out of good will or simply to avoid heavy taxation.[49] Although the govern-

---

[46] *PSPR*, vol. 2 (1722), no. 713, p. 400; no. 888, p. 578. Peter I's decree of 1718 ordered non-Christians to be assigned to work in shipbuilding, while exempting the Russian peasants from this hard labor. Numerous complaints from non-Christians went unanswered and conversion remained the only way to avoid this onerous work. Ibid., vol. 3 (1746–52), no. 1233, pp. 387–92 Tax exemptions upon conversion were offered as early as 1681. *PPSZ*, vol. 2, no. 867, p. 313; *Dopolneniia k aktam istoricheskim*, vol. 8, no. 89, pp. 310–11.

[47] Khodarkovsky, *Where Two Worlds Met*, 172, 183, 184.

[48] One of the most striking accounts came from the Kazan metropolitan Sil'vestr in 1729. He reported that 170 years after their conversion to Christianity, the old converts (*starokreshchennye*) continued to reside in their old villages far from the churches, remaining wholly ignorant of the Russian language and Christian laws. "Luka Konashevich, Episkop Kazanskii," in *Pravoslavnyi sobesednik*, October 1858, 234–37.

[49] *Opisanie dokumentov . . . v arkhive sviateishego synoda*, vol. 1, no. 157, pp. 141–43; ibid., pp. cccv–cccxiv, appendix, no. 27.

ment and the church had worked hand in hand in the past, cooperation between the two improved further when the Synod officially became a part of the government in 1721. Senate decrees instructed that non-Christians be baptized only with the permission of the Synod, and the latter did not hesitate to ask the Senate to dispatch the military to search for converts who had fled and hidden among their non-Christian kin.[50]

The interests of the Synod did not always coincide with the concerns of other branches of the government. When in 1724 the Navy Department ordered a priest to baptize all Tatar youth recruited as sailors, he refused and asked the Holy Synod for instructions. Unwilling to bow to Navy Department demands, the synod instructed the priest to withhold baptism until these Tatars were taught Christian precepts.[51]

Peter I, the first tsar to realize that non-Christians had to be introduced to Christianity beyond the mere ritual of baptism, ordered the synod to find missionaries who could learn the local languages, translate the Bible, and live among and teach the natives. Some natives were sent to be educated in St. Petersburg, and schools were set up at local monasteries to teach Christian laws and the Russian language to young non-Christians.[52]

In a further effort to secure converts as Christians and to protect them from their kins' revenge, the converts were moved from their villages and settled in towns founded especially for this purpose. On government orders, the fortress of Nagaibak in Ufa province was built for the Bashkir converts in 1736. There, at a safe distance from their relatives, converts could be watched by the authorities and had little chance to flee back to their homes. Three years later, the town of Stavropol' was founded to settle Kalmyk converts near the Volga River north of the city of Samara.[53]

Despite the new efforts and a more focused approach, the conversion of non-Christians proceeded slowly. The burdens of everyday missionary life tended to restrain the zeal of many priests. After several years of work, they would complain of the hardships involved in living among the natives and of the difficulty of learning their languages, often requesting transfers back to their monasteries in St. Petersburg, Moscow, or Kazan.

---

[50] *PSPR*, vol. 5 (1725–1727), no. 1897, p. 481; ibid., no. 1928, pp. 511–12. In his revisionist article, Gregory Freeze showed that, although formally incorporated into the state, the Synod stood operationally parallel to the government and the church and that the clergy constituted a separate institution and a separate social group. "Handmaiden of the State? The Church in Imperial Russia Reconsidered," *Journal of Ecclesiastical History* 36, no. 1 (1985): 82–102.

[51] *PSPR*, vol. 4 (1724–January 1725), no. 1192, pp. 51–52. For complaints about local authorites, see ibid., vol. 2 (1722), no. 484, pp. 133–34.

[52] Ibid., vol. 4 (1724–January 1725), no. 1245, p. 104; ibid., no. 1321, p. 150; ibid., vol. 5 (1725–1727), no. 1590, p. 125.

[53] *RGADA*, f. 248, op. 126, no. 135 Dela i prigovory Pravitel'stvuishchego Senata po Orenburgskoi gubernii, 1735–37 gg., l. 78; V. N. Vitevskii, *I. I. Nepliuev i Orenburgskii krai v prezhnem ego sostave do 1758 g.*, 3 vols. (Kazan, 1897), 2:439. Khodarkovsky, *Where Two Worlds Met,* 208–9.

Limited support by the government also disappointed the missionaries, who reported that they had insufficient funds to build new churches and reward converts.[54]

Non-Christians continued to be deterred from converting because they were afraid of opening themselves to more abuse from the local authorities and retaliation from their kin. Their hopes to improve their lot unfulfilled, many non-Christians who converted chose to return to their original faiths. The government's numerous orders failed to prevent the growing enserfment of non-Christians by local officials; in 1737, the Senate conceded and ruled that converts could be purchased and enserfed.[55]

Widespread corruption in the Russian frontier towns and fortresses subverted efforts to convert the natives. Local officials abused the rights of the converts, often withholding their due rewards or continuing to collect taxes instead of offering the promised exemptions. Corruption worked both ways: Non-Christians also often bribed officials and priests so that pagans could continue their traditional practices and Muslims could build new mosques and religious schools.[56] Aware of this corruption and unsatisfied with the progress of its proselytizing efforts, the government once again resorted to coercive measures and centralized missionary policies under a newly created umbrella organization, the Agency of Convert Affairs.

The Agency of Convert Affairs, 1740 to 1764

In September 1740 the Russian government created a new mission that was supposed to operate in four provinces: Kazan, Astrakhan, Nizhnii Novgorod, and Voronezh. This new mission formed the backbone of the organization which became known as the Agency of Convert Affairs. The mission consisted of three priests, five translators, several staff members, and couriers, with a budget of ten thousand rubles and five thousand *chetvert'* (about seven hundred tons) of flour allowance. Instructions to the agency consisted of twenty-three detailed articles explaining how to proceed with conversion. About one-fourth of their budget was to be used to pay the salaries of agency employees, while the rest was allocated to-

---

[54] *PSPR*, vol. 5 (1725–1727), no. 1846 pp. 416–18; ibid., no. 1908, pp. 487–88.

[55] Ibid., vol. 2 (1744–45), no. 933 p. 448; vol. 6 (1727–30), no. 2214, pp. 313–16.

[56] One priest was paid off in furs and cash by the Ostiak people, who continued to worship their idols. *PSPR*, vol. 5 (1725–27), no. 1475, p. 10. A 1736 decree of the Russian government forbade the construction of new mosques and religious schools. However, the decrees were easier issued than followed, and six years later a new decree ordered the demolition of mosques built since 1736. Ibid., vol. 2 (1744–45), no. 540, pp. 15–16.

ward founding four schools for non-Christians in addition to the rewards bestowed upon conversion.[57]

The period between 1740 and 1764 marked one of the most violent assaults against non-Christians' religious beliefs. The government put new emphasis on using force and legislative decrees, rather than teaching Christian doctrine. Missionary activity focused on the Kazan province, which was, in the words of the Father Dmitrii Sechenov, the first head of the Agency of Convert Affairs, "a center of all the non-Christians residing in south-eastern Russia."[58]

Orders to destroy mosques and forcefully resettle non-Christians indicated a renewal of efforts to expedite the conversion of the natives to Christianity. These polices were implemented with particular enthusiasm by the Kazan bishop, Luka Konashevich, whose name became synonymous for Russians with righteousness and missionary zeal, and for non-Christians with intolerance and oppression. In 1743, the government ordered 418 out of 536 mosques in the Kazan region demolished. The remaining 118 mosques were left untouched because they had been built prior to the Kazan conquest, and the government feared that their destruction would cause a popular uprising. In other Volga provinces only one mosque was allowed in each village, but only if the village had an exclusively Muslim population with no less than two to three hundred males.[59]

A series of legislative decrees was once again aimed at encouraging conversion of non-Christians, and the government used Russian criminal and military systems for this purpose. Thus, those convicted of petty crimes, and from 1741 even capital offenses, continued to receive pardons upon conversion, while non-Christians who converted to Islam, as well as the Muslims who converted them, were punished. Non-Christian recruits who converted to Christianity received an exemption from military service, while the non-Christians drafted in their stead faced additional pressure to convert from priests in the Russian army.[60]

The overenthusiastic proselytizing of Dmitrii Sechenov and Luka Kona-

---

[57] *PPSZ*, vol. 11, no. 8236 pp. 248–56; Mozharovskii, "Izlozhenie," 61–62; Efim Malov, "O novokreshchennykh shkolakh v 18 veke," *Pravoslavnoe obozrenie* 26 (July 1868): 354–57.

[58] "Luka Konashevich," 233.

[59] *Polnoe sobranie postanovlenii i rasporiazhenii po vedomstvu pravoslavnogo ispovedaniia Rossiiskoi imperii. Tsarstvovanie Elizavety Petrovny*, 4 vols. (St. Petersburg, 1899–1912), vol. 2 (1744–45), no. 662, pp. 143–45 (hereafter *PSPREP*). Separating converts from non-Christians was seen as another important way of securing the success of the mission. In 1740 the Senate decreed appointing a trustworthy person who would not take bribes and would supervise the resettlement of converts ("Luka Konashevich," 464–65).

[60] Ibid., vol. 1 (1741–43), no. 17, pp. 21–22; ibid., no. 70, p. 85; ibid., vol. 3 (1746–52), no. 1007, pp. 83–85; ibid., no. 1115, pp. 200–202; *PPSZ*, vol. 11, no. 8349, pp. 369–70. The 1760 law superseded the previous law and stated that conversion should no longer serve as

shevich led to a series of violent clashes and revolts by the local population. One episode in 1743 exemplified Russia's policies in the region. Eight Mordvin villages complained that they could not accept Christianity, explaining that they had no mosques, and they continued to worship in the fields and forests. They further warned that if forced to convert, they would follow the example of their ancestors and would burn everything and flee, or even set themselves afire, as some had done in the Arzamas district. Their complaints, however, failed to move the authorities, and when it was discovered that the Mordvins continued to practice old customs at their cemetery next to the church, bishop Dmitrii Sechenov ordered the cemetery burned. The ensuing revolt was suppressed when one hundred Russian soldiers arrived to offer the Mordvins pardons, if they agreed to be baptized. At least, this was the explanation that the regional Russian authorities gave for the Mordvin revolt.[61]

The Mordvin account of this event was different from the official version. According to this account, upon the suppression of the revolt twenty Mordvins were arrested, sent to Nizhnii Novgorod, kept in jail for seven weeks, and baptized by force. Meanwhile, Russian soldiers burned the Mordvin village cemeteries, cut down the trees and groves around them, beat the Mordvins, including pregnant women, and then arrested and baptized them. Those who refused to convert were beaten with the knout, and salt was rubbed into their wounds. The two Mordvin messengers sent with the complaint to Moscow were captured by Russian soldiers and severely beaten. After a warning to the Mordvin villagers that they would be similarly dealt with if they refused to convert, the soldiers were ordered to shoot, killing several Mordvins and wounding eleven. When the incident became known a year later in St. Petersburg, the Senate and the Synod ordered local officials to watch carefully that the Mordvins did not rebel again and to refrain from converting them by force.[62]

Although the government's fear of revolts in the end compelled it to issue orders urging local authorites to exercise restraint, gruesome stories of violence similar to the one above were frequent. The government had created an atmosphere of intolerance that allowed the abuses to continue, and no evidence suggests that the perpetrators of abuses ever suffered the consequences of their actions in cases of religious conversion.

In the frontier regions, particularly in the south, geopolitical considerations compelled the government to exercise more caution than in the ar-

---

a reason for commuting capital punishment. *PSPREP*, vol. 4 (1753–62), no. 1735, pp. 497–98.

[61] *Dokumenty i materialy po istorii Mordovskoi ASSR*, vol. 2 (Saransk, 1940), nos. 64–72, pp. 289–99. A Russian regional commander admitted that the recruit system was ruining the Mordvins.

[62] Ibid., nos. 75–78, pp. 301–6; no. 82, p. 313; no. 96, p. 326.

eas already under Russia's firm administrative control. When the issue of sending a mission to the Ossetian people in the north Caucasus came up in 1744, the Senate instructed the synod to send only Georgian priests, not Russian ones, and to give them no written instructions, so as to avoid any suspicion on the part of the Ottoman or Persian governments.[63]

This desire to avoid diplomatic confrontation with neighboring Muslim states and to convince them that Russia's Muslims were being converted of their own volition was probably behind the government's decision to formalize the conversion procedure.[64] A 1750 decree stipulated that non-Christians should not be baptized without first submitting a voluntary petition in writing. The contents of the petition were prepared in advance, and a petitioner only needed to add his or her name to it. The prescribed form required that a Muslim petitioner first denounce and reject "the most false Prophet (Muhammed) and his most false and ungodly laws (the Quran)," and then state his or her "sincere desire to be baptized into the Christian faith of salvation." Apparently, it was decided that pagans did not have to denounce their idols or to praise the virtues of Christianity at any great length, as their petitions were much shorter than those required of Muslims.[65]

Reports of the Agency of Convert Affairs boasted of the large numbers of converts. In 1747 there were more than a hundred thousand converts in Kazan province,[66] yet there was a striking contrast between Muslim and pagan populations of the region. In 1763, converted Tatars represented about one-third of the Tatar population of the province (13,615 converts and 35,079 Muslims), while almost 95 percent of the pagan Mari, Mordvins, Chuvash, and Votiaks were registered as converts.[67] The government's draconian laws favoring neophytes did not stop Muslim Tatars and Bashkirs from continuing their vigorous resistance to missionary activity. They revolted numerous times throughout the seventeenth and eighteenth centuries, and together with other non-Christians, were a crucial force in Russia's two largest popular uprisings, those of Stepan Razin in the early 1670s and of Emel'ian Pugachev a century later.[68]

---

[63] *PSPREP*, vol. 2 (1744–1745), no. 651, pp. 123–28; no. 805, pp. 310–3.

[64] It was at this time that the issue of the status of Christians within the Ottoman empire became a growing concern among the European states. In response, the Ottomans raised the issue of the status of Muslims within the Russian empire.

[65] *PSPREP*, vol. 3 (1746–52), no. 1174, pp. 283–85; no. 1193, pp. 310–13.

[66] Only a few years before, converts in the region numbered 13,322 out of a total non-Christian population of 285,464 ("Luka Konashevich," 233).

[67] *Istoriia Tatarii v materialakh I dokumentakh* (Moscow, 1937), 190–91.

[68] During the Razin uprising the non-Christian gentry chose to join the rebels. Michael Khodarkovsky, "The Stepan Razin Uprising: Was It a 'Peasant War'?" *Jahrbücher für Geschichte Osteuropas* 42, no. 1 (1994): 13–17. In the Pugachev uprising, non-Christians turned their rage against the church officials, murdering 132 of them in the Kazan region alone (Mozharovskii, "Izlozhenie," 98).

Preventing the spread of Islam and discouraging its practice remained one of the government's highest priorities. In 1756 the government added its own bleak statistics to the agency's reports on the Muslim converts. In addition to the mosques destroyed in Kazan province, the authorites destroyed 98 of 133 mosques in the Siberian provinces of Tobol'sk and Tara and 29 of 40 mosques in Astrakhan province.[69]

It is not surprising that conversions induced either by force or through promises of rewards were less than earnest. Government officials reported that the converts did not choose to receive baptism voluntarily but did so in order to avoid punishment for their crimes.[70] Local missionaries complained that since the agency did not keep a register of converts by name, it was difficult to keep track of non-Christians, who often came to convert several times in order to receive benefits. The government responded to these complaints by ordering in 1757 that those who had converted more than once be sent to perform hard labor in monasteries. The missionaries complained further that the converts did not allow preachers into their villages and houses, claiming that they had been granted exemptions by the government. The converts even threatened to beat the priests if they failed to provide the rewards that the converts considered to be their right.[71] The excessive force used by the Agency of Convert Affairs, the complaints against each other of church officials and converts, and the large but nominal character of conversion make it clear that missionary work in Russia in the middle of the eighteenth century was flawed.

Tolerance and Education

In April 1764, Empress Catherine II instructed the government to issue a decree that inaugurated the most tolerant period in Russia's relations with non-Christians since the middle of the sixteenth century. The decree also ended the twenty-four-year existence of the Agency of Convert Affairs. This put converts under the governance of the same civil and religious administration that oversaw all other Russian state peasants. Missionary activity was to be continued by educating non-Christians, not by force. For this purpose, the decree stipulated that preachers with annual salaries of 150 rubles should be sent to spread the Gospel without any coercion and that schools for the converts should continue to teach their children. The government recognized that the number of converts had grown to such an extent that those who remained unbaptized could no longer carry the burden of paying taxes or supplying military recruits in

[69] *PPSZ*, vol. 14, no. 10,597, p. 608.
[70] *RGADA*, f. 248, op. 113, no. 257, l. 5.
[71] "Luka Konashevich," 239–40, 469–70; *PSPREP*, vol. 4 (1753–1762), no. 1550, p. 291.

the converts' stead. The neophytes would continue to receive a three-year tax exemption but no rewards for their decision to convert. They were to be given an icon and a cross, and instead of any rewards a voucher that would be credited against their future taxes when their tax exemption expired.[72]

The cumulative effects of the government's policies of religious conversion became fully apparent in 1766, when delegates from different corners of the Russian empire arrived in the capital to petition a Legislative Commission in charge of compiling new laws. The delegates from the Penza province, representing local Tatars in Russian military service, complained that Muslims who had committed crimes chose to convert to Christianity in order to escape punishment. The delegates suggested that such criminals should be punished.[73] The Tatars from Orenburg explained that although they were experiencing a severe labor shortage, they were forbidden from hiring converted Mordvins, Mari, or Votiak. The delegates requested that they be allowed to hire converts and promised to let them practice Christianity. The Chuvash of Kazan province who paid *iasak* (a tax on non-Christians) complained that, due to the converts' tax exemption, they had to pay additional taxes and provide recruits and means of transportation in the converts' stead.[74]

The most detailed grievances were submitted by the Tatars of Kazan province. They complained that they suffered as a result of the privileges granted to converts, such as exemptions from taxes, military service, and existing debts, and because of land speculation by converts, who were selling land to Russian gentry. The Tatars objected to the discrimination in taxation that required them to pay 1.10 rubles per serf, while Russian landowners paid only 70 kopecks per serf. They asked for permission to cut the forest and to bear sabers and arms at home and on the road. Their most urgent request was one for greater religious freedom: they asked the government for permission to construct mosques, send their elders on pilgrimage to Mecca, and punish those who mocked their religion.[75]

Complaints were not limited to non-Christians; converts, too, submitted numerous grievances. Those from Siberia lamented that their ignorance of the Russian language and laws opened them to abuse by Russian peasants and landlords. In one instance, converts were lured for a one-year contract to work at an ironworks and then not allowed to return home. Other converts complained that they lost their lands to Russian

---

[72] *Polnoe sobranie postanovlenii i rasporiazhenii po vedomstvu pravoslavnogo ispovedaniia Rossiiskoi imperii. Tsarstvovanie Ekateriny Alekseevny,* 3 vols. (St. Petersburg, 1910–15), vol. 1 (1762–72), no. 176, pp. 217–18.

[73] *Sbornik imperatorskogo russkogo istoricheskogo obshchestva,* vol. 32, no. 76, pp. 541–44

[74] Ibid., no. 147, pp. 221–2l; no. 115, pp. 379–80.

[75] Ibid., no. 115, pp. 311–12, 319–28.

landlords, that their farming and forest lands were taken away from them for the use of the factories, that the merchants did not allow them to trade, that officers stationed to protect them took food and fodder by force, that the judges kept them in jail for months, and that their well-to-do people were ruined by jealous Russians.[76]

Catherine II showed a personal interest in the non-Christian subjects of the Russian empire. Having cast herself in the role of an enlightened monarch, she could not but regard religious persecution as unacceptable. Shortly before the Legislative Commission gathered in St. Petersburg, Catherine undertook a journey along the middle Volga River to see some of the regions of her empire for herself. She later described her impressions of the travel in correspondence with French *philosophes.* Catherine found the city of Kazan, the diversity of its population, and the complexity of the entire region fascinating. She confided in her letters her sudden realization that Russia was so much a part of both Europe and Asia that it would be difficult to apply general laws throughout the disparate regions of the Russian empire.[77]

Religious tolerance under Catherine II was not only a product of her enlightened ideas but was also driven by sheer pragmatism. The introduction of reforms, the incorporation of the new territories of the Crimea and Poland, and the importation of German colonists required a manifestation of toleration toward the new non-Christian subjects of the expanding empire. In addition, Russia's military advantage over its Islamic neighbors and a greater sense of security in the south led the government to try to ensure the loyalty of its Muslim subjects through toleration and the collaboration of the Islamic clergy rather than through the previous discriminatory and antagonizing laws. Missionary work did continue, although less by force and more by the teaching of the Gospel.[78]

The results of Russia's proselytizing of its non-Christian subjects were summarized in 1776 by Prince Mikhail Shcherbatov. He was unsurprised

[76] Ibid., no. 115, pp. 353–56, 421–24, 448.

[77] Solov'ev, *Istoriia,* bk. 14, vol. 27, pp. 49, 52. The empress found it appalling that, two decades before, Bishop Luka Konashevich of Kazan in violation of the decrees issued by Peter I, had torn apart the remains of the ancient city of Bulgar, and used the stones to construct a church and a monastery (ibid., 53).

[78] The recognition of religious differences among its own subjects did not prevent Russia from seeing itself as a protector of all Orthodox Christians. Thus, four years after the conquest of the Crimea in 1774 and in spite of promises to grant the Crimea an autonomous status, the Russian government insisted on expatriating all Christians who lived there. More than thirty-one thousand of these Christians were reluctantly delivered to the Russians by the Crimean khan (Solov'ev, *Istoriia,* bk. 15, vol. 29, p. 235). One particular provision, which eventually led to the Porte's recognizing Russia's right to be a protector of Orthodox Christians within the Ottoman empire, was negotiated in the 1774 treaty of Küchük-Kaynarja. This provision of the treaty later served as Russia's justification for laying imperial claims to much of European territory under the Ottoman dominion. John T. Alexander, *Catherine the Great: Life and Legend* (New York, 1989), 141.

that non-Christians remained attached to their native beliefs, observing that it could not have been otherwise because they had been converted by force. He lambasted the Russian Orthodox Church, which neither attempted to teach converts first, nor sent preachers who knew their language, and instead brought them to baptism in the same way they would have been brought to a bath; gave them a cross, which, in their ignorance, they considered some kind of talisman, and an image of Christ, which they regarded as an idol; and forbade them from eating meat on fast days, a prohibition that they did not follow, while the priests took bribes from them for overlooking this. Likewise, no attempt was made to translate the Holy Scriptures into their languages, nor to teach these to the priests, so that they would be able to preach.[79]

At the same time Prince Shcherbatov was pointing out the reasons why the church had failed to achieve a genuine conversion of non-Christians, Amvrosii Podobedov, the newly appointed archbishop of Kazan, simply observed the facts when he reported to the synod on the situation in his archdiocese: "I find that the ignorant [*neprosveshchennye*] non-Christian peoples, the Chuvash and Cheremis who reside here, have not only insufficient, but not even the slightest notion about the precepts of the faith into which they were converted by holy baptism."[80] Such was the state of affairs after the church and government had attempted to convert non-Christians to Christianity for two and a half centuries.

Conclusions

Modern nation-states require nonnatives to be naturalized and attain citizenship before they can enjoy equal opportunities and rights. Religious conversion in pre-nineteenth-century Russia, where the church could not be easily divorced from the state, was just such "naturalization"—a politico-religious act couched in theological terms. In the eyes of the Russian church and state, conversion was the most important rite of passage for non-Christians, whether as the ultimate test of their loyalty to the state, as was the case in the sixteenth and seventeenth centuries, or as a sign of their embrace of civilization and Christianity in the eighteenth century when Russia launched its own *mission civilisatrice*.

Conversion policies and their implementation represented only one aspect of the colonial encounter between the expanding Russian empire and the non-Christian peoples who were to be made "Russian" through conversion to Christianity. Government policies based on the preferential

[79] Shcherbatov, "Statistika," 64.
[80] Mozharovskii, "Izlozhenie," 107.

treatment of converts had a significant impact on the non-Christian population, driving a wedge between converts and those members of the community who refused to convert. However, the policy of cooptation through religious conversion was never a one-way street. In time, many non-Christians learned to use the terms of encounter to their own advantage. They insisted on exemptions, avoided paying taxes, and resorted to multiple baptisms, developing what may be called a strategy of "take the money and run." In the end, conversion policies became a costly undertaking for Russia, reducing the number of taxpayers and leading to frequent revolts and uprisings.

Conversion in Russia was not synonymous with assimilation. Shedding one's previous identity and acquiring a new one proved to be a long and difficult process. Conversion, it appears, was most successful not for communities as a whole but for individuals both at the top and at the bottom of their native societies. The non-Christian elites were able to make a transition relatively quickly. Upon conversion they retained their privileged status, received additional benefits, intermarried with the Russian nobility, and were fully assimilated within two or three generations. Those who for various reasons found themselves transplanted from their native societies as slaves or serfs in Russian households were also rapidly assimilated upon conversion. For other non-Christians, however, conversion meant little beyond receiving temporary benefits. Christianity attracted commoners because it promised exemption from taxes, corvée, or military service; the local gentry converted to avoid having their lands and property confiscated. Non-Christians were designated as "new converts," and remained in this transitional category for generations, alienated from both their former kin and their new coreligionists. Even those whose ancestors had converted centuries previously were still referred to as the "old converts."[81]

Despite the government's efforts to resettle converts and introduce them to the Russian way of life, both the new and old converts had little or no knowledge of the Russian language, law, lifestyle and, most important, their new faith. It was not until the middle of the nineteenth century that the growing number of schools and churches, and rising employment opportunities elsewhere allowed for increased geographical and social mobility of the converts and led to their more successful integration.

From the 1550s onward, the Russian government continuously en-

---

[81] It is instructive to compare the fate of converts in Russia with that of the *conversos*, the Jewish converts in late fifteenth-century Spain. Spanish authorities considered *conversos* a distinct and separate group. *Conversos* were discriminated against and their lack of "purity of blood" (*limpieza de sangre*) remained a disability in terms of their advancement until the early twentieth century. Angus McKay, *Spain in the Middle Ages: From Frontier to Empire, 1000–1500* (New York, 1977), 185–87.

gaged in policies encouraging its non-Christian subjects to convert to Orthodox Christianity. Pursued throughout centuries with various degrees of zeal, Russia's missionary activity was spurred at first by its encounter with the vast pagan world that the tsar suddenly found within his domain. It was incumbent upon the increasingly self-conscious Muscovite Orthodox state to make sure that these numerous pagan peoples ended up in the bosom of the Orthodox Church and not that of Islam. Similar considerations and an additional concern over the increasing influence of Islam among non-Christians led Peter I to adopt a more confrontational attitude toward the Muslim subjects of his empire and to encourage more active missionary work among non-Christians in the 1690s. Thirty years later the enthusiastic missionary work of the Catholic Church compelled the Russian government and church to reinvigorate its own missionary efforts once again. Finally, the idea of civilizing the "savage" and "unenlightened" became a major driving force behind proselytizing throughout the eighteenth century. At all times, however, the preferential policies of the Russian state, motivated as they were by political and theological considerations, were pursued at the expense of fiscal pragmatism.

The single most striking feature of Russia's missionary activity remains the unusual degree of government involvement. In a country in which the church was firmly wedded to the state, religious identity and religious conversion were at the core of many state policies. In the North Caucasus, for instance, the government encouraged non-Orthodox Christians, such as Catholics, Lutherans, Armenians, and Georgians, to settle the frontier region, while specifically forbidding Muslims from doing so. In order to convert the non-Christians, the government was willing to make exceptions even when it came to the nobility's exclusive right to own serfs. In 1755, the Foreign Ministry advised the Senate that new laws extended the right of serf ownership to priests, merchants, and Cossacks, as long they agreed to purchase, convert and teach Christianity to the numerous non-Christians of the Russian empire: "Kalmyks, Kumyks, Chechens, Kazakhs, Karakalpaks, Turkmens, Tomuts, Tatars, Bashkirs and other Muhammadans and idol-worshippers."[82] Russian colonial policies could not be separated from the issues of religion and ethnicity.

While offering converts a wide range of economic benefits and even pardons for crimes, the government imposed extra burdens on those who refused to convert. The further integration of non-Christians into the empire's fiscal and administrative system, the increased attractiveness of Russian markets and goods, and thus the greater importance of benefits offered upon conversion were among the reasons for the growing number

---

[82] Arkhiv vneshnei politiki Rossiiskoi Imperii, f. 118, Kizliarskie i Mozdokskie dela, op. 1, 1762–72 gg., d. 1; f. 119, Kalmytskie dela, op. 119/5, 1755 g., d. 17, ll. 4, 17, 20.

of converts in the eighteenth century. Yet conversions that had little to do with religion were largely nominal, and backsliding remained a recurring problem.

To be sure, the nominal character of conversion and backsliding were not unique to Russia but were also typical in New France, New Spain, and South America. In the New World, however, the missions founded by the religious orders of the Dominicans, Franciscans, and Jesuits intended to teach and civilize natives, and provide them with farming skills. These missions were frontier institutions dependent on Rome rather than on any specific government. In fact, the missions in the Americas were often in conflict with the interests of the local authorities as well as those of the settlers, who were more concerned with the supply of furs, as in New France, or the supply of slaves, as in Brazil.[83]

By contrast, missions in Russia were not frontier institutions. Indeed, the New World type of mission, as a special settlement of converts guided by missionaries and guarded by soldiers, did not exist in early modern Russia. Russian missionaries did not reside with converts but stayed in Russian towns, forts, and villages. Missions in Russia were part of a concerted colonization process directed by the state and, as such, were subservient to government interests. These missions were the third-tier institution that always followed in the footsteps of the military and the government officials, and they were dispatched to territories already under Russian military and administrative control. To this extent, evangelization in Russia was conducted more in the manner of Charlemagne than that of the contemporary New World.

Few missions had sufficient resources to do their job, and few missionaries approached their task in good conscience. Russian missionaries were sent to the remote parts of the empire with no training and often against their own will. Their numbers were inadequate and their churches were located far from the villages of the converts. Russian missionaries rarely attempted to study the language of the people amongst whom they lived or to teach the natives the precepts of Christianity. In-

[83] Like missions in Russia, the New World missions had also relied on the crown's financial and military support. However, unlike Russia, where the tsar or the emperor was in charge of both the secular and spiritual worlds, the Catholic Church preserved independence from the secular authorities and cherished its ecclesiastical immunities. Herbert E. Bolton, "The Mission as a Frontier Institution in the Spanish-American Colonies" *American Historical Review* 23, no. 1 (1917): 46–49; N. M. Farris, *Crown and Clergy in Colonial Mexico, 1759–1821* (London, 1968), 5–6, 19–20; Leslie Bethel, ed., *Colonial Brazil* (Cambridge, 1987), 22–23; W. J. Eccles, *The Canadian Frontier, 1534–1760* (New York, 1969), 35–59; Harry W. Crosby, *Antigua California: Mission and Colony on the Peninsular Frontier, 1697–1768* (Albuquerque, N.Mex., 1994), 178–220. For comparison with conversion process in the Islamic world and in southeast Asia, see Nehemia Levtzion, ed., *Conversion to Islam* (New York, 1979), and Vicente L. Rafael, *Contracting Colonialism: Translation and Christian Conversion in Tagalog Society under Early Spanish Rule* (Ithaca, N.Y., 1988).

stead, missionaries were content to have the natives memorize a few prayers in Russian. The language of the missionaries and of the Bible thus remained a mystery to converts.

Throughout the period under discussion, the Russian state and church were able to attract large numbers of the empire's non-Christian subjects to Christianity. Most converts were pagans, who after conversion continued to worship their old gods and goddesses along with the new ones. Muslims proved to be much more difficult to convert and their numbers were fewer; for them conversion meant abandoning the world of Islam, with its literary culture, abodes of worship, and educated clergy. In regard to both groups, however, the Russian state lacked sufficient resources and dedicated missionaries to implement its missionary policies systematically and was unable to protect converts from being maltreated by its own officials, to teach them the Russian language and the Scriptures, or to assure their assimilation into Russian society.

CHAPTER SIX

Big Candles and "Internal Conversion": The Mari Animist Reformation and Its Russian Appropriations

PAUL W. WERTH

In the late 1880s and early 1890s, a group of Mari peasants from Iaransk district in Viatka province filed a series of petitions to the emperor requesting both permission to perform pagan rituals and protection from local clergy and officials who, they claimed, "oppress us so that we will confess the Christian religion" and "threaten to exile us from our homes to faraway places in Siberia."[1] The petitioners became known as the "Kugu-Sorta" or "Big Candle" sect, because a large candle occupied a prominent place in their religious ceremonies. Since the petitioners were formally Orthodox Christians, and since "apostasy" to other religions was explicitly prohibited by the Russian empire's civil and religious laws, their petitions were unequivocally rejected. Moreover, the bishop of Viatka, convinced of the "noxious" character of the group's activities and the "uselessness of thorough pastoral admonitions and persuading," pushed hard for their prosecution as "apostates."

Funding for the research on this article was provided by the American Council of Teachers of Russian (ACTR), and by the International Research and Exchanges Board (IREX) with funds provided by the National Endowment ofr the Humanities, the United States Information Agency, and the Department of State, which administers the Russian, Eurasian, and East European Research Program (Title VIII). A shorter version of this paper was presented at the American Association for the Advancement of Slavic Studies National Convention in Washington, D. C., October, 1995. I would like to thank Jane Burbank, Allen Frank, Robert Geraci, Marianne Kamp, Michael Khodarkovsky, Virginia Martin, William Rosenberg, and especially Valerie Kivelson for reading earlier drafts of the present paper and providing useful suggestions and criticisms.

[1] Rossiiskii Gosudarstvennyi Istoricheskii Arkhiv, St. Petersburg f. 796, op. 172, d. 2686, l. 4–40b. (hereafter RGIA).

Eventually, eight of the animist reformers were exiled to Siberia without trial.[2]

This curious animist movement raises a series of questions concerning religious identity, the fate of small ethnic minorities in Russia, and the nature of subject status in the empire.[3] In this essay, I will address these questions by analyzing this animist revival in terms of the "internal conversion"—or rationalization of indigenous religion—that Clifford Geertz has described in a Balinese context.[4] In response to religious challenges and rapid social and economic change, a small group of Mari peasants chose to initiate a radical reform of their native beliefs, rather than practice Christianity or Islam. This reform entailed the articulation of a more coherent theology and the recasting and presentation of their teachings in the idiom of religion employed by official Russia, in particular the forwarding of their cause as a matter of *faith*. As we shall see, although this presentation involved the largely successful deployment of a colonizing discourse in defense of indigenous belief and practice, on another level it represented an incorporation of the reformers into the conceptual modes expressed by that discourse. On a more theoretical level, our discussion suggests that we should analyze non-Russian identity as constructed and refracted through practice, rather than as containing its origins within itself. This paper, in short, analyzes the syncretic manner in which the social identities, cultural styles, and ritual practices of some Maris were transformed by both material changes and the missionary encounter in Russia.

Maris and Religious Rationalization

Maris, or Cheremis, are a linguistically Finnic people occupying an area northwest of Kazan, around the bend of the Volga river. The vast majority

[2] RGIA, f. 796, op. 172, d. 2686, l. 12. These exiles were allowed to return from Siberia in 1896, but not to their original villages. After a period of unspecified residence, they were finally allowed to return to those villages in 1906. I deal here with the first few years of the group's appearance, roughly until the 1893 exile. I use the term "animist" in this essay to signify pre-Christian Mari religious beliefs, and the word "pagan" to refer to official confessional status and at times to refer to the tenets of the Kugu Sorta sect, since its own adherenets adopted this term.

[3] Kugu Sorta has produced a considerable literature. For a listing, see Ia. Ialkaev, *Materialy dlia bibliograficheskogo ukazatelia po marivedeniiu, 1762–1931* (Ioshkar-Ola, 1934), 56–57; N. S. Popov, "K voprosu o religioznom dvizhenii v Mariiskom krae vo vtoroi polovine XIX–nachale XX veka: Istoriografiia i istochniki," in *Istoriografiia i istochnikovedenie po arkheologii i etnografii Mariiskogo kraia*, Arkheologiia i etnografiia Mariiskogo kraia, vol. 7 (Ioshkar-Ola, 1984), 174–92; and V. M. Vasil'ev's critical survey in *Mariiskaia religioznaia sekta "Kugu Sorta"* (Krasnokokshaisk, 1927), 71–84.

[4] Clifford Geertz, " 'Internal Conversion' in Contemporary Bali," in *The Interpretation of Cultures* (New York, 1973), 170–89.

was nominally converted to Orthodoxy in the eighteenth century through a combination of tax breaks, exemption from military service, and payment in money and goods during an aggressive missionary campaign undertaken by local secular and religious figures.[5] By the early nineteenth century, aside from a sizeable group that had escaped baptism by fleeing eastward into Bashkiria,[6] only a relative handful of Maris were recognized officially as pagans (*iazychniki*).

My discussion draws on Max Weber's observations concerning two idealized polar types of religion, the "traditional" and the "rationalized." Traditional religions, in Geertz's summary of Weber, "consist of a multitude of very concretely defined and only loosely ordered sacred entities . . . which are able to involve themselves in an independent, segmental, and immediate manner with almost any sort of actual event." Thoroughly intertwined with the concrete details of everyday life, these religions approach spiritual concerns in a "piecemeal" fashion, addressing each individual occurrence as it arises. Rationalized religions, in contrast, "are more abstract, more logically coherent, and more generally phrased." Narrow and concrete questions receive broader formulations and become conceptualized as universal and inherent qualities of human existence. The process of rationalization in effect involves a transfer and concentration of sacredness, from the shrines, groves, and streams—from the countless spirits and spells through which it was vaguely diffused—to "a nucleate . . . concept of the divine." As the physical-concrete realm is divested of sacredness (or "disenchanted," in Weber's phrase), the relationship between humans and the sacred becomes more distant, thereby requiring more explicit and self-conscious explication.[7] Thus Weber saw doctrinal revelation—the initial creation or revivalist reformulation of religious truths—and the introduction of a transcendental vision putting greater distance between the mundane and the spiritual as hallmarks of rationalization.[8]

Weber's categories are of course ideal types and should be construed as

---

[5] These conversions are covered in greater detail in A. Mozharovskii, *Izlozhenie khoda missionerskago dela po prosveshcheniiu kazanskikh inorodtsev s 1552 po 1867 godu*, in *Chtenia v Imperatorskom Obshchestve istorii i drevnostei Rossiskikh pri Moskovskom Universitete* 112–13 (1880); E. A. Malov, *O novokreshchenskoi kontore* (Kazan, 1878); S. L. Ursynovich, "Novokreshchenskaia kontora: K voprosu o roli pravoslavnogo missionerstva v kolonizatsionnoi i natsional'noi politike samoderzhaviia," *Ateist* 54 (1930): 22–50; and G. N. Aiplatov and A. G. Ivanov, eds., *Istoriia Mariiskogo kraia v dokumentakh i materialakh*, vol. 1 (Ioshkar-Ola, 1992), 214–34.

[6] On these migrations see G. A. Sepeev, *Vostochnye mariitsy* (Ioshkar-Ola, 1975); U. Kh. Rakhmatullin, *Naselenie Bashkirii v XVII–XVIII vv: Voprosy formirovaniia nebashkirskogo naseleniia* (Moscow, 1988).

[7] Geertz, "Internal Conversion," 172–74.

[8] See the discussion in Robert F. Hefner, "Introduction: World Building and the Rationality of Conversion," in *Conversion to Christianity: Historical and Anthropological Perspectives on a Great Transformation*, ed. Robert F. Hefner (Berkeley, Calif., 1993), esp. 10–22.

terminal points on a spectrum of religiosity. It would be wrong to suggest that such doctrinal systematization automatically produces rationality in all believers' worldviews, or that traditional religions lack any and all such systemization. Nor can one ignore the specific historical conditions that render doctrinal revelation compelling for a given group of people.[9] As Geertz remarks, religious rationalization "is not an all-or-none, an irreversible, or an inevitable process."[10]

Native Mari belief, on the whole, conformed to Weber's understanding of traditional religion. It included a range of spirits, each responsible for different realms of life, to whom prayers were directed depending on the concrete concerns at hand.[11] Although Maris conceived of something resembling a supreme god, Kugu Jumo, this being did not occupy a prominent or overarching place in Mari conceptions, either theologically or functionally, and according to most accounts Maris had difficulty explaining its nature. As one ethnographer noted, "The Great God appeared for the Cheremis as something spectral, extremely unclear, and its functions come down to virtually nothing."[12] The sacred, according to Mari beliefs, was located in the physical world and could even inhabit specific objects.

By far the most significant single spiritual entity was the *keremet'*, which demanded blood sacrifices performed in a sacred grove located near each village. These gatherings, often undertaken in response to agricultural crisis or natural calamity, could take significant proportions, attracting Maris from distant villages and requiring the sacrifice of a tremendous number of animals.[13] The influence of the *keremet'* on Maris can hardly be overestimated, and is underscored by the fact that unbaptized Mari were

---

[9] See ibid., 14, 19.

[10] Geertz, "Internal Conversion," 172–74. Indeed, Birgit Meyer has recently pointed out that Weber himself recognized a tension between the ideal type of religious development and the practical-historical manifestation of religion in everyday life, and that some social scientists have appropriated only Weber's ideal type abstraction without appreciating this tension. See Birgit Meyer, "Modernity and Enchantment: the Image of the Devil in Popular African Christianity," in *Conversion to Modernities: The Globalization of Christianity*, ed. Peter van der Veer (New York, 1996), 199–230.

[11] For a listing of these various spirits, see "Imena bogov Cheremisskikh," *Zavolzhskii muravei* 16 (1833): 924–25.

[12] S. K. Kuznetsov, "Cheremisskaia sekta kugu sorta," *Etnograficheskoe obozrenie* 4 (1908): 19. Znamenskii likewise claimed that Maris' understanding of the higher God was "very crude." See P. Znamenskii, "Gornye cheremisy kazanskago kraia," *Vestnik Evropy* 4 (1867): 38. According to Sergei Nurminskii, himself a Mari, Jumo was a prosperous peasant with much livestock, who differed from mortals in that he lived in the sky. See Nurminskii, "Ocherk religioznykh verovanii cheremis," *Pravoslavnyi sobesednik* 3 (1862): 251.

[13] One gathering in 1828, for example, involved the slaughter of ninety-nine of each kind of domestic animal. RGIA, f. 797, op. 3, d. 12654. This gathering is also described in A. Andrievskii, "Dela o sovershenii iazycheskikh obriadov i zhertvoprinoshenii," *Stoletie Viatskoi gubernii, 1780–1880: Sbornik materialov k istorii Viatskago kraia*, vol. 2 (Viatka, 1881), 5–37. See also N. S. Popov, "Na mariiskom iazycheskom molenii," *Etnograficheskoe obozrenie* 3 (1996): 130–45; and A. G. Ivanov, "Vsemariiskoe iazycheskoe molenie 1827 i deistviia vlastei," *Mariiskii arkheograficheskii vestnik* 8 (1998): 48–74.

sometimes referred to as "people of the *keremet'* " (*keremetniki*). The cult of the *keremet'*, according to one observer, was "the essence of the entire religion."[14] On numerous occasions missionaries sought official permission to destroy the sacred groves and encouraged local Maris to participate in this destruction, but the latter almost without exception categorically refused.

The concerns behind these religious rites appear to have been very concrete. Offerings were usually conducted with some immediate goal in mind, whether to ensure a good harvest, to promote the well-being of livestock and bees, or to facilitate the payment of taxes.[15] One observer explained Mari animism as "exclusively practical. The dogmatic, mythological aspect of it occupies the lowest place; in the first place is ritual, token, offering, by means of which one can acquire from a deity one or another benefit, or defense from some misfortune. The relation to the gods is purely utilitarian."[16] Although this view fails to appreciate that the well-being of family and community could itself be invested with sacred significance, it does appear that Maris viewed religious rituals in more immediate than transcendental terms, and thus exhibited comparatively little interest in doctrine, or generalized interpretation of the events that made up their existence.[17] This is not to say that Maris lacked legends and stories accounting for the components of their religion, or that they performed these rituals in some purely mechanical or reflexive way. Nor do I hold that Christianity and Islam (especially in their local and popular forms) were any less concerned with immediate and material issues. Rather, I mean to suggest that Christianity and Islam could address these concerns at a level of considerably greater abstraction than could traditional Mari belief. So too, as we shall see shortly, could the teaching of Kugu Sorta.

In Weber's formulation, conversion to a "world religion" was perhaps the principal way that the religious beliefs of peasant and tribal peoples

---

[14] Znamenskii, "Gornye cheremisy," 50. See also Petr Dimitriev, "Missionerskaia deiatel'nost' cheremisina Petra Dimitrieva sredi lugovykh cheremis Kazanskoi gubernii, Kozmodem'ianskago uezda v 1873," *Izvestiia po Kazanskoi eparkhii* 1 (1876), 16, where Dmitriev calls animists *keremetchiki*. Russian sources occasionally refer to animist Maris as *keremet-stvuiushchie cheremisy.*

[15] See, for example, the Mari prayers collected in the 1830s, "Sobranie molitv, chitaemykh Cheremisami kreshchenymi i nekreshchenymi pri zhertvoprinoshenii Keremeti," *Zavolzhskii muravei* 10 (1833), 584–7. See also the "Encyclopedia of the Sacred" in Thomas A. Sebeok and Frances. J. Ingemann, *Studies in Cheremis: The Supernatural* (New York, 1956).

[16] Znamenskii, "Gornye cheremisy," 47.

[17] Maris' concern with the correct performance of each detail of the prescribed ritual was so great that on the day after a sacrifice they usually performed an apologetic prayer in the sacred grove, asking forgiveness for any mistakes that might have occurred in the ritual the day before. Kuznetsov, "Kugu sorta," 13–14.

became rationalized. And indeed, Maris in some cases did convert to Islam and Christianity. To the east, in Ufa and Perm provinces, though animism occupied a prominent place well into the twentieth century,[18] Islam came to exert a profound influence over those who had settled among the predominant Tatar population.[19] Much in their habits and dress became visibly Islamic, many became proficient in the Tatar language, and Orthodox missionaries eventually began to speak ominously of the "Tatarization of non-Russians" (*tatarizatsiia inorodtsev*).[20] At the western extreme of Mari settlement, on the other hand, the so-called highland Maris had begun to exhibit a strong attachment to Orthodox Christianity, and by the 1860s a number of the most zealous activists in this so-called "religious movement" had established an Orthodox monastery.[21] In both of these cases, Maris exhibited a new religious consciousness, characterized by a striving for literacy, greater questioning, and a condescending attitude toward their old animism. But the largest group of Maris, the meadow Maris settled in the heavily forested region along the border between Kazan and Viatka provinces, continued to exhibit strong attractions for their native animist beliefs more than a century after their formal conversion.

Kugu Sorta's Doctrinal Revelations: A Case of "Internal Conversion"

If for most peoples religious rationalization has entailed conversion to a "world religion," then what happens when circumstances preclude such a

[18] The Finnish scholar Uno Holmberg photographed pagan ceremonies in Birsk district of Ufa province in the 1920s. See Holmberg, *Die Religion der Tscheremissen*, FF Communications no. 61 (Porvoo, 1926). On the currency of these religious beliefs among Maris more recently, see Allen Frank, "Traditional Religion in the Volga-Ural Region: 1960–1987," *Ural-Altaic Yearbook* 63 (1991): 168–71.

[19] See P. Eruslanov, "Magometanskaia propaganda sredi cheremis Ufimskoi gubernii," *Pravoslavnyi blagovestnik*, nos. 8, 9, 12, 13, 14, 16, 18, 19, 21, 22 (1895); and Paul W. Werth, "Tsarist Categories, Orthodox Intervention, and Islamic Conversion in a Pagan Udmurt Village, 1870s–1880s," in *Muslim Culture in Russia and Central Asia from the 18th to the Early 20th Centuries*, vol. 2: *Inter-Regional and Inter-Ethnic Relations*, ed. Anke von Kügelgen, Michael Kemper, and Allen J. Frank (Berlin, 1998), 385–415.

[20] Perhaps the most famous of such statements were those of N. I. Il'minskii in his letters to K. P. Pobedonostsev, in *Pism'a Nikolaia Ivanovicha Il'minskago k Ober Prokuroru Sviateishago Sinoda Konstantinu Petrovichu Pobedonostsevu* (Kazan, 1895). See also materials in *Missionerskii s''ezd v gorode Kazani* (Kazan, 1910); and B. Iuzefovich, "Khristianstvo, magometanstvo, i iazychestvo v vostochnykh guberniiakh Rossii," *Russkii vestnik*, no. 164 (1883): 5–64.

[21] I address this "religious movement" and the creation of the monastery in *At the Margins of Orthodoxy: Christian Mission, Imperial Governance, and Confessional Politics in Russia's Volga-Kama Region, 1827–1905* (Ithaca, N. Y., forthcoming). "Highland Maris" (*gornye cheremisy*) were referred to as such because the right bank of the Volga had a much more rugged terrain than the left bank.

route? This was the case in Bali, Geertz tells us, where Christianity's association with a discredited colonial regime and Islam's threat to native identity impelled the Balinese to begin rationalizing their religious system through "internal conversion." Conversion to either Christianity or Islam was "tantamount, in their eyes, to ceasing to be Balinese." Faced with the elimination of their cultural heritage, the Balinese began to produce "a self-conscious 'Bali-ism' which, in its philosophical dimensions, will approach the world religions both in the generality of the questions it asks and in the comprehensiveness of the answers it gives." This process began with greater religious questioning, and led in turn to the systematization of doctrine, the spread of religious literacy, a more formally organized institutional structure, and finally to the recognition of "Balinese Religion" as an official "Great Religion" in Indonesia in 1962.[22] "Internal conversion" thus describes the process of religious rationalization not through the adoption of an external religious system, but through a fundamental reworking of one's own religious beliefs. My contention here is that although Kugu Sorta was of course never recognized as a "Great Religion,"[23] "internal conversion" is nonetheless a useful starting point for our understanding of the pagan reformers.

The early history of Kugu Sorta is obscure. While archival evidence suggests that baptized Maris around the village of Upsha, where Kugu Sorta came to be centered, exhibited particularly strong attachment to pagan beliefs in the 1830s to 1850s, nowhere is there any reference to a new teaching or a disengagement from more traditional beliefs.[24] By the 1860s, however, sources show a growing consciousness among Maris that their traditional beliefs had been altered in fundamental ways. As one observer noted in 1866, "Cheremis are convinced that their present faith is not at all the one that was before, when people were righteous; today, in their opinion, the faith has already lost its purity and has become the kind [of faith] that one finds among sinful people."[25] While it would be wrong to posit a pure and unsullied Mari traditional religion, Maris' *own* notion

[22] Geertz, "Internal Conversion," 181–9.

[23] In the early Soviet years, authorities eventually came to view the Kugu Sorta group as a threat. N. Matorin, in his 1929 survey of religion in the middle Volga, concluded that the adherents of Kugu Sorta were a "reactionary sect, a typical manifestation of the 'peasant narrow-mindedness' about which Lenin warned." N. Matorin, *Religiia u narodov volzhsko-kamskogo kraia* (Moscow, 1929), 68. Similarly, N. A. Martynov wrote in 1940 that the group was fundamentally "reactionary" and had hindered collectivization and "socialist construction." See Martynov, "Perezhitki religioznoi sekty 'Kugu Sorta' I ee reaktsionnaia rol' v sotsialisticheskom stroitel'stve," *Trudy Mariiskogo Nauchno-issledovatel'skogo Instituta*, vol. 1 (1940): 82–92.

[24] Based on missionary reports in RGIA, f. 796, op. 117, d. 1345; f. 796, op. 118, d. 73; f. 796, op. 123, d. 1216.

[25] P. D. Shestakov, "Byt cheremis Urzhumskago uezda," *Tsirkuliar po Kazanskomu uchebnomu okrugu* 17 (1866): 140–41. See also Nurminskii, "Ocherk," 278–82.

that their faith had lost its purity produced a strong incentive for religious reform.

The group's more immediate origins were located in a kind of Mari religious gathering around 1877–78, when adherents of different animist trends came together to discuss their beliefs and forge some kind of religious unity. The main issue appears to have been the question of blood sacrifice. Though no agreement was reached on this question, a number of the participants, led by a Mari who had recently returned from military service, Andrei Iakmanov, formed a new religious group that rejected blood sacrifice as unpleasing to God.[26] Numbering around three hundred formal adherents at its height, the group began to draw the attention of state authorities only when its members petitioned the emperor in 1887, requesting permission to confess their beliefs openly,[27] and when shortly thereafter they refused to pay the local clergy for the performance of Orthodox rites.

The name "Kugu Sorta" evidently came from those Maris who did not join the group, and who defined the latter by a big candle that occupied a prominent place in its ceremonies.[28] The reformers, at least initially, did not use this appellation, calling their beliefs instead *toshto chii Mari vera,* or "ancient pure Mari faith," and in their Russian petitions "customary ancient white-cheremis-oral-pagan faith and ritual" (*obychnaia drevne belo-cheremissko-izustno-iazycheskaia vera i obriad*). They called themselves "our white-cheremis-oral-pagan community" (*nashe belo-cheremisko-izustno-iazycheskoe obshchestvo*).[29] We shall return to this curious appellation below.

The petitioners described the Kugu Sorta revival as a necessary response to Maris' fall into sin, which could only be remedied by appealing to God. As one petition stated, "Lately among the people truth has disappeared; sin has befallen us, [we] must give repentance to God, but we do

[26] See Yrjö Wichmann, "Über eine Reformbewegung der heidnischen Tscheremissen," *Journal de la Société Finno-Ougrienne* 45 (1932): 21–46; and Kuznetsov, "Kugu sorta," 2–5. Kuznetsov's source for this early history was a letter written by a local teacher, A. Zhilin, to the ethnographer V. K. Magnitskii, who at the time was serving as the school inspector for Urzhum district.

[27] A copy of this original petition is in RGIA, f. 821, op. 133, d. 429, ll. 55–59. Popov cites one petition that was filed as early as 1879, requesting the right to perform Mari rituals. See Popov, "K voprosu o religioznom dvizhenii," 189–90.

[28] Vasilii Iakmanov told Wichmann in Finland that Russian missionaries gave them the name "Kugu Sorta" (Wichmann, "Über eine Reformbewegung," 41). Since the term itself was Mari, it seems more likely that other Maris would have been the source of the name, as Kuznetsov suggests.

[29] All references in this section come from the petitions in RGIA, f. 796, op. 172, d. 2686, ll. 3–11, 63–70, 75–84, 92–5, 99–105, 117–18, 135–36. See also Vasil'ev, *Mariiskaia religioznaia sekta "Kugu Sorta,"* 11, and Kuznetsov, "Kugu Sorta," 44. Given the cumbersome nature of these self-designations (especially when rendered in English translation), I have retained "Kugu Sorta" as a convenient shorthand.

not have the freedom to pray; day and night only bitter tears flow from our eyes."[30] A similar idea emerges in the following passage from a different petition, which I cite here at greater length despite its idiosyncrasy. The petitioners did not wish to confess Christianity, they wrote,

> because we understand nothing and we cannot honor and repent before Almighty [*Vsevyshnii*] God with zeal through the Christian religion, and [because] we have not lived [well, but] have only come to ruin in all respects—that is, from Almighty God we could not receive any recovery, especially since all Cheremis and we are only sinners and wretched; therefore our white-cheremis-oral-pagan community, that is, we, came to the conviction to remain only in the customary ancient white-cheremis-oral-pagan faith and ritual, established long ago . . .[31]

This passage exhibits both older Mari understandings and newer ones as well. On the one hand, the concern with material well-being and the idea that Maris could not communicate with God through Christianity were fairly standard elements in Mari rejections of Christianity. On the other hand, the notion of sin, the clearly expressed monotheism, and the insistence on the exclusive practice of paganism all represented significant innovation. Most importantly, their present misfortune was construed as a moral crisis, necessitating, as we shall see, not just a rejection of Christianity, but a reform of Mari animism. The publicist A. Baranov was probably right to see in the emergence of Kugu Sorta "an extraordinarily important spiritual crisis" that generated new spiritual inquiry among eastern non-Russians. "Not satisfied with their old pagan beliefs and at the same time not knowing the true Christian religion, *inorodtsy* (aliens, or non-Russians) in their striving to satisfy those inquiries are creating new dogmas, putting into them their new outlook."[32] Some of the more concrete reasons for this crisis will be addressed below.

Let us turn now to the actual tenets of the new religion, which most clearly reflect "internal conversion."[33] The most radical innovation was the assertion of monotheism, by which Jumo now occupied a central

---

[30] RGIA, f. 796, op. 172, d. 2686, l. 40b. This passage contains numerous grammatical and syntactical mistakes that are not clearly reflected in the translation.

[31] RGIA, f. 796, op. 172, d. 2686, l. 630b.

[32] A. Baranov, "Otpavshie ot pravoslaviia v iazychestvo i magometanstvo," *Russkoe bogatstvo* 9 (1902): 215. Baranov had some experience with Finnic peoples in the Volga-Kama region, since he had served on the defense team for a number of Udmurt peasants accused of performing a human sacrifice in the 1890s. See L. S. Shatenshtein, *Multanskoe delo, 1892–1896* (Izhevsk, 1960) and Robert Paul Geraci, "Window on the East: Ethnography, Orthodoxy, and Russian Nationality in Kazan, 1870–1914" (Ph.D. diss., University of California at Berkeley, 1995), chap. 4.

[33] Vasil'ev, in his 1927 study of Kugu Sorta, identified three subgroups or doctrines (*tolki*), characterized by the different degrees of strictness and asceticism to which they adhered.

place and became the referent for all religious activity. The reformed religion called upon its adherents to lead a life pleasing to God, and all offerings were directed toward him. The reformers were particularly eager to stress their monotheism in their petitions: "Truly we write that our Faith is [devoted] to Almighty God alone, and does not allow worship of any idol or object . . ."[34] The flip side of this new monotheism was the elimination of all smaller gods and most significantly of the *keremet'* itself. Thus the reformers concentrated sacredness into a single being and dispensed with the most important spiritual entity of the older pantheon, the *keremet'*. As much as the reformers retained important elements of the older animism, then, Kugu Sorta nonetheless constituted a fundamental innovation in Mari theology.

The reformers erected an entire set of ethical demands, including cleanliness, brotherly love, tolerance for other religions, hard work, and the rejection of alcohol, tobacco, coffee, and tea.[35] They viewed nature as pure and as a conduit between humans and God, considering it a great sin to misuse or destroy natural objects, especially without the permission of God.[36] Although the specifics of afterlife according to Kugu Sorta remained unclear, the reformers articulated the idea of achieving a "Heavenly Kingdom" (*Tsarstvo Nebesnoe*), which suggests a significant departure from the older Mari conception of the afterlife as simply a continuation of earthly life independent of a person's moral behavior.[37] The clear articulation of a moral system constituted a considerable break from the greater utilitarianism of the older beliefs, where animists had stood in a mostly functional relationship to the gods.

Moreover, Kugu Sorta was egalitarian with respect to women, who had been excluded from participation in some of the public prayers of the old animism.[38] The exact position of women in Kugu Sorta is not clear, but

---

See Vasil'ev, *Mariiskaia religioznaia sekta "Kugu Sorta,"* 3–5. Since these distinctions appear to have arisen after the exile of the most important reformers to Siberia in 1893, and since the distinctions are ones of degree more than qualitative differences, I do not address them here.

[34] RGIA, f. 796, op. 172, d. 2686, l. 700b. The trend toward monotheism was also observable among Udmurts in the early twentieth century, as the observer S. Chicherina noted in 1904. See S. Chicherina, *U privolzhskikh inorodtsev: Putevyia zametki* (St. Petersburg, 1905), 188.

[35] RGIA, f. 796, op. 172, d. 2686, l. 650b. A list of prohibitions and directives is in Wichmann, "Über eine Reformbewegung," 32–33. The prohibition of alcohol prevented many who were sympathetic from joining. As Kuznetsov related, "I know families, the female half of which long ago sided with the sect, but the adult men, despite great sympathy for it, cannot do so, since they are not in a position to reject vodka and tobacco" ("Kugu sorta," 27). Another observer concurred that Maris were heavy pipe smokers. See K. M., "Cheremisy Iaranskogo uezda, Viatskoi gubernii," *Russkiia vedomsti*, no. 130 (1872): 3.

[36] Vasil'ev, *Mariiskaia religioznaia sekta "Kugu Sorta,"* 32–33.

[37] Kuznetsov, "Kugu Sorta," 9, 24.

[38] See Aiplatov and Ivanov, *Istoriia Mariiskogo kraia*, 464, 480–81.

the ethnographer S. K. Kuznetsov asserted that women were equal members in the religious order and were among the most zealous adherents of the new faith.[39] While the group ascribed different roles to men and women during ceremonies, the very establishment of a feminine sphere of religious activity in the group may have given women a more important place in the ceremonies than they had enjoyed previously, and may thereby help to explain their enthusiasm.[40]

But perhaps one of the greatest indications of the reformers' rationalizing was their effort to codify and present the new religion to outsiders. While earlier Maris had been very secretive about their religion, the reformers, through their many petitions and their readiness to speak openly, attempted to explain their teaching and to counter claims of the Orthodox clergy that they posed a threat to the Russian state. To the emperor they offered a detailed description of their beliefs together with their petitions,[41] and after some initial apprehension spoke with ethnographers openly. But their most remarkable act in this regard was to present their religion at the Kazan Scientific and Industrial Exhibition in 1890. For this purpose, Iakmanov and his comrades drew up a short description of the faith and brought a number of artifacts to Kazan to show at the exhibition. Kuznetsov, who attended the exhibition, recalls how Iakmanov was completely open and declared "there is nothing secret in our faith; everyone can come and ask whatever he wants; we conceal nothing."[42] They explained the reason for their presentation thus: "We wanted to acquaint Russian society with [the artifacts], we wanted to show that in our faith there is nothing harmful, disgraceful, or prohibited."[43] The description of the faith, though only about half a page long and deeply concerned with the specific form of Kugu Sorta prayer, nonetheless constituted "something akin to a Kugu Sorta 'creed.'"[44] Here, in short, was an attempt by Iakmanov to codify and systematize the tenets of the new Mari faith.

The reformers received several certificates and badges from the organizers of the conference expressing gratitude and praise for their display. They referred to these "papers of approval and badges" in their petitions to the emperor, and used them to further their cause within the village.

[39] Kuznetsov, "Kugu sorta," 51.

[40] These distinctions appear to have echoed prevailing gender divisions of labor. For example, for the offering women prepared bread while men would prepare and arrange candles. The reasons for other distinctions seem less clear. For example, during one ritual men were to hold kernels of rye, while women had kernels of oats. See Vasil'ev, *Mariiskaia religioznaia sekta "Kugu Sorta,"* 34, 44.

[41] This description was written in Mari and to this day remains untranslated in the Synodal file. RGIA, f. 796, op. 172, d. 2686, ll. 6–11.

[42] Kuznetsov, "Kugu sorta," 7.

[43] Cited in Baranov, "Otpavshie ot pravoslaviia," 219.

[44] Kuznetsov, "Kugu Sorta," 8. Kuznetsov reproduces this document on 9–10, with a lengthy commentary.

The clergy reported that one Mari had received a medal at the exhibition and was now wearing it on his chest and explaining to villagers that it was given to him "for pagan faith." Others displayed the certificate on their gate a few days before Easter and explained "that although there were many people at the exhibition, the authorities recognized only their faith as correct."[45] The reformers also invoked the authority of recent ethnography, as they commented in one petition, referring to a brochure about the Kazan exhibition: "[W]e have not remained forgotten in the ethnography of N. I. Smirnov, and on pages 29–31 the harmlessness of our faith is discussed directly."[46] As local clergy became more concerned about the movement and attempted to portray it in the most dangerous light, the reformers actively countered these assessments. Though Maris had in the past resisted the clergy's efforts to disengage them from paganism—sometimes violently—never had they engaged in this kind of external ideological campaign in defense of their belief.

But however much was new in the group's teachings and activities, they were motivated by the idea of preserving old beliefs and even construed their practice as a return to an older, pristine, more genuine Mari past. It was for this reason that they deployed a discourse of purity, whiteness, and authenticity, and associated Christianity with "blackness." Thus the reformers declared in an 1892 petition that they "will never be untrue to our Faith and religion and blacken our conscience, as other Cheremis have done. . . ."[47] They argued that their ancestors had been baptized through force and deceit, and that "our fathers [and] we were Pure Cheremis, and not Orthodox."[48] The authority of ancestors, so important to Maris in general, was especially prominent in the reformers' texts and statements. As they explained in a document submitted to the Iaransk court in Russian that was less than graceful but nonetheless expressive: "We have been brought to judgment in the district court for the perfor-

[45] RGIA, f. 796, op. 172, d. 2686, l. 43–43ob. The tsarevich was the patron of the exhibition, and thus his title appeared on the certificate, which probably emboldened the pagan reformers. RGIA, f. 796, op. 172, d. 2686, l. 430b. Despite their expressed religious tolerance, the reformers in several instances asserted the exclusive correctness of their faith. Thus in 1888–89, members of Kugu Sorta buried various Christian and old pagan religious objects (icons, crosses, etc.). This burial signified the death of these religions, while Kugu Sorta itself was believed to remain alive and vibrant. See Vasil'ev, *Mariiskaia religioznaia sekta "Kugu Sorta,"* 35.

[46] RGIA, f. 796, op. 172, d. 2686, l. 5. The reference is to I. N. Smirnov's publication, *Etnografiia na Kazanskoi nauchno-promyshlennoi vystavke* (Kazan, 1890). Smirnov's brochure is summarized in "Osobennosti byta inorodtsev Volzhsko-Kamskago kraia," *Pravitel'stvennyi vestnik,* 22 and 23 September 1890. The petitioners were apparently referring to the following passage in Smirnov: "The concern among these interesting and touchingly naive sectarians for an accurate acquaintanceship with their beliefs goes to the extent that one of them—literate—even composed a short description of the prayers." (*Etnografiia,* 31).

[47] RGIA, f. 796, op. 172, d. 2686, l. 68.

[48] RGIA, f. 796, op. 172, d. 2686, ll. 64, 4.

mance of ancient-Cheremis-pagan faith and ritual, as our ancestors earlier believed and held their customary ritual, but as we descendants of our
ancestors, that is of our parents, and by their blessing we have performance of pagan ritual."[49] To the missionary Ia. Koblov, members of the
group explained in 1905 that the words of their fathers were the ultimate
referent in matters of the faith.[50] However much their program may have
constituted innovation, they presented it as the true belief of their ancestors, in conscious opposition to contemporaneous Mari practices, which
they openly derided as a deviation from the true path. The members of
Kugu Sorta, it seems, could "invent traditions" as well as anyone else.[51]

Thus I would argue that Kugu Sorta can at least partially be considered
a case of "internal conversion," to the extent that its leaders created, clar-
ified, and systematized a set of religious understandings, and articulated a
more transcendental vision involving the desire to live as was pleasing to
God. In Weber's terms, a leading reformer like Iakmanov played the role
of a prophet, i.e., one who rejects blind conformity and promulgates a
higher and more deliberate religious ideal.[52] True, the members were not
able to institutionalize a canon; nor were they able to effect the socialization of these principles into the ideas and actions of all rank-and-file believers. The exile of the most important members in 1893 prevented such
processes from occurring on a broader scale. Most of Kugu Sorta's followers returned to Christianity, at least officially, after the exile,[53] and the
group was not able to construct a numerically strong following. Yet for all
this, we can view Kugu Sorta as the first step in a more lengthy process of
"internal conversion."

The Emergence of Kugu Sorta

Having considered Kugu Sorta's specific doctrinal revelation, we must
now illuminate the broader circumstances that rendered this revelation
compelling to at least some Maris. In other words, rather than ascribe
Kugu Sorta's even limited success exclusively to the charisma of its

---

[49] Cited from court documents in S. M. S——v, "Cheremisskoe iazycheskoe verouchenie
'Kugu-Sorta,'" *Istoricheskii vestnik* 61 (1895): 730. My translation is designed to convey the
character of the original, which was written by Andrei Iakmanov.

[50] Ia. Koblov, "Cheremisskaia sekta 'Kugu-Sorta,'" *Pravoslavnyi sobesednik* 1 (1905): 528.

[51] The reference here is to Eric Hobsbawm and Terence Ranger, eds., *The Invention of Tradition* (Cambridge, 1983).

[52] See the discussion in Hefner, "Introduction," 10–22.

[53] According to the local clergy, many Maris were waiting to see what would happen to the
members of Kugu Sorta, and one Mari told a priest that "if nothing happens to Fedor Alekseev [one of the reformers then under prosecution in the courts], then we will all go to his
faith." RGIA, f. 796, op. 172, d. 2686, l. 440b. The exile evidently convinced Maris like this
one not to embrace Kugu Sorta openly.

"prophets," we must consider how and why this new vision was salient for the broader mass of Maris. According to Geertz's theoretical elaboration, "[T]he process of religious rationalization seems everywhere to have been provoked by a thorough shaking of the foundations of social order."[54] While the aspiration to indigenous religious practice among Finnic peoples was not new,[55] I believe that Kugu Sorta's appearance should be situated in the specific historical context of the mid- to late nineteenth century, characterized on the one hand by more rapid social and economic change, and on the other by a more concerted and open effort by clerics and officials to assimilate non-Russians to Russian language and culture.

While the economic condition of the postemancipation peasantry remains a question of historical debate, even some of the more positive assessments of peasants' living standards acknowledge a significant downturn in the late 1880s, when Kugu Sorta went public.[56] The situation of course only became worse when famine hit the region in the early 1890s. Moreover, several sources point directly to increasing "impoverishment" and "economic disorder" (*razstroistvo*) of peasant households in Mari regions.[57] The most dramatic account is provided by M. F. Kandaratskii, a doctor who visited meadow Mari settlements in the late 1880s and described tremendous hardship, destitution, and indeed the near extinction (as he saw it) of the meadow Mari people.[58] In addition, the replacement of *obrok* (quitrent) by redemption payments from state peasants in 1887, even while not accompanied by a significant increase in tax burden, may have been *perceived* by peasants as an important economic and social shift.[59]

---

[54] Geertz, "Internal Conversion," 173.

[55] Some cases involving Udmurts and Mordvins from earlier in the nineteenth century—albeit with much less detail than we have about Kugu Sorta—can be found in RGIA, f. 796, op. 105, d. 481, ll. 1–2, and Paul W. Werth, "Armed Defiance and Biblical Appropriation: Assimilation and the Transformation of Mordvin Resistance, 1740–1810," *Nationalities Papers* 27, no. 2 (1999): 245–70.

[56] For views on peasant economy, see Steven Hoch, "On Good Numbers and Bad: Malthus, Population Trends and Peasant Standard of Living in Late Imperial Russia," *Slavic Review* 53 (1994): 42–75; Steven G. Wheatcroft, "Crises and the Condition of the Peasantry in Late Imperial Russia," in *Peasant Economy, Culture, and Politics of European Russia, 1800–1921*, ed. Esther Kingston-Mann and Timothy Mixter (Princeton, N.J., 1991), 128–76, who notes that crisis at this time was greatest in what he designates the Central Producer Region, which included Viatka province.

[57] I. N. Smirnov, *Cheremisy: Istoriko-etnograficheskii ocherk* (Kazan, 1889), 155; M. I. Tereshkina, "Osvobozhdenie gosudarstvennykh krest'ian Mariiskogo kraia," *Trudy Mariiskogo Nauchno-issledovatel'skogo Instituta Iazyka, Literatury i Istorii*, vol. 9 (Ioshkar-Ola, 1956): 3–35 (quote, 34). Tereshkina's observation cites Tsarevokokshaisk and Urzhum districts, which bordered Iaransk district to the south and east.

[58] M. F. Kandaratskii, *Priznaki vymiraniia lugovykh cheremis* (Kazan, 1889). Another observer, writing in the early 1870s, concurred that Maris, "are presently close to disappearance." See K. M., "Cheremisy Iaranskago uezda," *Russkiia vedomosti* 113 (1872):3.

[59] After their "emancipation" in 1866, state peasants continued to make *obrok* payments to the state for the next twenty years. Redemption payments introduced in 1887 exceeded

There were other large-scale changes that should be noted here as well. First, many of the large forests in the Volga-Kama region were depleted in the nineteenth century, thereby exposing the native population to external influences to a greater degree and eliminating the very focus of indigenous religious practice. Such deforestation had already altered both the economy and the religiosity of highland Maris, and was now rapidly changing the topography of Iaransk district as well.[60] Second, Mari regions were increasingly subject to encroachment by Russian peasant settlers, especially in Iaransk and Tsarevokokshaisk districts.[61] Finally, the construction of more roads rendered otherwise remote areas of native settlement increasingly accessible to external influences. Thus the spread of the Russian language (and presumably Christianity) among the highland Maris has been attributed by a number of researchers to the region's many postal and trade routes.[62] While these issues require further study, the available evidence suggests that Kugu Sorta's appearance was at least partly rooted in these processes of change.

Indeed, there were distinctly economic dimensions to Kugu Sorta's appearance. First, as noted above, the reformers attracted attention precisely when they refused to pay fees to their local clergy. As they themselves explained in a petition submitted to the Iaransk court, "[W]e rejected church dues and work [requirements] on account of our ancient Cheremis faith."[63] Though the collection of church dues had long been resisted by non-Russian parishioners,[64] Maris now put forward their faith as an explicit justification for their refusal to pay. Moreover, it appears that local officials had become more adept in recent years at securing bribes and in effect assessing an informal tax on the large-scale Mari gatherings

---

obrok payments by over 40 percent in most areas of Mari settlement, but even Terëshkina, committed to showing the "predatory" nature of the emancipation, acknowledged that this increase was offset by the elimination of the soul tax. See Terëshkina, "Osvobozhdenie gusudarstvennykh krest'ian," 27. More research on these conditions is still needed.

[60] P. Znamenskii, "Gornye Cheremisy," 36; K. M., "Cheremisy Iaranskago uezda," *Russkiia vedomosti* 113 (1872):3.

[61] The population of Iaransk district increased by 47 percent over the years 1811–34 and by another 62 percent over the period 1834–58. This colonization was due in large measure to an influx of Russians from the northern and central portions of Viatka province to the south. See D. E. Kazantsev, *Formirovanie dialektov mariiskogo iazyka* (Ioshkar-Ola, 1985), 134–35; and N. Romanov, *Pereselenie krest'ian Viatskoi gubernii* (Viatka, 1880), 124–25.

[62] Of particular significance was the Moscow postal road, which united Moscow with almost all the provinces of eastern European Russia. See Kazantsev, *Formirovanie dialektov,* 137; K. I. Kozlova, *Ocherki etnicheskoi istorii mariiskogo naroda* (Moscow, 1978), 227, 239–40.

[63] S——v, "Cheremisskoe iazycheskoe verouchenie 'Kugu Sorta,'" 725. See also Baranov, "Otpavshie ot pravoslaviia," 219, and Vasil'ev, *Mariiskaia religioznaia sekta "Kugu Sorta,"* 219.

[64] On the difficulties of collecting church dues among non-Russians, see Terëshkina, "Osvodozhdenie gosudarstvennykh krest'ian," 24; S. Nurminskii, "Inorodcheskie prikhody," *Pravoslavnoe obozrenie* 12 (1863): 254–55; and RGIA, f. 383, op. 3, d. 2332.

so important to the old religion.[65] Charged with both supporting the Orthodox clergy in their parishes (in accordance with their formal Christian status) and providing livestock and goods for sacrifice by the tenets of the older animism, baptized Maris were stuck with a double burden. From a purely economic standpoint, then, the stage was set for some kind of religious innovation that might free them from this dual obligation.

Kuznetsov, in fact, considered economics to have been the main reason for Kugu Sorta's appearance and spread. Simply stated, the sacrifice of livestock required by the old animism was becoming too expensive.[66] In important ceremonies, Maris had traditionally offered large animals, such as sheep and horses, and even smaller offerings usually required the sacrifice of smaller animals and fowl. Already before Kugu Sorta's open appearance, Maris were trying to lessen the cost of sacrifices, by offering only parts of animals as sacrifices rather than the whole thing, or through symbolic offerings such as cakes that were shaped like horses.[67] Kugu Sorta offerings consisted simply of items such as bread, butter, and candles, and thus could be conducted weekly with comparatively little expense. Kugu Sorta's success, from this perspective, was to articulate a theology that allowed Maris to dispense with blood sacrifice while remaining true to the faith.

Moreover, Kugu Sorta was very explicitly opposed to processes of modernization. Imbued with strong respect for nature, the reformers firmly opposed the use of factory-made goods, above all in their religious ceremonies. They resorted to medicine only in dire circumstances and considered it a sin to wear colored clothing. Their tables and buckets "are all unpainted and are prepared with our own hands from the purest and healthy birch and lime trees." Their commitment to self-sufficiency was so great, in fact, that they rejected the use even of matches and kerosene. In explaining their rejection of factory goods, the reformers told Kuznetsov, "we do not know what they are made of, and besides our ancestors avoided factory goods."[68] Thus the Soviet historian N. S. Popov is at least partially correct to view Kugu Sorta as a form of peasant protest against the growth of capitalist relations of production.[69]

---

[65] Kuznetsov, "Kugu Sorta," 50–51. See also Kuznetsov's "Otryvki iz dorozhnykh zametok vo vremia etnograficheskoi ekskursii po Viatskoi gubernii v 1880," *Izvestiia Obshchestva Arkheologii, Istorii i Etnografii pri Imperatorskom Kazanskom Universitete* 3 (1884): 260–76, in which he describes how a local police official [*uriadnik*], a post introduced in 1878, was prohibiting Mari prayers unless he got his cut.

[66] Kuznetsov, "Kugu sorta," 50.

[67] Smirnov, *Cheremisy*, 155–158.

[68] RGIA, f. 796, op. 172, d. 2686, l. 64–64ob.; Vasil'ev, *Mariiskaia religioznaia sekta "Kugu Sorta,"* 21–27; Kuznetsov, "Kugu Sorta," 41.

[69] But Popov undoubtedly overstates the case when he remarks that Kugu Sorta was "religious in form only." Popov, "K voprosu o religioznom dvizhenii," 174–75, 191–92.

If these broad economic changes constituted one important basis for Kugu Sorta's emergence, then missionary activity and administrative reform in the nineteenth century formed another. Beginning in the 1820s, the Russian state had initiated a deeper intervention into the lives of non-Russians in the Volga-Kama region. In 1829 missionaries began to visit Mari settlements regularly, encouraging parishioners to reject paganism openly and persecuting them when they engaged in native religious practice. Several religious texts in Mari were published and distributed at this time, and efforts were made to educate Mari boys in the Viatka seminary for the purposes of preparing non-Russian clergy. Meanwhile, the reform of state peasants under P. D. Kiselev established a new administration in the countryside, charged with exercising "tutelage" (*popechitel'stvo*) over the peasant population. The reform established new peasant schools, promoted agricultural innovation, and promulgated plans for the "correct" construction of villages and homes. While the success of these policies was mixed, they nonetheless forced Maris to interact with missionaries and state representatives, exposed them to Russian conceptions of religion, and increasingly drove native religious practice underground.[70]

By the 1860s the ante was raised considerably, as officials and clergy began to speak more openly about the *obrusenie* (Russification) of non-Russians in the Volga-Kama region. This discourse was especially pronounced in debates leading to a new educational statute in 1870.

Educational experts expected that the introduction of native-language schooling, combined with Orthodox instruction for baptized non-Russians, would lead to their eventual Russification.[71] Moreover, where the Russian population was significant, Maris were already exhibiting varying degrees of *obrusenie*. Especially in larger villages, one ethnographer noted, one could encounter Maris "who have broken all religious connection with their tribe."[72] In short, the pace of assimilation was increasing.

All of these circumstances constituted a threat to Mari identity. Much like the Balinese, Maris traditionally viewed religious practice as the principal determinant of their identity. Indeed, for the peoples of Inner Asia generally, the origin of the communal group was one of the central elements of religious life.[73] By this understanding, God had granted a sepa-

---

[70] These interventions form the subject of inquiry in my *At the Margins of Orthodoxy*.

[71] Two dissertations that discuss an education of non-Russians in considerable detail are Geraci, "Window on the East," esp. chaps. 2 and 5; and Isabelle Kreindler, "Educational Policies toward the Eastern Nationalities in Tsarist Russia: A Study of Il'minskii's System" (Ph.D. diss., Columbia University, 1969).

[72] Kuznetsov, "Kugu Sorta," 29. Or as Nurminskii wrote already in 1862, "The Cheremis nation . . . as a consequence of constant external influence, has already lost its pure Mari type and has forfeited the ancient fatherly faith" ("Ocherk," 279).

[73] See the fascinating discussion in Devin DeWeese, *Islamization and Native Religion in the Golden Horde: Baba Tükles and Conversion to Islam in Historical and Epic Tradition* (University

A missionary school for Mari (Cheremis) girl converts in the Middle Volga region. *Pribavleniia k Tserkovnym vedomostiam* 13, pt. 2, no. 43 (1900).

rate religion to each people—seventy-seven faiths in all, each of them equally pleasing to God. Religions were accordingly designated in what we would regard as ethnic terms: "Tatar faith" (Islam), "Russian faith" (Christianity), and "Mari faith" (animism).[74] From this perspective those who converted to another religion had not only changed faith, but, in ef-

Park, Pa., 1994), esp. 27–39. Though DeWeese deals mostly with Turkic peoples and their historical narratives of conversion to Islam, the Inner Asian understandings that informed those narratives had currency among Finnic peoples as well.

[74] On the significance of the numbers seven and nine for the peoples of the Volga-Kama region—of which the belief in the existence of seventy-seven faiths is but one example—see N. I. Zolotnitskii, *Kornevoi chuvashsko-russkii slovar'* (Kazan, 1875), 181–90. For the members of Kugu Sorta, the number seventy-seven was sooner allegorical than actual. As Tikhon Iakmanov explained to the missionary Ia. Koblov, "When we say that there are seventy-seven faiths on the earth and that each tribe must confess its own faith . . . that does not mean that there are precisely seventy-seven faiths, but just signifies that there are many faiths, corresponding to the number of tribes and peoples." Koblov, "Cheremisskaia sekta "Kugu Sorta," 526.

fect, ethnicity as well: converts to Christianity had "made themselves Russians [*sdelalis' russkimi*]," as a group of Maris stated explicitly in 1829.[75] Those Maris who retained indigenous beliefs and practice were called *chii Mari*, literally "pure" or "genuine Maris."

The pagan reformers retained this outlook and complained about local authorities that "out of Cheremis they want to remake us into Russians [*peredelat' na ruskova*]." According to a local missionary, the reformers contended that there was an "Old Bible" that established seventy-seven different faiths and that "the existing Bible was thought up by priests in order to Russify the Cheremis [*dlia obruseniia cheremis*]." Faith, for these reformers, was "a force for the preservation of the tribal peculiarities of each people."[76] "As Cheremis," the reformers rejected the Savior, the cross, icons, Christian prayer, fasts, and "church-civil enactments" (i.e., civil laws regulating the religious life of Orthodox Christians). That is, the reformers did not consider themselves obligated to observe these enactments *precisely because they were Maris*, and not Russians. For them to accept Christianity, in short, was to cease being Mari, or at the very least to become "Russian Maris" (*russkie cheremisy*), as they put it.[77] Religious practice constituted perhaps the most effective way for Maris to delineate and maintain their identity in opposition to Russians and to invest the differences between Russians and Maris with a primordial character.

Both detractors and sympathizers, in fact, understood the group's aspirations principally in national terms. The clergy itself identified the group's alleged separatism as its most dangerous trait. As Bishop Sergii of Viatka contended, the movement, "under the guise of a *national faith*, has as its goal the union of the Cheremis tribe and strengthening of its language, the peculiarity of its way of life, customs, and so on."[78] Publicists who latched on to this interesting story were more sympathetic to the group, but they, too, viewed it as a manifestation of national aspirations. One article, noting the continued failure to provide Maris with access to Christianity in their native language, concluded, "[I]t will not be surprising for us that Cheremis have come to see in Christianity a danger for their nationality [*natsional'nost'*]."[79] Thus while treating the group with varying degrees of sympathy, Russian clergy, officials, and publicists all

---

[75] RGIA, f. 797, op. 3 d. 12654, l. 1150b. See also N. I. Il'minskii's assessment in 1863 that conversion for non-Russians constituted a change in nationality (*narodnost'*): "Ob obrazovanii inorodtsev posredstvom knig, perevedennykh na ikh rodnoi iazyk," *Pravoslavnoe obozrenie* 10 (1863): 137.

[76] RGIA, f. 796, op. 172, d. 2686, l. 690b, 140b. Citations come from an account of Kugu Sorta written by local clergy.

[77] RGIA, f. 796, op. 172, d. 2686, l. 200b.

[78] RGIA, f, 796, op. 172, d. 2686, l. 16 (emphasis added).

[79] D. Z., "Iazychestvo v Viatskoi gubernii (pis'mo iz provintsii)," *Zhizn'* 12 (1900): 400.

identified its goal as the preservation of Mari ethnic identity in the context of assimilation.[80]

Here a few words need to be said about the particular outlook of N. I. Il'minskii, who in the 1860s became perhaps the most influential educator of non-Russian peoples. While many clerics and officials explicitly sought the Russification of non-Russians, Il'minskii was decidedly more concerned with their Christian education. He actively promoted the translation of Orthodox texts into their languages, and the ordaining of non-Russian clergy—in short the idea that Orthodox Christianity be made available to non-Russian peoples on their own terms.[81] Il'minskii's outlook was most directly realized in the activities of the Brotherhood of Bishop Gurii, a group of priests, officials, and educators who took upon themselves the task of the Christian "enlightenment" among non-Russians.[82]

But while this educational approach by most indications deeply affected the communities into which it was introduced, its specific geographic scope needs to be noted as well. Historical sources suggest that while the brotherhood's efforts among baptized Tatars and Chuvash were substantial, comparatively little attention was devoted to the Mari population, especially in Viatka province. In 1869, there were only eleven schools with 167 Mari pupils, mostly serving the highland Mari population, which was culturally and linguistically distinct from meadow Maris. There were no schools at all for Maris in Viatka province in 1869.[83] Even by 1892, the activities of the brotherhood had not made significant inroads among meadow Maris. From 1883 to 1892 fewer than 100 Mari pupils attended the brotherhood's schools annually. Only two out of nine native Mari clerics by 1892 served among the meadow population, and none of them in Viatka province.[84] In 1900, a correspondent from Viatka province wrote

---

[80] It should be noted here that events like the appearance of Kugu Sorta provided ethnographers with a way to establish their authority deriving from unique knowledge of their subjects of study. As Kuznetsov wrote in concluding that Kugu Sorta was harmless: "In such a live affair, as with sectarianism in general, it is always useful to listen to the opinion not only of missionaries, but also of private observers, more or less acquainted with the life [*byt*] of aliens [*inorodtsy*]." Kuznetsov, "Kugu Sorta," 58.

[81] Aside from the citations above on the question of education more generally, see also *Perepiska o trekh shkolakh Ufimskoi gubernii: k kharakteristike inorodcheskikh missionerskikh shkol* (Kazan, 1885); and *Iz perepiski ob udostoenii inorodtsev sviashchennosluzhitel'skikh dolzhnostei* (Kazan, 1885).

[82] The brotherhood was founded in 1867. For a survey of its activities over its first twenty-five years, see M. Mashanov, *Obzor deiatel'nosti Bratstva Sv. Guriia za 25 let ego sushchestvovaniia, 1867–1892* (Kazan, 1892).

[83] P. D. Shestakov, "Soobrazheniia o sisteme obrazovaniia inorodtsev, obitaiushchikh v guberniiakh Kazanskago uchebnago okruga: Predstavlenie Popechitelia Kazanskago uchebnago okruga Ministru narodnago prosveshcheniia ot 3 dekabria 1869," RGIA, pechatnye zapiski, papka 3103, 83.

[84] Mashanov, *Obzor deiatel'nosti*, 74–75, 183.

that Il'minskii's precepts were not prevalent in Viatka province: there was no liturgy in Mari or Udmurt, and some missionaries did not know these languages. Russian was the language of instruction in most schools, and some of the so-called non-Russian schools, ironically, were located in predominantly Russian areas. Indeed, the correspondent considered the failure to implement Il'minskii's ideas to be a contributing factor to Kugu Sorta's appearance.[85] S. Chicherina, who traveled extensively in the Volga region in 1904, likewise reported that despite official claims, the Il'minskii system was in effect only in a few places in Viatka province, and that the Mari and Udmurt languages were for the most part disregarded in local schools.[86] In short, the Il'minskii system's presence was tenuous at best in the regions where Kugu Sorta arose. As a result, the members of Kugu Sorta continued to see in Christianity the specter of Russification.

Kugu Sorta thus appears to have been a consciously nativistic response to socio-economic change and the prospect of Maris' conversion and thus, as they believed, their elimination as a distinct group. But on one level even this "internal conversion" in fact signified a greater incorporation into Russianness than either the missionaries or the reformers themselves realized. It is to this incorporation that we now turn.

Kugu Sorta's Russian Appropriations

Religious rationalization for Maris entailed as much as anything else the appropriation of Russian understandings of "religion" and "faith" for their own belief system and its defense. "Internal conversion" was thus more than just an attempt to give the old beliefs greater conceptual generalization, tighter formal integration, and a more explicit sense of doctrine. However explicitly the reformers rejected Orthodox Christianity, that rejection, as well as the articulation of Kugu Sorta tenets as a viable alternative, were expressed to an increasing degree using Russian terms and conceptual understandings. In other words, however much we may wish to ascribe agency to the reformers and thus to see them engaged in a process of "making their own history," we must nonetheless consider that it was the interventions of the Russian state and church into the lives of non-Russians and, concomitantly, the particular world that was thereby fashioned, that provided new forms of language and understanding in which the reformers conceived of themselves and their project. The range of possible ways of thinking and indeed acting was structured in ways logically independent of the consciousness of the reformers themselves. In short, the members of

[85] D. Z., "Iazychestvo," 399–400.
[86] Chicherina, *U privolzhskikh inorodtsev*, 188–89, 214, 228–29, 235.

Kugu Sorta, even in rejecting Christianity, accepted considerably more from Russian discourse than they themselves realized.[87]

To situate the reformers fully in context, we need to acknowledge at least briefly that Islam, too, had a deep historical influence on Maris. Especially from the days of the Bulgar state (tenth to thirteenth centuries) and the Kazan Khanate (1445–1552), a number of Turkic and Arabic words made their way into the Mari language.[88] Perhaps most illustrative is the word *keremet'* itself, the quintessential animist spirit, which derives from an Arabic word meaning "miracle."[89] More immediately, the members of Kugu Sorta appear to have formulated their view of Christianity at least partly based on Islam's example. While they rejected the cross, icons, and all Orthodox prescriptions, they nevertheless accepted significant portions of the Old Testament as well as its prophets. They acknowledged Christ himself as the greatest prophet, but rejected the notion of his divine origin, much as Muslims did. The prohibition on alcohol may also have been an Islamic borrowing. In addition, the attempts by baptized Tatars over the course of the nineteenth century to be recognized as Muslims may have served as a model for the reformers' requests for formal recognition as members of Kugu Sorta. Though much from Islam probably entered Mari vocabulary and practice centuries earlier, these borrowings suggest that the reformers turned to Islam for inspiration in constructing arguments against the claims of the Orthodox Church.

But since the areas where Kugu Sorta took hold were relatively far from Tatar settlements, it seems likely that the specific elements of Kugu Sorta's rationalization were sooner the result of Christian influence. The reformers were, after all, officially Orthodox Christians and had at least gone through the motions of Christian practice in the years leading up to their open "apostasy." Their knowledge and acceptance of the Old Testament could just as well have resulted from Christian influence, as from Islamic, especially given their greater contact and geographical proximity to Christians and the publication of religious books in Mari.[90]

---

[87] My attempt here to qualify the autonomy and consciousness of the reformers as agents and subjects of their own history draws on Talal Asad, *Genealogies of Religion: Discipline and Reasons of Power in Christianity and Islam* (Baltimore, 1993), esp. 7–17; and on Rosalind O'Hanlon in "Recovering the Subject: *Subaltern Studies* and Histories of Resistance in Colonial South Asia," *Modern Asian Studies* 22, no. 1 (1988): 189–224.

[88] See Martti Räsänen, "Die tatarischen Lehnwörter im Tscheremissischen," *Mémoires de la Société Finno-Ougrienne* 50 (1923).

[89] *Keremet'*, then, was a spirit that could produce miracles. See N. Zolotnitskii, "Nevidimyi mir po shamanskim vozzreniiam cheremis," *Uchenye zapiski Imperatorskago Kazanskago Universiteta* 4 (1877): 735–59; Il'ia Sofiiskii, "O keremetiakh kreshchennykh tatar Kazanskago kraia," *Izvestiia po Kazanskoi eparkhii* 24 (1877): 674; R. G. Akhmet'ianov, *Obshchaia leksika dukhovnoi kul'tury narodov srednego Povolzh'ia* (Moscow, 1981), 31–33.

[90] Although a fair number of religious texts had been published in meadow Mari by the 1880s (for a listing, see I. G. Ivanov, *Istoriia mariiskogo literaturnogo iazyka* (Ioshkar-Ola,

There is indeed considerable evidence of Christian influence in the reformers' own teachings. The notion of sin, for example, appears to have been a borrowing, since prior to the reform Maris had contemplated only deviation from ritual, which they had held to be a *mistake* lacking a moral component.[91] The notion of sin now permeated their religious conceptions and constituted the basis for the prohibitions enumerated above, and one of the basic reasons for Kugu Sorta prayer was to request forgiveness of sins from God. The reformers even continued to celebrate several important Christian holidays, such as Easter and Christmas, albeit in their own way and using their own names. As one of the reformers explained, "[W]e wish to celebrate that time in some way, in order not to remain far from other people and alien to them."[92] They recognized Christian saints as persons pleasing to God, although they considered it a sin to pray to them.[93] Their monotheism and the practice of praying for others also appear to have developed under Christian influence. The reactions of publicists to Kugu Sorta in this regard are telling, for most of them viewed the group's teachings as "a mixture of Christianity and paganism," or even held them to be "in essence Christian." One even asked rhetorically: "Does the worship of a single, supreme God, without making for oneself an idol, . . . still constitute paganism?"[94]

Beyond this direct Christian influence, the reformers also appropriated Russian religious discourse more generally, in order both to assert the difference between themselves and Christians, and to invest their teaching with greater legitimacy. For one, they explicitly used the word "pagan" (*iazycheskii*) as part of their self-designation. The local clergy and secular authorities, they explained, "constantly oppress us and persecute [us], not permitting *us pagans* to execute our religious obligations . . ."[95] Similarly, they at one point used the term *inovercheskii* to refer to their beliefs. While this Russian term can be conveniently translated as "non-Christian," in more literal terms it meant "a person of a different faith." From a strictly semantic perspective, therefore, this term could only be applied to

---

1975), 248–53), I unfortunately have little information on the distribution and appropriation of these texts by Maris. There may well have been a greater Islamic influence on Kugu Sorta than the existing sources allow me to surmise here. But it is worth noting that Russian authorities were at this time very worried about the spread of Islam and "Tatarness" among the Finnic peoples and presumably would not have hesitated to ascribe episodes like Kugu Sorta to Islam's "pernicious" influence if they thought this was the case.

[91] Kuznetsov, "Kugu sorta," 13.

[92] Koblov, "Cheremisskaia sekta 'Kugu Sorta,' " 536.

[93] Vasil'ev, *Mariiskaia religioznaia sekta "Kugu Sorta,"* 29.

[94] Citation from S——v, "Cheremisskoe iazycheskoe verouchenie 'Kugu Sorta,' " 736. See also D. Z., "Iazychestvo," 402; Koblov, "Cheremisskaia sekta 'Kugu-Sorta,'" 526; Baranov, "Otpavshie ot pravoslaviia," 218.

[95] RGIA, f. 796, op. 172, d. 2686, l. 4 (emphasis added).

someone *other* than oneself. But the reformers' use of it in this articulation demonstrates the extent to which Maris were now conceptualizing the religious terrain (or at least expressing themselves) in terms that the Russian state and Russian missionaries had established.

Their most remarkable appropriation from this discourse, however, concerned the terms "faith" and "religion." Over the course of the nineteenth century Maris had begun to use the Russian word for "faith" (*vera*) in their own language, and thus had come to call their own beliefs *marla vera*, or "Mari faith."[96] The very application of this new term to native belief systems suggests the beginnings of changes in Mari religious consciousness. The notion of faith, as introduced by Russians, must have seemed to Maris sufficiently new for them to use it not only with respect to Christianity, which after all was indeed new to them, but ultimately to their own beliefs as well. Yet it appears that Maris continued to conceptualize "faith" in their own idiosyncratic ways for the better part of the nineteenth century. It was the members of Kugu Sorta who openly asserted that their beliefs constituted "faith," in the sense of internal conviction and a concrete set of propositions about the relationship between humans and the spiritual world, as opposed to a set of ritual sacrifices demanded by the *keremet'* and similar spirits. The extent to which Kugu Sorta represented a break from the past is underscored by the Maris' use of the term "religion" (*religiia*) as well, which had *not* been applied to indigenous belief systems earlier, and was in fact a relatively recent introduction into the Russian language itself.[97] *Religiia*, more than *vera*, implied institutions and official recognition, structure, and coherence—in short, the major elements of rationalization. The reformers frequently used the

[96] This borrowing seems traceable to the early nineteenth century and was probably the result of increasing efforts to translate religious works into Mari at this time, for example a catechism in 1808 and the Gospel in 1821. A recent Mari etymological dictionary lists the term as a borrowing of the nineteenth century, but is not more specific. See F. I. Gordeev, ed., *Etimologicheskii slovar' mariiskogo iazyka*, vol. 2 (Ioshkar-Ola, 1983), 91. The first Mari grammar of 1775, *Sochineniia, prinadlezhashchie k grammatike cheremiskogo iazyka* (reprinted in facsimile as Thomas A. Sebeok and Alo Raun, eds., *The First Cheremis Grammar, 1775* [Chicago, 1956]), does not list the Russian word, but rather *inianymash* (*vera*, "faith") and *inianem* (*veriu*, "I believe"), which were themselves of Turkic origin. I. G. Ivanov notes that of the approximately one thousand Mari words presented in the 1775 grammar, only about 1 percent were borrowings from Russian. See Ivanov, *Istoriia mariiskogo literaturnogo iazyka*, 16. By 1808, a catechism designed for Maris of Nizhnii Novgorod province used *verem* as "I believe," and contained a significant number of other Russian borrowings. But whether these represented actual Mari usage at the time or an imposition of the work's author is unclear. See Ivanov, *Istoriia mariiskogo literaturnogo iazyka*, 21, as well as portions of the text itself in N. I. Il'minskii, *Opyt perelozheniia khristianskikh verouchitel'nykh knig na tatarskii i drugie inorodcheskie iazyki v nachale tekushchego stoletiia* (Kazan, 1885).

[97] The term *religiia* appears to have entered the Russian language from Polish by the early eighteenth century. See Max Vasmer *Etimologicheskii slovar' russkogo iazyka*, trans. O. N. Trubacheva, vol. 3 (Moscow, 1971), 466; and P. Ia. Chernykh, *Istoriko-etimologicheskii slovar' sovremennogo russkogo iazyka*, vol. 2 (Moscow, 1993), 109.

terms "faith" and "religion," sometimes combining the two to make sure the point got across: "[W]e will never betray our Faith and religion [*Vera i religiia*]."[98] To drive the point home completely, they almost always capitalized the term "Faith."

By using the terms "faith" and "religion" the reformers sought to assert the institutional and religious equality of their teaching with Christianity. They used the notion that their teachings constituted "faith" in order to argue for protection under the empire's laws on religious tolerance. These laws prohibited the use of force in the promotion of Orthodoxy and guaranteed to the adherents of all religions recognized by the state, including most indigenous religions, the right to worship without interference. At the same time, those laws prohibited conversion from Orthodoxy to any other faith—or, as church officials called it, "apostasy."[99] The reformers clearly were aware of these legal provisions. While the bishop of Viatka asserted that they had "a false understanding of religious tolerance" (since tolerance did not extend to "apostates"), in fact the reformers' understanding was considerably more sophisticated than that. The violation of religious tolerance, as they saw it, was rooted in the spurious baptism of their ancestors "through force or deceit."[100] Thus the reformers declared in one petition from their exile in Siberia:

> We understand perfectly well that if our ancestors had accepted Christianity voluntarily then [our] solicitation of permission to confess the faith "Kugu Sorta" would amount to a solicitation for permission of a crime, but the essence of the matter is that neither our great-grandfathers, nor our grandfathers, nor our fathers, nor we ourselves have ever entered Orthodoxy by free will, as we were pagans [in the past], we remain so to the present day.[101]

This last passage, especially when compared to some of the earlier statements, demonstrates that the reformers' argumentation was becoming more sophisticated. If in early petitions they struggled to express their ideas in awkward prose, the style of later petitions was more articulate and the ideas more complex. Most significantly, the reformers significantly broadened the range of justifications for their practice of Kugu Sorta. If previously they had pointed to their own "ruin" and their desire to remain "pure" Maris, then they subsequently claimed that local authorities, by persecuting them and confiscating their religious possessions, cause "harm and animosity" for society and state, "from which occur all kinds of

[98] RGIA, f. 796, op. 172, d. 2686, l. 68–68ob.
[99] *Svod Zakonov Rosisskoi Imperii* (1832), vol. 1, arts. 40, 44–45; vol. 10, art. 70; vol. 14, art. 73.
[100] RGIA, f. 796, op. 172, d. 2686, l. 34, 44.
[101] RGIA, f. 796, op. 172, d. 2686, l. 136. Petition from Tomsk, dated 16 March 1894, in the name of four of the exiles.

treason and misfortune in the Empire."[102] Thus while the clergy tried to portray Kugu Sorta as "harmful" (*zlovredna*) to the state, the reformers now articulated a response that conceived of state interest in different terms and offered a poignant diagnosis of the discontent afflicting the empire. Their focus on the wider consequences of such imperial misman-agement suggests that they were thinking in broader terms, even if only for the purpose of forwarding their own cause. In yet another petition, they argued that the confiscation of their religious goods was not only wrong, but also "not rational," since it punished their families as well as the reformers themselves.[103] From all this they concluded that "in re-straining [someone] in a Faith, or in converting [someone] from one [faith] to another, it is necessary to act through moral suasion [*deistvovat' na moral'nuiu storonu*], and all of this is completely the right and responsi-bility of the religious administration . . ." It was inappropriate, in other words, for the civil authorities to confiscate their religious artifacts in an affair concerned with *faith*.[104] In short, these were fairly complex argu-ments that required knowledge of Russian laws and conventions, under-standings of distinction between civil and religious realms of law, and a sense for the well-being of the empire as a whole.

In this respect, Kugu Sorta can be viewed as part of a process whereby Maris applied Russian-Christian concepts to themselves, and it demon-strates the extent to which religious rationalization for Maris—even when it came in the ostensible form of "internal conversion"—was based to a sig-nificant degree on Russian paradigms and modes of conceptual under-standing. Kugu Sorta represented a modernist understanding of faith, one that construed faith as a matter of "conscience" and inner conviction as much as religious practice, and one that attempted to draw a clear distinc-tion between religious and secular realms. It was for this reason that Kugu Sorta initiated an internal critique of the older animism by standards that the reformers had adopted from this Russian discourse. It was for this rea-son that they could hold their regular animist counterparts in disdain: it was less that the other animists had abandoned some ancient, pure and pristine ideal type of Mari beliefs—although the reformers themselves may truly have seen it this way—than that their practices did not measure up to the standards that the reformers had now adopted for themselves.

Lest the incorporation of the reformers into the Russian worldview seem too complete, however, there were also peculiarities that demon-

[102] RGIA, f. 796, op. 172, d. 2686, l. 950b.
[103] The amount of material confiscated was evidently great. A fairly large inventory of items was produced, and the reformers estimated the value of the confiscated goods at 9797 rubles and 77 kopecks (a curious sum that just happened to include the sacred numbers 7 and 9). RGIA, f. 796, op. 172, d. 2686, l. 1020b.
[104] RGIA, f. 796, op. 172, d. 2686, l. 105.

strate the reformers' desire to hold on to certain indigenous modes of religious understanding. In other words, Kugu Sorta was not just Christianity in Mari guise, and the emphatic assertion by the reformers of their non-Christian identity should be taken seriously. One of the more curious aspects of the various names the reformers gave to their teaching was the omnipresent use of the term "ritual" (*obriad*), often used in combination with the terms "faith" and "religion." Thus, the reformers wrote, at the Kazan exhibition they had been "representatives of our *faith and ritual.*" Or as they described their teachings at one point, "our pagan-ancient-Cheremis non-Christian holy *ritual and religion.*"[105] The contrast between ritual, as a set of concrete acts performed in a prescribed manner, and faith, as a set of beliefs internal to a person's constitution, would seem to highlight the contrast between Weber's theoretical model of "traditional" and rationalized religions. And it almost seems as though Maris themselves on one level understood this when they used both "faith" and "ritual" simultaneously to characterize their teaching. It was as if they wanted to elevate their beliefs to the level of "faith" and "religion," by the Russian understandings of these words, while at the same time retaining the ritualistic conception that made their beliefs unique and indigenous. They were trying, it would seem, to have it both ways.

While Kugu Sorta should be understood in the context of a very lengthy and complex process of syncretic change, the new teaching did represent a break with the "dual faith" more characteristic of Mari religious experience some decades earlier. At that time, Maris had been more religiously pluralistic, attending church one day and pagan sacrifices the next. They do not appear to have been troubled then by the "cognitive dissonance" in these different practices, but rather took an instrumental view of religion and were willing to try out techniques that seemed promising. The reformers of Kugu Sorta, on the other hand, embarked on an attempt to reconcile these different religious elements: the standards of Christianity, which included monotheism and exclusivity, and their own indigenous traditions, which they treasured as the basis for their ethnic identity and in whose efficacy they still had faith. Kugu Sorta, in other words, represented religious synthesis and integration rather than cultural mosaic.[106] This, then, was a transitional time in religious consciousness, when Maris were adopting more from Russian religious experience without themselves being fully aware that these processes were

[105] RGIA, f. 796, op. 172, d. 2686, ll. 4–50b (emphasis added).

[106] See the following discussions of syncretism: J. D. Y. Peel, "Syncretism and Religious Change," *Comparative Studies in Society and History* 10, no. 2 (1968): 121–41; Jerald Gort et. al., eds., *Dialogue and Syncretism: An Interdisciplinary Approach* (Grand Rapids, Mich., 1989); and Charles Stewart and Rosalind Shaw, eds., *Syncretism/Anti-Syncretism: The Politics of Religious Synthesis* (London, 1994). The term "cognitive dissonance" is Peel's ("Syncretism and Religious Change," 130).

under way. While contesting the idea of Christianity's universality, the reformers also accepted the standards and the discourse that Christianity had helped to establish. Kugu Sorta affirmed that syncretism may function in more than one way. On the one hand, it can be a form of resistance, since hegemonic practices are never simply absorbed wholesale and passively, but in part selectively and for particular purposes. But on the other hand, attempts to resist subordination with syncretized elements of the dominant language may be caught up in contradictions whereby the contested hegemonies are reasserted in another form.[107]

Not all Maris were interested in maintaining cultural differences between themselves and Russians; some strove instead to show that these differences had ceased to be relevant. Even in their own villages, the reformers did not achieve any kind of dominance, and it is worth underscoring that their exile was secured by a resolution (*prigovor*) passed by their local community. While the reformers contested this decision and claimed that the clergy and the trustees of their confiscated property had bribed and incited other villagers into voting for the exile, the outcome suggests that the reformers were unable to generate the solidarity among Maris needed to prevent the vote from occurring.[108]

By way of conclusion, I wish to offer two brief hypotheses concerning the particular ways that Russian understandings made their way into Mari consciousness. The first involves the growth of ethnography in Russia. While the state and clergy had previously shown comparatively little interest in the specific content of native beliefs and practices, around midcentury interest in these native belief systems grew immeasurably.[109] Partly this interest arose out of a new curiosity and desire to know the basic contours of the empire's population, but it also had to do with specifically missionary concerns—i.e., the notion that effective missionary work required a fuller understanding of native belief systems. Thus clergy and ethnographers (who were often one and the same) began to observe native religious practices and to ask non-Russians questions about their beliefs— questions that were determined by the ethnographers and not by the natives themselves. Natives were thus forced to answer these questions, to

[107] See Stewart and Shaw, "Introduction: Problematizing Syncretism," in *Syncretism/Anti-Syncretism*, 20–22.

[108] RGIA, f. 796, op. 172, d. 2686, ll. 137–54. In general, the passage of this resolution was characterized by irregularities. While the reformers accused the local clergy of bribery, Iakmanov himself was accused of having treated local Maris to vodka in order to prevent the peasant gathering from having the quorum needed to vote on the resolution. Meanwhile, the Ministry of Internal Affairs argued that the exile was itself improper, since cases of "apostasy" were supposed to be handled in the courts. RGIA, f. 796, op. 172, d. 2686, l. 132.

[109] On the emergence of ethnography as an independent discipline in Russia, see Nathaniel Knight, "Constructing the Science of Nationality: Ethnography in Mid-Nineteenth Century Russia" (Ph.D. diss., Columbia University, 1994), esp. 337–68 on the study of non-Slavic nationalities.

the best of their abilities or to the extent they wished to cooperate, in terms and circumstances not of their own choosing. More than likely, Maris had not understood or talked about these matters in the ways that ethnographers and clergy were now requesting them to do. There had not been a theology, as such, since there was no need for one. Everyone understood the beliefs (albeit in his or her own way) and experienced religiosity in ways that differed from those prescribed by official Orthodoxy.

More concretely, the reformers were required to defend themselves from the accusations of the clergy—accusations that quickly produced a court case and led to the confiscation of their property and the threat of exile. In producing the new religion and above all in presenting it to outsiders, the reformers had to adopt certain basic elements of the Russian religious and ethnographic discourse which they then applied to their beliefs, thereby transforming them. Thus in their defense—undertaken in court, at the Kazan exhibition, and in petitions to the emperor—the reformers were required to make the new teaching intelligible to outsiders and to explain how their teaching differed from the older paganism *on the terms of the outsiders*, rather than on their own. This very act necessitated the greater codification and conceptual generalization that Geertz associates with rationalization. This may have been the first time that Maris had actually attempted to explicate the relationships between different spiritual entities and practices that characterized their beliefs, in such a way that these could make sense to, and ultimately generate sympathy with, the emperor, or the district court, or "Russian society." Needless to say, the reformers were selective and calculating in deciding how to present their beliefs. But the presentation itself had a transformative effect on the teaching; it was not merely representational, but productive of new understandings, outlooks, and modes of consciousness as well. Thus even the selective appropriation of Russian concepts and understandings affected those beliefs as they were presented.

Thus, the members of Kugu Sorta forged their identity and their beliefs not just prior to dealings with Russian authorities and society, but precisely through those dealings. In short, their identity was constructed and refracted through practice. Clearly Maris were able to use elements of the prevailing Russian conceptions to their own advantage. Their appropriation of the idea of "faith" allowed them to counter the demands of the Orthodox clergy, and their cultivation of the conviction that they were protected by the laws of the empire strengthened their resolve, even in the years of exile. Yet however much these internalized norms became a basis for resistance and a source for the construction of a Mari alternative to Christianity, the adherents of Kugu Sorta remained a part of the dominant culture and its discourse. Mari "internal conversion," occurring as it did within the Russian empire, was shaped by both social conditions and a discursive milieu not entirely of Maris' own making.

CHAPTER SEVEN

Russian Orthodox Missionaries at Home and Abroad: The Case of Siberian and Alaskan Indigenous Peoples

SERGEI KAN

The Russian Orthodox Church has always considered proselytizing activities among the indigenous peoples of Siberia as one of the most important aspects of its missionary endeavor.[1] From the fourteenth century to the 1917 revolution, Orthodox clergymen made repeated attempts to replace "pagan" religions of Siberian natives with Christianity. After the establishment of the Russian presence in Alaska in the eighteenth century, the Orthodox mission extended its reach across the Bering Straits. In their work, the clergy were confronted not only with severe weather and huge distances between settlements, but with a wide linguistic and cultural gap between themselves and the indigenous peoples, or *inorodtsy*.

Within the Russian Orthodox missionary tradition, two different approaches to evangelization can be identified. The first favored a more forceful elimination of "pagan" religions and emphasized the missionar-

---

[1] Many of the arguments presented in this paper are further elaborated in my monograph on the history of Orthodoxy among the Tlingit of southeastern Alaska: Sergei Kan, *Memory Eternal: Tlingit Culture and Russian Orthodox Christianity through Two Centuries* (Seattle, 1999); also cf. Kan, "Russian Orthodox Brotherhoods among the Tlingit: Missionary Goals and Native Response," *Ethnohistory* 32, no. 3 (1985): 196–223; idem, "Memory Eternal: Russian Orthodoxy and the Tlingit Mortuary Complex," *Arctic Anthropology* 24, no. 1 (1987): 32–55; idem, "Recording Native Culture and Christianizing the Natives—Russian Orthodox Missionaries in Southeastern Alaska," in *Russia in North America: Proceedings of the 2nd International Conference on Russian America*, ed. R. Pierce (Kingston, Ont., 1990), 298–313; idem, "Russian Orthodox Missionaries and the Tlingit of Alaska, 1880–1900," in *New Dimensions in Ethnohistory: Papers of the Second Laurier Conference on Ethnohistory and Ethnology*, ed. B. Gough and L. Christie, Canadian Ethnology Service, Mercury Series Paper 120 (Ottawa, 1991); idem, "The Russian Orthodox Church in Alaska," in W. Washburn, ed. *Handbook of North American Indians*, vol. 4: *History of Indian-White Relations* (Washington, D.C., 1988), 506–21.

ies' role as both messengers of the Word of God and representatives of the Russian state whose job included introducing natives to the Russian language and culture and thus speeding up their incorporation into the Russian empire. The second approach stressed the importance of a more gradual and cautious missionization, which included tolerating the less objectionable indigenous customs (at least temporarily) and using native languages in communicating with the new converts and in the church service. This latter tradition drew on the legacy of SS. Cyril and Methodius, who used a vernacular language to bring the Gospel to the Slavs,[2] and the experience of the Russian clerics who had been obliged to tolerate some of the pre-Christian beliefs and practices of the Orthodox Russian peasants.[3] It also emphasized the need for missionaries to distance themselves somewhat from the local secular Russian authorities and not to identify Christianization with Russification. Adherents of this approach were particularly conscious of the need to discourage converts from accepting "harmful" Russian customs, on the one hand, and abandoning "useful" indigenous economic and social traditions, on the other.

The focus of this essay is the Orthodox missionary work in Alaska. Missionary work in Siberia remains largely beyond the scope of this work and serves mostly as a point of comparison.[4] For instance, in contrast to the enormous territory of its Siberian counterpart, the Orthodox mission in Alaska was confined mainly to coastal areas and interacted with only a few indigenous peoples, such as the Aleuts, the Pacific Yup'iks (Alutiiq), the Yup'iks of the Kuskokwim and the Nushagak rivers, the Athapaskans of

[2] See Michael J. Oleksa, *Orthodox Alaska: A Theology of Mission* (Crestwood, N.Y., 1992).

[3] B. A. Rybakov, *Iazychestvo Drevnei Rusi* (Moscow, 1987).

[4] There are several reasons why I discuss Siberia only briefly. First, the three-hundred-year-old Siberian mission operated in very diverse geographical areas, from the Ural Mountains to Chukotka Peninsula, and dealt with a variety of indigenous societies and cultures, many of them radically different from each other. Secondly, the number of serious and relatively unbiased scholarly publications on the Orthodox missionization of Siberia is small. Most of the prerevolutionary Russian works on the subject were written by the clergy and their lay sympathizers or by the church's staunch social critics. The majority of the pre-1917 ethnographers were much more concerned with the study of the "traditional" elements in the culture of the indigenous Siberians than with documenting the effects of Christianization on it. The same is true of most Soviet scholars, who tended to see manifestations of Christianity in the native Siberian cultures as "superficial," destined for rapid extinction, and not particularly worthy of serious scholarly investigation. One major exception is a collection of essays edited by I. S. Vdovin: *Khristianstvo i lamaism u korennogo naseleniia Sibiri* (Leningrad, 1979). See also I. I. Ogryzko, *Khristianizatsiia narodov Tobol'skogo Severa v XVIII v.* (Leningrad, 1941). As one of the authors in the Vdovin collection admitted, studying indigenous Christianity in the field had never been part of his research agenda; see E. A. Alekseenko, "Khristianizatsiia na Turukhanskom Severe i eio vliianie na mirovozzrenie i religioznye kul'ty ketov," in Vdovin, *Khristianstvo i lamaism,* 51. One would hope that in the post-Soviet era more careful and less biased works on the subject would appear; however, so far only a few publications have come out, several of them marked by a renewed patriotic and nationalist bias. See, e.g., A. D. Dridzo and R. B. Kinzhalov, eds., *Russkaia Amerika* (Moscow, 1994).

the Kenai Peninsula, the Tlingit of southeastern Alaska, and a few other smaller groups. Compared to the Siberian mission, the Alaskan one was much more cohesive. It traced its origins to a single group of monks who had come from the Valaam monastery in Russia in the late eighteenth century and for much of the nineteenth century, the mission bore a stamp of the ideas and activities of a single missionary thinker and organizer, Ivan Veniaminov. Unlike the archival records of the Siberian mission, which are stored in various locations throughout Russia, those of the Alaskan mission, which were well represented in the documents that remained in the United States after Russia's sale of Alaska, are mostly concentrated in a single archive, the so-called Alaska Russian Church Archive.[5]

While my comparison of the Siberian with the Alaskan missions remains tentative, several propositions and hypotheses are presented here. First, I argue that the more tolerant approach to missionization seems to have been more prominent in Alaska than in Siberia, where the state tended to exercise greater control over the indigenous peoples and where the church often directly promoted the state's interests. Secondly, this essay demonstrates that missionization is both a sociopolitical and an ideological process and cannot be properly understood without an analysis of the wider colonial endeavor and the missionizers' culture.[6] In Alaska, the central role in this endeavor was taken by the Russian-American Company (RAC) as the sole agent of Russian colonialism between 1799 and 1867 and, after the sale of Alaska, by the American government and the Protestant missionaries who competed with their Orthodox rivals for native converts. With the exception of the Aleuts and the Kodiak Alutiiqs who were in the RAC's service, other native Alaskans remained rather independent from the company, a fact that makes their conversion and especially their continued loyalty to the Orthodox Church after 1867 particularly interesting. Finally, this essay demonstrates that an ethnohistory (or a cultural history) of Christianization must also pay careful attention to the culture of the missionized and their perceptions of and attitudes toward the missionizers.

---

[5] The original documents of the Alaska Russian Church Archives are located in the Library of Congress; copies are available on microfilm. Another important body of documents dealing with the Orthodox mission in Alaska is the M. Vinokouroff Collection, located in the Alaska State Historical Library in Juneau. Over the years I have also been able to consult documents located in the local parish archives of the Alaska Diocese of the Orthodox Church in America, particularly those of Sitka and Juneau.

[6] Cf. Jean Comaroff and John Comaroff, *Of Revelation and Revolution: Christianity, Colonialism and Consciousness in South Africa*, vol. 1 (Chicago, 1991); Robert Hefner, ed., *Conversion to Christianity: Historical and Anthropological Perspectives on a Great Transformation* (Berkeley, Calif., 1993).

Russian Orthodox Missionaries and the Conquest of Siberia

Standard histories of Russian missionary work usually begin with an account of the life of St. Stefan of Perm who in the late fourteenth century volunteered to preach the Gospel to the Komi people near the Urals.[7] With the conquest of Siberia in the sixteenth and seventeenth centuries, Orthodox missionary activities spread all the way to the far eastern border of the state.

Since the acquisition of valuable furs was the main objective behind the Russians' rapid eastward expansion, the delivery of an annual tribute in furs, known as *iasak*, was imposed on most of the indigenous Siberians. In addition to its important economic function, this tribute was also seen by Moscow as a "tangible manifestation of the natives' subject status vis-à-vis the Russian suzerain."[8] *Iasak* was a heavy burden on many of the natives and various forms of resistance against it took place, from complaints to central authorities to actual warfare. Of course, in order to remain good producers of *iasak*, the *inorodtsy* had to be allowed to continue their hunting way of life. Consequently, with few exceptions, there was little effort to interfere with or modify their economy, social organization, or religion.[9]

Another method of symbolically affirming the suzerain-subject relationship between Russia and the native peoples was the taking of hostages (*amanat*) from among the local elite. This action also served as a guarantee against the natives' possible violations of peace treaties.[10] While hostage taking had been practiced by indigenous Siberians prior to the

[7] The standard histories of the Russian church's missionary activities are E. Smirnoff, *A Short Account of the Historical Development and Present Position of Russian Orthodox Missions* (London, 1903); Sergei Bolshakoff, *The Foreign Missions of the Russian Orthodox Church* (London, 1943); Josef P. Glazik, *Die russisch-orthodoxe Heidenmission seit Peter dem Grossen* (Münster, 1954). Two recent American studies offering a detailed discussion of the Russian colonization of Siberia, including missionization, are James Forsyth, *A History of the Peoples of Siberia: Russia's North Asian Colony, 1581–1990* (Cambridge, 1992) and Yuri Slezkine, *Arctic Mirrors: Russia and the Small Peoples of the North* (Ithaca, N.Y., 1994); see also Richard Pierce's survey article, "Russian and Soviet Eskimo and Indian Policies," in Washburn, *Handbook of North American Indians*, 4:119–27. For a Soviet perspective on Orthodox missionization, see Vdovin, *Khristianstvo i lamaism*, and for a recent American evaluation of the Orthodox Church's missionary policies in the sixteenth through the eighteenth centuries, see Michael Khodarkovsky, "The Conversion of Non-Russians in Early Modern Russia," in this volume.

[8] Michael Khodarkovsky, "From Frontier to Empire: the Concept of the Frontier in Russia, Sixteenth–Eighteenth Centuries," *Russian History* 18, nos. 1–4 (1992): 115–28. Khodarkovsky makes an interesting argument that since the Russians usually feasted and distributed various compensatory gifts to the deliverers of furs, the latter might have interpreted *iasak* not as a symbolic statement of their subordination to the newcomers but as a gift exchange or a form of trade.

[9] Forsyth, *History of the Peoples of Siberia*; Pierce, "Russian and Soviet Eskimo and Indian Policies."

[10] Khodarkovsky, "From Frontier to Empire," 122; Pierce, "Russian and Soviet Eskimo and Indian Policies," 118–19.

Russian conquest and hence made sense to them, mistreatment and neglect of hostages did provoke resistance, at least in the early era of native-
Russian interaction. These hostages, who spent considerable periods of
time living in the Russian forts, were among the first natives to be baptized, with the ceremony often performed by the laity rather than the
clergy. Attempts to ensure peace with the local population included not
only hostage taking but the courting of native leaders by means of gift giving and feasting. The fact that baptism was accompanied by lavish gifts
and feasts made it quite attractive to the local elite, even though the
meaning of this ritual was rather vague to them.

Another category of early converts were the native wives and concu-
bines of the Cossacks. By baptizing them, the Russians transformed them
from aliens (*inorodtsy*) into "subjects" of the Russian state, thus also giving greater legitimacy to the children born of these relationships. In addition, natives who became slaves or indentured servants of the Russians
were also often baptized. Because the law required that the baptized *inorodtsy* were to be exempt from paying *iasak*, however, until the eighteenth century the state did not encourage mass baptism of Siberian
aborigines.[11]

Missionary work received a new impetus under Peter I who saw civilizing his non-Russian subjects as an important task of the state. Thus in
1702 the new Siberian metropolitan, Filofei Leshchinskii, received the
emperor's permission to convert the *iasak*-paying peoples without lifting
their tribute obligations. Four years later Leshchinskii traveled to the
Khanty people in Western Siberia to "burn down their idols" and baptize
them "big and small."[12] Many Khanty and Mansi trying to escape conversion and assault on their beliefs took their sacred effigies and hid them
deep in the woods. Some, provoked by the desecration of their sanctuar-
ies, resorted to violence; in 1717 they murdered an Orthodox official in
charge of new converts in the Konda region. Yet the government policies
of carrots (gifts, rewards, and temporary exemption from *iasak*) and sticks
induced many to accept baptism.[13]

At the same time, Peter I was the first Russian ruler to argue that the
non-Christians had to be introduced to Orthodoxy beyond the mere baptismal ritual, and he ordered the Synod to find missionaries who could
learn local languages, translate the Bible, live among the *inorodtsy*, and
teach them the Scriptures. Some indigenous Siberians were even sent to

---

[11] Slezkine, *Arctic Mirrors*, 11–45.

[12] A 1710 ukase by the emperor to the new metropolitan proclaimed that those interfering with and opposing evangelization of the Siberian natives would be subject to the death
penalty. See P. P. Liubimov, "Religiia i veroispovednyi sostav naseleniia Aziatskoi Rossii," in
Aziatskaia Rossiia, ed. G. V. Glinka, vol. 1. (St. Petersburg, 1914), 208.

[13] Forsyth, *History of the Peoples of Siberia*, 154; Slezkine, *Arctic Mirrors*, 49.

St. Petersburg to be educated there, and schools were set up in some local monasteries to teach the natives' children the rudiments of Christianity and the Russian language.[14]

Educating the natives, however, remained a remote ideal, and direct and brutal attacks on "pagan" religious practices were far more common. Aggressive conversion reached its peak in the 1740s and was abated only during the reign of Catherine II. The empress abolished most of the privileges once granted to the natives converting to Orthodoxy. She also confiscated many of the lands owned by Siberian monasteries, further weakening these major centers of missionary activity.[15]

The most enlightened document dealing with the state's treatment of the Siberian natives was drafted in 1822 by Alexander I's reform-minded governor of Siberia, Mikhail Speranskii. Speranskii's statutes for governing indigenous Siberians emphasized indirect rule (i.e., reliance on local elites) and placed many of them into a category of "not fully dependent aliens" who were granted substantial freedom in running their own affairs. The statutes also encouraged local Orthodox clergymen not to interfere in the internal affairs of the *inorodtsy*, and to convert by persuasion alone. However, the Speranskii statutes could not be fully enforced and the natives continued to languish, abused by local officials and clergy and ignorant of the Russian laws.[16] In the early 1880s, one critic of the early nineteenth-century government policies toward aboriginal Siberians wrote:

> The old self-government system was disappearing, the old social union was crumbling; no new one was being created, and the natives were like a herd terrorized by the local police. . . . neither the monarch's decrees, nor legislation, nor Speranskii's humane constitution, nor fear of the law, nor the stirrings of human conscience have succeeded in protecting the native and enforcing respect for his human rights.[17]

The government itself soon returned to more oppressive and conservative policies toward Siberia's indigenous population. St. Petersburg began to view with suspicion the church's attempts to translate the scriptures into the indigenous languages of the empire. Twelve years after the Russian Bible Society was established in 1812, the government criticized it for

---

[14] Vdovin, *Kristianstvo i lamaism*, 3–11; Khodarkovsky, "Conversion," 131; Liubimov, "Religiia i veroispovednyi sostav," 200–225.

[15] Forsyth, *History of the Peoples of Siberia*, 155; Liubimov, "Religiia i veroispovednyi sostav," 213–14.

[16] Forsyth, *History of the Peoples of Siberia*, 156–157; Slezkine, *Arctic Mirrors*, 83–88.

[17] N. M. Iadrintsev, *Sibir' kak koloniia* (St. Petersburg, 1882), 108.

translating the Bible and Christian prayers into "non-Christian" languages and ordered it shut down.[18]

Repeatedly, church officials pointed to the state of indigenous Christianization as "superficial" and its pace as "slow." They frequently lamented the widespread "return to paganism" and *dvoeverie* ("double faith," or a mixture of pre-Christian and Christian beliefs) and referred to the Orthodox *inorodtsy* as "Christians practicing paganism" (*iazychestvuiushchie khristiane*).[19] On the whole, the Russian church's proselytizing activities in Siberia were much more modest than those of either the Catholic or the various Protestant churches in the New World, and adherence to Orthodoxy in many cases appears to have been nominal at best.

Russian Expansion into Alaska and the Orthodox Church

The "discovery" of Alaska in 1741 was a natural consequence of Russia's eastward march toward the Pacific Ocean. A rush of hunters and traders (*promyshlenniki*) from Siberia to the Aleutian Islands began when the survivors of the second Bering expedition brought back with them fifteen hundred sea otter pelts, which they sold at the Chinese trading post near Lake Baikal for nearly one thousand rubles each. While the Russian government was preoccupied with European ventures and unable to invest the resources and manpower for expanding into America, Siberian merchants quickly seized the new opportunity to make a handsome profit. Backed by private companies organized in Irkutsk and Okhotsk, parties of *promyshlenniki* moved from island to island in the Aleutian chain and in 1762 reached the Alaska Peninsula.[20]

The peoples encountered by the Russians in the Aleutians had a rather complex social organization and had been engaged in sophisticated warfare prior to the Russian "discovery." However, the fact that they had inferior weapons, were occupying relatively defenseless villages scattered over a series of islands, and were divided into quite distinct kinship groups and

---

[18] Vdovin, *Khristianstvo i lamaism,* 5.

[19] *Eniseiskie Eparkhial'nye Vedomosti,* 1886, no. 12:161; V. V. Soliarskii, *Sovremennoe pravovoe i kul'turno-ekonomicheskoe polozhenie inorodtsev Priamurskogo Kraia* (Khabarovsk, 1916). See also E. E. Alekseenko, "Khristianizatsiia na Turukhanskom Severe i ee vliianie na mirovozzrenie i religioznye kul'ty ketov," as well as several other chapters in Vdovin, *Khristianstvo i lamaism;* Liubimov, "Religiia i veroispovednyi sostav," 233; Oleg Kobtzeff, "La colonisation russe en Amérique du Nord, 18e–19e siècles" (Ph.D. diss., University of Paris 1, 1984).

[20] Russian penetration of the Aleutians tended to follow a pattern of exploiting one group of islands of the chain until the supply of animals became exhausted, and then moving eastward to the next group, eventually reaching the mainland. See Margaret Lantis, "Aleut," in *Handbook of North American Indians,* vol. 5: *Arctic,* ed. D. Damas (Washington, D.C., 1984), 161–84.

residential units meant that their resistance could not prevent the new-comers from establishing their domination over the area.[21] Some of the Russian-Aleut encounters were friendly and involved exchanges of gifts and feasting, while others were hostile, with the Russians capturing native women and supplies. Seeing the success of the Russian traders in the Aleutians, the government instructed the *promyshlenniki* to obtain *iasak* from the Aleuts (Unangan), thus bringing to the New World the same pattern that had characterized Russian-native relations in Siberia. Russian sovereignty over the Unangan was also marked by the taking of hostages to ensure peace.[22]

In the 1740s to 1760s most of the sea otter hunting and some fox trap-ping was done by the Russians themselves. However, by the mid-1760s Aleut men were forced to devote much of their time and energy to procuring sea otters for the various independent fur-trading companies. Government regulations prohibiting the abuse of Aleuts, including force-ful resettlement, tended to be ignored by most of the independent skip-pers. In addition to treating the Aleuts as their subordinate serf-like pop-ulation, Russian commercial companies used them as an auxiliary military force in confrontations with the Alutiiq (Pacific Yup'ik) people of Kodiak, and eventually also with the Tlingit. All of these activities contributed to a serious decline of the Aleut population.[23]

The *promyshlenniki* began to baptize the Unangan early and for various reasons: some out of piety, others out of a need to establish peaceful rela-tionships. Among the first baptized Aleuts were women living with Rus-sians and children born from these alliances. Settling down and intermar-rying with natives were rather common for the *promyshlenniki*, who were usually of low social classes and indigenous Siberian ancestry. For ex-ample, a *promyshlennik* named Glotov reached the Fox Islands in 1759 and stayed there for three years, baptizing many of the Aleuts and instructing

[21] Nevertheless on several occasions, for example in 1761 on Inalak Island, the Unangan managed to annihilate large numbers of *promyshlenniki*. See Oleksa, *Orthodox Alaska*, 85–86.

[22] In fact, the Russians borrowed many terms derived from their earlier interaction with in-digenous Siberians to describe the lifeways of native Alaskans, such as *toion* for "chief," and *barabora* for "native dwelling." Lantis, "Aleut"; Douglas W. Veltre, "Perspectives on Aleut Cul-ture Change during the Russian Period," in *Russian America: The Forgotten Frontier*, ed. B. S. Smith and R. Barnett (Tacoma, Wash., 1990), 175–83.

[23] While the extent of the Russian mistreatment of Aleuts and its negative effect on Aleut population figures remain a hotly debated topic, Lantis and Veltre make a persuasive argu-ment that there was an 80 percent decline in the indigenous population in the first two gen-erations of the era of Russian domination, i.e., between the middle of the eighteenth cen-tury and the 1790s when Shelikhov's Russian-American Company gained control (Lantis, "Aleut," 180–83; Douglas W. Veltre, "Perspectives," 177–81). See also Lydia Black, *Atka: An Ethnohistory of the Western Aleutians* (Kingston, Ont., 1984); Oleksa, *Orthodox Alaska*, 81–93; S. A. Mousalimas, *The Transition from Shamanism to Russian Orthodoxy in Alaska* (Providence, R.I., 1995), 27–82.

them in the rudiments of Christianity.[24] Likewise, many Aleuts welcomed the opportunity to establish a client-patron relationship with their Russian godfathers and to improve their lot. During an era of labor shortages and competition among fur-trading companies, baptized natives represented a submissive and reliable labor force.

By 1770, when the cost of outfitting expeditions to increasingly distant places had driven smaller companies out of business, a few stronger companies had come to dominate the Alaska fur trade. Of all the Russian companies operating in the area, one headed by Shelikhov and Golikov proved most successful. In 1784 Shelikhov established a settlement on Kodiak island and named it Three Saints Bay. Alternately using brute force and generous gifts, he skillfully exploited intervillage and intertribal enmities and recruited male Kodiak Islanders as hunters and fighters against hostile neighbors. Shelikhov encouraged marriages between Russian men and Alutiiq women and began baptizing the local people: children of mixed marriages, native women, and hostages. He also established a school on the island where the native children were taught literacy, navigation, and the basic precepts of Christianity.[25]

During this time the government in St. Petersburg began to take a closer interest in "Russian America." The newly enthroned Empress Catherine II proclaimed that the inhabitants of the Aleutians were Russian subjects and issued decrees terminating their *iasak* payments and demanding their better treatment. In petitions to the government in the 1780s, Shelikhov, seeking to win imperial patronage and receive a monopoly, emphasized the Alaskans' willingness to be baptized.[26] He asked that a clerical mission or at least a priest be assigned to the Aleutian Islands and Kodiak, and that his best students be permitted to study for the priesthood in the Irkutsk seminary in Eastern Siberia, and agreed to bear the expenses involved in maintaining churches. In a far-reaching proposal Shelikhov also described how his company would establish permanent Russian settlements on the islands, how Russian ships would supply these settlements and bring back furs, and how these settlements would become part of the Russian empire.[27]

---

[24] Ivan Veniaminov, *Notes on the Islands of the Unalashka District*, trans. L. T. Black and R. H. Geoghegan (Kingston, Ont., [1840] 1984), 233–34.

[25] Mousalimas, *The Transition from Shamanism*, 44–63.

[26] The chaplain of the Joseph Billings expedition reported that traveling in 1790–91 along the range of the Fox Islands and Unalaska and on the western side of Kodiak Island, he baptized over a hundred natives, some of whom had already accepted Christianity from the *promyshlenniki*, and married four couples. Gregory Afonsky, *A History of the Orthodox Church in Alaska (1794–1918)* (Kodiak, Alaska, 1994), 18; see also Mary E. Wheeler, "The Russian American Company and the Imperial Government: Early Phase," in *Russia's American Colony*, ed. S. Frederick Starr (Durham, N.C., 1987), 43–62.

[27] Wheeler, "The Russian American Company," 45.

In 1790 Alexander Baranov, a person with considerable experience in various mercantile enterprises in Siberia, became chief manager of Shelikhov's North American enterprise. He brought some order and discipline into the ranks of the *promyshlenniki* and into the company's operations, and showed genuine, if paternalistic, concern for his workers —Russian and non-Russian alike. Under the new chief manager, the use of native labor increased significantly, as many Russian northerners and Siberians returned home unhappy with the difficult living conditions in Alaska.

Baranov continued to treat his employees in the same authoritarian manner as his predecessors in Alaska and Siberia. He used brutal methods to maintain discipline; lashing and running the gauntlet were common practice for native and Russian workers alike. To maximize profit, he also began sending native hunting crews to obtain sea otter pelts further away from their home territory, where the risk of losing life to a storm, a hostile attack, or food poisoning increased. Baranov became a virtual dictator on Kodiak and other Russian establishments in Alaska. But excessive violence and disregard for natives' hunting grounds and ancestral territories led some Alaskans to rebel against the company. The natives found allies in a missionary party that arrived in the 1790s.

Shelikhov's request for clergymen to be sent to Alaska had been received favorably by Catherine II and the Holy Synod. The government had agreed to establish a separate see in America and appoint a prelate, subordinate to Irkutsk diocese, with the new title of bishop of Kodiak. St. Petersburg awarded about four thousand rubles annually for the upkeep of the bishop; additional funds were supposed to be provided by the Shelikhov-Golikov company. In 1793 Metropolitan Gabriel of St. Petersburg selected a group of ten monks and two novices to travel to Kodiak under the direction of Archimandrite Iosaf Bolotov.[28] These missionaries came from the Valaam Monastery in northern Russia, known for its emphasis on spirituality, simplicity, and strict discipline.[29]

On their way to Kodiak the missionaries baptized over one hundred Aleuts in Unalaska and consecrated the first Alaskan Orthodox Church in St. Paul's Harbor. In 1795 Iosaf reported that on Kodiak, the nearby islands, and the Alaska Peninsula 6,740 natives (mostly Unangan and Alutiiq) had been baptized. In the same year Hieromonk Iuvenalii baptized 700 Alutiiq (Chugach Yup'ik) of Prince William Sound, and from there

[28] *The Russian Orthodox Religious Mission in America, 1794–1837*, trans. Colin Bearne, ed. Richard A. Pierce (1894; reprint ed., Kingston, Ont., 1978); Afonsky, *History of the Orthodox Church*, 16–39; Mousalimas, *The Transition from Shamanism*, 212–13 n. 2.

[29] The Russian Orthodox Church considers the arrival of this group of monks on Kodiak on 24 September 1794 the beginning of its first overseas mission and the start of its mission in Alaska.

went to the Kenai Peninsula, where a substantial number of Tanaina Athapaskans were brought into the church. In the meantime, Fr. Makarii labored with the Aleutians, baptizing 2,442 persons and performing 536 marriages, including 36 between Russians and Aleutians.[30]

When the missionaries arrived in Kodiak, they were shocked by what they perceived as the "wild frontier" atmosphere of Baranov's rule. They were particularly incensed by the *promyshlenniki*'s "immoral" behavior and the various forms of mistreatment of native hunters. The missionaries also tried to establish a parish school on Kodiak and argued that the best of the native students should be taught religious subjects in preparation for becoming clergymen in Alaska. Instead of sending these young people to Russia, they suggested, a religious school or even a seminary should be established on Kodiak.[31] Soon Fr. Iosaf began complaining to the government about Baranov and Shelikhov. Angered by their criticism and especially their attempts to defend the natives and even incite them against him, Baranov threatened the missionaries with arrest and expulsion back to Russia.[32] Such defense of the natives had rarely occurred in Siberia. The fact that the missionaries were criticizing private management rather than state officials, the unsettled nature of the Russian colony in America, and Baranov's crude and violent methods may explain the missionaries' unusual courage in trying to stem the abuse of the natives.[33]

Apparently, these complaints fell on deaf ears in St. Petersburg. In 1799 an imperial decree granted the company a monopoly, thus chartering the Russian-American Company. Placed "under the supreme protection of His Imperial Majesty," the company was given the sole right to trade in and administer the newly discovered region for the next twenty years.[34] The colonial system created by the charter of 1799 resembled those of the Hudson's Bay Company and the British East India Company. The RAC became the only representative of the crown within the designated area and exercised quasi-governmental authority.[35]

---

[30] Kan, "The Russian Orthodox Church," 506–7.

[31] Oleksa, *Orthodox Alaska*, 106–18.

[32] He was particularly incensed by Father Makarii's criticism of his employees' activities in Unalaska, where the priest had been laboring since 1796. Eventually, Father Makarii organized and led an Aleut delegation to relate the abuses of the Aleut people to Emperor Paul in St. Petersburg.

[33] A modern-day church historian attributes the boldness of Alaskan missionaries to an old Orthodox tradition of the monastic's "right and obligation to intercede with secular authorities on behalf of the poor and the persecuted" (Oleksa, *Orthodox Alaska*, 106).

[34] Tikhmenev, *A History of the Russian-American Company*, 2 vols. (Seattle and Kingston, Ont., 1978–79), 1:41–61.

[35] Pierce, "Russian and Soviet Eskimo and Indian Policies," 121. One significant difference between the RAC and the main Western European colonial commercial companies was the fact that the former did not receive any contribution from the Russian government. In contrast, the British government contributed 20 percent to the East India Company's capital. See Wheeler, "The Russian American Company," 61.

The company's 1799 charter did not contain elaborate or definitive regulations on the status of the Alaska natives. Consequently Baranov established his own strict order under which the Unangan and the Alutiiq people came under the company's paternalistic control. Thus all able-bodied men and women were required to perform work for the company: service in sea otter hunting teams, bird hunting, fox trapping, or the like. Some provisions and reimbursement for these native employees were provided by the company. As with the Unangan, the company's exploitation of the Alutiiq people and their dispersal over coastal Alaska disrupted the traditional way of life and resulted in a substantial population decline.[36]

In 1798 Archimandrite Iosaf returned to Siberia to be consecrated as a bishop, but a year later on the return voyage to his new diocese in Alaska he and most members of the Kodiak mission perished in a shipwreck. The two priests and two monks who remained on Kodiak continued to criticize Baranov's and the RAC's mistreatment of the natives. In 1804, in response to their collective memorandum concerning abuses, the Holy Synod sent one Hieromonk Gideon to investigate the situation and to revive missionary activities in Russian America. Despite his instructions to maintain cooperative relations with RAC officials, Gideon added his strong voice to the earlier criticisms of Baranov's policies in the company.[37] Gideon stayed in Kodiak between 1804 and 1807 and achieved some cooperation between the clergy and the company. He organized a two-grade school for native children where he taught literacy, Christianity, history, geography, and several other secular subjects. By 1807 the school had enrolled one hundred students students and was maintained by the RAC.[38] By that time the RAC's center of operations had shifted to Novoarkhangel'sk (Sitka), in the heart of Tlingit territory. Orthodox missionary activities in Alaska, with the exception of Kodiak, gained new momentum only in the 1820s with the arrival of Fr. Ivan Veniaminov.

The Veniaminov Era, 1820s–1867

Fr. Ivan (Ioann) Popov (Veniaminov) (1797–1871), was undoubtedly the most important figure in the history of the Russian Orthodox mission in Alaska. It was his vision and labor that were largely responsible for the establishment of the Alaska diocese, with him as its first bishop. This son of a rural Siberian church sexton ended his career occupying the most in-

[36] Donald W. Clark, "Pacific Eskimo: Historical Ethnography," in Damas, *Handbook of North American Indians* 5:185–87.

[37] Dridzo and Kinzhalov, *Russkaia Amerika*, 33–39.

[38] Hieromonk Gideon, *The Round the World Voyage of Hieromonk Gideon, 1803–1809*, trans. Lydia T. Black, ed. Richard A. Pierce (1894; reprint ed., Kingston, Ont., 1989).

fluential ecclesiastical office in nineteenth-century Russia—that of the Metropolitan of Moscow.[39] A charismatic priest, an outstanding scholar, and an astute politician, Veniaminov tried to rely on a more enlightened approach to missionization, which had been advocated by some of his superiors and teachers in Irkutsk but had rarely been put into practice in Siberia.[40] Born in Irkutsk province, Ivan Popov in 1806 entered the Irkutsk seminary, a major center of clerical education in Siberia, whose many graduates served as parish priests and missionaries in Siberia and Alaska. Despite his humble social background, Popov (whose last name was changed to Veniaminov in 1814 to keep alive the memory of a popular Irkutsk bishop, Veniamin) soon demonstrated his outstanding intellectual abilities and became the best student at the seminary. In addition to standard theological and liturgical subjects, he studied natural history, geography, physics, Latin, and German.[41] Veniaminov's substantial, if rather eclectic, education was later manifested in his views on human nature and society which combined Orthodox theology with Enlightenment rationalism. In 1821 he was ordained as a priest to serve in one of Irkutsk's churches. Until 1840 Alaska churches were part of the Irkutsk diocese, and it was allegedly from one former *promyshlennik* that Fr. Ioann first heard about Russian America and the simple but deeply devout Aleuts. Having been inspired by these stories, Veniaminov answered the call of the bishop of Irkutsk to go and serve as the parish priest of the island of Unalaska.

After spending a year in Novoarkhangel'sk, Veniaminov finally arrived at his ultimate destination in the summer of 1824. He was warmly welcomed by the Aleuts, most of whom had been baptized for quite some time (mostly by laymen) and had maintained their devotion to the religion of the Russians, despite the absence of a resident priest. While their knowledge of Orthodox dogma was rather limited, their religiosity was quite strong and appeared sincere. According to Veniaminov himself as

[39] In 1977 the Orthodox Church in America canonized him as "St. Innocent, Apostle to America, Enlightener of Alaska."

[40] Because of St. Innocent's stature and his prominence in the history of the Orthodox Church in both Alaska and Russia, a great deal has been written about him, and his life and works have acquired a somewhat mythical quality. See., e.g., I. P. Barsukov, *Innokentii, Mitropolit Moskovskii i Kolomenskii* (Moscow, 1883); Paul Garrett, *St. Innocent, Apostle to America*, (Crestwood, N.Y., 1979); Richard Pierce, *Russian America: A Biographical Dictionary*, (Kingston, Ont., 1990), 521–27; Michael Oleksa, *Alaska Missionary Spirituality* (New York, 1987); S. A. Mousalimas, "Introduction," in *Journals of the Priest Ioann Veniaminov in Alaska, 1823 to 1836*, ed. S. Mousalimas, trans. J. Kisslinger (Fairbanks, Alaska, 1993), xiii–xxxix. However, a more critical analysis of his writing, missionary as well as ethnographic, has only begun; see Kan, "Recording Native Culture."

[41] This broad curriculum was the product of rather progressive educational reforms of the reign of Catherine II and Alexander I which were inspired to some extent by the Enlightenment. See Gregory L. Freeze, *The Russian Levites: Parish Clergy in the Eighteenth Century* (Cambridge, Mass., 1977).

well as secular Russian observers, much of their pre-Christian religion had already been abandoned, while their material and social culture had already become a synthesis of indigenous and Russian ideas and practices.[42] Using his skills as a carpenter, Veniaminov built the first church in the Aleutians in 1825. He learned Aleut and, with the help of several Aleut men, designed an alphabet and translated the Scriptures into that language.[43] By 1840 he had translated and published several major religious texts in Aleut and had recruited the talented Iakov Netsvetov, the first "Creole" priest, to continue his linguistic and educational work.[44] A man of many talents, Fr. Ioann spent his ten years in the Aleutians administering sacraments throughout the islands and the adjacent areas, writing textbooks, teaching in school, and conducting meteorological, zoological, linguistic, and ethnographic research.[45]

Transferred to Novoarkhangel'sk in August of 1834, Veniaminov arrived there with not only a great deal of missionary experience but also a strong interest in continuing to collect linguistic and ethnographic data on the local inhabitants. While anxious to begin his proselytizing work among his Tlingit neighbors, he favored a slow and cautious approach to Christianization. Inspired by instructions given to him upon his departure for Alaska in 1823 by Bishop Mikhail of Irkutsk, Veniaminov outlined his ideas about the theory and practice of missionary work in various writings, from official ecclesiastical correspondence and personal letters to his own well-known "Instruction to Alaskan Missionaries."[46]

One of the cornerstones of Veniaminov's evangelizing method was the idea that a clergyman had to gain the natives' trust and a sense of their culture and language, and should explain to them in simple words (instead of preaching) the "Light of Truth."[47] After establishing a rapport with the natives he was visiting, a missionary should ask his hosts ("with curiosity") about their own "faith and religious practices [*zakon i bogosluzhenie*]." Having learned about them, he should initiate an argument about

[42] Veniaminov, *Notes on the Islands*, passim.

[43] Lydia T. Black, "Ivan Pan'kov: An Architect of Aleut Literacy," *Arctic Anthropology* 14, no. 1 (1977): 94–96.

[44] "Creole" was a standard term used in Russian America to refer to the persons of mixed Russian–Native Alaskan ancestry. Lydia T. Black, ed. and trans., *The Journals of Iakov Netsvetov: The Atkha Years, 1828–1844* (Kingston, Ont., 1980); Oleksa, *Orthodox Alaska*; Mousalimas, *Journals of the Priest Ioann Veniaminov.*

[45] Veniaminov, *Notes on the Islands*; M. V. Stepanova, "I. Veniaminov kak etnograf," *Trudy Instituta Etnografii*, n.s. 2 (1947): 295–314; A. A. Arsen'ev, "Etnograficheskoe nasledie I. E. Veniaminova," *Sovetskaia Etnografiia* 5 (1979): 76–89; Kan, "Recording Native Culture."

[46] Bishop Mikhail of Irkutsk, "Instruktsiia Missioneram." A copy of this unpublished document, cited here, is located in the Vinokouroff Collection, box 33, f. 22. I. P. Barsukov, ed., *Pis'ma Innokentiia, Mitropolita Moskovskogo i Kolomenskogo*, 3 vols. (St. Petersburg, 1897–1901); I. Veniaminov, *Nastavlenie* (New York, 1899).

[47] Veniaminov, *Nastavlenie*, 35.

the "falseness [*nepravost'*] of their opinions, using natural arguments." The missionary was supposed "to listen to them patiently and tolerantly," while telling his own story "without rudeness and use of offensive words but in a kind and friendly manner." Only after spending a considerable amount of time in these dialogues with the natives was the missionary advised to offer them the sacrament of baptism.[48]

Although neither Mikhail nor Veniaminov encouraged the missionaries to tolerate pre-Christian religious practices or to incorporate them into Christianity, as a number of modern Orthodox or pro-Orthodox scholars have suggested,[49] both emphasized that conversion had to be voluntary, without threats or violence. New converts were not to be asked to observe fasts and fulfill other religious duties as strictly as Russians or those natives who had already become Christians. Like the apostle Paul, the missionary was not to force the newly baptized "to turn away all of a sudden from customs that were not contrary to Christianity" but had to explain to them that those customs *"should not be considered religious"* (italics mine). The simple Ten Commandments (rather than the New Testament) were supposed to be the essence of the newly baptized people's religious observance; old "idols" should be abandoned and forgotten, parents must be revered, neighbors loved, and so on.

Throughout his missionary career, Veniaminov insisted on making important allowances for new converts, adjusting church law to local conditions. For example, since most Native Alaskans could not survive on a vegetarian diet, they should be allowed to limit their consumption of meat during certain Orthodox fasts rather than abstain from it altogether. Veniaminov also encouraged missionaries not to be too harsh in their criticism of polygamy, which was widespread among the American natives, and "given the small size of the local population (which is reminiscent of patriarchal times), do not broaden too much the categories of relatives who are forbidden to marry each other."[50]

Unlike many Western missionaries of his era, Veniaminov did not equate Christianization with the imposition of European culture, arguing that it did not make any sense for Native Alaskans to abandon their traditional subsistence activities. Like other conservative Russian thinkers of

---

[48] Bishop Mikhail, "Instruktsiia," 1–2.

[49] Black, "Ivan Pan'kov," 1–4; Barbara S. Smith, *Russian Orthodoxy in Alaska* (Anchorage, Alaska, 1980), passim; Mousalimas, *Journals of the Priest Ioann Veniaminov*, xvii–xxxii; Mousalimas, *The Transition from Shamanism*, 219–25; Oleksa, *Alaska Missionary Spirituality*, 15–16 et passim; idem, *Orthodox Alaska*, 127–42.

[50] Veniaminov, *Nastavlenie*, 24–25; cf. Veniaminov, *Tvoreniia Innokentiia, Mitropolita Moskovskogo i Kolomenskogo*, ed. I. P. Barsukov, 3 vols, in 2 (Moscow, 1886–88), 2:178. For more details on the matrimonial regulations that were developed by Veniaminov for Russian America and remained in effect after the sale of Alaska to the United States, see documents in ARCA, D 404.

the time, Veniaminov was deeply troubled by the revolutionary movements of the 1840s in Western Europe, seeing them as a sign of Western secular civilization's decline. He contrasted the corrupt modern Europeans with the simple but morally pure natives, especially his favorite Aleut people. As he wrote in an 1843 letter, "The more I become acquainted with the savages, the more I become convinced that, as far as morality is concerned, the so-called wild ones [*dikie*] are much better than many of the so-called enlightened ones. Does this mean that we, with our enlightenment, are moving away from, rather than approaching perfection?"[51]

The Russian priest was also concerned with the style or tone in which the essentials of Christian faith were presented to the unbaptized. Drawing on an Orthodox view of the role of religion in human life, he argued that "Christianity is a need, satisfaction, and consolation primarily of the heart, and not the mind alone, and hence when instructing [the heathen] in matters of faith, you should try to influence the heart rather than the mind."[52]

Baptism as such was only the beginning of the conversion process. Only when the new Christians expressed their wish to have a priest live among them and demonstrated their devotion to Orthodoxy could their conversion be considered complete. Veniaminov strongly opposed the prevailing RAC practice of offering gifts to the newly baptized. Determined to eliminate any possibility of material interest on the part of converts, he argued against the practice of giving a new shirt and insisted that a simple cross for wearing underneath the clothing was sufficient.[53] At the same time he demanded that missionaries accept only voluntary contributions, pay natives for their services (so that they would not conclude that by accepting Christianity they were simultaneously becoming slaves or servants), and avoid engaging in any trade relations with new or prospective converts.[54]

Veniaminov repeatedly emphasized the importance for the Russian clergy of training local laity to serve as interpreters and catechists.[55] Eventually some of these people, American-born natives and especially Creoles

---

[51] Barsukov, *Pis'ma Innokentiia*, 1:97.

[52] Veniaminov, *Nastavlenie*, 9–10. Another reason for this emphasis on the emotional rather than the intellectual in proselytizing among the natives was his notion that the non-Western ("primitive") peoples were not yet intellectually ready to comprehend the more complex theological concepts. In fact, Veniaminov says so in the following passage: "As far as their habits and ideas are concerned, the people you will be dealing with are pagans and strayed [*zabludshie*] souls, and as for their level of education, they are children." Ibid., 10.

[53] Ibid., 28–29.

[54] While accepting voluntary donations, the missionary had to make sure that the donors understood that their gifts were different from the offerings to the pagan spirits—i.e., the Christian God did not have to be placated with gifts. Ibid., 34–35.

[55] Ibid., 3.

(a rising social class that was becoming increasingly important for the RAC's operations in the New World), were to become the new generation of Alaskan clergy. To train such church workers, who would speak to their flocks and conduct church services in their own languages and have an understanding of the local culture, Veniaminov established a seminary in Novoarkhangel'sk in the mid-1840s.[56]

While Veniaminov emphasized the spiritual goals of Christianization throughout his "Instruction," he did not forget the interests of the state. According to Veniaminov's mentor, Bishop Mikhail, by enlightening the "lost ones" with the "knowledge of the Saving Truth" and thus pointing the way for them to the "Heavenly Kingdom" and "confirming them in the perfection of faith and true virtues," an Orthodox missionary would also "encourage them to share in the [Russian] faith [*edinomyslie*] and be concerned with acting in ways that are beneficial for the State."[57] At the same time, the missionary was not to tell the natives that he had been sent to them by government order but was only to let them know that he had come "because of the duty imposed upon him as a priest." Veniaminov advised clergymen "not to interfere in settling secular affairs" and "not to undermine any local leaders," whether traditional ones or those established by the RAC. Only if the head of a post was too cruel in his treatment of the natives should the missionary try to change his ways through friendly conversations; if the man remained incorrigible, then the clergyman could report him secretly to church authorities who would then make their own report to colonial officials.[58] Thus, while reserving the right to criticize local secular authorities, Veniaminov advocated (and practiced) greater caution in his dealings with them than had his predecessors from Valaam. In fact, with the departure of Baranov, the church established much more amicable relations with the RAC, whose chief managers were now being recruited from the ranks of officers of the Imperial Navy, and finally put a stop to the abuse of the company's native workers.

Veniaminov's first opportunity to put his elaborate missionary ideas into practice presented itself during his encounters with the Yup'ik Eskimos of the mouth of the Nushagak River and in his subsequent labors

[56] Oleksa, *Orthodox Alaska*, 127–71.

[57] Bishop Mikhail, "Instruktsiia Missioneram," 5. Compare the following advice given to Orthodox missionaries by Metropolitan Filaret of Moscow in his own 1840 instruction: "All the peoples inhabiting our Russian colonies are considered to be subjects of Russia; but those who have not yet been enlightened with Holy Baptism do not yet know that they are under the mighty protection [*pokrov*] of Russia and that in the security they are enjoying, they are Russia's beneficiaries; hence you must impress upon them this idea and in general at every opportunity you must try to present to them the superiority of our type of government in comparison with the other ones, as well as its selfless care for them, its protection, etc." Metropolitan Filaret, *Instruktsiia missioneram* (Beijing, 1905), 1.

[58] Veniaminov, *Nastavlenie*, 29–36.

among the Tlingit and other indigenous peoples of Alaska and eastern Siberia. In his efforts to convert the Tlingit, Veniaminov faced serious difficulties of a kind he had not encountered in other parts of Russian America. From the very beginning of the RAC's presence in the Tlingit territory, Alaskans had offered considerable resistance to the newcomers, and in 1802 they burned the Russians' fort to the ground. Russians were never able to exercise any control over southeast Alaska's indigenous peoples and the RAC's six and a half decades of operation in the region were periodically interrupted by skirmishes with its original inhabitants. The RAC charters assigned the Tlingit (along with several other Native Alaskan peoples) to the category of "independent" tribes whose way of life was not supposed to be disturbed by the Russians.[59]

Given such a relationship between the Russians and the Tlingit, it is not surprising that during the RAC era the influence of Orthodoxy on this Native Alaskan people was weaker than on the subjugated and heavily Russified Aleuts and Alutiiqs.[60] Not until the late 1830s, when a devastating smallpox epidemic weakened the Tlingit trust in their own medicine men (shamans) and gave the Russians an opportunity to show their good will by administering vaccine, did a significant number of Sitka natives and other small groups begin to convert.[61]

Seizing the new opportunity for proselytizing, Veniaminov obtained the permission of the Sitka Tlingit headmen to visit their homes and meet with their people. In his efforts to open up a real dialogue with the Tlingit, Veniaminov was a true pioneer. His willingness to be a guest in their homes made him unique in the eyes of his hosts. His courage and eloquence as well as ability to conduct elaborate rituals appealed to them as well. So did his insistence on using good interpreters and his efforts to learn the Tlingit language, even though he never mastered it as he did Aleut.[62] In the eyes of the Tlingit, his "respectful" behavior called for highly courteous treatment in return.[63]

The way Veniaminov presented Orthodox Christianity to the Tlingit

[59] The history of Russian-Tlingit relations is detailed in a recent Russian study by A. V. Grinev, *Indeitsy tlinkity v period Russkoi Ameriki, 1741–1867* (Novosibirsk, 1991), and in my forthcoming monograph, *Memory Eternal;* see also Tikhmenev, *History of the Russian-American Company;* Jonathan Dean, "'Their Nature and Qualities Remain Unchanged': Russian Occupation and Tlingit Resistance, 1802–1867," *Alaska History* 9, no.1 (Spring 1994): 1–17; J. Gibson, "European Dependence upon American Natives: The Case of Russian America," *Ethnohistory* 25(1978): 359–85.

[60] In fact, one of the obstacles to Tlingit conversion was their view that their former enemies, the Aleuts and the Alutiiqs living in Sitka, were Russian slaves.

[61] J. Gibson, "Smallpox on the Northwest Coast, 1835–1838," *BC Studies* 56, no. 1 (1982–83): 61–81. Veniaminov, *Notes on the Islands,* 434–38.

[62] Ibid.

[63] "Respect," which implied deferential and courteous treatment, has always been one of the key values of Tlingit culture; see Sergei Kan, *Symbolic Immortality: the Tlingit Potlatch of the Nineteenth Century* (Washington, D.C., 1989), 25–26.

followed the order that he eventually outlined in his "Instruction."[64] Thus he began his explanation of religion with a discussion of God's creation of the world, followed by an explanation of the notions of the immortality of the human soul and the sinfulness of the human being, and ended with the introduction of Christ the Savior. Pointing out that all of the "American savages" had some concept of immortality and life after death, Fr. Ioann also emphasized the importance of Christ's own death, resurrection, and second coming, and especially the idea that Christ would save them. Here he seems to have understood the centrality of eschatology and death-related beliefs and observances in both Orthodoxy and indigenous Alaskan cultures (especially that of the Tlingit).[65]

According to Veniaminov, the Tlingit had always appreciated and enjoyed eloquent public speaking and masterful storytelling, and were therefore impressed and intrigued by the Russian priest's presentation of the rudiments of Christianity. For a people who had witnessed the havoc wrought by a smallpox epidemic and were exposed to a culture different from their own, however, Veniaminov's stories raised difficult new questions with no satisfactory answers to be found in the traditional Tlingit ideology.

Most Tlingits' relationship with the church was heavily influenced by their experiences with the RAC and especially its leadership. Tlingit aristocrats insisted that top company officials serve as their godfathers and took advantage of their special ties to these Russian men to ask for gifts, feasting, and other favors. Despite Veniaminov's opposition, baptized Tlingit, especially those of high rank, often did receive presents. Social divisions among the Tlingit had also to be taken into account. Even though a special church was constructed for the Tlingit on the border between their village and the Russian fort, their aristocracy resented having to attend services with people of lower rank and preferred to wait for rare opportunities to take part in holiday services inside St. Michael's Cathedral in Novoarkhangel'sk.[66]

Veniaminov's own missionary efforts as well as those of several of his successors notwithstanding, only about half of Sitka's Tlingit population had joined the Orthodox Church by the 1860s and most of these converts had a very vague understanding of Christianity. Only a small portion of these converts were willing to bury rather than cremate their dead, while shamanism, witchcraft accusations, polygamy, and even slave sacrifices continued despite the clergy's attempts to gently discourage those "heathen" practices. Generally speaking, the limited amount of interaction be-

---

[64] Veniaminov, *Notes on the Islands,* 434–38.
[65] Cf. Kan, *Symbolic Immortality,* passim.
[66] Kan, *Memory Eternal,* 145–73.

tween Russians and Tlingits during the RAC era and the periodic confrontations between them were not conducive to native conversion, and even less so to Tlingit appropriation of Orthodox dogma and rites. Paradoxically, many Orthodox beliefs and rituals eventually did take root, but only after the Russian departure from Alaska and the arrival of the much more powerful *Waashdan Kwaan* (the Tlingit term for the Americans, literally "Washington People").

. The state of Tlingit Orthodoxy on the eve of the American arrival resembled that of several other native Alaskan groups that had managed to maintain a fair amount of independence from the RAC, such as the Nushagak and the Kuskokwim Yup'iks. At the same time, it contrasted sharply with that of the Aleuts, the Alutiiqs, and to some extent the Kenai Athapaskans, all of whom found themselves under much greater Russian economic, political, and cultural influence and/or domination.[67]

Russian Orthodox Missionaries in American-Dominated Alaska, 1867–1917

The sale of Alaska to the United States radically altered the Russian church's status. The RAC withdrew completely from the New World, while the Orthodox mission was now forced to operate in a foreign country. The church did retain the right to serve the needs of its members, native and nonnative alike, but it had lost its economic base as well as its prestige. In fact, with the arrival of well-endowed and well-staffed Presbyterian and other Protestant missions, it became the subject of harsh criticism for its alleged inefficiency, excessive emphasis on ritual, and anti-American spirit. Much of this criticism was unfair and had more to do with the rivalry between missions and the chauvinistic anti-Catholic and anti-Orthodox ideology of many late nineteenth-century American Protestants.[68] Particularly strong anti-Orthodox views were espoused by the powerful Presbyterian mission led by Sheldon Jackson (later General Agent for Alaska Education), who resided in Sitka among the Tlingit and whose educational activities enjoyed considerable support from local American officials.[69]

In the first few decades after the sale of Alaska, the Orthodox Church was one of the few voices to speak out against the mistreatment suffered

---

[67] Kan, "The Russian Orthodox Church in Alaska," 511–14. According to an 1860 estimate, there were 11,562 Orthodox Church members in Russian America, including 784 Russians, 1,676 Creoles, and 9,102 natives. See Tikhmenev, *History of the Russian-American Company,* 1:384.

[68] Oleksa, *Orthodox Alaska,* 171–87; Kan, *Memory Eternal,* 236–37.

[69] T. Hinckley, *The Americanization of Alaska, 1867–1897* (Palo Alto, Calif., 1972), 155–68.

by Native Alaskans at the hands of American commercial firms and zealous officials. Orthodox clergy helped draft petitions from the natives to the president of the United States describing this mistreatment and asking for federal help.[70] The most famous appeal by an Orthodox Church official to the U.S. president was a stern letter sent in 1897 by Nikolai, bishop of Alaska, to President McKinley. The letter accused the Alaska Commercial Company and Sheldon Jackson of antinative and anti-Orthodox propaganda and activities.[71]

After 1867 many Orthodox clergymen returned to Russia, so that in 1870 only four priests remained in Alaska. Eventually, the Orthodox Church revived its moribund Alaska mission, establishing a new diocese of Alaska and the Aleutians in the early 1870s. By decree of the Russian government, the State Council had to provide financial support for the Alaska churches, whose parishioners were either very poor or not yet accustomed to contributing money to their parish treasuries. Additional financial help came from the Orthodox Missionary Society, established in Russia in 1869. Nevertheless, the Alaska mission remained poor, with its priests often complaining about their low salaries and many of its sacristans and teachers forced to resign or take on additional jobs outside the church in order to survive. Despite these difficulties, between 1867 and 1917 the church managed to establish a number of new parishes, build new churches and chapels, and open parish schools. In the early twentieth century it even established a small seminary/boarding school in Sitka, where Alaska-born Creole and native Orthodox boys were trained to become church workers. Several Orthodox clergymen continued Veniaminov's work of translating and publishing Orthodox prayers and hymns into indigenous Alaskan languages.

The Alaska clergy during this era consisted of two types. The first was the Alaska-born Creole and native priests, deacons, and lay readers who served in various parishes, especially in the Aleutians and on the Yukon. These men tended to speak the local languages and be tolerant of their parishioners' transgressions from church rules and the persistence of indigenous customs and beliefs.[72] The others were Russian-born priests who served in most of the parishes of southeastern Alaska, Kodiak, and the Aleutians. Many of these priests viewed their jobs as temporary assignments and longed for their native land. Some were well educated and urbane, which made it even more difficult for them to cope with their assignments at "the end of the world." Politically many of these priests were

---

[70] A. Kamenskii, *Tlingit Indians of Alaska*, trans. Sergei Kan (1906; reprint ed., Fairbanks, Alaska, 1985), 132–36.

[71] Afonsky, *History of the Orthodox Church*, 76–90; M. Oleksa, *Alaska Missionary Spirituality*, 326–28.

[72] Kan, "The Russian Orthodox Church," 514–18; Oleksa, *Orthodox Alaska*, 143–71.

conservative monarchists and Russian nationalists, who lamented the passing of the Russian language and cultural influence in Alaska and never tired of contrasting the "golden days" of paternalistic RAC rule to the unbridled exploitation of Alaska and its indigenous inhabitants by greedy and unscrupulous Americans. Many of them were appalled and confused by America's freedom of religion, its lack of a single government-supported church, and its democratic political system. Thus they pointed to the refusal of many young Russians and Creoles to submit to their church's moral authority as a manifestation of their increasing Americanization.[73]

Some priests shared the views of the nationalist missionaries in Russia proper whose voices became louder during the conservative reign of Alexander III. These missionaries subscribed to the old conservative triad of Orthodoxy, Autocracy, and Nationality, and insisted that it was their job to instill in Siberian natives "loyalty to the tsar, obedience to government officials, and a feeling of brotherly love towards the Russians."[74] The *Russian Orthodox American Messenger*, the official newspaper of the newly established North American diocese of the Orthodox Church, frequently reprinted such Russian statements along with supportive editorial comments. Because of these views, officials of the Alaskan diocese insisted that the Russian language continue to be taught in the parish schools, even though most Native Alaskans, with the exception of some of the Aleut and Kodiak Alutiiqs, did not use it.

Yet even the most ardent Russian nationalists among the Alaska clergy realized that in order to survive under the American flag their church had to be loyal to Alaska's new masters. Hence, following the old Russian tradition of church loyalty to the state, they introduced English into the parish schools' curriculum and included prayers for the president of the United States in the liturgy.[75] To demonstrate their loyalty to the new regime, high Orthodox clergy emphasized that, unlike the Western churches, the Russian church was concerned only with spiritual and not political issues. As Bishop Nikolai put it in his letter to President McKinley, "our Church never interferes in politics and clergy never gets involved in political intrigues, whether at home or abroad. We should not be confused with the Jesuits. Our Church allows us only to intercede with the

---

[73] Kan, "Translator's Introduction," in Kamenskii, *The Tlingit Indians*, 3–17.

[74] *Eniseiskie Eparkhial'nye Vedomosti*, 1885, no. 94:1. Compare the following statement made by the bishop of Irkutsk in an 1885 publication: "the Orthodox mission to the *inorodtsy* is a mission of Russification." See Archbishop Veniamin, *Zhiznennye voprosy pravoslavnoi missii v Sibiri* (St. Petersburg, 1885), 2.

[75] For a strongly articulated argument for the need to teach English to Native Alaskans, see Innokentii Pustynskii's article "Priemyshi" in the *Russian Orthodox American Messenger* 9 (1905): 89–95, 104–9, 124–33. Bishop Pustynskii, known for his liberalism, was the head of the Alaska diocese in the early 1900s.

higher secular authorities on behalf of the oppressed and the innocent sufferers, as I have done in the United States, but never permits us to incite these people to rebellion and treason."[76]

Service outside the borders of the Russian empire and political and financial weakness forced the missionaries to soften their antiheathen stand. They realized that the destruction of pagan religious artifacts and other attacks on indigenous religions, which were being advocated and practiced by a significant number of late nineteenth-century missionaries in Siberia,[77] would only further weaken the church's influence on Native Alaskans.[78] Hence, much of the celebrated tolerance of the Orthodox missionaries in Alaska during the post-1867 era was to a large extent a direct result of weakness.[79]

At the same time, Veniaminov's tradition of greater tolerance of pre-Christian native cultures remained alive among some of the Russian-born missionaries of this era. This is particularly true of those who labored among the Tlingit, the Yup'ik Eskimos, and other native Alaskan peoples still clinging to some pre-Christian beliefs and rituals. For example, the priest Grigorii Chudnovskii, who served in 1889–90 in a recently organized Tlingit parish on the island of Killisnoo, tolerated the persistence of the memorial potlatch, the central native ceremony, which included offerings of food and property to the spirits of the ancestors. To contrast his tolerant stand with that of the local Presbyterian minister who was berating the Indians for participating in this ceremony, Fr. Grigorii told them the following,

My children, I do not interfere in your native festivities [*narodnye gulian'ia*]. The most important thing for you to do is to avoid drinking, which leads to the worst kinds of evil. Love each other, since all of you were born in one spiritual [i.e., baptismal] font and have one Holy Church which protects you and gives you spiritual food and all of the heavenly benefits. Treat your pagan brothers with honor and teach them to lead a good life. Your chiefs will take my place in my absence and keep a strict watch over your behavior. If you be-

[76] *Russian Orthodox American Messenger* 5 (1901): 90.

[77] Archbishop Veniamin, *Zhiznennye voprosy*; K. Kharlampovich, *O khristianskom prosveshchenii inorodtsev: Iz perepiski arkhiepiskopa Veniamina s N. I. Il'minskim* (Kazan, 1904); Alekseenko, "Khristianizatsiia na Turukhanskom Severe," 50–61.

[78] Prior to 1867, some of the Alaska missionaries did commit such excesses as interfering with native religious rituals, and destroying shaman masks. See, for example, Iakov Netsvetov's experience among the Yukon Yup'iks, described in *The Journals of Iakov Netsvetov: The Yukon Years, 1845–1863*, trans. by L. T. Black (Kingston, Ont., 1984).

[79] This understanding of the need to be realistic and adapt to local conditions was also manifested in the fact that many Alaskan missionaries refused to deny communion to native couples married according to the native law, rather than in church. Only an occasional zealot, often a recent arrival from Russia, would protest against this tolerance but would usually be reprimanded by his superiors who argued that such strictness would drive native parishioners away. See Kan, "Translator's Introduction," 3–17.

Father Ioann Sobolev with the St. John the Baptist Killisnoo Indian (Tlingit) Brotherhood, Alaska, c. 1904. Alaska State Library, collection M2 (Vinokouroff), photo # PCA 243-80. Courtesy Alaska State Library.

have well, I will be happy and will praise you. But if you behave badly, I will, as your father, give you a fatherly punishment in order to save you from the punishment on the Judgment Day.[80]

In a letter to his superiors, Chudnovskii offered the following telling comment on his speech: "Of course, in five or ten years I will not talk about the Indian dances anymore, but right now I want to be a pagan among the pagans in order to save them."[81] Like most other Orthodox missionaries in Alaska, this priest was most concerned with rampant native alcoholism and the social disorganization it produced, both of which were common in much of Alaska in the late nineteenth and early twentieth centuries.

Some of the adherents of this more liberal missionary tradition found inspiration in the ideas of Nikolai Il'minskii, which had considerable support among missionaries laboring in Russia during this period.[82] Others looked to the Russian government's paternalistic policies toward Siberian

[80] Fr. Grigorii Chudnovskii's letters to his superiors, ARCA, D 316, p. 11.

[81] Ibid.

[82] Slezkine, *Arctic Mirrors*, 121–22; Alekseenko, "Khristianizatsiia na Turukhanskom Severe." Il'minskii's writings on the need to produce high-quality translations of Orthodox

inorodtsy for models of how to improve the lot of Alaska Natives who were both exploited and Westernized by the Americans. A number of Russian priests in Alaska advocated the old tsarist policy of indirect rule (i.e., reliance on the local native leaders as intermediaries between their communities and government officials) and argued that the traditional subsistence activities of native peoples had to be preserved. Thus they differed rather sharply from their Protestant rivals who were anxious to transform Native Alaskans into Christian Americans who would abandon hunting and fishing in favor of various trades, commerce, wage labor, and even agriculture.[83] To protect the native land base and resources, some Russian clergymen even advocated the establishment of reservations, an idea that was totally opposed by Sheldon Jackson and other Protestant missionaries who wanted to speed up natives' entry into the mainstream of American life rather than slow it down.[84] Of course, such proposals by the Orthodox clergy carried little weight, since the real power and control over the life of Native Alaskans was in the hands of the Protestants and their allies within the territorial administration.[85]

Given the weak position of the Orthodox mission in the post-1867 Alaska, how can one explain its rather substantial success in maintaining and even expanding its base among the indigenous population of the territory? Part of the answer to this question has already been suggested here: the fact that the Russian church did not, by and large, interfere in native socio-economic and spiritual life made it attractive to the more conservative segment of the native population. Of course, it is important to differentiate between those ethnic groups that had already become heavily Russified by the end of the RAC era and those that retained a great deal of their pre-and early-contact culture.

Thus, the Aleuts, the Alutiiqs, and some of the Athapaskans of the Kenai Peninsula remained strongly committed to Orthodoxy because for them Orthodoxy was part of Russian culture, which they had been incorporating into their own culture since the days of Shelikhov and Baranov. In fact, in the late nineteenth and the beginning of the twentieth centuries, some of these communities continued to use the Russian language and were not enthusiastic about sending their children to American schools. In the Aleutians, literacy in Russian and Aleut survived into the

---

texts into native languages and train native clergy were cited approvingly in several articles published in the *Russian Orthodox American Messenger* in the early 1900s.

[83] Hinckley, *The Americanization of Alaska*, passim; idem, *Alaskan John G. Brady: Missionary, Businessman, Judge, and Governor, 1878–1918* (Columbus, Ohio, 1982), passim.

[84] Kamenskii, *Tlingit Indians*, 117–23; Kan, "Recording Native Culture and Christianizing the Natives."

[85] By the 1890s Sheldon Jackson did lose some of his influence on Alaska politics. However, many of his reformist ideas continued to be put into practice by government officials, schoolteachers, and other American agents of social change.

1930s.[86] Consequently, despite their strong efforts, Protestant missions had very little success in this part of Alaska. The fact that Protestant churches were often identified, in the eyes of the natives, with the newcomers who were exploiting them further undermined their efforts to pull the Aleuts, the Alutiiqs, and others away from Orthodoxy.

For other ethnic groups, and particularly the Tlingit, Orthodoxy offered a model of a more gradual acceptance of Western religious ideology and broader cultural values. In the last two decades of the nineteenth century, the Tlingit community was split between the younger, more Americanized (and often American-educated) people who favored the Presbyterian Church, and the more conservative and less-schooled individuals who resented the Presbyterians' heavy-handed control over their lives. For the latter group, many of them people of high rank who continued practicing the memorial potlatch, Orthodoxy was easily combined with traditional practices. These Tlingit embraced enthusiastically the Orthodox funeral and memorial rites, including the observances on the fortieth day after death. Similarly, Orthodox icons, holy water, and other sacred objects and substances made a great deal of sense to the Tlingit and other Native Alaskans (such as the Yup'ik Eskimos) whose own indigenous spirituality centered on and was expressed through ritual action rather than abstract theology.[87]

Another example of native reinterpretation of Orthodox institutions and rituals was the church brotherhoods and temperance socities introduced by the Russian clergy at the turn of the century. While their primary goal was to fight native drinking and encourage mutual assistance and cooperation, the great popularity of these sodalities stemmed from the fact that they allowed their members to wear distinctive uniforms and assume leadership positions within their parishes. This was particularly true among the Tlingit, where the traditional aristocracy quickly took over the brotherhoods and used them to strengthen their influence in communities and parishes where they were competing with Creoles for power and influence.

By 1917, Protestant opposition to Orthodoxy weakened, and many local American officials and educators began to accept the natives' membership in the Russian church. An analysis of Orthodox parish records for the 1890s to 1910s clearly indicates that Orthodoxy in southeastern

[86] The Aleut alphabet, developed by Veniaminov and other missionaries, was based on the Cyrillic one. See Jay Ransom, "Writing as a Medium of Acculturation Among the Aleut," *Southwestern Journal of Anthropology* 1, no. 3 (1945): 333–44; Richard Dauenhauer, "The Spiritual Epiphany of the Aleut," *Orthodox Alaska* 8 (1979): 13–42; Oleksa, *Orthodox Alaska.*

[87] Cf. Ann Fienup-Riordan, *The Real People and the Children of Thunder: The Yup'ik Eskimo Encounter with Moravian Missionaries John and Edith Kilbuck* (Norman, Okla., 1991), passim; Kan, "Russian Orthodox Christian Brotherhoods."

Alaska continued to grow and to enjoy the natives' support.[88] Despite the lack of resources and trained priests, the end of financial support from Russia after 1917, and the loss of some Orthodox Church members, it seems that Orthodoxy has been more successful abroad (in Alaska), where it has not been identified with an authoritarian and oppressive Russian state, than at home (in Siberia), where on the eve of the 1917 Revolution, it still had a fairly limited influence on the *inorodtsy*.[89]

After 1917 the Orthodox influence in Siberia was further undermined by the new state's antireligious propaganda, while in the last few years it has suffered from the rise of indigenous nationalism and the revival of (neo-)pre-Christian religions.[90] In Alaska, on the contrary, the native political and cultural renaissance of the last thirty years has tended to boost the Orthodox Church's image as a religion of the more traditionalist natives and a protector of the indigenous peoples against American abuses.[91] Of course, the church itself has encouraged such sentiments, while at the same time reviving its activities in Alaska.[92]

Conclusion

While the Orthodox mission in Alaska was in many ways the continuation of the Russian church's project of proselytizing among the indigenous peoples of Siberia, it differed from the Siberian mission in several key areas. Prior to 1867 it had to coexist with and was supported by a paternalistic commercial company rather than by the government. Consequently, the first cohort of Alaska missionaries was more willing to criti-

---

[88] Kan, *Memory Eternal*, 245–366.

[89] Thus, a Russian observer of the Eastern Siberian native scene wrote in 1916: "The *inorodtsy* have accepted only the outer, ritual aspects of Christianity; its inner meaning and essence remain foreign to them; Christian *inorodtsy* have retained to this day their pagan religious beliefs and most of them still adhere to shamanism, attributing the same mysterious meaning to the Christian rites and the shamanic ones." See Soliarskii, *Sovremennoe pravovoe i kul'turno-ekonomicheskoe polozhenie*, 156. Another Russian observer characterized native Christianity in the Eniseisk *guberniia* in the 1890s as very superficial. See V. N. Latkin, *Eniseiskaia guberniia, ee proshloe i nastoiashchee* (St. Petersburg, 1892), 143. For other examples of this phenomenon, see Vdovin, *Khristianstvo i lamaism*.

[90] Marjorie M. Balzer, "Dilemmas of the Spirit: Religion and Atheism in the Yakut-Sakha Republic," in *Religious Policy in the Soviet Union*, ed. S. P. Ramet (Cambridge, 1993), 231–51; Slezkine, *Arctic Mirrors*, 371–85.

[91] Oleksa, *Orthodox Alaska*, 187–205; N. M. Dauenhauer and R. Dauenhauer, eds., *Haa Kusteeyi, Our Culture: Tlingit Life Stories* (Seattle, 1994). 30–119; Kan, *Memory Eternal*, 519–47.

[92] The church opened a seminary on Kodiak which has already produced a large cohort of native priests, deacons, readers, and teachers. To further "indigenize" its image, the Alaska diocese has recently canonized an Aleut martyr, Peter, as well as a Creole priest, Iakov Netsvetov. Several Russian-born missionaries have been canonized as well (Kan, "The Russian Orthodox Church," 518–21).

cize Russian abuses of the indigenous population than were their Siberian counterparts.[93]

If in Siberia the extent of Orthodox influence on specific native peoples corresponded with the degree of the Russian government's influence and control, in Alaska it was the RAC that played a similar role. Thus the church's influence on the Aleuts, who were fully dependent on the RAC and heavily Russified, was much stronger than on the Tlingit who maintained an almost total political, economic, and ideological independence from the Russians. Given their significant role in setting up policies toward the natives, the Alaska missionaries favored a more cautious approach to missionization. Innokentii Veniaminov was the most prominent advocate of such an approach, and his ideas continued to influence the work of the Alaska mission long after his return to Russia in the 1850s.[94]

After the sale of Alaska to the United States, the Orthodox mission lost most of its political power and clout but was able to benefit from native resentment of the Americans' economic, political, and ideological domination. Veniaminov's legacy of tolerance and patience was further reinforced when the Orthodox missionaries' lack of power and control over their native parishioners, and their desire to contrast their work with those of their Protestant rivals, pushed them toward increasing tolerance of the indigenous cultures. Finally, the post-1867 Orthodox mission in Alaska relied more heavily on native church workers, particularly those in the lower ranks of the ecclesiastical hierarchy, than did its Siberian counterpart. It is these workers who are often credited with Orthodoxy's surprising survival in twentieth-century American Alaska.[95]

[93] In fact, prior to 1917, the clergymen's salaries in Alaska were higher than those of their colleagues on the Russian mainland.

[94] In the 1850s and 1860s Archbishop Innokentii Veniaminov was also instrumental in spreading Orthodoxy among the *inorodtsy* of Chukotka, Kamchatka, and the newly acquired Russian Far East.

[95] Oleksa, *Orthodox Alaska*, 187–205; Kan, "The Russian Orthodox Church," 518–20; idem, *Memory Eternal*, 454–547.

CHAPTER EIGHT

The Orthodox Church, Lamaism, and Shamanism among the Buriats and Kalmyks, 1825–1925

DITTMAR SCHORKOWITZ

Two Mongol-speaking peoples lived in the Russian empire: the Buriats on both sides of Lake Baikal in Eastern Siberia, and the Kalmyks in the steppes north and west of the Caspian Sea. Both peoples were Tibetan Buddhists and shared other similarities—a shamanist past, a pastoral-nomadic economy and sociopolitical structure—yet the two peoples' historical experiences within the Russian empire proved to be quite different.

In the seventeenth century the Buriats found themselves subjugated by Cossack forces led by Kozlov (1623), Perfil'ev (1627–30), Khripunov (1628), Beketov (1628–31), Ivanov (1643–44), and Firsov (1654), among others, and forced to pay *iasak* (fur tribute) to the Russian government. The Kalmyks, on the other hand, were moving forcefully westward during this time, eventually occupying pastures in the Caspian steppes and laying the foundations for their own government (khanate). The paths of the two peoples diverged further in the nineteenth and early twentieth centuries, when the Russian and Soviet governments pursued the transformation of native administration, land ownership, economy, taxation, education and religion. This essay will discuss these policies, focusing particularly on the effects they had on the religion of the Buriats and Kalmyks.

Shamans and Lamas before the Nineteenth Century

In the seventeenth century, the shamanist religion traditional to the native residents of Siberia was entering a steep decline. Among the Buri-

This essay is part of a comprehensive research project generously supported by the Deutsche Forschungsgemeinschaft.

ats, the expansion of Lamaism (also known as Tibetan or Mahayana Buddhism) and the beginning of Russian Orthodox missionary work were not the only causes of this process; it was also closely linked to the political changes and socio-economic transformations induced by contact with Russian civilization. Shamanism was, in effect, the religion of a people still living in a communal social order. Under Russian influence, the traditional Buriat clan structure began to be transformed into a socially more complex and differentiated aristocratic society, and religious practices changed accordingly.[1]

Lamaism spread rapidly among the Eastern (Tümed, Ordos), Western (Oirat- Kalmyks) and Northern (Khalkha, Buriat) Mongols from the second half of the sixteenth century to the first half of the seventeenth century.[2] The Russian officials P. Beketov and N. Spafarii, stationed in the Transbaikal area, described the initial expansion of Lamaism there between 1640 and 1670. Even after the Treaty of Nerchinsk of 1689, which divided disputed territories between Russia and China and thus turned the Buriats into the subjects of either Moscow or Beijing, Mongol and Tibetan clergymen (lamas) and medicine men (emchi) continued to migrate into the area. Such migration was not curtailed until 1727, when a new treaty with China at Kiakhta forbade the arrival of new lamas. Instructions of Count S. V. Raguzinskii-Illiiskii to the Russian border patrols (30 June 1728) categorically prohibited the *iasak*-paying, non-Christian subjects of the Russian empire (*"iasachnye inorodtsy"*) from accepting new

---

[1] Good introductions to Buriat shamanism are M. N. Khangalov, *Sobranie Sochinenii*, 3 vols., ed. G. N. Rumiantsev (Ulan-Ude, 1958–60); G. D. Sanzheev, "Weltanschauung und Schamanismus der Alaren-Burjaten," trans. R. Augustin *Anthropos* 22 (1928): 576–613, 933–955; 23 (1928): 538–60, 967–86. B. E. Petri, *Staraia vera buriatskogo naroda: Nauchno-populiarnyi ocherk* (Irkutsk, 1928); Lawrence Krader, "Buriat Religion and Society," *Southwestern Journal of Anthropology* 10, no. 3 (1954): 322–51; idem, "The Shamanist Tradition of the Buryats (Siberia)," *Anthropos* 70 (1975): 105–44; idem, "Shamanism: Theory and History in Buryat Society," *Bibliotheca Uralica*, vol. 1: *Shamanism in Siberia*, ed. V. Diószegi and M. Hoppál (Budapest, 1978), 181–236.

[2] Some believe this development began in the 1570s. See Giuseppe Tucci and Walther Heissig, *Die Religionen Tibets und der Mongolei*, vol. 20 of *Die Religionen der Menschheit*, ed. Ch. M. Schröder (Stuttgart, 1970), 327; G. Sh. Dordzhieva, "Sotsial'nye korni lamaizma i osnovnye vekhi ego rasprostraneniia sredi oiratov i kalmykov," in *Lamaizm v Kalmykii* (Elista, 1977), 5–13; V. P. Sanchirov, "Teokratiia v Tibete i rol' Gushi-khana v ee okonchatel'nom utverzhdenii," ibid., 17; T. D. Skrynnikova, "Osnovnye tendentsii v razvitii lamaistskoi tserkvi Khalkhi XVIII–nachala XX v.," in *Istochnikovedenie i istoriografiia istorii buddizma: Strany Tsentral'noi Azii* (Novosibirsk, 1986), 73–84; Dittmar Schorkowitz, *Die soziale und politische Organisation bei den Kalmücken (Oiraten) und Prozesse der Akkulturation vom 17. Jahrhundert bis zur Mitte des 19. Jahrhunderts: Ethnohistorische Untersuchungen über die mongolischen Völkerschaften*, Europäische Hochschulschriften, ser. 19, Volkskunde, Ethnologie, sec. B, Ethnologie, vol. 28 (Frankfurt, 1992), 369ff.; idem, "Konsanguinal-politische Organisation und Grenzen der Souveränität bei den Kalmücken-Oiraten," *Asiatische Forschungen* 126 (1993): 231ff.

lamas. Instead, the Buriats had to rely on the services of those lamas who had come before the demarcation of the border with China.[3]

As a result of the treaty, the Buriats had to petition St. Petersburg to request that 150 Mongol and Tibetan lamas, having fled civil war in Mongolia in 1712, be allowed to stay with them. In 1741, the Empress Elizabeth decreed that all of these clergymen be permitted to stay, given tax exemptions, and confirmed as lamas.[4] Oddly, it is this event that in Russian historiography marks the beginning of Lamaist missionary work among the Buriats of the Transbaikal.

Along with the lamas' subordination to Russian authority came exemption from the payment of *iasak* and other obligations, and the permission to build temples (*datsans*). The clergy was also explicitly permitted to convert the shamanist Buriats and Tungus "and to persecute shamanism among the *inorodtsy* of Eastern Siberia in order to convert them to Lamaism, and even to apply force in doing so."[5] Early nineteenth-century reports of English missionaries indicate that such conversions to Lamaism were not particularly gently pursued.[6]

It is beyond the scope of this work to describe the expansion of the Lamaist ecclesiastical hierarchy and the foundation of temples and monasteries in the eighteenth century. Suffice it to say that the Gusino-Ozero (Goose Lake) *datsan* won out over others to become the clerical center of Lamaism among the Buriats. In light of political conflict between the old shamanist elite and the Lamaist clergy, the support of the Russian government until the 1830s was crucial in helping to consolidate Buddhism in the Transbaikal region.[7]

[3] M.N. Bogdanov, *Ocherki istorii buriat-mongol'skogo naroda: S dopolnitel'nymi stat'iami B. B. Baradina i N. N. Kozmina* (Verkhneudinsk, 1926), 107.

[4] *Letopisi khorinskikh buriat: Khroniki Tuguldur Toboeva i Vandana Iumsunova*, trans. N. N. Poppe, Trudy Instituta Vostokovedeniia, vol. 33: Materialy dlia istorii Buriat-Mongolii, vol. 4 (Moscow, 1940), 49.

[5] Rossiiskii Gosudarstvennyi Istoricheskii Arkhiv, St. Petersburg, f. 821, op. 133, d. 409, l. 41a (hereafter RGIA).

[6] Charles R. Bawden, *Shamans, Lamas and Evangelicals: The English Missionaries in Siberia* (London, 1985), 165.

[7] RGIA, f. 821, op. 133, d. 409, l. 115a, b; Bogdanov, *Ocherki*, 107f. *Letopisi*, 22f., 37, 48ff; *Istoriia Buriat-Mongol'skoj ASSR*, vol. 1, ed. P. T. Khaptaev, 2d ed. (Ulan-Ude, 1954), 157f; K. M. Gerasimova, *Lamaizm i natsional'no-kolonial'naia politika tsarizma v Zabaikal'e v XIX i nachale XX vekov*, (Ulan-Ude, 1957), 22; Bawden, *Shamans*, 166. Günther Schulemann, *Geschichte der Dalai-Lamas* (Leipzig, 1958), 346, 374; N. L. Zhukovskaia, "Iz istorii religioznogo sinkretizma v Zabaikal'e," *Sovetskaia etnografiia* 6 (1965): 120–21; Hans Bräker, "Der Buddhismus in der Sowjetunion im Spannungsfeld zwischen Vernichtung und Überleben," *Berichte des Bundesinstituts für ostwissenschaftliche und internationale Studien* 36 (1982): 3; G. R. Galdanova, K. M. Gerasimova, D. B. Dashiev, and G. Ts. Mitupov, *Lamaizm v Buriatii XVIII–nachala XX veka: Struktura i sotsial'naia rol' kul'tovoi sistemy* (Novosibirsk, 1983), 12–26.

Celebration at the Gusino-Ozero (Goose Lake) *datsan*. Rossiiskii Gosudarstvennyi Istorich-eskii Arkhiv, f. 1293, op. 169, d. 450a.

Administrative and Ecclesiastical Regulations

With the ascension of Tsar Nicholas I and the dissolution of the Russian Bible Society in 1826, the power of the Russian Orthodox Church was on the rise. Now the Russian government began to pay more attention to the increased influence of Lamaism in Eastern Siberia and the lamas' ties to Mongolia, Tibet, and China. In 1826, the governor general of Eastern Siberia, A. S. Lavinskii, suggested the introduction of legislation restricting influence from the outside. The Ministries of the Interior and Foreign Affairs, however, rejected the idea, fearing a massive exodus of Buriats and potential damage to the commerce at Kiakhta. Four years later, the Asiatic Department of the Ministry of the Foreign Affairs dispatched its first special representative, Baron P. L. Schilling von Canstadt, to the Transbaikal region to study the situation and to draw up a "Memorandum on the Lamas of Eastern Siberia." The liberal baron, a corresponding member of the Russian Academy of Sciences and a friend of Alexander Pushkin and Nikolai Bichurin, also undertook the collection of valuable Chinese, Tibetan, and Mongolian manuscripts for the Museum of the Academy of Sciences. Well disposed towards the Lamaist clergy, he recommended that the government continue supporting the Lamaist mission among the shamanistic peoples.[8]

Of course, such a pro-Lamaist proposal stood no chance of becoming law given Nicholas I's reactionary policies. Reacting to the widespread accusations of the Russian Orthodox Church against the Lamaist clergy, conservative forces within the government took decisive action in 1844 by dispatching Senator Tolstoi to inspect the administration of Eastern Siberia. Under pressure from Tolstoi, the Buriat *taiishi* (local nobleman) R.-D. N. Dymbylov, who had converted to Russian Orthodoxy in St. Petersburg in 1842, charged that the Lamaist clergy "exist only to enrich themselves, and therefore their number should be reduced."[9] This proposal to reduce drastically the number of Lamaist clergy and datsans gave rise to an opposition movement led by Bandido-Khambo-Lama (the title of the highest-ranking cleric) D. Ch. D. Ishizhamtsoev against Dymbylov and the Russian officials who stood behind him.

By the end of the 1840s, the Buriat and Kalmyk Lamaist communities had their most important state representation in the Lamaist section of the Department of Spiritual Affairs of Foreign Confessions of the Ministry of the Interior—a department established in 1832 to oversee non-Orthodox religious institutions in the Russian Empire. Despite the efforts of the Russian Orthodox Church to check the expansion of Lamaism by administrative means, the number of monks exempted from state taxes increased and Lamaism continued to grow, claiming by 1849 as many as 124,916 followers with 34 monasteries, 146 *sumes* (chapels), and 4,546 clergy (291 on state salaries and 4,255 financed by local communities).[10]

As conflict grew between the Russian church and administration on the one side, and the Lamaist clergy on the other, Minister of the Interior L. A. Perovskii sent his own special representative, Levashev, to investigate the matter. The results of Levashev's investigation were spelled out in his decree of 15 May 1853, "On the Lamaist Clergy in Eastern Siberia." In accordance with the geographic peculiarities of the region, the memoran-

---

[8] *Letopisi*, 54, 95 n. 58; *Entsiklopedicheskii slovar'*, 78:568.

[9] *Letopisi*, 55; D. S. M. Williams, "The Mongolian Mission of the London Missionary Society: An Episode in the History of Religion in the Russian Empire," *Slavonic and East European Review*, 56, no. 3 (1978): 342. On the basis of archival materials of the London Missionary Society, Charles R. Bawden reported that Dymbylov, who had attended the English Missionary School for ten years and was appointed a *taiishi* in 1838, had made similar statements against the English missionaries, "making representations to the Russian government, that our labours are not needful among the Boriats." See "English Mission Schools among the Buriats, 1822–1840," *Zentralasiatische Studien des Seminars für Sprach- und Kulturwissenschaft Zentralasiens der Universität Bonn* 16 (1982): 216, 237.

[10] RGIA, f. 821, op. 133, d. 394, ll. 24a, 25a; f. 796, op. 445, d. 306, l. 6b.; f. 821, op. 133, d. 409; T. Berezin [Sviashchennik], "Zabaikal'skaia pravoslavnaia missiia v tsarstvovanie Imperatora Aleksandra II (1855–1881)" *Pravoslavnyi blagovestnik* 22 (1893): 19–32; 23 (1893): 11–26; 24 (1893): 5–19. In the first half of the nineteenth century there had been several attempts to reduce the number of lamas on state salaries.

OF RELIGION AND EMPIRE

dum dealt with the Buriats and Tuvinians but not the Kalmyks in European Russia. Levashev's position was that the Russian government should not seek to undermine the Lamaist clergy per se, but to cut their contacts with clergy in Mongolia and Tibet, which were under Chinese control. This was easier said than done, however, as the porous frontier between the Russian- and Chinese-controlled areas was virtually impossible to guard.[11] Levashev also showed that the charges laid against the lamas by the Russian church and local administration had been based only on rumors or simply fabricated. He confirmed that the lamas obeyed the Russian authorities, who forbade the construction of new *datsans* and admission of new lamas, and "as for the slow pace of Christianization among the non-Christians, regrettably, for this I must blame our Orthodox clergy, who have contributed to it neither by word nor by deed."[12]

Further entrenched by the "Official Nationality" policy of Minister of Education S. S. Uvarov and the transformation of the office of Supreme Procurator of the Holy Synod into a ministerial position by Count N. A. Protasov, the Orthodox Church continued in the second half of the nineteenth century to enjoy the support of the monarch and the government at the expense of the non-Christian population of the empire.[13] In the Transbaikal region lamas' requests for the construction of clerical buildings were treated extremely restrictively by the Department of Spiritual Affairs of Foreign Confessions (in accordance with the 1853 decree), always under the pretext of "the damaging impact of Lamaism upon the successful civil development of the local non-Christian population."[14]

The first aggressive persecutions of Lamaists took place in the early 1870s under Governor-General N. P. Sinel'nikov, who did not limit himself to administrative regulations but even undertook the destruction of

[11] RGIA, f. 796, op. 197-VI-3, d. 311, l. 34a; f. 821, op. 133, d. 409, ll. 115b–117a.
[12] RGIA, f. 821, op. 133, d. 409, ll. 43b–44a.
[13] On the influence of German-English Pietism-Protestantism in St. Petersburg through the Russian Bible Society (Prince A. N. Golitsyn, I. Ia. Schmidt, V. M. Popov) and in the Transbaikal under the aegis of Count M. M. Speranskii, I. B. Tseidler, Baron P. L. Schilling von Canstadt, R. Iuille and others; developments in church policy after 1824 and the anti-Protestant mood kindled at first by Francophobes and then by Anglophobes (Metropolit Serafim, Arkhimandrit Fotii, Count A. A. Arakcheev); and the end of Protestant influence in Russia and of the Protestant mission to the Buriats, see Williams, "The Mongolian Mission," 335, 337ff.; Bawden, "English Mission," 212, 224; idem, *Shamans,* 51–53, 329–334; Josef Glazik, *Die russisch-orthodoxe Heidenmission seit Peter dem Grossen: Ein missionsgeschichtlicher Versuch nach russischen Quellen und Darstellungen,* Missionswissenschaftliche Abhandlungen und Texte, vol. 19 (Münster, 1954); Helen Sharon Hundley, "Speransky and the Buriats: Administrative Reform in Nineteenth Century Russia" (Ph.D. diss., University of Illinois, 1984); Igor Smolitsch, *Geschichte der russischen Kirche, 1700–1917,* vol. 1, ed. W. Philipp and P. Scheibert, Studien zur Geschichte Osteuropas, vol. 9 (Leiden, 1964); idem, *Geschichte der russischen Kirche,* vol. 2, ed. G. L. Freeze, Forschungen zur osteuropäischen Geschichte: Historische Veröffentlichungen des Osteuropa-Instituts der Freien Universität Berlin, vol. 45 (Wiesbaden, 1991).
[14] RGIA, f. 821, op. 8, d. 1234, ll. 3b–4a.

206

Lamaist places of worship. It was during this time that the Buriats (both laity and clergy) started to organize themselves to protect these places.[15] From that time onward, the church more than ever focused its efforts on portraying the Lamaist clergy as the prime hindrance to Orthodox missionary work, and the government issued decrees limiting the mobility of the lamas. At the same time, both church and state tried to discredit the work of the local medicine men and sent missionaries with medical knowledge and skills to work among the Buriats.

The policy of heavy regulation by local authorities and the Ministry of the Interior complemented the goals of the Transbaikal mission, refounded in 1862, and the founding of missionary societies in 1865 and 1869. Beginning in 1867, church and government authorities helped Buriat converts to be elected into the steppe councils (dumas) in the hope of implementing Russification policies through them and thus influencing the development of the mission and the related questions of land and settlements. These attempts, however, proved to have little success.

At the same time, the church launched an open attack on liberal central and local officials, accusing them of noncompliance with the 1853 decree. (Later in the nineteenth century, church propagandists would charge that the legalization of Lamaism and the lamas' work among the Buriats, and the allocation of state budgets and lands to the *datsans* and their clergy, had prepared the ground for the rise of Buriat nationalism.) Attempting to limit the power of the Bandido-Khambo-Lama (whose position, according to the 1853 law, included control of the Lamaist clergy for all of Eastern Siberia), the Holy Synod, led by Supreme Procurator K. P. Pobedonostsev and Archbishop Veniamin of Irkutsk, succeeded in obtaining a new government decree of 7 July 1889 excluding the Lamaists of Irkutsk province from the Bandido-Khambo-Lama's jurisdiction (in effect restricting the latter's influence to the Transbaikal).[16] Though this decree caused numerous complaints from the Buriats, their demands to restore the status quo ante were ignored until the Edict of Toleration of 17 April 1905.[17]

Similarly, the Russian Orthodox Church used personal and political in-

---

[15] *Letopisi*, 56.

[16] RGIA, f. 1276, op. 14, d. 657, ll. 4a, b, 22a. The cooperation of Pobedonostsev and Veniamin, "who gave to the Holy Synod in the winter of 1886–87 several suggestions regarding the improvement and new construction of missionary stations in Siberia" is also mentioned in Gerhard Simon, "Konstantin Petrovič Pobedonoscev und die Kirchenpolitik des Heiligen Sinod 1880–1905," *Kirche im Osten: Studien zur osteuropäischen Kirchengeschichte und Kirchenkunde*, vol. 7 (Göttingen, 1969), 66.

[17] Even in 1905, however, the influence of the church was so strong that the suggestion of the appointed Committee on Confessional Affairs (*Osoboe Soveshchanie po Delam Very*) supporting restoration of the status quo ante was not accepted by the government: cf. RGIA, f. 1276, op. 14, d. 657, l. 23a. This question was decided in favour of the Buriats only at a

fluence in St. Petersburg and Astrakhan to obtain from the government severe regulations concerning the Kalmyk Lamaist clergy. Decrees of 1825 and 1834 placed the clergy under strict government control.[18] A Chancellery of Lamaist Spiritual Affairs (1836–1847) was required to report regularly to the Council of the Kalmyk Administration on the number of *khuruls* (monasteries) and clergy. In 1836 there were reported to be 5,270 clergymen and 105 *khuruls*, but a decree of March 4, 1838 restricted the numbers to 30 large *khuruls* and 46 small ones, and reduced the size of the salaried clergy to 2,650. By 1843, the latter number had been further reduced to 2,503.[19]

Although regulations of 1847 reforming the administration of the Kalmyk people placed special emphasis on freedom of religion as a personal right, at the same time the Ministry of State Domains was empowered to ensure that the number of Lamaist clergy and *khuruls* did not increase. The ministry had the right to give permission for the construction or renovation of *khuruls*, which were to be financed only by the voluntary donations of the Kalmyks or from assets belonging to the clergy. The lamas' complaints about a continuous reduction of clergy went unheeded. When in 1852 Lama Dzhinzan sent such a complaint to the Ministry of State Domains and raised his objection to the policy requiring the number of lamas to be in a certain proportion to the number of Kalmyk households, he was offered a higher salary instead of an increase in clerical personnel. He turned down the offer, refusing to be co-opted.[20]

In the decree of 1847 the government forbade the Lamaist clergy to write petitions on behalf of the Kalmyks and to interfere in secular matters. The Lama was explicitly ordered not to intervene in property or criminal proceedings of either laypeople or clergy. Violation of public order was penalized with revocation of the privileges guaranteed to the clergy, and the accused were handed over to the administration of the *ulus* (the main Kalmyk social and administrative unit). The aims of these regulations were obvious. The Russian empire tolerated Kalmyk Lamaism as an organization inasmuch as it offered a reliable guarantee of self-government in religious affairs. Yet the ultimate goal was to complete the sec-

---

meeting of the Provisional Government on 16 August 1917; it was formalized by the decree of 14 September 1917.

[18] *Polnoe sobranie zakonov Rossiiskoi imperii: Sobranie pervoe* (St.Petersburg, 1830), vol. 40 (1825), no. 30,290 (hereafter *PPSZ*). *Polnoe sobranie zakonov Rossiiskoi imperii: Sobranie vtoroe* (St.Petersburg, 1830–85), vol. X (1835), no. 7,560a (hereafter *VPSZ*).

[19] Tsentral'nyi Gosudarstvennyi Arkhiv Respubliki Kalmykiia, Elista, f. 42, op. 1, d. 31, ll. 4a, b (hereafter TsGARK). L. S. Burchinova, "Lamaistskaia tserkov' Kalmykii v sisteme Rossiiskoi gosudarstvennosti (Razrabotka pravovogo statusa kalmytskogo dukhovenstva v pervoi polovine XIX v.)," in *Lamaizm v Kalmykii*, 27–30.

[20] *VPSZ*, vol. 22 (1847), no. 21,144; TsGARK, f. 42, op. 1, d. 43, ll. 5a, b.

ularization of the clergy and to put it under the control of state authorities. In the long term it was a question of weakening the influential, more educated monks, who (with the cooperation of much of the Kalmyk aristocracy) was increasingly coming to play the role of a Kalmyk sociocultural elite. The opportunities for Kalmyk clergymen to influence government policies were naturally limited. Nevertheless, they learned to utilize the weaknesses and contradictions within the system to their advantage in at least three ways: winning a foothold in the Ministry of the Interior, gaining personal access to the tsar, and later on exploiting the academic interest of the increasingly important departments of Oriental Studies at the Academy of Sciences and St. Petersburg University.

The first coordinated efforts of the Ministries of State Domains and the Interior and the Holy Synod to enforce limitations on Kalmyk Lamaism were carried out in the early 1860s by Colonel K. I. Kostenkov, an energetic advocate of the law-and-order principle. Kostenkov's plans included reduction of the Kalmyk clergy by more than 50 percent and its social isolation: he decreed that "all Kalmyk clergy should roam [*kochevat'*] only together with the *ulus* administration, in other words in the steppe," far from Kalmyk groups on the Volga who were undergoing acculturation.[21] Charging that Kalmyk boys were being brought to the *khuruls* against their wills, he suggested that parents should not be allowed to bring their children and that boys entering *khurul* schools be no younger than sixteen. With proposals such as this, the Ministry of State Domains was certain to meet with the approval not only of the Ministry of the Interior; the Holy Synod and the Ministry of Education were also happy to support a decree that aimed in effect at prohibiting the Lamaist clergy from educating Kalmyks between seven and sixteen years old.

Missionary and Conversionary Work: The Buriats

The first mission among the Buriats of the Transbaikal, the so-called "Dauri mission," was founded in 1680, sixty years after the foundation of the diocese of Tobol'sk by Archbishop Kiprian. The mission was initiated by Metropolitan Pavel and Patriarch Ioakim, and headed by Abbot Feodosii, who with eleven other monks reached Selenginsk in February 1681 and built a monastery there a year later. [22]

[21] RGIA, f. 821, op. 8, d. 1235, ll. 4b–5a; Dordzhieva, "Lamaistskie khuruly," 27. The number of 1,530 clergy allowed in 1847 was to be reduced to 744 persons.

[22] Prokopii Gromov [Protoierei], *Nachalo khristianstva v Irkutske, i Sviatyi Innokentii, pervyi episkop Irkutskii: Ego sluzhenie, upravlenie, konchina, chudesa i proslavlenie* (Irkutsk, 1868), 4–19, 24–28, 36; Bogdanov, *Ocherki*, 156–60.

Under bishops Mikhail (1814–30), Irinei (1830–31) and Meletii (1831–35), the mission acquired new vigor, stimulated by competition with English missionaries based along the Selenga, Khodon, and Onon rivers. Even then, the resurgence of missionary work could not be sustained. Government support was unsystematic and limited, so that missionary work was instead left to local Russian priests.[23] Moreover, the process of missionizing remained purely formal. Shocked English missionaries reported in the 1820s that the church had no intention of converting the non-Christians to Christianity, but only of making them "real" Russian subjects through mass baptism:

> No systematic efforts were made by the Russians to convert the Buriats, but 'many hundreds' entered the 'Greek church' by baptism. However, no attempt had been made to instruct the converts or to encourage Christian practise. Consequently, converts differed from their heathen fellow-countrymen only by certain outward marks, such as the wearing of a small cross, allowing the hair to grow, and dressing partly in Russian manner.[24]

No less important was the fact that the church had to turn its efforts additionally to converting the Old Believers. The Old Believers had begun to arrive in Eastern Siberia in the middle of the eighteenth century as peasants and merchants, and settled in the Transbaikal regions of Tarbagatai, Bichur, and Mukhorshibir, where they were known as *semeiskie* ("families").[25]

Until the end of the 1850s missionary work concentrated on the conversion of those who could be easily coopted: the Buriat aristocracy, their families, clan members, and dependents employed in the Buriat administration. Parallel to economic, legal, and social assimilation, conversion represented the chief cultural means of administrative integration and Russification of the Buriat elite. Such a strategy of acculturation aimed at baptizing the top of the Buriat social hierarchy in order to take advantage of the aristocracy's authority over clans and *uluses*. The resulting factions and fissions within native society were useful by-products of such colonial policies. The priests and missionaries cooperated directly with district governments, the governors of Eastern Siberia, and the imperial ministers and ministries, creating an institutional structure for the government's growing interest in the mission, its success, and its organizational forms. As a result, the state began to consider the mission a part of its own realm. For example, in 1843 the tsar personally decreed that an annual budget

---

[23] Berezin, "Zabaikal'skaia pravoslavnaia missiia"; Bawden, *Shamans*, 327f.

[24] Williams, "The Mongolian Mission," 340.

[25] Gromov, *Nachalo khristianstva*, 10–14, 41–44, 75, 78, 81f.; Zhukovskaia, "Iz istorii religioznogo sinkretizma," 121; Simon, *Konstantin Petrovič Pobedonoscev*, 71, 79f., 165f., 168–87; M. V. Lysekno, *"Semeiskii" kompleks Zabaikal'ia*, (Ulan-Ude, 1982).

be set aside for presents to Buriat converts, and obliged the local administration to submit reports on the pace of conversions.[26]

With the foundation of a state-sponsored missionary society in 1865, the mission was officially declared a part of government policy. The missionary society was under the direct patronage of the Empress Maria Alexandrovna and governed by a council based in St. Petersburg. Its purpose was to spread the Orthodox faith among the pagans and other non-Christians of the Russian empire and even outside it. In accordance with new Russian imperial ambitions, Central Asia was now considered within the reach of missions, and the mission in China was to be intensified later as well. In the Altai and Transbaikal the goal was to counteract the influence of Islam and Lamaism among those Kazakhs, Kirgiz and Tuvinians who had remained shamanists.[27]

In addition, the Buriat mission turned from the aristocracy, many of whom were by now already converted, to the common indigenous people. In this sense the old mission had reached its limits. Spectacular mass baptisms, still common as recently as the 1840s, were not practiced for the time being. By the early 1870s, however, the church was ready to strengthen its position by drastic and aggressive means. Annual numbers of conversions increased throughout the Baikal region. The head of the mission and the diocesan administration supported forced baptisms by the missionaries, so that the mission could formally claim great successes. A crucial factor in the support of local authorities was their desire to impress the Grand Duke Aleksei Alexandrovich, who was touring Eastern Siberia in 1873. In Irkutsk, mass baptisms were staged for his benefit.[28] Such forced conversions created nominal Christians who had baptism certificates and were entered into the registers as Christians but received no further guidance and continued to worship their old gods. The government authorities were well aware of the formality of such conversions and the new converts' lack of understanding of the Christian precepts.[29]

Under Count D. A. Tolstoi as minister of education and supreme procurator of the Holy Synod from 1865 to 1880, both agencies worked hand in hand to create favorable political and financial conditions for the

[26] RGIA, f. 383, op. 9, d. 8079, ll. 2–3a. The emperor's decree regarding the budget was extended every ten years, documented for the years 1853 and 1863. RGIA, f. 383, op. 15, d. 18279, l. 8a; op. 25, d. 39588, l. 3a.

[27] *VPSZ*, vol. 40 (1865), no. 42, 309. "The Society for the Restoration of the Orthodox Faith in the Caucasus" was founded in the same year (ibid., no. 41,733). For more information on the Orthodox mission among the Muslim population of Central Asia and the Caucasus, see Simon, *Konstantin Petrovič Pobedonoscev*, 235–48.

[28] Natsional'nyi Arkhiv Respubliki Buriatiia, Ulan-Ude, f. 171, op. 1, d. 147, l. 2a (hereafter NARB); Ioann Kosygin [Missioner sviashchennik], "Ocherk istorii rasprostraneniia khristianstva mezhdu Tunkinskimi buriatami na Torskoi stepi za istekshee piatidesiatiletie (1827–1877)," *Trudy Pravoslavnykh Missii Irkutskoi Eparkhii*, vol. 3 (Irkutsk, 1885), 558–99.

[29] RGIA, f. 796, op. 197-VI-3, d. 311, l. 15a.

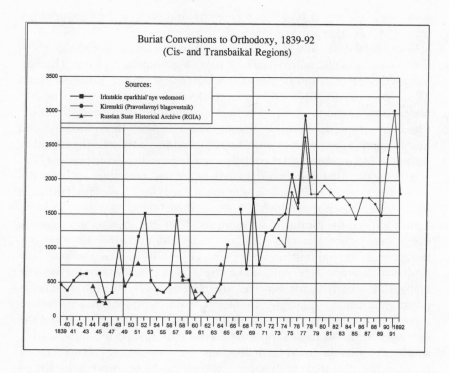

Buriat Conversions to Orthodoxy, 1839-92
(Cis- and Transbaikal Regions)

Sources:
■— Irkutskie eparkhial'nye vedomosti
●— Kirenskii (Pravoslavnyi blagovestnik)
▲— Russian State Historical Archive (RGIA)

Transbaikal mission. Even after leaving both these posts, Tolstoi continued to influence policy regarding the mission as minister of the interior and a member of the State Council.

The mission received further impetus when the post of supreme procurator was assumed by K. P. Pobedonostsev (1881–1905), an adviser to the emperors Alexander III and Nicolas II, both of whom had personal interest in Eastern Siberia.[30]

The graph shows the yearly numbers of baptisms of Buriats to Orthodoxy from 1839 to 1892. It illustrates the sharp increase in baptisms related to the foundation of the Orthodox Missionary Societies (1865–69) and the tours through Siberia of Tsar Alexander III (1873) and the future Nicholas II (1891). It shows clearly that the average number for the period 1869–92 is about three times higher than for 1839–68.[31]

---

[30] Simon, *Konstantin Petrovič Pobedonoscev*, 15f., 18f., 21, 25, 37, 39, 45.

[31] The data in the graph come from governors' reports and published clerical sources. RGIA, f. 383, op. 9, d. 8079, l. 2; op. 10, d. 9375, ll. 2a, b; op. 15, d. 18279, l. 2a; op. 22, d. 33036, ll. 1a, b; op. 24, d. 37714, ll. 1a–3b; f. 796, op. 132, d. 1831, ll. 1a, b; f. 797, op. 17, d. 39331, l. 26b; "Statisticheskaia vypiska iz otchětov Ober-Prokurorov, skol'ko v kakom godu bylo kreshcheno iazychnikov v Irkutskoi eparkhii," *Pribavleniia k Irkutskim Eparkhial'nym Vedomostiam* 51 (1879): 623; Agafangel Kirenskii [Episkop], "Otchět o sos-

After the greater part of the shamanist Cisbaikal Buriats had been baptized, the Orthodox Church began to focus its mission on the Lamaists. (Despite the unfavorable circumstances of the 1870s, the influence of Lamaism in the Transbaikal had not diminished; in fact, it may have increased as Buriats expressed their resistance to Orthodox missionaries by turning to it clandestinely.) For this purpose, Pobedonostsev convened a meeting under the leadership of Irkutsk Archbishop Veniamin to discuss "the issues of the mission, Old Belief, and the foundation of new parishes." In July–August 1885, seven Siberian bishops and governors (including the governor general of Eastern Siberia) met in Irkutsk. Veniamin saw the cause of the mission's crisis in a lack of support from the local authorities in challenging Lamaism. Furthermore, he considered D. G. Anuchin and Baron A. N. Korf to be secret patrons of Lamaism. Veniamin found a strong ally in Pobedonostsev, who himself complained in 1887 of the growing "power" and "influence" of Lamaism at the imperial court. After some shuffling behind the scenes, Pobedonostsev in 1889 secured the appointment of a new governor general for Eastern Siberia, A. D. Goremykin, whom he described to Veniamin as "a man of the church spirit."[32]

Archbishop Veniamin and Bishop A. Kirenskii saw Goremykin's appointment as an opportunity to renew missionary efforts among the Lamaist population in the old style. The new wave of mass conversions pleased the heir to the throne Nikolai Aleksandrovich, who traveled through Irkutsk province in the summer of 1891. Goremykin and local authorities ignored Buriat petitions complaining of forced baptisms and violence. On the contrary, following the suggestion of the Holy Synod, an imperial decree of 12 March 1894 established an independent Transbaikal diocese in Chita headed by the bishop of Transbaikal and Nerchinsk (formerly the first vicar of Irkutsk diocese). Further support of the Transbaikal mission came from the new Chita seminary, for which the State Council provided a credit of up to three hundred thousand rubles.[33] Support for the missionaries was also improved, which must have made it even harder for them to accept the aftermath of the 1905 Toleration

toianii i deiatel'nosti Irkutskoi dukhovnoi missii za 1892 god," *Prilozheniia k Pravoslavnomu Blagovestniku* 20 (1893): 80–90; 21 (1893): 90–98; 22 (1893): 98–108; 23 (1893): 108–18.

[32] V. P. Girchenko, "Stranitsa iz istorii khristianizatsii buriatskogo naseleniia v kontse XIX-go veka: po neizdannym arkhivnym materialam," *Zhizn' Buriatii* 1–3 (1926): 98–107 (quotation, 104). Compare also P. Kudriavtsev, "Stranichka iz istorii nasil'stvennogo kreshcheniia buriat" ibid., 6 (1929): 63–66; Simon, *Konstantin Petrovič Pobedonoscev*, 46, 71. Pobedonostsev also undertook the replacement of the incumbent minister of the interior, I. N. Durnovo, by I. L. Goremykin, a relative of A. D. Goremykin.

[33] *Polnoe sobranie zakonov Rossiiskoi imperii: Sobranie tret'e*, vol. 21 (1901), no. 20,912; vol. 23 (1903), no. 23,616 (hereafter *TPSZ*).

A Buriat lama of the Transbaikal region. This lama was one of those paid by a local community, not by the imperial budget. Rossiiskii Gosudarstvennyi Istoricheskii Arkhiv, f. 1293 (Technichesko-stroitel'nyi komitet MVD, 1768–1917 gg.), op. 129, d. 456.

Edict. With the system of coercion lifted, thousands of formally and forcibly baptized Buriats turned away from the church and returned to Lamaism and shamanism. The "fruits of the missionary cause" were put to ruin at one blow.

The Kalmyks

The conversion of the Kalmyks began under quite different historical and political circumstances from that of the Buriats. Given the political independence of the Kalmyks, no missionary work among them was possible in the seventeenth and eighteenth centuries, and the government and church made few attempts to convert them. Those Kalmyk nobles who chose to convert (usually in order to separate themselves and their clans from the authority of the Kalmyk khan) found themselves joining the Russian nobility in the capital, while most converted commoners were registered as Cossacks and sent to the hosts of the Don, Stavropol' on the Volga (today Tol'iatti), and Orenburg.[34]

The first signs of serious missionary activity among the Kalmyks date to the 1820s. In August 1824, Supreme Procurator P. S. Meshcherskii asked the Ministry of Finance to allot over nine thousand desiatinas of state land in Tsaritsyn district (Saratov province) to settle twenty-five Kalmyk converts.[35] In 1840, the issue of renewing missionary work among the Kalmyks was again raised when the Holy Synod, in the hope of obtaining more administrative and financial help, submitted a memorandum to the Ministry of State Domains explaining that the conversion of the Kalmyks was difficult "in part because of their religious fanaticism, in part because of their relationship with their nobles."[36] As a result, the ministry asked military governor Temiriazev to submit a proposal for the Kalmyks' conversion to Christianity. In his 1843 report to Supreme Procurator N. A. Protasov, Temiriazev bemoaned the unavailability of comprehensible prayerbooks and textbooks in Kalmyk and the Russian clergy's ignorance of the Kalmyks' language and religious beliefs. Temiriazev denounced the Holy Synod's description of the Kalmyks' "religious fanaticism" as a ruse to protect itself against criticism and to conceal the church's own inactivity and incompetence.

---

[34] For a more detailed history of the Russian mission among the Kalmyks see Arkhimandrit Gurii [Stepanov], *Ocherki po istorii rasprostraneniia khristianstva sredi mongol'skikh plemen,* vol. 1: *Kalmyki: izsledovanie,* pt. 2: *Rasprostranenie khristianstva sredi kalmykov* (Kazan, 1915); Michael Khodarkovsky, *Where Two Worlds Met: The Russian State and the Kalmyk Nomads, 1600–1771* (Ithaca, N.Y., 1992), 177, 180–83, 197f., 205f., 208f.; Schorkowitz, *Die soziale und politische Organisation bei den Kalmücken,* 414–21, 509, 511, 521, 523.

[35] *VPSZ,* vol. 5 (1830), no. 3,653.

[36] RGIA, f. 1589, op. 1, d. 1016, l. 2a.

The above episode illustrates two important differences in comparison with the mission to the Buriats. First of all, the Kalmyks were under the administration of the Minsitry of State Domains. Insofar as the ministry was able to defend its particularistic interests against the state, the Kalmyks and their self-administration were sheltered from the effects of Nicholas I's policies as executed by the church and the Ministry of the Interior. The powerful troika of governor general, vice governor, and archbishop so typical in East Siberian administration did not exist in Astrakhan. Secondly, unlike the Buriats, the Kalmyks were no longer in a frontier region, and therefore attracted little government concern regarding national security.

The church had serious difficulties getting the mission to the Kalmyks off the ground. Despite Protasov's efforts, the church remained in a subordinate position to the Ministry of State Domains. An 1846 resolution of Minister P. D. Kiselev referred only vaguely to the forthcoming administrative and economic reforms of 1847, "which were to bring the Kalmyks closer to the Russian way of life and the Christian religion," and stated that for the time being there was no need for the Kalmyk administration to undertake active missionizing.[37] The experience of Russian missionary efforts in Eastern Siberia also played an important part in the decision making of the Ministry of State Domains. Unwilling to deprive the Kalmyk nobles of their taxpaying subjects or to risk submitting Kalmyk converts to the abuses of Russian priests, the ministry stated that "priests often make demands on converts for their own gain and then persecute the converts under the pretext that they do not follow the fasts, while *inorodtsy* such as the Kalmyks, because they practice animal husbandry in the steppes, do not and can not use any other food but meat and milk."[38]

In 1847 an important decree of the Ministry of State Domains provided a set of regulations and incentives for conversion among the Kalmyks. Kalmyk nobles were assured that in the case of their conversion they would lose neither their hereditary rights nor their subjects. If a converted noble wished, he could turn his subjects into state peasants and receive an annual compensation for the amount of lost income. Converted subjects of Lamaist nobles were allowed to decide for themselves whether to stay with the nobles or become state peasants and be settled on state land allotted in proportion to the number of tents in the *ulus*.

If they chose the latter alternative, the noble received a single payment

---

[37] RGIA, f. 1589, op. 1, d. 1016, ll. 17a, b; *VPSZ*, vol. 22 (1847), nos. 20,758, 21,144, 21,145.

[38] RGIA, f. 1589, op. 1, d. 1016, ll. 19a–20a. Brief accounts regarding the status and morale of the clergy and church are in Simon, *Konstantin Petrovič Pobedonoscev*, 8off.

equivalent to five years of tax revenue lost for each of his converted subjects.[39] Converts were also entitled to a payment of baptism money of eight rubles per person or fifteen per family. Initially, they were given permanent exemption from taxes and obligations, but in 1851 the exemption was limited to only eight years. To encourage the Kalmyks' intended transition to peasant status, the exemption could be extended to twenty years if within three years they were settled and began farming.

As in the past, however, the conversion of Kalmyks remained little more than a formality. Chief Overseer of the Kalmyks M. I. Tagaichinov complained in a letter to the Ministry of State Domains in 1853 that poor Kalmyks were accepting baptism in order to evade taxes and receive privileges, and as a result they paid taxes neither to their nobles nor to the state. He further charged that converts were maintaining their nomadic lifestyle, were not separating from Lamaist Kalmyks, did not baptize their children, and neither married nor lived in accordance with Christian customs.[40]

The ministry's attempts to combine conversion with settlement produced little result. At the same time as thousands of Buriats were being baptized, only a few hundred Kalmyk families converted to Christianity. A more determined missionary policy for the Astrakhan Kalmyks began under Count D. A. Tolstoi. Tolstoi sent a confidential letter to the Ministry of the Interior on 10 November 1866, the result of which was the formation of the Planning Committee on the Spread of Christianity among the Lamaist Kalmyks, which included Archbishop Afanasii of Astrakhan, civilian Governor A. L. Degai, and Chief Overseer of the Kalmyks K. I. Kostenkov.[41] The committee pursued intensified missionary activities aimed at aggressively undermining the social influence of the Lamaist clergy. The mission was not as extensive or as violent as that among the Buriats, though it would gain intensity in the 1880s. But the political conditions had already changed decisively in favor of Russification, and the Holy Synod cooperated congenially with the Ministries of Education and State Domains.

The missionaries' activities exceeded the usual pastoral and liturgical tasks. Converts required continuous supervision even after accepting baptism. The missionaries' work was made especially difficult because of the hostile attitude of Lamaist Kalmyks toward the newly converted and lack of interest in convert affairs on the part of local *ulus* overseers.

Discord created by the missions placed low-ranking state officials in the

---

[39] *VPSZ*, vol. 22 (1847), no. 21,144, paras. 32–38; RGIA, f. 381, op. 16, d. 9401, ll. 1a, 3a, b.

[40] Ibid., f. 383, op. 14, d. 16041, ll. 12a, b, 20a–21b; ibid., op. 16, d. 20108, ll. 1a, b.

[41] RGIA, f. 821, op. 8, d. 1235, ll. 1a, b.

steppes in an especially difficult position. The church completely ignored the fact that Kalmyk Lamaism was under the legal protection of the state and that Ministry of State Domains officials were required to protect the interests of Lamaists. The situation changed, however, in 1902 when the administration of the Kalmyks was handed over to the Ministry of the Interior, which was now supposed to protect the converts from the hostilities and assaults of Lamaist Kalmyks.

Usually the missionaries propagated the Christian faith among the Kalmyks of the scattered *khotons* (the smallest social and administrative units) by traveling across the steppes. Whenever possible, they stayed with Kalmyk communities or extended families. Beginning in 1891, Kalmyks were obliged to provide missionaries with horses, food, and shelter (previously, state officials but not clergy had enjoyed these privileges). This made possible extended journeys, the expansion of the missionary area, and increased opportunities for religious discussion with the Kalmyks. In time, it led to greater numbers of conversions, primarily of nuclear families. Socio-economic and moral ties within communities collapsed. Converted families were regarded as foreigners (*khari*) by their still-Lamaist extended families, and lost access to social welfare and to joint property such as herds, land, equipment, inheritance, *kalym* (bride price), and dowries. They had to earn their living, however, on the same pastures and in their usual districts, in conflict with their relatives, as well as the local aristocracy, judiciary, and Lamaist clergy. As with the Buriats, therefore, the Missionary Committee was preoccupied with state regulation of the "land question." Converts were supposed to receive an allottment of land for settlement and farming in the vicinity of the missionary stations or frontier parishes. But such allottments could take place only at the expense of neighboring Kalmyk communities, which led to inevitable tensions between Lamaist Kalmyks and their converted relatives. As a result, the tensions within communities reverberated on the *ulus* and governmental levels as well.

Lamaism Between Blossoming and Persecution, 1903–1925

Despite state regulations in its favor, the mission among the Kalmyks, unlike the one in the Transbaikal region, could boast only very moderate success. It suffered a further setback in the 1890s when the Russian Foreign Ministry began to permit easier access to Tibet.[42] On the occasion of his supposed first journey to the Astrakhan Kalmyks in 1898, Bandido-

[42] Arash Bormanshinov, "A Secret Kalmyk Mission to Tibet in 1904," *Central Asiatic Journal* 36, no. 3–4 (1992): 169–73.

Khambo-Lama Agvan Dorzhiev laid the foundations for united Buriat-Kalmyk efforts to strengthen Lamaism in the Russian empire (in St. Petersburg as well as in the east). His popularity among the Kalmyks was manifest in acts of hospitality and in the many donations presented to him. The Astrakhan governor, M. A. Gazenkampf, alarmed by the Lama's presence and convinced that "this was an unadultarated manipulation of the Kalmyks' religious feelings," expelled him from the region.[43]

The Manifesto on the Reestablishment of Domestic Order of 26 February 1903 brought about a modicum of religious tolerance. The first Lamaist high school, founded in the late 1890s, was finally legalized in 1903.[44] The most significant change came with the uprisings of 1905. Under pressure, Nicolas II was compelled to put an end to the policy of Russification in the controversial fields of education and religion, and to issue edicts guaranteeing freedom of religion and civil liberties to Old Believers and all other confessions. Formally, the Russian Orthodox mission ceased to exist. Thanks to the efforts of Count Sergei Iu. Witte, an article was inserted into the April 17 Edict of Toleration promising revision of the 1853 decree on Lamaism and forbidding any future reference to the Lamaists as "idolaters" (*idolopoklonniki*) or "pagans" (*iazychniki*).[45] In addition, a special committee under the guidance of Count A. P. Ignat'ev developed a "Small Legal Reform" that guaranteed the right of the *datsans* and *khuruls* to have their own presses and uncensored religious literature, to import cultural and religious objects, and to increase the number of Lamaist clergy.[46]

The Orthodox Church, the Holy Synod, and the missionaries launched a rearguard action against the secularization policies of the government and against the forcefully converted *inorodtsy*, Balts, and Poles who now sought to return to their original faiths as Lamaists, Muslims, shamanists, Protestants, or Catholics. It is apparent from correspondence between the Holy Synod, the dioceses, and the Ministry of the Interior that the Buriats' exodus from the Orthodox Church began spontaneously and collectively.[47] As a result of political and legal battles with the Russian clergy and administration, the exodus increasingly assumed the form of a politically organized movement. This was accompanied by a campaign for Buriat education, and both were branded by the church as "national movements." By politicizing the Buriat apostate movement and portraying

---

[43] RGIA, f. 821, op. 133, d. 394, l. 7b; compare with RGIA, op. 138, d. 115; see also A. N. Komandzhaev, "Polozhenie lamaistskoi tserkvi v kalmytskom obshchestve (konets XIX–nachalo XX v.)," *Orient* 1 (1992): 145–51.

[44] RGIA, f. 821, op. 133, d. 394, l. 9a.

[45] RGIA, f. 1276, op. 14, d. 657, l. 2a.

[46] *TPSZ*, vol. 25 (1905), no. 26,136; vol. 27 (1907), no. 28,758.

[47] Komandzhaev, "Polozhenie," 146; Bogdanov, *Ocherki*, 161. A similar process took place in the Baltic and Volga regions; see Simon, *Konstantin Petrovič Pobedonoscev*, 252.

these Buriats as no longer loyal Russian subjects, the church attempted to enlist the support of the government ministries. Thus, beginning in 1903 and continuing with the 1905 toleration law, Lamaism occupied an ambiguous position in the Russian empire that resulted in its simultaneous blossoming and persecution, until the systematic purge of its leaders in the 1930s.

The crucial Article 3 of the 1905 Toleration Edict provided that converts (or descendants of converts) who were formally considered to be the members of the Russian Orthodox Church, but in practice had remained true to their former faith, could return to their old faiths if they wished. Following a Department of Spiritual Affairs of Foreign Confessions circular of 18 August 1905 (which was accepted by the Holy Synod on December 14 and sent to the dioceses), those who could prove the above condition were issued letters permitting their reconversion.[48]

In 1907, Archbishop Tikhon reported to the Holy Synod that Buriats of Tunkinsk district had begun to abandon Russian settlements and to break off contacts with the church in order to evade the one-month application deadline provided by the Department of Spiritual Affairs of Foreign Confessions circular and pursuit by missionaries. Tikhon was furious about "Lamaist agitators" who he said were taking advantage of popular ignorance and telling people that the Toleration Edict was a decree ordering them to return to their old faith. On one occassion more than three thousand Buriats signed and submitted a petition to the Irkutsk governor stating their collective wish to return to Lamaism.[49] In 1913, Archbishop Serafim confirmed that the number of Buriats who had left the church was indeed large. In Tunkinsk district, most of the ten thousand Christian Buriats had reconverted to Lamaism before the end of 1905. The secessions had been carried out according to regulations and with the active support (maybe even encouragement) of Buriat officials who regarded them as a matter of course, a turning of Buriats "to their ancestral and national [natsional'naia] religion".[50]

The governors were instructed to ask the local church offices for monthly reports about the number of Buriats leaving the church. Seeing this as an infringement of their own authority, bishops crusaded vociferously against this obligation. Tikhon charged that the Buriats' return to Lamaism was merely a means for political plotters to create out of "calm and passive Buriats" a Buriat-Mongol nation (narodnost'). The conver-

[48] RGIA, f. 796, op. 189, d. 8494, l. 10a. Compare also Ralph Tuchtenhagen, *Religion als minderer Status: Die Reform der Gesetzgebung gegenüber religiösen Minderheiten in der verfassten Gesellschaft des Russischen Reiches 1905–1917*, ed. B. E. Pfeiffer, Friedensauer Schriftenreihe, ser. B: Gesellschaftswissenschaften, vol. 1, (Frankfurt, 1995), 95, 284.

[49] RGIA, f. 796, op. 188, d. 7837, l. 1b.

[50] Ibid., op. 197–VI-3, d. 311, l. 3b; ibid., f. 821, op. 133, d. 394, ll. 24a, 25a; Bogdanov, *Ocherki*, 161.

sions, in his words, "have nothing to do with freedom of conscience, which naturally presupposes full consciousness."[51] The Synod reacted maladroitly: Supreme Procurator S. M. Luk'ianov declared in a 1908 decree that the church could not let go of baptized Christians and must do everything possible to save their souls from destruction. This applied primarily, of course, to those who had always belonged to the church, but also to *inorodets* converts, and "therefore the point of view of the Ministry of the Interior is contradictory to the teachings of the Orthodox Church."[52]

When Luk'ianov again raised the issue in 1910 in a letter to Prime Minister P. A. Stolypin, he received a decisive response in which Stolypin objected to any interference in his sphere of competence. Stolypin stated that he closely supervised all branches of the government, and particularly carefully "the application of the present laws and regulations concerning departure from the Orthodox Church." As for setting the criteria of the legitimacy of such departures, "it was entirely within the jurisdiction of the civil authorities and did not depend on the judgment of any diocese."[53] Finally, Stolypin reiterated that a declaration of intent to leave the church was formally sufficient to withdraw the person making such a declaration from the church's jurisdiction and for the church to lose its rights over that person. The Buriats, in any case, did not understand either the Russian language or the church liturgy, did not go to church and "were only nominal Christians, in fact behaving no differently from other Lamaists"; understandably, therefore, they had interpreted the manifesto as permission to return to their old faith.[54]

Self-critical explanations for the collapse of the mission remained a rare exception within the church. One such exception was Archbishop Serafim, who in 1913 submitted to the Holy Synod a lengthy report analyzing the reasons for the Buriats' mass exodus from Christianity. Even then, his comments were relatively late and despite his unusually frank tone he chose to avoid any criticism of the policies of his predecessor, Archbishop Tikhon.[55] This dispute between the church and the government certainly would have led to an open rift if not for the revolutionary events of 1917. Stolypin had put forth his arguments too uncompromisingly.

In the meantime, the resurgence of Lamaism was not limited only to the Buriats and Kalmyks. In 1908 the government approved Dorzhiev's petition to have a *datsan* built in St. Petersburg. In a confidential letter to Stolypin on 12 June 1908, Foreign Minister A. P. Izvol'skii stressed the political significance of this project: it would enable Russia to maintain good

---

[51] RGIA, f. 796, op. 188, d. 7837, ll. 2a, 3b, 7a.
[52] RGIA, f. 796, op. 188, d. 7837, l. 16a.
[53] RGIA, f. 796, op. 189, d. 8494, ll. 18a,b.
[54] RGIA, f. 796, op. 197-VI-3, d. 311, l. 2a.
[55] RGIA, f. 796, op. 197-VI-3, d. 311, l. 3a.

relations with the Dalai Lama and thus to have greater influence on China and on Russia's Lamaist subjects.[56] Rising phoenix-like from the ashes of persecution, Lamaism gained strength under the guidance of the Buriat clergy and began to unite its Buriat, Kalmyk, and Tuvinian believers.

This provoked a strong counterattack, in the form of an increase in state regulations that would turn to open persecution after the October Revolution. After all, freedom of religion and assembly were creating openings for organizations that had begun to develop political programs under the mantle of religious and cultural-educational goals. Ignoring the inner connections between culture and politics, the government in theory allowed the former and at the same time thought it could disallow the latter. In practice, however, local authorities felt obliged to embrace repression "in the interest of the state" because they believed that the Lamaist clergy was emerging as a "political-national danger."[57]

It was not until after the February Revolution of 1917 that all residents of the Russian empire were granted freedom of confession and conscience as a fundamental right regardless of religion or nationality.[58] In August 1917 the Provisional Government secularized the synodal administration and established a Ministry of Confessions with two departments, one for the Russian Orthodox religion and one for the others (under the old name of the Department of Spiritual Affairs of Foreign Confessions), plus a legal department. The new minister's competence combined those of the former supreme procurator of the Holy Synod and the director of the Department of Spiritual Affairs of Foreign Confessions.[59]

With regard to the Buriats and Kalmyks, the Provisional Government aimed at close cooperation between state officials and organs and the Lamaist clergy. On 22 July 1917, the First Convention of Kalmyk Lamaists was held in Astrakhan, attended by clerical and secular representatives of the Kalmyks of the Astrakhan, Stavropol', and Terek regions. The assembly adopted a new constitution for Kalmyk Lamaist administration, resolved to increase the number of *khuruls* and registered clergy, and established a State Confessional Commission.[60] Soon afterward, government representatives and Buriat-Kalmyk clergy formed a special commission

---

[56] A. I. Andreev, "Iz istorii Peterburgskogo buddiiskogo khrama," *Orient* 1 (1992): 6, 12. The first plans to found a Buddhist place of worship in St. Petersburg were already circulating in 1898. The construction of the *datsan* in the Russian capital represented Tibet's reaction to Britain's Himalayan adventurers and to indecisive Russian diplomacy.

[57] RGIA, f. 821, op. 138, d. 115, l. 35a; Bogdanov, *Ocherki*, 162.

[58] *Sobranie uzakonenii i rasporiazhenii pravitel'stva, izdavaemoe pri Pravitel'stvuiushchem Senate* (Petrograd, 1914–17), no. 188, art. 1099, 14 July 1917.

[59] Ibid., no. 190, art. 1134, 5 August 1917.

[60] I. I. Orekhov, "Lamaistskoe dukhovenstvo Kalmykii v nachale XX veka," in *Lamaizm v Kalmykii*, 51–54.

which on 2 August 1917 repealed 1889 and 1890 restrictions on the registered Lamaist clergy and their head, the Bandido-Khambo-Lama.[61]

As a result of the October Revolution and unique geopolitical conditions in Eastern Siberia, Lamaism was able temporarily to strengthen its position there, and to resume its mission among Buriat and Tuvinian shamanists.[62] Of no less importance was the development of a reform movement in Cisbaikal shamanism that proved flexible enough to adapt to the "new psychology of the Buriat masses formed during the revolution." In 1922, a young female shaman characterized the change as follows: the "new shamans" first helped the poor, and then the rich, and they drastically restricted the use of expensive *tarasun* (an alcoholic beverage) and tobacco in healing ceremonies, as well as animal sacrifices.[63]

In January 1918, the Soviet government enacted a Decree on Separation of Church from State and School from Church which brought the decisive secularization of both the European and Asian (Soviet-controlled) parts of Russia. In a pragmatic and populist manner, local authorities were entrusted with the determination as to whether religious customs and institutions presented a threat to public order; thus the right to practice a religion openly became directly dependent on the forces controlling local organs.[64] This, along with an August 1918 decree on nationalization of church property, aimed at banning religious communities and churches as corporate bodies, removing the basis of their social influence, and dissolving their internal organizational structures. But the right of individuals to practice their religions in private or in small groups was as yet untouched. While the Soviet government planned to fight the church using state-institutional means, individual beliefs and religions themselves were to be handled by the ideological means of scientific atheism and organizations such as the Godless (*Bezbozhniki*), Atheists (*Ateisty*), and "Adversaries of Religion" (*Antireligiozniki*). A decree of the Central Committee of the Russian Communist Party of August 1921 defined the ideological goal of atheist propaganda as "the replacement of religious beliefs by the well-ordered Communist scientific system, to explain the questions for which the working peasant masses have until now sought answers in religion."[65]

Under War Communism and amid the Red-White conflicts that contin-

[61] NARB, R. 483, op. 1, d. 16, l. 15a.

[62] Ibid., R. 643, op. 1, d. 7, ll. 2a–b, 4a.

[63] Ol'khonets, "Ol'khonskii krai: kraevye dela," *Krasnyi Buriat-Mongol: Organ Burrevkoma i Buroblkoma RKP* 12, no. 3 (27 April 1922): 3.

[64] *Sobranie uzakonenii i rasporiazhenii rabochago i krest'ianskago pravitel'stva* (Moscow, 1917–1938), no. 18, art. 263, 23 January 1918.

[65] S. I. Ubushieva, "Ateisticheskoe vospitanie trudiashchikhsia Kalmykii v period stroitel'stva sotsializma (1917–1937 gg.)," in *Lamaizm v Kalmykii i voprosy nauchnogo ateizma*, ed. U. Erdniev (Elista, 1980), 52.

ued in 1918–20 among both Buriats and Kalmyks, the decrees originally enacted against clerical organizations were in revolutionary, proletarian, and nationalistic practice redirected against people and property in the form of excesses of one kind or another. Very early on, Kalmyk territory was turned into the central theater of war on the southeastern front. It therefore suffered the ravages of war (committed primarily by the Red Army) far more than the Baikal region. Dorzhiev, seeing that Lamaist clergy and believers were being physically threatened, traveled into the Kalmyk steppe in the spring of 1919 to prevent the worst. Many lamas requested dismissal from their posts to avoid impending purges. In October 1921, Dorzhiev wrote to Stalin, as an accredited representative of the Tibetan government, openly complaining about the behavior of the Red Army toward Kalmyk Lamaists: "All social, administrative, private, and monastic buildings have been subject to devastation. Walls, roofs, doors, and other parts have become firewood for units of the Red Army holding the front along the Kalmyk steppe."[66]

The fate of Lamaism in the Soviet Union—like that of Islam—was until the end of the 1920s closely intertwined with Soviet policies regarding national minorities and policies toward Asia in general. The contradictory interests of domestic and foreign policy were brilliantly exploited by some national deputies to guarantee a respite for Lamaism. Despite the onset of antireligious persecution, the Soviet government, desiring the support of Muslims and Buddhists, stopped short of launching an all-out war against their religious beliefs and institutions.[67] However, it was predictable that such a situation would be only temporary. As Sovietization advanced further into Buriat and Kalmyk regions, the number of Lamaist clergy and *khuruls* was reduced. Antireligious propaganda was especially successful among assimilated Kalmyk fishermen in the Iandyko-Mochazhnyi *ulus*, who in the last decades had had intensive contact with the Russian fishing industry. When the registration of denominations began there in 1924, twelve of nineteen *khuruls* were closed without difficulty, and 143 clergy transferred to secular status.[68] Letters of complaint written to the Central Confessional Commission on 17 June 1924 show that clergy bitterly resisted decrees of the Soviet government undermining the activities of the *emchi*, limiting the importation of Tibetan medicine, and imposing a minimum age requirement of eighteen for monastic educa-

[66] NARB, R. 643, op. 1, d. 6, l. 2a.

[67] Hans Bräker, *Kommunismus und Weltreligionen Asiens: Zur Religions- und Asienpolitik der Sowjetunion*, 2 vols. (Tübingen, 1969–71), 1:90–95 et passim. According to Walter Kolarz, *Religion in the Soviet Union* (London, 1961): "Winning Asian support has seemed at times more important to the Kremlin than conducting an all-out attack on Buddhist beliefs and institutions" (448).

[68] Rossiiskii Tsentr Khraneniia i Izucheniia Dokumentov Noveishei Istorii, Moscow, f. 17, op. 16, d. 352, ll. 27a, b (hereafter RTsKhIDNI).

tion. One letter remarked that persecution had become more extreme under the Communists: "even in the old days, when Buddhism was under attack by the missionaries, we never had to experience such oppression."[69] In its physical assault on Buddhist clerical influence, the party intended "to allow only the strongest and most resilient of the clergy to remain."[70] A pogrom-like atmosphere prevailed, and in 1925 some Kalmyk officials were cautioning against committing atrocities against Lamaist monks.[71]

In August–September 1925, the Fifth All-Kalmyk Conference of Lamaist Clergy was held. Even in the preparation stage, it was dominated by the Bolsheviks, who determined the location of the conference, its participants, and the topics to be dealt with. The conference elected as Lama of the Kalmyk People the moderate L. S. Tepkin, who had gone to Tibet in 1911 to pursue his education and had returned to Petrograd in 1922 as representative of the Tibetan ambassador to the USSR, the former Bandido-Khambo-Lama Dorzhiev. Thanks to Dorzhiev's position, the conference approved combining the smaller *khuruls* into several large ones, a proposal that had already been supported by the State Confessional Commission and decided by the Fourth All-Kalmyk Conference.[72] This was the first conference in which party policy had a crucial influence not only on form and procedure but also on content, reducing it to predetermined propaganda. Reports of later conferences show an even stronger party influence, increasing ideological control of the participants, and a further widening of the gap between "modernist" and "traditionalist" forces. In 1926 and 1927, a group of "reformers" (A. Dorzhiev, S. F. Ol'denburg, F. I. Shcherbatskii, and O. O. Rozenberg) made a strained attempt to subordinate the Lamaist religious system to philosophy, placing Buddhism into a modern scientific frame and putting it into the service of atheist ideology. This may have been the last attempt to rescue Lamaism until the collapse of the Soviet Union.

[69] TsGARK, R. 112, op. 1, d. 49, l. 13a.
[70] RTsKhIDNI, f. 17, op. 31, d. 22, l. 4a. See also Ubushieva, "Ateisticheskoe vospitanie," 58f.
[71] TsGARK, R. 112, op. 1, d. 49, l. 3a.
[72] Gosudarstvennyi Arkhiv Rossiiskoi Federatsii, Moscow, f. 1318, op. 9, d. 42, l. 1a; RTsKhIDNI, f. 17, op. 31, d. 22, l. 50a; Bormanshinov, "The Lamas," 19f. Another conference was held in 1929.

III

Facing Islam

CHAPTER NINE

Colonial Dilemmas:
Russian Policies in the Muslim Caucasus

FIROUZEH MOSTASHARI

The Russian administration of nineteenth-century Caucasia faced a formidable dilemma: should it attempt to convert its Muslim subjects to Christianity? Or would it be more judicious to co-opt local religious leaders in the interest of bureaucratic administration? Should Russian imperial rule, in other words, be consolidated with or without the introduction of the Orthodox faith?

The proper answer seemed to vary depending on the ethno-religious groups and geographical areas under consideration. Thus in Ossetia and Ingushetia, where the population was nominally Muslim with continued strong attachment to polytheistic practices, the Russian administration supported and financed some missionary activities among the Muslim highlanders (*gortsy*). The officials justified their plans by claiming that the areas in question had once been Christian and that they were simply facilitating the "re-Christianization" of erstwhile Christians. By contrast, the rebellious areas of Chechnia and Daghestan remained beyond such consideration. Nor did the government make any serious efforts to convert to Orthodox Christianity the Muslim population in the Baku and Elizavetpol' provinces of eastern Transcaucasia (roughly the territory of today's Azerbaijan). Islam was deeply entrenched here and gravitated toward the Muslim religious leaders of the neighboring Persian and Ottoman empires.

The geographic positioning of Caucasia at the frontier with the two Islamic empires contributed to an uneven strength of Islam in the eastern and western Caucasus. In the western and central regions the religious and cultural legacy of Christian Byzantium was still evident, whereas eastern Caucasia had been influenced by Sufism, a branch of mystical Islam spread by the Naqshbandi Brotherhood. The eastern regions were politically volatile, especially after the resurgence of the Sufi brotherhoods under the legendary guerrilla leader Sheikh Shamil in the nineteenth century.[1]

In view of the precarious political and military position, the Russian government was compelled to pursue a more flexible policy toward the Muslims of the eastern Caucasus. Avoiding direct involvement, the Russian policy was to win the support of the offical Muslim clergy, the *ulema*, against the popular preachers of Sufi Islam. Until the demise of the old regime, Russian administrators cautiously proceeded with their efforts to control the Muslim religious hierarchy of the Caucasus. We shall examine below how these policies were articulated, deployed, and finally resisted by the local population.

Attempting Evangelization: "Re-Christianizing" Central Caucasia

Located at the crossroads of the Persian, Byzantine/Ottoman, and Russian empires, the Caucasus had historically been an arena of competing religious and political interests, and the ebb and flow of Islam and Christianity had depended upon the relative fortunes of these empires. Islam had first been introduced to the region in the seventh century by the expanding empire of the Abbasids, while eastern Christianity made inroads in the Caucasus under the Byzantines. Yet both religions could claim at best moderate success among the largely illiterate and animist highlanders.[2]

With the fall of Byzantium in 1453, the influence of Christianity waned and its evangelizing activities ceased. To the contrary, the rise of the Ottoman empire meant a further strengthening of Islam in the Caucasus. Observing the Circassian highlanders, the Dominican friar Johann of Luki wrote in 1637: "The Circassians speak both Circassian and Turkish. Some of them are Muhammedan and others are Greek Orthodox. But there are more Muhammedans. The Orthodox priests, who live in Tereki, sometimes baptize them but rarely explain the holy scriptures. With each

---

[1] For scholarship on Shamil see Thomas M. Bartlett, "The Remaking of the Lion of Daghestan: Shamil in Captivity," in *Russian Review* 53, no. 3 (July 1994): 353–67; Moshe Gammer, *Muslim Resistance to the Tsar: Shamil and the Conquest of Chechnia and Daghestan* (London, 1994); and Uwe Halbach, "Holy War against Czarism: The Links between Sufism and Jihad in Nineteenth-Century Anticolonial Resistance against Russia," in *Muslim Communities Reemerge*, ed. Andreas Kappeler et al. (Durham, N.C., 1994), 251–76.

[2] "Nachalo khristianstva v Zakavkaz'e i na Kavkaze," *Sbornik svedenii o Kavkazkikh gortsakh* 2 (1869): 20–23.

passing day, the number of Turks (Muslims) grows. All that remains of Orthodox belief is the custom of carrying food to the graves . . ."[3]

It was through interaction with the Cossack community on the Terek river that the Caucasian highlanders came into contact with Russian Orthodox Christianity.[4] By the seventeenth century, priests residing among the Terek Cossacks were the primary agents in the conversion of the highlanders. According to the observation of a diplomat visiting from the German principality of Holstein in 1636, the Cossacks had even built a monastery in the town of Terki, to baptize the Caucasian highlanders.[5] Initially, the Muscovite tsars had been reluctant to antagonize the Ottoman Turks by openly admitting their ambitions to convert neighboring Muslims to Orthodoxy.[6] In time, however, as Russia's hold over the Caucasus strengthened over the next centuries, so did the boldness with which the Russian state approached the question of missionary activity along the southern frontiers of the empire.

It was in the eighteenth century that the Russian government began to pay attention to the "revival" of Christianity in central Caucasia, focusing its efforts on the Kabardinians, Ossetians, and Ingush. According to nineteenth-century historians, many of these highlanders (the Ingush and Ossetians in particular) exhibited previous religious influences in their eclectic practices. While observing Islam, they also rested on Sundays and observed pagan holidays. Physical remains, such as ruins of churches, chapels, and crosses, seemed to point to a previous period of Christianity.[7]

Russian government officials claimed that because the highlanders had once been Christians, they would therefore "baptize with great willingness." In 1744 the Holy Synod was instructed to organize Georgian priests for converting the highlanders and constructing schools and churches in their midst.[8] The choice of Georgian priests betrayed the timidity with which the Synod took these initial steps toward missionary activity in the Caucasus. The Georgians, who were also Orthodox Christianians, could act as suitable surrogates for Russian missionaries and appear less intrusive.

In 1752, in order to facilitate the conversion of the Ossetians and the Ingush, the Holy Synod founded the Ossetian Commission under the aus-

---

[3] Ibid., 22.

[4] W. E. Allen, "The Volga-Terek Route in Russo-Caucasian Relations," in *Russian Embassies to the Georgian Kings (1589–1605)*, ed. W. E. D. Allen, (Cambridge, 1970), 162.

[5] Ibid., 164.

[6] Michael Khodarkovsky, " 'Not by Word Alone': Missionary Policies and Religious Conversion in Early Modern Russia," *Comparative Studies in Society and History* 38, no. 2 (1996): 273.

[7] "Ingushi," *Sbornik svedenii o Kavkazskikh gortsakh* 9 (1876): 21–22.

[8] P. G. Butkov, *Materialy dlia novoi istorii Kavkaza s 1722 po 1803 god*, pt. 1 (St. Petersburg, 1869), 266.

pices of the Georgian church.[9] In its attempt to attract the highlanders to Orthodox Christianity, the Ossetian Commission relied heavily on material incentives. Upon baptism, new converts received fifty kopecks, a new shirt, and a copper cross which they believed to be gold. Many volunteered for baptism several times in order to receive more gifts.[10] Parents consenting to send their children to the missionary schools appeared less interested in a Christian education than in the monthly stipend of two rubles, food and clothing allowed for their children.[11] Between 1746 and 1764, the Ossetian Commission boasted slightly over two thousand converts.[12]

The failure of the Ossetian Commission to win genuine converts provoked the personal intervention of Catherine II. Concerned by the Synod's report that "the local inhabitants convert for the most part out of their greed in order to obtain provisions, and then remain in their former ungodliness," Catherine recognized that it was essential to train the converts from a young age. She instructed the governor of Astrakhan province to allocate more resources to the education of the young converts, to increase the stipend for students and teachers in the Russian school in Mozdok, and to secure for them sufficient supplies and comfortable living quarters.[13]

During Catherine II's reign, the government's missionary policy centered on educating non-Christians in the precepts of Christianity, rather than emphasizing the formalities of baptism. The Synod's secret instructions to the Ossetian Commission on how to approach the nonbelievers emphasized teaching the commandments as well as obedience to God, church law, and one's parents. The instructions cautioned against the use of religious symbols such as icons, as the Synod was concerned that the animist population would begin to worship them as idols.[14] Moving away from its former ritualistic approach to Christianity, the Synod instead concentrated on conveying the basic tenets of the Orthodox Christian religion.

The new approach presented different problems. The main obstacle to the teaching of Christianity was the paucity of language skills among the Georgian and Russian missionaries. After Russian priests were assigned to the Ossetian Commission in 1771, church services began to be held in Russian. Occassionally, translators provided short explanations in the na-

[9] "Ingushi," 22.
[10] Ibid., 25.
[11] Butkov, *Materialy*, 268–270.
[12] Ibid., 438.
[13] Ibid., 439–44.
[14] Ibid., 445–47.

tive languages,[15] yet the use of the Russian language and poor translations prevented effective communication.

Not surprisingly, the Christianity practiced by the new converts was hardly Orthodox. The Caucasian highlanders adapted Christianity to their pagan ways, and celebrated Christian holy days by bringing their animal sacrifices to church. Their marriage rituals included combining the blood of bride and groom, which put the highlanders' practices in direct contradiction to church doctrine.[16] Islamic rituals were also retained and practiced alongside the Christian and the pagan ones. One official publication of the Russian administration in the Caucasus explained this confusing state of affairs as follows: "The old beliefs of the Caucasian highlanders have not yet disappeared and their practice is allowed in our times. Even though they had once been called Christian and they are now considered Muslim, a significant portion of the highlanders are pagan."[17] Nevertheless, claiming that Orthodox Christianity was not so much being introduced as resurrected in the Caucasus, the government and church continued their missionary efforts in the region.

Obstacles to Missionary Activity in the Muslim Caucasus

In the last two decades of the eighteenth century, Russian involvement in the Caucasus brought Russia into proximity and further conflict with the Persian and Ottoman empires. A series of military victories and diplomatic treaties at Turkmanchai in 1828 and Adrianople a year later left Russia in political control of Greater Caucasia.[18] Despite the nearly complete Russian military conquest of the Caucasus, missionary efforts had yet to bear fruit. One report delivered to General Ivan Paskevich, administrator in chief of the Caucasus (1827–31), openly admitted that there were no differences between the baptized and nonbaptized highlanders. Baptized highlanders continued to abide by their polytheistic customs and were Christian in little more than name. In southern Ossetia, the churches built during the previous century were empty and the priests

---

[15] Ibid., 272.

[16] "Nachalo khristianstva," 17–19.

[17] Ibid., 18.

[18] In this essay, "the Caucasus" refers to Greater Caucasia or Kavkaz, as it was known to the Russians. This area extended from the Black Sea to the Caspian Sea and south of the Caucasus Mountains to the Aras River. For accounts of Russia's conquest of the Caucasus see John F. Baddeley, *The Russian Conquest of the Caucasus* (London, 1908); N. G. Dubrovin, *Istoriia voiny i vladychestva russkikh na Kavkaze*, 6 vols. (St. Petersburg, 1871–88); V. A. Potto, *Istoricheskii ocherk Kavkazkikh voin ot ikh nachala do prisoedineniia Gruzii* (Tiflis, 1899); and V. A. Potto, *Utverzhdenie russkago vladychestva na Kavkaze 1801–1901*, 4 vols. (Tiflis, 1901–8).

idle. The Russians began to view even the baptized highlanders as "Christians gone astray."[19]

The conversion of the Caucasian highlanders was further thwarted by the activities of mystical Islamic movements in the northern Caucasus. The Muslim highlanders were unwilling to accept Russian sovereignty and under the influence of Naqshbandi Sufis began a "holy war" against the Russians. Known as Muridism, this movement did not recognize any worldly laws other than those laid down by the prophet Muhammed in the Shari'a.[20] In Muridism, social and religious protest had merged to create formidable anti-authoritarian and egalitarian tendencies. Muridism, in the words of one early twentieth-century historian, "proclaimed equality for all Muslims, rich and poor alike; the new teaching was therefore essentially popular, and from this time onward Muridism was a political movement grafted upon a purely religious one."[21] Insofar as it opposed Russian rule, Muridism was a political movement, and took a stance against local oppressors supported by Russian power.

In late 1829, the highlanders chose Ghazi Mohammad as the *imam* of Daghestan. Attempting to unite the Muslim population and resist Russian expansion, Ghazi Mohammad and his successor Hamzad Bek led military campaigns against the Russians in Daghestan and Chechnia between 1829 and 1834.[22] In his call for a "holy war" or *ghazavat* against the Russians, Ghazi Mohammad evoked the pains of tainted honor in order to rally the highlanders against Russia. He declared:

> People, we are not Muslims! Muslims cannot be under the rule of infidels. Only free persons are Muslims. For such a person the first task is *ghazavat* against the nonbeliever and then the fulfillment of the Shari'a. Without Ghazavat the Shari'a cannot be saved. True Muslims must arm themselves and fight the infidel, not sparing themselves or their families. And what are you doing? You pitiful cowards![23]

Ghazi Mohammad and Hamzad Bek were among the most popular religious leaders of the early nineteenth century. But the most successful military and religious leader was Shamil, a bearded man of medium height with piercing blue eyes. In September 1834, Shamil was elected the third *imam* of Daghestan, and for the next quarter-century the Russian commanders of the Caucasian Corps were preoccupied with defeating

[19] V. N. Ivanenko, *Grazhdanskoe upravlenie Zakavkaz'em ot prisoedineniia Gruzii do namestnichestva velikago kniazia Mikhaila Nikolaevicha* (Tiflis, 1901), 196–98.

[20] The term "Muridism" is derived from the Arabic *murid*, which means student or follower of a mystic teacher or *murshid*.

[21] Baddeley, *The Russian Conquest*, 237.

[22] Gammer, *Muslim Resistance*, 39–74.

[23] Ivan Ivanin, *Kavkazskaia voina i eia geroi* (Moscow, 1904), 110.

this enigmatic figure, who became known to the Russians as "the lion of the Caucasus."[24] Shamil's ascendancy presented not only a military threat to Russia, but it also thwarted the cause of Christianity in the Caucasus. In the territories occupied by his warriors, Shamil energetically enforced the Muslim laws of the Shari'a. In these lands the population received a religious education, and learned to pray and read the Quran.[25]

The appeal and spread of Muridism was more than a domestic threat. During the years of the Crimean War (1854–56), internal instability in the vicinity of the Russo-Ottoman frontier was of especial concern to the Russian government. Prince A. I. Bariatinskii, third viceroy of the Caucasus (1856–62) and a childhood friend of Alexander II, candidly admitted to the tsar that "the legal influence of Russia on the neighboring Muslim countries is weak, especially when it is unable to suppress the union of rebellious mountain tribes within its interior." Bariatinskii feared that the existence of an armed Murid movement within the Caucasus would entirely cripple the Caucasian army in the event of an external war.[26]

In order to provide a counterbalance to the Murid leaders, the Caucasian administration, under the stewardship of the first viceroy of the Caucasus, Mikhail S. Vorontsov (1844–55), promoted the interests of the official Muslim clergy, as this mosque-based group did not consider Sufi Islam to be legitimate. Under Vorontsov, Muslims were allowed into the lower and middle ranks of local administration, promoted, and given land rights in order to dissuade them from joining the ranks of the insurgents. It was not until Shamil had been captured in 1859 and Muridism quelled that the Russian administration again considered the issue of missionary activity in the Caucasus.

The Society for the Resurrection of Orthodox Christianity in the Caucasus

On 9 June 1860, Tsar Alexander II approved Bariatinskii's plans for founding the Society for the Resurrection of Orthodox Christianity in the Caucasus (*Obshchestvo Vosstanovleniia Pravoslavnago Khristianstva na Kavkaze*), which was to be based in Tiflis. In a royal rescript Alexander wrote: "In olden times Orthodox Christianity prevailed in those areas of the Caucasus that are now Muslim. In the mountains, to this time, many traces of the past remain, but the light of Christianity is inextinguishable.

---

[24] Baron August von Haxthausen, *Zakavkazskii krai—zametki o semeinoi i obshchestvennoi zhizni*, pt. 2 (St. Petersburg, 1857), 208.

[25] Gammer, *Muslim Resistance*, 232–33.

[26] *Otchet namestnika Kavkazskago i glavnokomanduiushchago Kavkazskoiu Armieiu za 1857–1859* (Tiflis, 1861), 19, 40.

With the conquest of the Caucasus, I desire that Orthodoxy be resurrected in this region."[27] "To spread the word of the Gospel" the tsar placed the society under the supervision of the viceroy of the Caucasus and the patronage of the tsaritsa, Maria Aleksandrovna. The Ossetian Commission was dissolved and its funds transferred to the new body.[28]

From its inception, the society was subject to the tensions and rivalries existing between the Caucasian administration and St. Petersburg. The society, after all, was the brain child of Bariatinskii, who ardently guarded his viceroyalty against the incursions of the central ministries. Bariatinskii's secular leadership of the society especially antagonized the Holy Synod, since ecclesiastical authorities no longer directed missionary activities in the Caucasus. Reacting to the encroachment on his sphere of influence, Metropolitan Filaret of Moscow was extremely critical of the society, its aims and organization. "Why resurrection of Orthodoxy?" he asked. "Does this mean that it is in decline?" "Would no efforts be made to convert the Muslims and pagans who had never been Christian?" And, above all, "why was the society headed by secular individuals?" Filaret argued that if the Russians were to examine the example of the Bible societies in England, they would see that these societies were led by members of the church hierarchy. Representing a centralizing perspective, Filaret demanded that the society's headquarters be transferred to St. Petersburg, where only one such society would operate for the entire empire.[29]

The viceroy of the Caucasus justified the existence of a separate organization based in his Tiflis headquarters by pointing out that in Siberia and western China, for example, Orthodox Christianity had not previously existed and that the tasks of his organization were entirely different from those in the empire at large. In addition, in the interests of political stability, the Caucasian administration could not openly aspire to convert the Muslims as this would invariably agitate the Muslim population. Bariatinskii wrote candidly: "If we openly express our desire not to resurrect but to spread Christianity in the mountains, we will justify the strongest prejudices of the Muslims and raise obstacles before the goals for which we have striven."[30] Bariatinskii was well aware that Muridism drew strength from the conviction that the Russians had planned to re-

[27] Kavkazskaia Arkheograficheskaia Komissiia, *Akty sobrannye Kavkazskoiu arkheograficheskoiu komissieiu*, vol. 12 (Tiflis, 1904), 526.

[28] Ibid., 526, 529. Another goal of the society had been the conversion to Orthodoxy of the exiled Old Believers, who had been sent to the Caucasus under Nicholas I as punishment for spreading their "heresy."

[29] A. L. Zisserman, *Fel'dmarshal Kniaz' Alexandr Ivanovich Bariatinskii: 1815–1879*, 3 vols. (Moscow, 1891), 3:121–24.

[30] Ibid., 129, 130.

place Islam with Christianity and that Islam was a "patriotic symbol" for the Caucasian highlanders, a sign of their independence and dignity.[31]

The tensions between central and regional authorities were also played out in the sphere of finance, when the Ministry of Finance withheld funds for priests proselytizing in the Caucasus. In response, Bariatinskii defended his local interests by arguing that if the government considered it essential that the priests of the interior regions of the empire be excellently educated, then this necessity was even more acute in the regions bordering Muslim populations. Otherwise, warned Bariatinskii, the priests would not only be unable to counter the spread of Islam, but would even fail at teaching their own followers.[32]

Bariatinskii was determined to learn from the experience of the Ossetian Commission. His new approach was to convey the necessity of learning local languages and the danger of appearing overtly interested in converting Muslims. He and his advisers drew plans for the missionaries to acquaint themselves with the local languages and customs and to translate major works of Russian literature and missionary writings into Azeri and Arabic.[33] Bariatinskii also ordered the society to translate the Orthodox liturgies into the Ossetian, Abkhaz, and Svanetian languages because he believed that these peoples, as well as the South Lezghins, Kabardinians, and some Chechens, had once been Christian.

To realize these plans, Bariatinskii organized the opening of seminaries in Tiflis and Stavropol', where missionaries would learn the languages of the highlanders. The Orthodox missionaries were even to learn medicine, so that they could render some practical assistance to the natives and appear less priestly. Bariatinskii's advisers even cautioned against the missionaries' garb resembling that of priests.[34] Overall, the society exercised extreme caution in its missionary overtures toward the highlanders.

Situated on the frontier of Christian and Muslim states, the Caucasus was especially susceptible to religious movements from neighboring countries. Areas close to the Black Sea were particularly vulnerable to Ottoman influence. Seeking to appeal to the religious sentiments of the Circassians, the Ottoman sultan generously bestowed the Muslim clergy with money and gifts.[35] In eastern Transcaucasia, it was Persian clerics who exercised moral influence over the predominantly Shi'ite population of the region. Reporting to Bariatinskii on the local state of affairs, one provincial governor lamented that "the influence of Islam has noticeably in-

---

[31] Ibid., 105, 129.
[32] Kavkazskaia Arkheograficheskaia Komissiia, *Akty*, 12:528.
[33] Ibid., 520.
[34] Zisserman, *Fel'dmarshal Bariatinskii*, 102, 138–39.
[35] Potto, *Utverzhdenie russkago vladychestva*, 143.

creased, to the detriment of Orthodoxy . . . weakening our political influence on the Christians of the neighboring Turkish provinces."[36]

When Bariatinskii departed from the Caucasus, the new viceroy, Grand Duke Mikhail Nikolaevich (1863–1881), abandoned the previous objectives of the society along with much of its ideal of proselytizing. Under the leadership of the realistic grand duke, the society limited its activities to refurbishing old churches and building new ones in Mozdok, Kuba, Ordubata, Kutais, and Piatigorsk. The society also aimed to ensure a satisfactory standard of living for its clergy, as the poverty of the Christian population reduced the means by which the clergy could gain additional income.[37] Altogether, the new objectives of the society were to uphold and strengthen Orthodox Christianity where it already existed in the Caucasus, and to develop plans for missionary activity among the Muslims.

By the late 1880s, the Caucasian administration had implicitly admitted the impracticality of attempting to proselytize among the Muslim highlanders, especially in view of the massive exodus of Caucasian Muslims to the Ottoman empire in the aftermath of the Russo-Turkish War of 1877–78. Under the administration of the grand duke's successor, Prince Dondukov-Korsakov (1882–90), the principal aim of the society remained defensive; it was to preserve Christianity in those areas of the Caucasus where it was already dominant. But after a long power struggle between the center and the periphery and between the ecclesiastical and secular establishments, Dondukov-Korsakov ceded his control of the society to the Holy Synod in 1885.[38] In the synod's report to the tsar, the society's goals were explained as follows: "The Society for the Resurrection of Orthodox Christianity in the Caucasus does not have an exclusively missionary character and is primarily concerned with supporting the existing churches, clergy and schools. . . . Its activities are directed not so much toward spreading Orthodoxy among nonbelievers, as restraining the Orthodox from being seduced by those of other belief."[39]

The society was not very successful in the first few decades of its existence; in fact, its achievements were modest even compared with those of the former Ossetian Commission. By 1900 only ninety-three Muslims had been converted to Christianity.[40] The weak position of Orthodoxy among

[36] Kavkazskaia Arkheograficheskaia Komissiia, *Akty*, 12:521–22.

[37] Velikii Kniaz Mikhail Nikolaevich, *Otchet po glavnomu upravleniiu namestnika Kavkazskago za pervoe desiatiletie upravleniia Kavkazskim i Zakavkazkim kraem ego velikim kniazem Mikhailom Nikolaevichem 6 dekabriia 1862–6 dekabriia 1872* (Tiflis, 1873), 93–99.

[38] This process had already begun in 1881 with the abolition of the viceroyalty of the Caucasus. It was not until 1905 that the viceroyalty was reinstated and local government gained control over the periphery.

[39] *Vsepoddanneishii otchet ober-prokurora Sviateishago sinoda K. Pobedonostseva po vedomstvu pravoslavnago ispovedeniia za 1884 g.* (St. Petersburg, 1886), 133–34.

[40] Alexandre Bennigsen and Chantal Lemercier-Quelquejay, "Musulmans et missions orthodoxes en Russe orientale avant 1917," *Cahiers du monde russe et soviétique* 13 (1972): 96.

An Orthodox bishop with converted animists of the Khevsur region in northeastern Georgia. *Pribavleniia k Tserkovnym vedomostiam* 27, pt. 1, no. 1 (1914).

the Caucasian highlanders and the decline of Christianity in the region had become apparent a decade earlier, as indicated in the yearly report of the society in 1890. Acknowledging that "Islam attracts highlanders from all walks of life," the society stated that "with each passing year, entire Christian villages go over to Muridism and, under the influence of the mullahs, harbor animosity toward the Russian state and especially its clergy."[41]

Caught between the contradictory aims of spreading, resurrecting, or preserving Orthodoxy, the Caucasian administration tempered its plans

[41] V. C. Krivenko, *Ocherki Kavkaza*, vol. 1 (St. Petersburg, 1893), 74–75.

for proselytism. Instead, it focused on finding support from within the Muslim community, a parallel process that had begun from the first days of the conquest of the Caucasus. Ultimately pragmatism and the interests of internal security outweighed the ideological predilection for propagating the Orthodox faith. On the frontier of the empire, the Caucasus proved resistant to the dictates of the imperial center.

Autonomy and Toleration

While the Caucasian administration was experimenting with missions in central Caucasia, it had adopted an entirely different policy in the eastern regions of the Caucasus, especially in eastern Transcaucasia.[42] Here Islam was deeply entrenched and neighboring Islamic states provided guidance and support for the Muslim clerics of the Caucasus. One high commissioner of the Caucasus reported to the tsar: "From the very beginning of Russian rule over the Caucasus, our government has been concerned with the moral dependence of the Muslims of this region on the clergy abroad, which is extremely hostile towards us. . . ."[43] Under these inhospitable conditions, the Russian administration viewed the question of proselytism from a more practical perspective. Here their task was limited to merely containing Islam rather than extending or even resurrecting Christianity.

The first half of the nineteenth century was a period in which the Caucasian administration, especially under the experienced viceroy Mikhail Vorontsov, sought to appease the traditional elites in order to win allies in the war against the Caucasian highlanders. Furthermore, by granting favors to the Muslim clerics, the Russians hoped to legitimize their rule in the eyes of a native population that suspected the government of conspiring to suppress Islam.

Vorontsov allowed the Muslim clerics to continue in their traditional roles as educators, judges, and social workers in their communities, particularly because the Caucasian administration was understaffed. During this period of Russian rule over the Caucasus, the official Muslim clerics enjoyed a degree of autonomy in their religious affairs that was unparalleled in the empire since the days of Catherine II. Both Sunni and Shi'ite clerics continued to exert considerable influence on their followers and

---

[42] Baku and Elizavetpol' provinces were the only areas in the eastern Caucasus where the government could have a religious policy. Areas to the north, including Chechnia and Daghestan, which were not under Russian control, were distinguished by an absence of official religious administration. Even after the defeat of Shamil, these areas were under special military rule and hence treated differently from areas under civilian rule.

[43] *Vsepoddanneishaia zapiska glavnonachalstvuiushchago grazhdanskoiu chast'iu na Kavkaze 1897–1902 gody* (Tiflis, 1903) 28.

elected their own members. The only exception to carrying on business as usual was the government's appointment of a liaison between the Muslim clergy and the administration. Typically there was one such cleric in each *uezd*, but his powers and responsibilities were not clearly specified.[44]

Guided by Vorontsov's ideas on civil rule, the Caucasian administration attempted to demonstrate the good will of the government toward the local Muslim clergy. In order to counter the Murid movement, it sought to give the official clergy a material stake in Russian rule. Thus lands that had been confiscated from mosques and gone to the Treasury after the initial conquest of the region were returned to the mosques. This move significantly increased the incomes of the mosques from their religious endowments, the *waqfs*.[45] The mosques were financially independent from the Russian administration, managed their own properties, and paid salaries to the Muslim clerics.

Numerous other concessions were enumerated in a project drawn up in 1849 for the organization of the Muslim clergy. These included a guarantee of full religious freedom, recognition of Muslim religious holidays, and protection of mosques, cemeteries, and shrines of Muslim saints. The administration also allowed the continued existence of *mektebs*, the mosque schools which provided children with basic literacy and a religious education. On the whole, the Russian administration allowed for a broad autonomy of the Muslim clergy.[46]

One of the most significant concessions made by the Russian authorities was accepting the continued existence of the Islamic justice system, the Shari'a religious courts. These courts were permitted to operate even after the incorporation of Transcaucasia into the imperial administrative structure. The Shari'a courts had jurisdiction over questions of a religious nature, marriage ceremonies, inheritance, wills, and the guardianship of minors, although they were excluded from the sphere of civil and criminal law. Even though the Shari'a courts coexisted with the Russian courts, the local population was reluctant to appeal to Russian-language courts in which the judges were ignorant of local languages and customs.[47]

The latitude given to the Muslim courts stimulated much debate within official circles. Proponents of centralization, like Minister of the Internal Affairs L. A. Perovskii, cautioned against the Muslim clergy's de facto substitution of the Shari'a for Russian law, and wrote that in view of the vagueness of Muslim law, "giving such powers to the clergy is danger-

---

[44] State Historical Archives of the Azerbaijan Republic, Baku, f. 289, op. 1, d. 1, l. 22 (hereafter GIA AR).

[45] *Kolonial'naia politika rossiiskogo tsarizma v Azerbaidzhane v 20–60 gg. XIX veka*, vol. 2, (Moscow, 1937), 341.

[46] Ibid., 345–47, 352.

[47] Ibid., 352–53; Russian State Historical Archive, St. Petersburg, f. 932, op. 1, d. 332, l. 2 (hereafter RGIA).

ous."[48] Others, like D. I. Bludov, the chairman of the Second Section of the Imperial Chancery, disagreed and claimed that the Russian civil courts were "incongruous with the inhabitants' understanding." Bludov argued that unlike their European counterparts, the Russians lacked the means to eliminate the religious courts at this time:

> The British in India and the French in Algeria constructed the courts differently for their Muslim subjects . . . but these governments had more capable administrators at their disposal, that is, judges devoted to service in India and Algeria, and well versed in Eastern languages and Islamic jurisprudence. We lack such officials, or at least their numbers are so limited, that they hardly suffice for staffing the viceroy's chancery.[49]

Russian local administration had little choice but to accept the participation of the Muslim clergy in the legal process.

Another Approach: Bureaucratization of the *Ulema*

For the Russian administrators of the Caucasus, the opportunity to limit the *ulema*'s sphere of activities presented itself after Shamil had been captured and the Murid movement defeated. To this end, the Russian administrators resolved to make the *ulema* dependent on the Russian state and to incorporate it into the imperial bureaucracy. The rationale for bureaucratic administration of the *ulema* was recognized early in the nineteenth century, but plans were put into effect only in 1864, after the Murid movement had been quelled. At this time the Caucasian administration took deliberate measures to curb the independence of the Muslim clergy and to minimize their judicial and educational functions. Bariatinskii even planned to weaken the influence of Islam by promoting local customary law.[50]

In April 1870 Grand Duke Mikhail Nikolaevich, who had a penchant for bureaucratic reorganization, submitted to the State Council a project titled, "On Regulations for Administering the Shi'ite and Sunni Muslim Clergy of Transcaucasia." Attempting to defend local interests against encroachments from the center, the viceroy tried to impress upon his colleagues in St. Petersburg that the question of the Transcaucasian Muslim clergy was of a unique nature and hence the region needed its own particular solutions. He demonstrated that the proportion of Muslims in

[48] *Kolonial'naia politika*, 390–91.
[49] Ibid., 392.
[50] Alfred J. Rieber, *The Politics of Autocracy: Letters of Alexander II to Prince A. I. Bariatinskii* (Paris, 1966), 69.

Transcaucasia was not comparable to that in the empire's interior provinces, where they constituted a minority surrounded on all sides by the Russian Orthodox population. In Russia, he explained, the Tatars had been under Russian rule for a longer period of time and did not "doubt the religious tolerance" of the Russian government. In Transcaucasia, the Muslims constituted the majority of the population; the area itself bordered on two Islamic powers; and after sixty years of continuous warfare, it had been only recently conquered. Therefore, the viceroy concluded, the issue of the Muslim clergy was not as urgent or politically charged in the interior provinces as it was in eastern Transcaucasia, where it constituted "one of the most important imperial issues."[51]

One of the government's major concerns was to break ties between the local Muslim clergy and their Islamic coreligionists in the Persian and Ottoman empires. Grand Duke Mikhail Nikolaevich proposed that "in order to avert dangerous consequences [of such relations], it is imperative to create within our borders a Muslim hierarchy, whose members are either chosen by the government, or are chosen under its supervision, and who would find it materially advantageous to cooperate with our government's goals."[52]

One year earlier, in a letter of January 1869 to the chairman of the Caucasian Committee, the viceroy had explained the rationale behind his proposed Muslim hierarchical organization as securing state surveillance and control over Muslim clerics who were hostile to the Russian state. Mikhail Nikolaevich also sought to counter the consolidation of a corporate identity among the *ulema*, and to limit as far as possible the sphere of activity of the Muslim clergy. These plans would entail monitoring the activities of religious schools as well as gathering information on religious endowments so as to control the flow of funds abroad for the support of foreign clerics.[53]

In order to safeguard against the influence of the Persian *ulema* in Transcaucasia, the viceroy proposed to abolish the position of *mujtahed*, the highest Shi'ite clerical authority. Mikhail Nikolaevich believed that the presence of the *mujtaheds*, who did not recognize the authority of the Russian state, was responsible for constant clashes between the Muslim clergy and the Russian administration. In addition, if the government were to recognize the Muslim religious hierarchies in the region, the Persian *ulema* would gain considerable influence, because no one could match the stature and prestige of the Persian *mujtaheds* in Transcaucasia. Hence, he decreed that foreign clerics were ineligible to hold office in

---

[51] Rossiia, Gosudarstvennyi Sovet, Departament Zakonov, *Materialy*, vol. 59 (1871), project no. 8, pp. 1–4. (hereafter *Materialy Gos Sov*).

[52] Ibid., project no. 8, p. 4.

[53] Ibid., project no. 33, p. 2.

Transcaucasia; only subjects of the Russian empire could join the ranks of the official clergy. The native *ulema* were not allowed to contact the clergy abroad or to rely on their financial assistance.[54]

These regulations were concerned only with offical Muslim clergy and did not extend to unofficial clerics or to the mystical sects such as the various Sufi and dervish orders. The Sunni and Shi'ite administrations were independent of one another, although they had parallel structures. At the apex of the Muslim religious administration stood the Shi'ite and Sunni Ecclesiastical Boards (*Dukhovnye Pravleniia*) chaired by a *sheikh ul-Islam* on the Shi'ite board and a *mufti* on the Sunni board. The viceroy and the minister of internal affairs jointly appointed the chairpersons of the ecclesiastical boards, thus bringing an end to the self-rule of the Muslim clergy. The *mufti* and *sheikh ul-Islam* were to report directly to the viceroy like other government officials and to provide him with yearly reports and copies of all the boards' decisions. In addition, they were held responsible for the orderly and peaceful practice of Muslim religious ceremonies in the region, as well as the interpretation and resolution of questions relating to Islamic law.[55]

The appointment of Muslim religious leaders by a Christian government and their transformation into civil servants was unacceptable to the Muslims of the Russian empire. Not only the Caucasian Muslims, but also the Tatars and Bashkirs objected to the subordinate position of the muftiate (Sunni Ecclesiastical Board) first established in Orenburg by Catherine II. The muftiate itself declared that appointment of the *mufti* by the government was in violation of Islamic law because according to the Shari'a the religious leaders were to be elected from among the *umma*, the Muslim community of believers.[56] Despite these protestations, however, the viceroy of the Caucasus continued to insist that the Muslim religious administration of the Caucasus was in a frontier region with fundamentally different versions of Islam, and therefore was different from both the Crimean and Orenburg muftiates.[57] Convinced by this argument, St. Petersburg proceeded with the previous plans.

The Caucasian administration expected high-level Muslim clerics to "instill trust and loyalty to the government in their coreligionists." They were to report all antigovernment propaganda to the authorities. The clergy was "forbidden without the special permission of the Caucasian

---

[54] Ibid., project no. 24, pp. 4–8; project no. 27, p. 3.

[55] Ibid., project no. 28, pp. 50–54. For information on the Muslim religious establishment also see Audrey L. Altstadt's *The Azerbaijani Turks: Power and Identity under Russian Rule*, (Stanford, Calif., 1992), 57–62.

[56] A. A. Rorlich, *The Volga Tatars: A Profile in National Resilience* (Stanford, Calif., 1986), 43, 58–59.

[57] *Materialy Gos Sov*, project no. 24, p. 6.

viceroy, to appeal to foreign clergy or to other powers . . ."[58] The Russian administration also expected the Muslim clerics to defend orthodox Islam against the "dangerous interpretations of impostor Islamic sects," such as Sufism and Muridism.[59] In return for its loyalty and the performance of administrative duties, the official Muslim clergy was exempt from property and municipal taxes, dues, and corporal punishment. Children of the clergy were also to benefit from these privileges as long as their fathers remained in service. And after twenty years of service, these rights were granted for life.[60]

The "higher" Muslim clergy benefited particularly from the government's incentives and rewards. The Russian administration was mainly concerned with appealing to the religious elite and not the rank and file. While the *mufti* and *sheikh ul-Islam* were entitled to two months' paid vacation per year, the use of six horses and an annual salary of 1,600 rubles, ordinary mullahs who served in the mosques could not take vacations exceeding one month and had salaries of 150 rubles per year.[61] This glaring inequality between ranks of the Muslim clergy created rifts among them and undermined the bureaucratization of the *ulema*.

The preferential treatment accorded to the higher official clergy brought about a general discontent among lower-level clerics and among the unofficial clergy, who were not in the state service and were part of the taxpaying population. As one provincial governor observed, the lower-level Muslim clergy "does not consider itself at all obligated to our [the Russian] government and appears discontented." The governor also indicated that these clergy encouraged the people to defy the authorities.[62] Indeed, the lower clerics encouraged the population to emigrate to neighboring Muslim countries. According to the *mufti* of the Caucasus, the lower-level Sunni clerics were especially drawn to the Ottoman empire and circulated rumors about the good life there.[63]

The bureaucratization of the *ulema* had estranged the lower clerics and the Muslim population from their religious leaders, who were considered to be on the Russian payroll. Disillusioned, the lower clerics turned to the Persian and Ottoman religious authorities for moral guidance. Foreign clerics were found circulating within the Caucasian region and delivering sermons in mosques, thus clearly defying Russian law.[64]

---

[58] Ibid., project no. 9, p. 9.
[59] Ibid., project no. 28, p. 21.
[60] Ibid., project no. 9, pp. 6–7.
[61] Ibid., project no. 28, pp. 15–16; project no. 99, p. 9.
[62] RGIA , f. 1268, op. 10, d. 127, ll. 270–271.
[63] GIA AR, f. 289, op. 1, d. 69, ll. 3, 5.
[64] GIA AR, f. 290, op. 1, d. 273, ll. 3–4.

In eastern Transcaucasia, the activities of the Persian *ulema* were so widespread that they began to alarm the authorities. In 1882, ten years after the foreign *ulema* had been legally banned from the region, the chairman of the Shi'ite Ecclesiastical Board, Akhund Ahmed Hosseinzade, was still warning the district *qadis* (Islamic judges) of the presence of the foreign *ulema* who were busy proselytizing and preaching in the mosques, performing religious rites, and collecting money from the Muslims of Transcaucasia by "deceiving them." Hosseinzade ordered all local clergy to prevent the foreign clerics from preaching in the mosques and to report the existence of all such persons to the authorities so that they might be driven out of the region.[65]

With the increasing presence of foreign clergy in the region, the official clergy found itself increasingly isolated and discredited. Few were willing to cooperate with local officials, and those who did expected the material benefits to outweigh the losses that they invariably incurred. In April 1881, the head of the Baku province *mejlis* (provincial Muslim assembly) petitioned the Shi'ite Ecclesiastical Board of Transcaucasia for an increase in its deputies' salaries. Writing in Persian, he argued that the current salaries did not suffice to attract competent mullahs, who demanded twice the amount offered. The petitioner hoped that the board would intervene on behalf of the *mejlis* with the administration and increase salaries so that the qualified members of the *ulema* would be drawn to government work, which they did not otherwise consider attractive or highly honorable.[66]

Muslim clerics in government service were placed in a disadvantageous position, having lost authority within their own communities and being insufficiently rewarded by the government. Their predicament was explained by the head of the Tiflis Shi'ite *mejlis*, who wrote to the Ecclesiastical Board in May 1881: "In order to fulfill the responsibilities placed upon us by the government, such as bookkeeping [of birth, marriage, and death records], we have neglected our own work and the people no longer pay us any money. We, the unfortunate ones, are neither considered to be part of the peasantry, in which case we would receive lands for agriculture and sustain ourselves, nor are we considered to be civil servants . . ."[67] Instead, the official clerics were expected to raise their own income in addition to serving the government; consequently, they had accumulated substantial debts.[68] Alienated from their communities and neglected by the Russian administration, the official clerics found themselves in a hopeless situation.

[65] GIA AR, f. 290, op. 1, d. 273, ll. 14–14b.
[66] GIA AR, f. 290, op. 1, d. 233, ll 1–1b.
[67] GIA AR, f. 290, op. 1, d. 233, ll. 2–2b.
[68] GIA AR, f. 290, op. 1, d. 233, ll. 2–2b.

By 1890, the Caucasian administration had acknowledged that the experiment with bureaucratizing the local religious elite lay in ruins. In his 1890 report to the tsar, Count S. A. Sheremetev, high commissioner of the Caucasus (1890–96), questioned the effectiveness of the regulations that had created the ecclesiastical boards and incorporated them into the local administrative apparatus. Conceding that this move might have compromised the Muslim clergy, he wrote: "The religious officials do not have the trust of the Muslim population, who as before continue to appeal to the mullahs who are not in state service as well as the foreign clergy for their spiritual needs."[69] Aware of the official clergy's diminishing influence, the Caucasian administration did little to bolster their image in the public eye. Instead of granting the Muslim clerics autonomy and allowing them to choose their own representatives as they had under Vorontsov, the Caucasian administration, influenced by the pervasive ethos of Russian nationalism, further circumscribed the actions of the *ulema*.

Between 1890 and 1905, the Caucasian administration redoubled its pressure on Muslim clerics to carry on official correspondence only in the Russian language. Before, both Persian and Azeri had been used and Russian translations seldom appeared. In September 1904, the Baku Shi'ite *mejlis*, coaxed by the Caucasian administration, issued a directive to all the *qadis* and mullahs ordering them to use Russian in all official correspondence with the provincial administration. The *qadis* protested. They argued that they did not know official Russian, had served without a salary, and had not received money from the government even for administrative expenses, such as hiring secretaries with a knowledge of Russian. As the *qadis* continued to carry on their correspondence in Persian and Azeri, the administration threatened to assign positions only to those *qadis* with a knowledge of Russian.[70]

The *qadis* petitioned to use their native languages in official correspondence, but the administration refused to compromise. The Russian governor of Baku wrote emphatically to the Baku provincial Shi'ite *mejlis* that the district *qadis* had submitted very few reports to the police administration, and that "writing in Russian does not incur substantial expenses for the *qadis*." The governor uncompromisingly stated: "I cannot express agreement with granting the district *qadis* the right to conduct official correspondence in the Muslim language."[71] A reference to Azeri as "the Muslim language" made it clear that its substitution for Russian as the language of Orthodox Christianity symbolized more than bureaucratic

[69] *Vsepoddanneishaia zapiska glavnonachalstvuiushchago grazhdanskoiu chast'iu na Kavkaze* (Tiflis, 1897), 28–29.
[70] GIA AR, f. 44, op. 2, d. 854, ll. 5–5b.
[71] GIA AR, f. 44, op. 2, d. 854, l. 4.

efficacy. This symbolism did not escape the attention of the Muslim clerics.

By the early twentieth century, the accumulated grievances of the Muslim clergy and the Muslim population grew into an open demand for autonomy in their own religious affairs. In February 1905 the Muslims of the Caucasus petitioned the Committee of Ministers:

> The Muslims are particularly constrained in their religious rights. Regardless of laws allowing for religious toleration for all, not one of the government's edicts permits the Muslims of Russia to perform their religious rites according to the laws of their Shari'a. . . . The Muslim clergy is so disdained and scorned by the government that it has lost all of its significance and authority.[72]

Like Muslims elsewhere in the empire, the Muslims of the Caucasus vehemently sought to reestablish the prestige and authority of their religious leaders by endowing them with real elected power and placing them in control of their religious establishments. They also demanded financial autonomy for the mosques, so that Muslims could decide questions concerning their religious endowments. Other points raised were the right to teach Islamic theology in the schools and the right of religious officials to work without the precondition of knowing Russian. The Muslims emphasized their right to practice their religion freely and fulfill their religious duties without interference from the authorities. The petition concluded:

> Previously, the higher religious persons, the *mujtaheds*, with which the government had to reckon as leaders of the clergy, had a strong moral and spiritual influence in the Caucasus. Now, however, the *sheikh ul-Islams* and the *muftis* are only administrative officials, from whom the fulfilling of clerical duties is demanded; they are denied influence in religious affairs and on other Muslim clerics. They do not have moral influence, as the Muslims themselves have taken no part in their appointment.[73]

The petitioners' concern for the Muslim clergy's loss of legitimacy was also recognized by the Russian press, which acknowledged that the clergy's appointment by the state had "greatly limited their authority."[74] Ultimately, the Caucasian administration's policy of bureaucratizing the Muslim clergy had proven unsuccessful. The state had failed to incorporate effectively the Muslim clergy into its administrative apparatus as the Muslim clergy were denied the privileges granted to other state bureau-

[72] RGIA, f. 1276, op. 1, d. 107, l. 65.
[73] RGIA, f. 1276, op. 1, d. 107, ll. 65, 70.
[74] G. Alisov, "Musul'manskii vopros v Rossii," *Russkaia Mysl'*, no. 7 (1909): 54.

crats and were troubled by the Russification campaigns which limited their freedom of expression. As a consequence, the official clergy was estranged both from the state as well as from its followers, who had lost faith in a clergy serving the "infidel." When in 1905 the Caucasian Muslims voiced their discontent at having been neglected as a people, along with other Muslims of the empire they demanded the reform of the Muslim religious establishment. The results of the Russian government's policies proved to be diametrically opposed to their initial goals.

Conclusions

The Russian administration used various approaches toward the Muslims of the Caucasus. These included benign neglect, conversion, and bureaucratic control over their religious establishments. Conversion mostly remained a desired objective rather than an actual policy. When it was briefly attempted, it proved to be unsuccessful. Efforts to control the activities of the Muslim clerics were also counterproductive, as the Russian administration was unable and unwilling to attract the lower-level clerics, who were in daily contact with the population. Given the proximity and influence of the two Islamic empires, Russian religious policy in the Caucasus was by necessity defensive. Similarly, the popularity of the mystical Islamic movement among the highlanders compelled the Russian administration to refrain from any aggressive policy of conversion.

In the eighteenth and early nineteenth centuries, plans for converting or "re-Christianizing" the Muslims of the western and central Caucasus had to be shelved in favor of preserving rather than spreading Orthodoxy. In the eastern Caucasus, serious proselytizing among the Muslims never took place. Fearing that the local religious and secular elites would turn against the government, the Caucasian administrators beginning with Vorontsov sought to co-opt and control these elites. The Muslim clerics were bureaucratized and brought under state surveillance, a process that was repeated elsewhere in the empire with other non-Orthodox Russian subjects.

Ultimately the bureaucratization of the *ulema* backfired. Among the Muslims of the Caucasus, the official clergy was diminished in stature and lost much of its following. Ironically, greater control over official Islam resulted in the greater popularity and influence of the unofficial clergy and foreign clerics within the Caucasus. Under the religious and military onslaught of Christian Russia, Islam in the Caucasus came to signify far more than a religion.

CHAPTER TEN

The Role of Tatar and Kriashen Women in the Transmission of Islamic Knowledge, 1800–1870

AGNÈS KEFELI

From the start of the nineteenth century, collective apostasies to Islam by some of the Kriashens (the descendants of the Muslim and animistic Tatars who had been baptized from the sixteenth through eighteenth centuries) shook the Orthodox Christian Tatar community of the Middle Volga. Orthodox missionaries, such as the Kriashen Vasilii Timofeev (1836–95) from Nikiforova (Mamadysh district), and the Russians Gordii Sablukov (1804–80), Nikolai Il'minskii (1822–91), Evfimii Malov (1835–1918), and Mikhail Mashanov (1852–1924) generally attributed these mass conversions to the cunning of Muslim Tatars who offered Kriashens gifts and jobs in their factories. At the same time as the Orthodox missionaries made the Muslims look like exploiters and the Kriashens like victims, they noticed that Muslims used literacy to spread their religion. Although the missionaries regarded Muslim Tatar schooling as backward, they recognized its powerful impact on illiterate peoples such as the Chuvash, Votiaks, Cheremis, and Kriashens.[1]

Indeed, social and cultural networks explain why conversion took place

---

[1] Vasilii Timofeev, "Iz Kazani: Poezdka v prikhody kreshchenykh tatar po povodu poslednikh otpadenii v magometanstvo," *Pravoslavnoe obozrenie*, 13 (September 1872): 488–89; *Materialy po istorii Tatarii vtoroi poloviny 19-go veka: Agrarnyi vopros i krest'ianskoe dvizhenie v Tatarii XIX veka* (Moscow, 1936), 220–25; Nikolai Il'minskii, ed., *Kazanskaia tsentral'naia kreshcheno-tatarskaia shkola: Materialy dlia istorii khristianskogo prosveshcheniia kreshchenykh Tatar* (Kazan, 1887), 300; "Izvlechenie iz vsepoddanneishego otcheta ober-prokurora Sviateishego sinoda po vedomstvu pravoslavnogo ispovedaniia za 1866 god," *Pravoslavnoe obozrenie* 25 (1868): 135–39; Mikhail Mashanov, "Sovremennoe sostoianie Tatar-mukhammedan i ikh otnoshenie k drugim inorodtsam," *Pravoslavnyi sobesednik* 57 (February 1911): 235–48; S. Bagin, "Ob otpadenii v magometanstvo kreshchenykh inorodtsev Kazanskoi eparkhii i o prichine etogo pechal'nogo iavleniia," *Pravoslavnyi sobesednik*, 56 (February 1910): 391–95.

A Kriashen (baptized Tatar) family in the village of Elyshevo, Mamadysh district, Kazan province. Rossiiskii Gosudarstvennyi Istoricheskii Arkhiv, f. 835, op. 4, d. 72.

among the Kriashens and other, Finno-Ugrian peoples of the Middle Volga. Too often, Tatar Islam is viewed by Tatar historians as a fixed identity defined by history, rather than a dynamic and evolving phenomenon. Tatar historians still consider the apostasies as a mere return of the Kriashens to the faith of their ancestors, i.e. Islam. But as Richard Eaton has shown in his recent study of the Bengal frontier, the conversion of an entire society is not simply the sum of personal experiences but a complex political and sociocultural process taking centuries to complete.[2] Eaton's approach may help to illuminate the case of the Kriashens in the Middle Volga. For Kriashens or Chuvash, conversion to Islam was not simply a choice between two world religions, but involved a complex dialogue between a variety of cultural systems (including mystical Islam and animism) that flourished on the Middle Volga.[3]

Various strategies and agents of Islamization were at work, such as the

---

[2] Richard M. Eaton, *The Rise of Islam and the Bengal Frontier, 1204–1760* (Berkeley, Calif., 1993); idem, "Approaches to the Study of Conversion to Islam in India," in *Approaches to Islam in Religious Studies*, ed. Richard C. Martin (Tucson, Ariz., 1985), 106–23.

[3] Ildus Zahidullin, "Jylysh avyly mäk'ruhlary" [The apostates of Elyshevo] in *Miras* [Heritage], no. 9 (1995): 111–15; no. 11–12 (1995): 138–48. In this article Zahidullin speaks of the "return" of the Elyshevite Kriashens to Islam, although the inhabitants of this particular

use of popular Sufi religious books, the appropriation of pre-Islamic and pre-Christian sacred places, and the development of economic networks.[4] The Christian-Muslim divide was not absolute among Tatars and Kriashens. Missionaries seem to have overemphasized the degree to which Kriashens were despised by their Muslim brethren and left alone—a view that contradicted the missionary assumption that Muslims were dangerous proselytizers. The frontier between the two world religions was continuously defined and redefined at the micro level, either at the expense of Christianity or at the expense of Islam. Agents of Islamization such as mullahs, traders, craftsmen, itinerant Sufi preachers, and women played a decisive role in turning various ethnic groups to Islam. The present article confines itself to an issue long neglected by historians—the role of Tatar and Kriashen women in Islamizing the Kriashens.

Most Western and Soviet historians and ethnographers have been interested only in the struggle of prerevolutionary Tatar women for equality and freedom. They have significantly neglected the devotion of women to Islam and their role as Muslim missionaries. The ethnographic literature, in contrast, emphasizes the oppression of women in prerevolutionary Tatarstan. But such a position, even when supported by facts, pictures women in traditional Islamic society as merely passive victims. In this respect, contemporary historiography is still under the influence of the Islamic reformist (*jadid*) and Western anti-Muslim literature of the nineteenth century. Prerevolutionary Tatar educators, for example, argued that women in traditional Islamic societies lived under the yoke of their fathers and their husbands, who kept them in total ignorance. These reformers attacked Muslim patriarchy, the cloistered lives of Tatar women, and the inadequacy of their education.[5] Before 1917, Russian Orthodox missionaries wrote similar accounts, but contended that only conversion

village were mainly of animistic background. Typically, the editors of *Miras*, a Kazan historical and literary journal, have placed Zahidullin's article in a section called "The movement of national liberation of the Tatar people."

[4] Sufism, a set of mystical movements that had arisen within Islam by the mid-eighth century, entered the Volga from Central Asia in the tenth and fourteenth centuries. Adherents of these mouvements sought to unite themselves with God through a variety of ritual practices, spiritual exercises, and ascetic disciplines. The most popular Sufi orders among the Tatars were the Yasawiya (which arose in the mid-twelfth century) and the Naqshbandiya (which emerged in the fourteenth century). Both orders played an important role in the conversion to Islam of Mongol and Turkic tribes. They are well known for their flexibility toward local customs, and their use of the native language as a tool of conversion. On Sufism on the Volga, see Alexandre Bennigsen and Chantal Lemercier-Quelquejay, *Le Soufi et le Commissaire: Les confréries musulmanes en URSS* (Paris, 1986).

[5] Ia. Abdullin, *Tatarskaia prosvetitel'skaia mysl'* (Kazan, 1976), 242–51; M. Kh. Gainullin, *Tatarskaia literatura XIX veka* (Kazan, 1975); Nikolai Ashmarin, "O sovremennoi literature Kazanskikh Tatar," *Zhurnal Ministerstva Narodnogo Prosveshcheniia*, no. 9, part 361, sec. 3 (September 1905): 10; Fatikh Ämirhan, "Khäiat" in *Äsärlär* [Works], 4 vols. (Kazan, 1985),

to Christianity could ultimately liberate Muslim women. However, they also noted that women offered greater resistance than did men to the spread of Orthodox Christianity among the native peoples of the Volga. This indicates that women were more than just "domestic slaves," but played an important role in the struggle against religious assimilation in the nineteenth century. Missionaries attributed women's devotion to Islam and pre-Islamic beliefs to their natural conservatism and innate predilection for superstitious beliefs, charms, and amulets.[6] Such appeals to gender differences, however, have little explanatory power and reveal nothing about women's position in the family or outside the home as carriers of Islamic literacy.

Until recently, ethnographic works on women in the Islamic world have tended to separate sharply the domestic from the public sphere; the former was the woman's domain; the latter, the man's. This approach assumed that women had no influence or power upon the outside world.[7] This study will argue that women's role was not limited to the domestic sphere, but had important repercussions on the future of their communities. First, I will show that there was a positive vision of woman in popular oral and written Tatar traditions; secondly that women embodied this image by actively proselytizing for Islam in both their households and their villages; and, thirdly, that family, sacred, and educational networks were essential to the spread of Islam. These conclusions will lead us to a tentative reinterpretation of gender roles in traditional pre-*jadid* Islam, and of the Kriashen apostasy movement as a whole.

For this preliminary study of the role of Tatar women in the spread of Islam, I have used five types of sources. Russian Orthodox missionary literature, even though biased and partial, provides valuable insight into the process of Islamization, since the missionaries were especially concerned about the phenomenon and recorded illuminating conversations with the native population of the Middle Volga. In addition, there are published and unpublished state reports on the Tatars. Since most of the Tatars were state peasants prior to emancipation, the Ministry of State Domains (the agency responsible for the state peasants) collected many valuable

---

2:119–75; idem, "Fätkhulla khäzrät," ibid., 2:7–118; "Tatar kyzy," [A Tatar girl], ibid., vol. 1 (Kazan, 1984), 47–56.

[6] Mikhail Mashanov, "Zametka o religiozno-nravstvennom sostoianii kreshchënykh tatar Kazanskoi gubernii Mamadyshskogo uezda," *Izvestiia po Kazanskoi eparkhii*, no. 1 (1875): 19; Il'minskii, *Kazanskaia tsentral'naia shkola*, 301.

[7] Recent studies have challenged this traditional dichotomy. See Leslie P. Pierce, "Beyond Harem Walls: Ottoman Royal Women and the Exercise of Power," in *Gendered Domains: Rethinking Public and Private in Women's History*, ed. Dorothy O. Helly and Susan M. Reverby (Ithaca, N.Y.,, 1992), 40–55; Cynthia Nelson, "Public and Private Politics: Women in the Middle Eastern World," in *Gender in Cross-Cultural Perspective*, ed. Caroline P. Brettell and Carolyn F. Sargent (Englewood Cliffs, N.J.,, 1993), 94–106.

statistics, especially concerning education. I have also used ethnographic literature produced at Kazan University (founded in 1804). The Turkologist, physician, and rector of the university, Karl Fuks (1776–1846), for example, made many important observations about Tatar women in his field studies in the 1840s.

Tatar sources consisting of Sufi literature and memoirs are scarcer, but they provide an important corrective to the more abundant Russian sources. A close analysis of popular Sufi works read widely on the Middle Volga provides a deeper understanding of the kind of Islam that prevailed among the Tatar peasants. By reading the Russian sources against this broader Islamic context, we can discover meanings in missionary reports that escaped the attention of the missionaries themselves. Nineteenth-century missionaries and twentieth-century historians alike have usually underestimated the importance of this material. On the one hand, missionaries referred exclusively to the Quran to expose the heretical nature of the Kriashens' Islamic faith, and ignored the links between popular Sufi Islam and learned Islam. On the other hand, Western, Tatar, and Russian historians have claimed that most Kriashens were originally Muslim and that their apostasy to Islam was simply an effort to force the Russian authorities to recognize their true faith. These historians have ignored the content of the Kriashens' Islam and their internalization of Islamic values.[8] Finally, Tatar memoirs and diaries, which remain almost

[8] A. N. Grigor'ev, "Khristianizatsiia nerusskikh narodnostei, kak odin iz metodov natsional'no-kolonial'noi politiki tsarizma," *Materialy po istorii Tatarii*, vol. 1, ed. I. M. Klimov (Kazan, 1948), 234; Alexandre Bennigsen and Chantal Quelquejay, *Les mouvements nationaux chez les Musulmans de Russie (Le "Sultangaliévisme" au Tatarstan)* (Paris, 1960), 24, 34–35; Jean Saussay, "L'apostasie des Tatars christianisés en 1866," *Cahiers du monde russe et soviétique* 9, no. 1 (January–March 1968): 20–45; Stephen J. Blank, "National Education, Church and State in Tsarist Nationality Policy: The Il'minskii System," *Canadian-American Slavic Studies* 17, no. 4 (winter 1983): 469; I. K. Zagidullin, "K voprosu otpadeniia kreshchenykh tatar Kazanskoi gubernii v musul'manstvo 1866 goda," in *Natsional'nyi vopros v Tatarii do oktiabr'skogo perioda*, ed. S. K. Abishev (Kazan, 1990), 66–78. The "Kriashen question" is a burning issue in contemporary Kazan that divides nationalist Tatar thinkers and the Kriashen community itself. Since perestroika, the Kriashens have challenged the idea that they were originally Muslim Tatars who were forcibly Christianized by Ivan the Terrible, and have claimed to be a separate nation. According to them, Islam was not the only religion among the tenth-century Bulgars, whom many historians regard as the direct ancestors of the contemporary Tatars; Christians lived on Bulgar lands before the Russian conquest of Kazan in 1552. Kriashen writers add that the Kriashens may have been the first Christians in Eastern Europe. V. M. Malakhov, "Kto krestil Kriashen?" *Keräshen süze (Slovo Kriashen)*, 9 April 1996, 2. In this view, the apostate Kriashens are not people returning to Islam, but people subjugated to the Islamic propaganda of Turkish agents and Tatar mullahs. Maksim Glukhov-Nogaibek, *Sud'ba gvardeitsev Seiumbeki* (Kazan, 1993), 194. Despite some incongruities in the Kriashens' self-identification, it has some value. It shows that Islamization was not complete the day when the Bulgars adopted Islam, and was still under way in the middle of the nineteenth century.

entirely unread in personal and state archives, furnish new information about the lives of Tatar women in the nineteenth century.[9]

Conversions to Orthodoxy and Apostasies

There were two major waves of conversion of Tatars to Christianity—in the sixteenth century and then in the eighteenth century. Those converted in the first wave (and their descendants) were known as *starokreshchennye* or *starokriasheny* (Old Converts); those from the second wave, as *novokreshchennye* or *novokriasheny* (New Converts). The Old Converts were primarily of animist background.[10] By contrast, the New Converts all came from peoples who had originally been Muslim.

Russian law forbade all forms of reconversion. Even after Catherine II had ended the destruction of mosques, proclaimed religious liberty, and favored the expansion of Tatar merchant colonies, apostates from Eastern Orthodoxy continued to be separated from their families and in the worst cases, exiled to Siberia.[11] In 1803, however, descendants of the converted Tatars began to apostatize en masse from Eastern Orthodoxy and to reembrace Islam. In vain they sent petitions to St. Petersburg asking permission to profess Islam openly. These collective apostasies followed one another in rapid succession in 1802–3, 1827–30, 1866–70, 1896, and 1905, each on a larger scale than the one before it. As shown in tables 1 and 2, there was a significant increase in the number of apostates in Kazan province between 1864 and 1901.

Obviously, population growth alone cannot explain the increased number of apostates. Before 1866, most of the apostates were New Converts; afterwards, the Old Converts also revolted against Orthodoxy. The growing number of apostates may have reflected rising hopes of government toleration of Islam after the repressive reign of Nicholas I. There is also an

---

[9] Written in Arabic script, these texts are incomprehensible to most modern Tatars who use the Cyrillic alphabet; I am fortunate to have procured one such diary thanks to the kindness of Mädinä Rähimkulova, who is laboring in Orenburg to make such works available to the younger generation: "Gabdräkhim Gabdrakhman ugly Välidovnyñ tereklektäge khäle häm Kargaly tarikhi" (Biography of Gabdräkhim, son of Gabdrakhman Välidov, and history of Kargala), unpublished manuscript (Kargala, 1924).

[10] Many of the Old Converts probably descended from the Sobekullian, Chelmat, and Temtiuzi peoples, mentioned in twelfth-century Russian chronicles, who had been distinct from the Tatars well before the Mongol invasion. F. S. Baiazitova, *Govory Tatar-Kriashen v sravnitel'nom osveshchenii* (Moscow, 1986), 16.

[11] The law remained unchanged until 1905. See "O preduprezhdenii i presechenii otstupleniia ot Pravoslavnoi very," *Svod zakonov*, vol. 14 (St. Petersburg, 1857), ch. 3, sec. 1, arts. 47–54, pp. 11–12; sec. 2, arts. 55–59, pp. 12–13; M. N. Palibin, *Ustav dukhovnykh konsistorii* (St. Petersburg, 1900), 23–30.

Table 1. Number of Apostates in Kazan Province in 1864

District	Baptized	Apostates	Muslims
Cheboksary	427		
Chistopol'	3,996	3,152	
Kazan	2,561	16	
Kozmodem'iansk		9	
Laishev	12,353	623	
Mamadysh	15,304	2,267	
Spassk	562	260	
Sviiazhsk	5,302		
Tetiushi	3,782	42	
Tsarevokokshaisk			
Tsivil'sk	1,090	897	
Total	45,377	7,266	399,204

Source: Complied from Evfimii Malov, "Staatisticheskie svedeniia o kreshchenykh tatarakh v kazanskoi i nekotorykh drugikh eparkhii, v volzhskom basseine." *Missionerstvo sredi mukhammedan i kreshchenykh Tatar* (Kazan, 1892), 400, 405–6.

Table 2. Number of Apostates in Kazan Province in 1901

District	Baptized	Apostates	Muslims
Cheboksary		800	3,040
Chistopol'	5,565	8,200	91,193
Kazan	1,521	1,541	151,576
Laishev	12,957	1,746	63,027
Mamadysh	22,125	3,515	115,050
Spassk	1,397	514	55,647
Sviiazhsk		6,743	37,642
Tetiushi	5	6,531	94,237
Tsarevokokshaisk		195	29,472
Tsivil'sk		1,952	12,950
Total	43,570	31,737	653,654

Source: Pamiatnaia knizhka Kazanskoi gubernii na 1901 g. (Kazan, 1901), 18–23.

economic explanation. The mobility of Kriashen society was increasing because of improvements in communications in the Russian empire and the formation of a dynamic Tatar bourgeoisie on the Middle Volga and in Central Asia.[12] Kriashens found employment among Tatars as seasonal workers in Menzelinsk or Ufa, and learned to live among them as religious Muslims. They returned home and shared their adventures and religious stories with their immediate families and neighbors.[13] Their expe-

[12] Bennigsen and Quelquejay, *Les mouvements nationaux*, 28.
[13] See my article "Constructing an Islamic Identity: The Case of Elyshevo Village in the Nineteenth Century," in *Russia's Orient: Imperial Borderlands and Peoples, 1700–1917*, ed. Daniel Brower and Edward Lazzerini (Bloomington, Ind., 1997), 271–91.

riences in Tatar lands would not have had any lasting impact if there had not been sympathetic recipients of Islam in their own households. Women had an important role in the fixation of Islamic knowledge in the village. They also helped to spread rumors of imperial edicts that supposedly permitted Kriashens to profess Islam officially. Tatar women maintained contact with their husbands when the latter were arrested or sent away to exile. But why were Kriashen women not deterred from supporting the apostasy by the negative legal and economic consequences? To answer this question we must make a foray into popular traditions.

The Role of Women in Written and Oral Tradition

Tatar and Kriashen peasants rarely left a written legacy; women did so even less than men. *Mentalités* and attitudes may be reconstructed, however, from popular literature, missionary diaries, and *jadid* accounts.

Two types of literature conditioned women's weltanschauung: Sufi books and folk tales. Sufi books constituted the bulk of Islamic knowledge among peasant women, as among men who had spent only two or three winters at the Quranic school in their village. While boys interested in becoming mullahs could pursue their schooling in more prestigious *medressehs* (Islamic seminaries), women's education did not go beyond the *mekteb* (Muslim primary school). Girls did not study the books of higher learning, but did read and sing from popular Sufi books, written in Jagatai Turkish (the Turkic literary language of Central Asia) that made the high tradition of Islamic knowledge available to them.

Sufi books were not specifically addressed to a female audience. For instance, *Bädävam kitaby* (Forever), written supposedly by an unknown Bulgar author around the twelfth century, and faithful to the letter of the Quran, explicitly demanded the same piety from men and women.[14] It was only at the end of the nineteenth century that early reformers started writing hygiene manuals for girls, and compiling biographies of famous women to serve as role models.[15] Sufi books did include female characters, however, and offered paradigms of female behavior in the religious sphere.

As Annemarie Schimmel points out in her works on Islamic mysticism, the attitude of Sufis toward women was ambivalent. In early Sufism, a majority of mystics viewed sex with women as a hindrance on the path toward

[14] *Bädävam kitaby* (Kazan, 1861), 1.
[15] The most prolific writer in this area was the *qadi* Rizaetdin Fäkhretdin (1858–1936). See *Tärbiiale ana* [The educated mother] (Kazan, 1898); idem, *Tärbiiale khatyn* [The educated wife] (Kazan, 1899); idem, *Gailä* (Orenburg, 1912); idem, *Mäshhür khatynnar* [The famous women], published in 1903 and dedicated to his daughter, Zäinäp.

God, and they considered "the weaker sex" inferior, unclean and dangerous. Later, some Sufis had a more positive attitude toward sex and
women, considering love for a woman as a manifestation of the divine.
Abu Hamid al-Ghazzali (1058–1111) used love for a woman as a
metaphor for the relationship between the believer and God. Both traditions were present on the Middle Volga. In *Qyssa-i Solomon* (The Tale of
Solomon), a folk tale popular among the Tatars, the writer warned men
not to follow women's advice because they were stupid and ignorant. Conversely, female characters in *Qyssa-i Iosyf* (The Tale of Joseph), *Kisek-bash*
(The Decapitated Head), and particularly Mariiam (Mary) in *Khasret
Mariiam kitaby* (The Book of Saint Mary) illustrated the positive role of
women in religious life.[16] These three books were widely circulated and
extremely popular on the Middle Volga.

The Tale of Joseph, which appeared in twenty-one thousand copies between 1854 and 1864,[17] was read and sung by female and male audiences
with equal frequency during popular religious feasts and evening gatherings. Attributed to the early thirteenth-century Bulgar poet Qol Gali
(1172–?), it refers to the story of Joseph in the twelfth sura, emphasizing
the struggle against paganism and the thaumaturgical powers of the
prophets. The central feminine figure in the tale is Zuleikha, the pharaoh's wife, who tries to seduce Joseph.

Zuleikha's story is above all about a conversion and a mystical experience. The pharaoh's wife, although pagan, becomes a Seeker of God. As a
woman, she is not excluded from the Sufi path. Her love for Joseph, her
husband's adopted son, exemplifies on one hand the temptation of sex,
and on the other the mystic's longing for the divine. It is one of the rare
instances in Sufi poetry in which both aspects of Eros—lust and desire for
God—are represented, and where the divine ecstasy of love is personified
by a woman.[18]

Zuleikha's conversion is described as a long, gradual and triumphant
process. First, she appeals to her idols to help her seduce Joseph, but they

---

[16] Annemarie Schimmel, *Mystical Dimensions of Islam* (Chapel Hill, N.C., 1975), appendix
2, "The feminine element in Sufism," 426–35; idem, "Eros—Heavenly and Not So Heavenly—in Sufi Literature and Life," in *Society and the Sexes in Medieval Islam*, ed. Afaf Lutfi al-
Sayyid Marsot, Sixth Georgio Levi della Vida Conference, UCLA, 1977 (Malibu, Calif.,
1979), 119–41; A. Mikhailov, "Kriticheskii razbor i perevod s tatarskogo iazyka na russkii
broshiury 'Rasskazy o Solomone,'" *Orenburgskie eparkhial'nye vedomosti*, no. 10 (15 May
1889): 280–84.

[17] Evfimii Malov, "Pravoslavnaia protivomusul'manskaia missiia v Kazanskom krae v sviazi s
istoriei musul'manstva v pervoi polovine XIX veka," *Pravoslavnyi sobesednik* 14, pt. 2, no. 7
(1868): 230, 232, 242–44, 246–49, 250–53.

[18] For a more detailed discussion of Eros in Sufi poetry, see Schimmel, "Eros—Heavenly
and Not So Heavenly," 124.

recognize his authority, declaring him a Prophet of the Truth. As punishment, Zuleikha's love for Joseph is never returned, and she turns into a blind and aged woman. But Zuleikha continues to love Joseph until she finally concludes that Joseph's God has paralyzed her idols' powers. She then breaks her idols, gives away her riches, and declares to Joseph: "I believe in one God and in you Joseph". These words, reminiscent of the Muslim creed (the *shahada*), purify Zuleikha, who regains her youth and beauty. Joseph marries her, and twelve children bless their union.[19] Only after her recognition of Allah's Oneness does she find happiness in marriage and childbearing. Before she broke the idols, her love for Joseph was pure incestuous lust, but after she decides to follow the God-given law, the *shari'a*, she finally enters the *tariqa* (path) on which mystics walk. She goes through the classical stations of the Sufi ladder: repentance, abstinence, poverty, patience, love, and fear, before she meets Joseph again, and surrenders her heart in the contemplation of the divine beloved. In the particular tradition represented by Qol Gali, Sufism did not exclude women from the path to God; in fact there was no distinction between men and women in their ability to reach the divine. Zuleikha was no less than a traditional Sufi disciple in search of unity with God—a female Joseph.[20]

Motherhood was another key theme in Tatar Sufi literature. When Joseph weeps at his mother's tomb, her voice sounds forth from the grave and teaches him patience and hope. In *The Book of Saint Mary*, Mary rises from the dead in response to the prayers of her desperate and lonely son, Gaisa (Jesus). She gently reproaches him for his lack of faith and summons him to continue his mission. In the supposedly twelfth-century epic *The Decapitated Head*, a wife and mother cries and prays until the prophet Ali comes with his sword and frees her from the *Div*, a mythological giant. Although in some respects a passive victim (unlike the princesses of some Tatar tales, the heroine does not take up the sword), she is spiritually ac-

---

[19] Kol Gali, *Kyissai Iosyf* (Kazan, 1989), 84, 103–18, 150–57.

[20] Ibid., 100–101, 154; Martin Lings, *What is Sufism?* (Berkeley, Calif., 1977); Schimmel, *Mystical Dimensions*, 98–186.

It is only in Persian and in Turkic tradition that Zuleikha reaches the final goal of any mystical quest, union with the divinity, since the prophet Joseph represents the divinity in human form. In Qol Gali's narrative, Zuleikha is not responsible for her insatiable sexual appetite, since her infatuation with Joseph's beauty springs from a divinely inspired dream she experienced while a mere child. In fact, Zuleikha is God's instrument to elevate Joseph to the status of saint. When she tries to seduce him, the latter repeats the main tenets of Islamic faith and overcomes his lower instincts (*nafs*). Gali, *Kyissai Iosyf*, 103–18; Djami, *Youssouf et Zouleikha* trans. from Persian by Auguste Bricteux (Paris, 1927), 189–209; *Shasenem i Garyp: Kasym-oglan i drugie turkmenskie povesti* (Moscow, 1991), 332 (Turkmen version of the story of Joseph, written by the poet Andalib in the eighteenth century).

tive. Her prayers keep the giant from raping and devouring her, and give Ali enough time to reach the well where she has been kept prisoner. Without her devotions, the tale would have ended with the giant's victory.[21]

In these accounts, mothers appear to be guardians of true religion. Their role consists in strengthening their children's faith when it is challenged by adversarial forces. They are the ones who bring up their children to serve God, and remind them of their duty toward God. In the fourteenth-century *qadi* Nasiruddin Rabguzi's *Qyssas al-anbiia* (Tales of the Prophets), Mary brings her son Jesus to school and advises the teacher to beat him less and teach him more. Above all, mothers are models of faith. In *The Book of Saint Mary*, Mary is the one who asks her son to build a mosque so that she can retire and pray.[22]

Finally, in Sufi tradition, women could also live alone as dervishes. In *The Tale of Joseph*, a rich woman converts to Islam after seeing Joseph and distributes her wealth to the poor and dervishes before she herself retires to a cell to become a Seeker of God. More importantly, women could also be miracle-workers. Fatima, the Prophet's daughter, was a popular female figure on the Middle Volga and in the Ural countryside. It was said that after she prayed, invisible hands built a mosque in one night.[23]

Tatar epics and historical traditions illustrated and added a new dimension to the Sufi tales. They showed in actual accounts how important the women's mission was in resisting invaders. The Tatar folklorist Fatykh Urmancheev has emphasized the importance of heroic maidens in Tatar epics. During the Mongol invasion, the Bulgar khan's daughter Altynchäch (Golden Hair) refused to marry the Mongol khan. She armed herself and entered the battle. Although wounded, she never subjugated herself to the infidel.[24] The same type of legends flourished with regard to Russians. The Soviet historian Mikhail Khudiakov described the roles of the *khansha* (princess) in their struggle against Russian invaders. Numerous traditions praised the princess Söembikä for her beauty, intelligence and courage. She predicted the fall of the Kazan kingdom and brought poisoned food to Shakh-Ali, Ivan the Terrible's candidate for the throne

[21] Gali, *Kyissai Iosyf*, 63–65; S. M. Matveev, "Mukhammedanskii rasskaz o Sv. Deve Marii: Tekst i perevod," *Izvestiia obshchestva arkheologii, istorii i etnografii* 13, pt. 1 (1895): 19–34; *Kisek-bash kitaby* (Kazan, 1846).

[22] Nikolai Ostroumov, *Kriticheskii razbor Mukhammedanskogo ucheniia o prorokakh* (Kazan, 1874), 179; Matveev, "Mukhammedanskii rasskaz o Sv. Deve Marii," 22.

[23] Gali, *Kyissai Iosyf*, 81–83; R. Ignat'ev, "Skazaniia, skazki i pesni, sokhranivshiesia v rukopisiakh tatarskoi pis'mennosti i v ustnykh pereskazakh u inorodtsev-magometan Orenburgskogo kraia," *Zapiski Orenburgskogo otdela Imperatorskogo russkogo geograficheskogo obshchestva* 3 (1875):191–192.

[24] F. I. Urmancheev, *Epicheskie skazaniia tatarskogo naroda* (Kazan, 1980), 81–82; see also Karl Reichl, *Turkic Oral Epic Poetry: Traditions, Forms, Poetic Structure* (New York, 1992), 298–301, on the heroines in Turkic epic poetry.

of Kazan.[25] In 1550, it was said, she appeared armed to defend the city of Kazan.[26] The famous epic of Söembikä told of her ordeal before and after the fall of the Khanate. Because the *mirzas* (Tatar princes) did not listen to her, Ivan the Terrible took Kazan. Her son was taken away by the priests (*popy*), who tried to turn him against his mother's religion. Söembikä's lament, written in the first person, symbolized the fate of the Tatars, from now on subjects of an infidel state.[27]

Tatar Women as Possessors and Transmitters of Islamic Knowledge

Sufi books had a great impact on popular religious knowledge, discourse, and conduct. Peasant women's Islamic knowledge per se did not differ much from men's. Like peasant men, they were the depositories of numerous Islamic folk stories drawn from Sufi literature that declared the final victory of Islam as a certainty. As seen above, these stories illustrated the power of Islamic prayers, the miraculous grace (*baraka*) of the prophets, and the deeds of famous women. Some also told of anonymous Russians who showed reverence toward Muhammed and his message.[28] These stories were passed down to daughters from mothers, visiting Sufis, or male seasonal workers who went to trade in places where Islam was dominant.

Contrary to what missionaries often implied, peasant women had a clear understanding of their faith. Because missionaries had a bookish, rationalized idea of Islam, they tended to counterpose "low" and "high" Islam. "Low" Islam meant popular Sufi books in Tatar and superstitious beliefs in amulets, charms, and evil spirits, whereas "high" Islam was the Islam taught in the *medressehs* of the Middle East or Central Asia, in Arabic or Persian.[29] In their approach to women, missionaries often associated women's worldview with so-called "low" Islam. However, contrary to what missionaries contended, the borders between high and popular Islam were often blurred. This is supported by scholarship on Islam in other parts of the world. Learned men in Algeria, Anatolia, India, or the

[25] Mikhail Khudiakov, *Ocherki po istorii Kazanskogo khanstva* (1923; reprint ed., Moscow, 1990), 179–82.

[26] Kanäfi Näfyikov, *Ütkängä säiakhät* [Journey to the past] (Kazan, 1993), 39.

[27] The text of *Söembikä bäete* has been published as an appendix to Ilgaz Bahan Näürüzkhan's historical novel, *Söembikä (Tarikhi roman)* (Chally, 1992), 120–25.

[28] Evfimi Malov, *Missionerstvo sredi mukhammedan i kreshchenykh Tatar* (Kazan, 1892), 25.

[29] Stefan Matveev, "Dva dnia sredi kreshchenykh i otpavshikh inorodtsev (iz dnevnika missionera)," *Pravoslavnyi blagovestnik*, no. 1 (1902): 21–24; no. 7 (1902): 304–7; Malov, *Missionerstvo*, 5–100 (to the missionary's amazement, Sagid, a middle-aged Tatar whose knowledge of Islam is mainly drawn from popular textbooks and whose mastery of Arabic is extremely poor, wishes to become officially a mullah).

Balkans used folk tales as media for popular instruction in Islam, since Arabic was not accessible to the average peasant.[30]

Similarly, in defending and explaining Islam Tatar peasant women and men referred to images drawn from Sufi books and tales echoing pre-Islamic beliefs. A Tatar woman from Artyk in Mamadysh district (Kazan province), for example, after reading a passage from *The Book of Baqyrgan* (an anthology of Sufi poetry) about the necessity of saying "Bismillah" ("in the name of God") before meals, explained that if one failed to say "Bismillah," the *päri* (house spirits) would steal the food. If a woman left her child in the field without saying "Bismillah," the *päri* would likewise steal the child and replace him with one of their monstrous offspring. Among the Tatars and other Middle Volga peoples, *päri* were known for living in abandoned houses or baths. For this woman, any action was incomplete without praising God; such incomplete actions attracted the *päri* who chose to live in empty places.[31] For the Orthodox missionary who recorded this story, it was proof that Tatar women did not know their religion and that their Islam was no more than a sophisticated written form of paganism or polytheism. In fact, this woman had given a clear, metaphoric explanation of the text she had read. Like Sufis on the Middle Volga and in India and Anatolia who spread the word by using images from daily life, this woman from Artyk resorted to imagery taken directly from Tatar folk tales.[32] As in the Quran, she proved that the spirits could be domesticated rather than annihilated, and served a unique God.

Even *shakirds* (students) of the *medressehs* used the same device to demonstrate the power of Muslim prayers against evil spirits.[33] This kind of discourse had a powerful impact on the non-Muslim Old Converts in Mamadysh district, and on other peoples like the Cheremis in Ufa province or the Chuvash and Votiaks in Kazan province. It often constituted the first step in their Islamization.[34]

---

[30] See also Annemarie Schimmel, *As Through a Veil: Mystical Poetry in Islam* (New York, 1982), 137; Fanny Colonna, *Savants paysans: Eléments d'histoire sociale de l'Algérie rurale* (Algiers, 1987).

[31] Vasilii Timofeev, "Dnevnik starokreshchenogo Tatarina," in Il'minskii, *Kazanskaia tsentral'naia shkola*, 57; *Baqyrgan kitaby* (Kazan, 1904), 13; R. G. Akhmet'ianov, *Obshchaia leksika dukhovnoi kul'tury narodov srednego Povolzh'ia* (Moscow, 1981), 40.

[32] For instance, the Tatar historian N. Khisamov has shown that Qol Gali's metaphors in *Qyssa-i Iosyf* go back to the Old Turkic poetic tradition of ancient epics that were popular in the thirteenth century. Qol Gali also Turkicizes the prophet Joseph, who wears braids, a Turkic custom. In addition, Gali often alludes to the animistic past of the Turkic peoples, as when he mentions Kylych, a dark spirit, or silver statues of bulls. N. Sh. Khisamov, *Poema Kyssa-i Iusuf Kul Ali* (Moscow, 1979), 50–51, 71, 170.

[33] Ia. D. Koblov, "Mifologiia Kazanskikh tatar," *Tsirkuliar po Kazanskomu uchebnomu okrugu* 2, no. 9 (September 1909): 407.

[34] P. Eruslanov (Cheremis), "Magometanskaia propaganda sredi cheremis Ufimskoi gubernii (iz lichnykh nabliudenii)," *Pravoslavnyi blagovestnik*, no. 8 (1895): 422–26; no. 9:

Schooling was the next important step in the fixation of popular Sufi knowledge. According to Karl Fuks, it was rare to find a girl who did not know how to read and write. Girls studied with the *abystai* (a female teacher, often the mullah's wife in a Quranic primary school) until the age of ten, or received private lessons. Very often, small children of both sexes studied side by side before the mullah took over the boys' education. The elementary program for girls was not fundamentally different from that for boys; the girls read and recited the same Sufi books they had heard in their early childhood when women gathered on Fridays, or when they cooked meals. Since girls were not supposed to become mullahs, it was common popular belief among peasants that they had no need for higher learning. Writing was considered superfluous as well. However, in the 1840s, Fuks met an *abystai* who taught her students to record Tatar popular songs. He also received love letters from women whose writing was conditioned by stereotyped Sufi images and popular songs.[35] Biographies of early *jadid* women show that mullahs' and also merchants' daughters had access to higher learning. Mullahs' daughters like the poet Galimätelbänat Biktimeriia (1876–1906) studied under their father, and merchants' daughters took private lessons. The poet Gazizä Sämitova, a merchant's daughter (1862–1929) kept a diary, learned Arabic and Persian, and read classical oriental poetry.[36] Fuks again noticed that mullahs' children, both boys and girls, could read the Quran and understand as much as their fathers.[37] Since a mullah's daughters were likely to marry mullahs and become *abystais*, their thirst for knowledge was encouraged.[38]

According to statistics of the Ministry of State Domains and the Muslim Spiritual Assembly, almost as many girls as boys studied in Quranic schools. In 1860 in Kazan province, 682 mosques had 483 Quranic schools with an enrollment of 16,326 boys and 13,946 girls. These statistics underestimate the number of such Muslim schools, since they did not include clandestine schools among Kriashen apostates or Islamicized

20–27; no. 12: 181–84; no. 13: 225–27; no. 14: 275–79; no. 16: 382–91; no. 18: 82–88; no. 19: 133–41; no. 21: 220–26; no. 22: 253–61.

[35] Karl Fuks, *Kazanskie tatary v statisticheskom i etnograficheskom otnosheniiakh* (Kazan, 1844), 39–43.

[36] *Ömet ioldyzlary* [Stars of hope] (Kazan, 1988), 18, 40.

[37] Fuks, *Kazanskie tatary*, 25.

[38] Peasant boys also learned to write, for purposes of trade. However, they often interrupted their education to work outside the village, unless their fathers were mullahs. As a general rule, Tatar peasants worked as seasonal laborers from October to March, and their sons accompanied them when they were old enough (between nine and fourteen). In general, boys stopped going to school at the age of thirteen or before. The result was that there was only a small gap between women's and men's Islamic knowledge. "Gabdräkhim Gabdrakhman ugly," l. 7.

Chuvash, Votiaks, and Cheremis; private courses for girls; or the schools attached to Tatar factories.[39]

In discussions reported by missionaries, women in average peasant families often appeared to be more knowledgeable about Islam than their husbands, probably because their education had not been interrupted by seasonal work and changes of teachers. Among Islamicized Kriashen women, many could read even when their husbands were illiterate. The Kriashen women in the village of Verkhnie Mashliaki in Mamadysh district strictly observed Islamic rites despite their husbands' indifference.[40]

The prolonged absence of male traders from their communities forced women (literate or not) to assume an important role in the transmission of Islamic knowledge. In the village of Elyshevo (Mamadysh district), an aged, illiterate, and blind woman of Kriashen origin imparted the basics of the Islamic faith to the children.[41] Very often, Tatar mothers taught their children to sing and read Sufi books before going to the *mekteb*. In a Tatar home, a missionary witnessed a scene where a grandmother taught her granddaughter to repeat the mullah Ishniiaz's *Shäraitu'l-iman* (Rules of the Faith) or (as it was known among the Tatars) *Iman sharty* (Principles of the Faith).[42] This Sufi primer, written in the eighteenth century, contained prayers in Turkic for those who had difficulty reading Arabic.[43] A Tatar craftsman of peasant origin from Kargala, near Orenburg, wrote in his memoirs that his mother, and not his father who was busy trading, made him recite the same book when he was five years old.[44] His mother also made him copy the alphabet, whereas at the traditional *mekteb* writing was taught long after reading, sometimes after four or five years of schooling. Partly thanks to his mother, the boy was able to make and sell talismans containing Quranic verses.[45] Women's involvement in their children's education was such that in non-Muslim areas where Islamized mothers had the choice between Russian missionary schools and clandes-

[39] Rossiiskii Gosudarstvennyi Istoricheskii Arkhiv, St. Petersburg, f. 383, op. 24, ed. khr. 37141, l. 1 and 2 ob.; f. 821, op. 8, ed. khr. 1093, l. 1 (hereafter RGIA).

[40] Mashanov, "Zametka," *Izvestiia po Kazanskoi eparkhii*, no. 2 (1875): 47.

[41] Evfimii Malov, "Ocherk religioznogo sostoianiia kreshchenykh tatar, podvergshikhsia vlianiiu magometanstva," *Pravoslavnyi sobesednik* 17, no. 11 (1871): 243.

[42] Iapei Babai [Evfimii Malov], "O kreshschenykh tatarakh (iz missionerskogo dnevnika)," *Izvestiia po Kazanskoi eparkhii* no. 18 (1891): 563–64. See also the Bashkir émigré historian Zaki Validi Togan's (born in 1890) recollections of his mother who knew Persian and Turkic Sufi poetry by heart. She recited for him poems by Ahmad Yasawi (d. 1166), Attar (d. 1229), Jalal al-Din Rumi (1207–73), and Nizam ad-Din Alisher Navoi (1441–1501). In her everyday speech and in her letters, she drew images and metaphors from their works. Zaki Validi Togan, *Vospominaniia* (Ufa, 1994), 34–36.

[43] *Shäraitu'l-iman* (Kazan, 1904).

[44] "Gabdräkhim Gabdrakhman ugly," l. 1.

[45] Ibid., ll. 1, 16.

tine *mektebs*, they had enough authority to keep their husbands from sending their children to the missionaries.[46]

Finally, women's role was not confined to the home. Some Tatar women were true missionaries of Islam who proselytized outside village boundaries. The learned Tatar women of Artyk were renowned for visiting the Kriashen village of Nikiforova in the district of Mamadysh.[47] Missionary accounts claimed that Tatar women promised paradise to any Kriashen who would repeat the *shahada* several times each day. Nothing else could be asked from them since theirs were simple minds. (Among Tatars, Kriashens had the reputation of being illiterate and ignorant of the Russian faith.) This type of proselytizing reflected the experience of *dhikr*, the recollection of God, used by many Sufi orders.[48] It also reflected the idea dear to Sufi mystics that knowledge from God could be immediate, and was not acquired only through books and formal education.[49]

Women with small businesses (usually selling sugar, tea, or candies) had contacts with and proselytized among women of different faiths as well. For instance, economic exchanges between Kriashens and Tatars in the village of Vladimirova (Mamadysh district) favored the spread of Islam.[50] Women who kept sacred shrines enjoyed great authority in their villages. In the village of Chally, the female heirs of a famous Sufi master (*ishan*) took care of his sacred shrine. They were thought to have healing powers, and even Kriashens (male and female) who diligently fulfilled their Christian obligations brought them offerings.[51] These women saints visited Tatar and Kriashen houses outside Chally, reading the Quran and spreading the word.[52] According to A. Iablokov, tombs of female Sufi saints were not uncommon on the Middle Volga even though they were not entered into official archaeological descriptions of Kazan province. Evfimii Malov, a graduate of the Simbirsk seminary and of the Kazan Theological Academy, mentioned the grave of Gaisha Bikä in Ishi village, near the ruins of Old Kazan. While alive, Gaisha had been particularly famous for her miracles. Her charisma was such that even Russian peasants feared to till the lands around her tomb.[53]

---

[46] Il'minskii, *Kazanskaia tsentral'naia shkola*, 81.

[47] Malov, *Missionerstvo*, 237.

[48] Ibn Arabi connected the bipartite profession of faith ("There is no god but God, and Muhammed is the Prophet of God") with the divine breathing (Schimmel, *As Through a Veil*, 59, 139).

[49] Il'minskii, *Kazanskaia tsentral'naia shkola*, 39.

[50] Ibid., 146.

[51] N. Odigitrievskii, "Kreshchenye Tatary Kazanskoi gubernii," *Pravoslavnyi blagovestnik* 3, no. 2 (February 1894): 110–11.

[52] Mashanov, "Zametka," *Izvestiia po Kanzanskoi eparkhii*, no. 4 (1875): 113–15.

[53] Malov as cited in A. Iablokov, "O pochitanii sviatykh v Islame," *Pravoslavnyi sobesednik* 29, no. 3 (1883): 424.

Mechanisms of Transmission on the Frontier

In light of the nineteenth-century apostasy movement, the importance of women in the reproduction of Islamic knowledge inside the family and in the community appears even greater. Like their Muslim brothers, the Kriashens practiced exogamy. A bride rarely remained in her home village, and so constituted an element of exchange between two communities. This practice could have two consequences: either it strengthened the integrity of the Kriashen community as a separate Tatar Christian group, or in the case of families already somewhat inclined to Islam, it contributed to further internalization of Islamic practices.

Parents in Kriashen families had the right to choose their children's spouses. Theoretically, both father and mother had equal responsibility for this choice, but in practice, the mother usually had the last word. Parents considered the potential spouse's village of origin, the family, and the degree of Islamization of the village that would receive the bride. On this point, the prospective groom's village often proved to be more important than his family. For example, the mullah Ivanov at Elyshevo, a village of apostate Old Converts in the Mamadysh district, thought about marrying one of his daughters to one of the sons of Arkhipov of Savrushi village. This family had not definitively accepted Islam and showed signs of being influenced by the proselytism of Orthodox missionaries. Ivanov did not cancel the plans for the wedding until the village of Savrushi decided to remain officially Christian.[54]

In the village of Nikiforova there lived a Kriashen whose father, Semën, was outwardly Christian, but continued to observe pagan rituals. Semën's wife, on the other hand, favored Islam. When the time came for their son to marry, Semën suggested a young woman from Nikiforova, but his wife opposed this since she felt that the village was too Christian, and ultimately convinced her husband to choose a girl from Elyshevo, where the families were more Islamized. The children born of this marriage were raised by their illiterate mother in the Islamic faith with the agreement of Semën's son, even though he had attended Russian parish schools. The mullah of the village of Satysh taught the boys, and an Islamized Kriashen of Staraia Ishkurma taught the daughter. Later, one of the boys was married to a Kriashen of Staraia Ishkurma who had studied with Biksutana, an *abystai* from the hamlet of Tri Sosny, and with the *abystai* of the village of Savrushi. Thanks to these two women, the young bride was able to read and recite her prayers.[55]

Semën's family was Islamized in only two or three generations. As the

---

[54] Malov, "Ocherk," *Pravoslavnyi sobesednik* 18, no. 1 (1872): 126; Il'minskii, *Kazanskaia tsentral'naia shkola*, 132.

[55] Il'minskii, *Kazanskaia tsentral'naia shkola*, 70–72.

person responsible for the physical and spiritual well-being of her children, his wife had considered prospective daughters-in-law very carefully. Wanting to approach the Quranic ideal as closely as possible, she chose a daughter-in-law whose adherence to Muslim culture was stronger than her own. Often, an illiterate mother-in-law would choose a daughter-in-law trained in the Muslim sciences.

To help their children find suitable mates, Islamicized Kriashens reconstituted the *jyen*, which had disappeared after their ancestors' conversion to Christianity, and which represented another system for spreading Islamic knowledge. The *jyen* were popular festivals which relatives and friends celebrated before the harvest, and which lasted from four to seven weeks from the end of May or the beginning of June. Beginning on a Friday, they moved from village to village within an established network; each village hosted the fair for three or four days. These feasts were occasions for Tatars to choose spouses or to contract marriages.[56]

By converting to Christianity, the Kriashens' ancestors had excluded themselves from the traditional *jyen* networks. However, on 18 June 1865, the Kriashen villagers of Elyshevo celebrated the *jyen* along with their Muslim neighbors. According to one witness, the Elyshevites had begun to celebrate the *jyen* on their own fifty years before.[57] In 1890, the *jyen* was the starting point of a new wave of apostasies in Apazovo (Kazan district), a village of Old Converts.[58] During these holidays, Christian and Muslim Tatars met and exchanged news about the progress of the apostasies. Merchants sold their wares, blind bards sang religious ballads (*mönäjät*) and epics (*bäet*), and people bought and read Sufi books such as *Forever* or *The Tale of Joseph*. All this activity helped to strengthen the Muslim faith of those who were already officially Muslim, but also of those who were inclined to Islam but had not internalized all of its principles.

Exogamy also facilitated the emergence of a new class of pedagogues who were exclusively Kriashen and, for the most part, women. The education of children occurred in two stages. In the first stage, women taught children the basic Muslim prayers at home. In the second, women opened underground *mektebs*. Biksutana (Evfimiia Ivanova),[59] one such *abystai*, who was about sixty years old in 1864, was originally from Elyshevo and had married a Kriashen of Tri Sosny (Mamadysh district). Her grandfather, a rich baptized Tatar, had founded numerous mosques in the area, notably that of Savrushi. In August 1864, she was teaching two boys

---

[56] *Tatary srednego Povolzh'ia i Priural'ia* (Moscow, 1967), 195.

[57] Il'minskii, *Kazanskaia tsentral'naia shkola*, 152–54.

[58] Iapei Babai, "O khreshchenykh tatarakh," 400.

[59] Apostate Kriashens bore two names, a Russian and a Muslim name. When questioned by missionaries, they often pretended not to remember their Christian name (Il'minskii, *Kazanskaia tsentral'naia shkola*, 297).

and fifteen girls for free, and accepted only occasional presents from the parents of her pupils as recompense for her labors. Her pupils showed great aptitude; they were able to recite an entire page of *Forever*.

Biksutana had studied with the *abystai* of the village of Ziuri in the Mamadysh district. After educating her eldest daughter herself, Biksutana sent her to the *abystai* of Savrushi to continue her studies. Later, this daughter married a Kriashen of Staraia Ikshurma, where she taught the children of her village. In this way, Biksutana established a dynasty of female pedagogues.[60]

The Tatar practice of exogamy encouraged the expansion of Islamic literacy over an ever greater territory. Biographies of early *jadid* Tatar women confirm that literate unmarried women who gave lessons in their native villages later pursued their pedagogical endeavors in the villages of their husbands. In this way, the practice of exogamy also contributed to the rapid spread of modernist schooling in the countryside at the beginning of the twentieth century. For example, Fatyjma Färidä (1889–1914), daughter of a merchant of Chistopol', had studied under a mullah's son from 1896 to 1903. In 1907, she opened a *jadid* school in the village of Karashly in the district of Bugul'ma (Samara province), to which her parents had moved, and in 1908, after her marriage, went to Tomsk where she taught in a girls' school.[61]

Biksutana understood her role in the spread of Islam. She explained to Vasilii Timofeev, himself a Kriashen who had studied in the parish school of Taveli village, that according to the Quran everyone would become Muslim before the end of the world. The mass conversions of the Kriashen seemed to confirm her apocalyptic hopes. Biksutana herself was deeply religious. She regularly visited the mosque in Savrushi, especially during Ramadan. Her life was an example of Muslim piety to the Kriashens in Tri Sosny. Her reputation as a teacher of Islam was such that Kriashens called her "Biksultan," a title of respect and affection.[62]

Biksutana also understood the threat posed by Nikolai Il'minskii's school system to the spread of Islam among the Kriashens. Il'minskii, a famous Turkologist trained at the Kazan Theological Academy, had introduced a phonetic method of reading Tatar texts in the Cyrillic alphabet that was far superior to the traditional education in the *mektebs*.[63] Thanks to this new approach, Il'minskii's pupils were able to read unfamiliar

---

[60] Ibid., 74–75.

[61] A. Makhmutova and V. N. Smirnova, "Tatarka-prosvetitel'nitsa (iz istorii bor'by za zhenskoe obrazovanie u Tatar)," *Voprosy istorii, filologii i pedagogiki*, 2 (1967): 21–25.

[62] *Istoriko-statisticheskoe opisanie tserkvei i prikhodov Kazanskoi eparkhii*, vol. 6: *G. Mamadysh i Mamadyshskii uezd* (Kazan, 1904), 34.

[63] Isabelle T. Kreindler, "Education Policies toward the Eastern Nationalities in Tsarist Russia: A Study of Il'minskii's System" (Ph.D. diss., Columbia University, 1970).

Tatar texts immediately, whereas pupils in the *mektebs* first named each letter (mim for m, nun for n, and so on), without understanding the sound represented by the letter. Unlike Il'minskii's students, they did not have immediate access to the meaning of what they read.[64] When Il'minskii opened a school for Christian Tatars in Kazan in the autumn of 1864, Biksutana spread rumors against the school partly because some of her students had been in contact with Timofeev's teaching.[65] Biksutana's activism was such that the state and the church made an example of her. In 1864, the Kazan vice governor Rozov confiscated the Quran that a Tatar from Tatarskie Savrushi had given her, and when she died, the priest of Abdi buried her in the Christian cemetery.[66]

Female teachers such as Biksutana helped their fellow villagers understand the importance of establishing permanent schools. In Elyshevo, for example, a woman from Tiamti, Laishev district, taught children from 1860 to 1864. She was replaced by the *shakird* Mukhi-ed-din; when he left Elyshevo, another woman, Matrena Ivanova, took his place as the local educator.[67]

Women's Direct Role in the Apostasy Movement

Womens' place in marriage negotiations helped to facilitate the flow of news from one village to another. The leaders of apostasies were often related by marriage; father-in-law and son-in-law stood side by side. Rumors spread by women were crucial before, during, and after rebellions. Avdot'ia Fedorova of the village of Kibiak-Kozi (Laishev district) was arrested because of her involvement in spreading rumors about a law supposedly allowing Kriashens to become officially Muslim.[68] Women also gathered information about the development of apostasy in the neighboring villages through family ties, which could involve several villages. For example, a woman in Elyshevo brought fresh news about the apostasy movement from her parents who lived in Kibiak-Kozi.[69] While visiting relatives in Elyshevo, another woman of Savrushi learned about the arrival of an Orthodox missionary and immediately reported the news to her fellow vil-

---

[64] The traditional method of reading was also criticized by the Crimean Tatar Ismail Gaspraly in the 1880s. Edward Lazzerini, "Gadidism at the Turn of the Twentieth Century: A View from Within," *Cahiers du monde russe et soviétique* 16, no. 2 (April–June 1975): 245–77.

[65] Il'minskii, *Kazanskaia tsentral'naia shkola*, 79, 88.

[66] *Istoriko-statisticheskoe opisanie*, 34.

[67] RGIA, f. 821, op. 8, ed. khr. 763, l. 289 ob.; Il'minskii, *Kazanskaia tsentral'naia shkola*, 153.

[68] RGIA, f. 821, op. 8, ed. khr. 763, l. 20b. –3.

[69] Malov, "Ocherk," *Pravoslavnyi sobesednik* 17, no. 11 (1871): 242.

Muslim apostates from the Orthodox Church gathered in front of their clandestine mosque in the village of Kibiak-Kozi, Laishev district, Kazan province. Rossiiskii Gosudarstvennyi Istoricheskii Arkhiv, f. 835, op. 4, d. 72.

lagers.[70] This information was carefully discussed in homes and at elders' meetings afterward.

Upon the arrival of Russian investigators, women came forward and, in villages where the decision to apostatize was not yet unanimous, swore that their husbands had never participated in the apostasy movement and knew nothing about Islam. If a woman's husband had already gone on seasonal work, she refused to tell where he was. Women also used other methods of passive resistance. In the village street, some women kept silent and refused any contact with missionaries. Others hid behind the curtain dividing the house into women's and men's quarters when missionaries entered, and came out only if the missionary showed them the Quran or other Muslim books. When the missionary started reading the Gospel of Matthew in Tatar, they hid again. In other instances, women would gather around the missionary to get more information about the investigation going on in the village. They would also ask him to read some specific texts from the Bible that would answer some of the questions they asked themselves about Islam (not about Christianity). Those

[70] Malov, "Ocherk," ibid., 18, no. 1 (1872): 66.

texts often referred to the story of Joseph, so popular in the Tatar villages. Since the biblical account almost completely ignored Zuleikha (known only as "Potiphar's wife" in Genesis), Tatars and Islamicized Kriashens concluded that Christians had indeed falsified the Word of Allah, as the Quran claimed. On the other hand, Jesus' miracles and Mary's miraculous pregnancy confirmed what the Kriashens had heard from Tatars. Enthusiastic missionaries often failed to sense that apostate Kriashens were interested in their readings not because they suddenly felt moved by the Bible, but because of possible connections with what they knew about the Quran. Moreover, Kriashens who owned Muslim books would ask the missionaries to translate some of the more difficult Arabic words, thus clearly demonstrating that they desired to learn more about Islam than about Christianity.[71]

Women's role was not confined to the gathering of information about police investigations or knowledge about Islam. When necessary, women took a more active role in the defense of their Islamic identity. They wrote their own petitions to the government to be recognized as Muslims. The petition of one woman (approved by the Senate, the highest government council, in 1807), served as a legal precedent for the Kriashens who apostatized en masse in 1827.[72] In another reported case in 1866, women's resistance could have violent consequences. When a Russian priest sought to bury Kriashen apostate women in a Christian cemetery, three women threw themselves on the dead bodies; the outraged men took up arms and chased the police. The three women were then arrested, together with Ibetulla Muksinov (Vasilii Vasil'ev), the leader of the apostasy in Bol'shoi Sulabash, Shepsheik, and Nurma (Kazan district), for their active involvement in the rebellion. The last names of two of the women (Khalitova) might indicate family connections with Muksinov, whose son-in-law, Menglybai Khalitov, lived in Nurma. The women may have served as informants among the inhabitants of the three villages implicated in the apostasy.[73]

Despite pressure from police and missionaries, women did not stop proselytizing. In 1872, a married couple in the village of Elyshevo went door to door, urging people to convert to Islam. The wife stood on the

[71] Malov, "Ocherk," ibid., 18, no. 2 (1872): 125; idem, "Prikhody starokreshchenykh i novokreshchenykh Tatar v Kazanskoi eparkhii," *Pravoslavnoe obozrenie* 12 (1865): 502; Iapei Babai, "O khreshchenykh tatarakh," 560.

[72] Malov, "Pravoslavnaia protivomusul'manskaia missiia," Pravoslamyi sobesednik, no. 10 (1869): 151–154; A. Mozharovskii, *Izlozhenie khoda missionerskogo dela po prosveshcheniiu Kazanskikh inorodtsev s 1552 po 1867 godu* (Moscow, 1880), 125–126; *Polnoe Sobranie Zakonov,* first series, 45 vols. (St. Petersburg: V Tipografii II-ogo otdeleniia Sobstvennoi E. I. V. Kantseliarii, 1830), vol. 16, no. 12126, pp. 704–7.

[73] *Materialy po istorii Tatarii vtoroi poloviny 19-go veka: agrarnyi vopros i krest'ianskoe dvizhenie v Tatarii XIX veka* (Moscow, 1936), 236–42.

bridge leading to the newly built church, and dissuaded women from going to services. The result was that women ceased to attend the newly created Orthodox Tatar liturgy.[74] Finally, when missionaries looked for pupils to teach in their newly opened girls' schools, they found greater resistance than with boys' schools. Boys needed to learn Russian to transact business, but girls did not. A girl was supposed to stay in the village unit, whether her parents' or her husband's, and be in charge of her children's religious education. Islam sufficed. Besides, sewing and other feminine crafts were taught in girls' *mektebs*.[75]

Conclusion

Women's elaborate communication networks were partly responsible for the expansion of the apostate movement. Contrary to the claims of missionaries and *jadids* alike, the traditional woman's world was not limited to the home. First of all, thanks to the Tatar and Kriashen practice of exogamy, the wife served as a link between her native village and her husband's village. Often, information and rumors about the apostasies spread from village to village because of these links. Secondly, mothers-in-law often chose Islamicized Kriashens as the only suitable wives for their sons. They helped to organize the *jyen*, local festivals that encouraged the contact between the Kriashens and their Muslim Tatar neighbors. Finally, they served as *abystais*, or teachers in Quranic schools.

At the turn of the twentieth century, modernist Tatars used the same female networks observed in the Kriashen apostate villages to spread their revolutionary ideas about schooling in the Kriashen and Tatar communities. In a book published in Tatar using the Cyrillic alphabet by the Kärimi brothers (well-known *jadid* publishing house) in 1906, Kriashens were advised to find a *shakird* to teach boys, and marry him to a literate native who would teach girls.[76] Exogamic kinship explains partly why the *jadid* movement spread so fast on the Middle Volga. After having been exposed to *jadid* schooling, literate women taught in their husbands' villages. *Jyens* as well as other popular festivals became places where *jadid* literature was sold and where money was collected for the building of new schools.[77]

Sufism, with its charismatic and superrational qualities, also provided women with opportunities for religious action; it provided the framework

---

[74] RGIA, f. 821, op. 8, ed. khr. no. 763, l. 2990b.

[75] Malov, "Ocherk," *Pravoslavnyi sobesednik* 17, no. 11 (1871): 243; Fuks, *Kazanskie tatary*, 119.

[76] S. Bagin, "Ob otpadenii," 235–36; Mashanov, "Sovremennoe sostoianie," 278–79. The title of the book was *Islam dine* (The religion of Islam).

[77] *Mir Islama* 2, no. 6 (1913): 408–11.

that Muslim women used to understand their world and to act in it. The missionaries, who were exclusively male, misunderstood and underestimated Sufism's power. By validating the woman's role as Seeker of God, guardian of the faith, and teacher in works such as *The Tale of Joseph*, Sufism gave women a vocabulary of images, metaphors, and behaviors. Women used these images for the mystical and ritual instruction of the common people, and to prepare young believers for formal theological training in the *medressehs*. Thanks to the separation of the sexes, the woman's world was closed to the male-dominated Russian authorities. Among the apostate Kriashens, the police could not easily check on female teachers' clandestine schools. This gave women greater freedom to teach and proselytize.

Thus Sufism, the Tatar kinship structure, and even the separation of the sexes created opportunities for women to change their world for the better. In the end, though, it was individual women who actively exploited these opportunities to hasten the victory of Islam and (as they saw it) the triumph of a just social order.

CHAPTER ELEVEN

Going Abroad or Going to Russia?
Orthodox Missionaries in the Kazakh Steppe,
1881–1917

ROBERT P. GERACI

One June morning in 1893, Father Sergii, a missionary to the Kazakh population of Tomsk diocese, was invited to visit the village of Karpovka, which had recently been founded by Ukrainian migrant settlers about fifty versts away. These Ukrainians (*malorossiiskie*), explained the priest in his memoirs, "the Cossacks [*kazaki*] refer to using the adjective *rossiiskie* ['the ones from Russia'], but . . . the Kazakhs [*kirgizy*[1]], who like to use abbreviations for everything, just call [them] 'Russia' [*Rossiia*]."

Sergii, who had begun his service in the mission only the previous November and had not yet been to Karpovka, set off for the village the same morning accompanied by servants. To get there from his post in the Russian village of Shul'ba, he had to cross the Irtysh river. Until the recent construction of a bridge, the river had been an obstacle between the Russian village and the steppe, where most of the Kazakhs lived as nomads, and was thus known colloquially as "the border" or "barrier" (*granitsa*). In Russian, to go "beyond the border"—*za granitsu*—is, idiomatically, to leave one's country, to go abroad. So to cross the river was, in local parlance, to move not only between two places, but also between two different nations or peoples. Crossing the river for the first time, thanks to the bridge, Father Sergii was struck by the irony of these colloquialisms.

[1] I am using the present-day designation "Kazakh" for the people known until 1925 as "Kirgiz." Occasionally, they were also referred to more specifically as "Kirgiz-kaisaks." The people now known as "Kyrgyz" were referred to previously as "Kara-kirgiz." See I. P. Poddubnyi, "Naselenie Aziatskoi Rossii: etnograficheskii ocherk," in *Aziatskaia Rossiia*, ed. G. V. Glinka, 3 vols. (St. Petersburg, 1914), 1:153.

... on the crossing the Russians asked me: "Father, are you going 'abroad'?" [*Vy, batiushka, edete za-granitsu?*] I was already used to this [expression] and answered, "Yes." And when we were crossing the Irtysh, we encountered some Kazakhs along the way who already knew that I had been invited to visit the settlers. They asked me: "Are you going to 'Russia'?" [*Vy edete v Rossiiu?*] And to this question, not afraid of contradicting ourselves, we also answered positively![2]

Father Sergii's joke—arguably, more than he himself may have realized—captured the predicament of Russian Orthodox missions in the borderlands of the empire during the last decades of tsarism. The missions were fraught with ambiguity, most notably with regard to the ostensibly central role of the Russian people and Russian nationality in the transformation of the missions' Muslim subjects. As the above anecdote implies, the mission's primary assumption of a stable gradient between colonizer and colonized was at odds with some aspects of everyday perception. Competing assumptions collided, resulting in uncertainty over names and identities. Were Cossacks and Ukrainians Russians or not? Was a Cossack, Ukrainian, or Russian in the borderlands the same as one in the heartland? Were Russians better defined in geographic terms (as *rossiiskie*) or in ethnic ones (as *russkie*)? Missionaries' consciousness of their work among the Kazakhs as a national or ethnic as well as religious crusade gave these seemingly philosophical quandaries an acute and immediate importance in the steppe.

In this essay we will examine such tensions and ambiguities in the Orthodox mission among the Kazakhs between 1881 and 1917. Our chief sources are the reports, letters, and diaries of the missionaries themselves, most of them published in *Pravoslavnyi blagovestnik* (The Orthodox Missionary), the leading Russian journal concerned with the church's work among non-Christian peoples.[3] The temporal, cultural, and geographical dimensions of this particular mission presented a unique challenge in the history of attempts to spread Russian Orthodoxy; however, a look at the mission will offer some insights on the broader issue of religious and ethnic diversity in tsarist Russia, and more generally on the dynamics of empire and nation-building and on the distinctiveness of the Russian case.

The steppe mission was fairly short-lived: it opened in the era of reactionary politics in the 1880s and was dismantled in the wake of the 1917 revolutions. The brevity of this career, among other factors, makes it unfair to judge the mission by the very small number of Kazakhs it converted

---

[2] "Zapiski Shul'binskogo missionera ieromonakha Sergiia za 1893-i god," *Pravoslavnyi blagovestnik*, no. 2 (1894): 100 (hereafter *PB*).

[3] The journal *Missionerskoe obozrenie* (The Missionary Review), published from 1889 to 1917, was the counterpart of *Pravoslavnyi blagovestnik* concerned primarily with the church's "internal" missions— those among Old Believers and other nominally Orthodox sectarians.

to Orthodoxy. Yet we also have a record of the missionaries' continual frustration and disappointment with their work, which gives us an additional frame of reference; their perceptions of their tasks may in fact tell us more than any objective measures. The mission's unimpressive performance for the thirty-odd years of its existence, therefore, we are inclined to see as evidence of a gap between the ideals of the missions and the reality of steppe society; it was a prognosis of difficulties that lay ahead, were the mission to exist longer than it did. Before delving into the missionaries' writings, however, we will discuss three contextual factors that will help us to understand why the work of these missionaries was especially challenging: the theory and practice of missions as they developed in nineteenth-century Russia; Russian ambivalence toward undertaking missions among Muslim peoples; and finally, the juxtaposition of the mission with large-scale peasant migration from European Russia into Siberia and Central Asia.

Missionary Reform: The Nineteenth-Century Legacy

Before the mid-nineteenth century, Russian missionary efforts were typically superficial and relied primarily on either force or material incentives.[4] Moreover, the Orthodox presence in border areas was usually not organized or consistent; as one historian has put it, there were missionaries but no missions.[5] These shortcomings became a source of great concern in both the Russian church and state in the opening decades of the nineteenth century, when numerous and visible instances of apostasy occurred in communities thought to have been Christianized in the sixteenth through the eighteenth centuries (particularly in the Volga region, which had been subject to missionary campaigns following the conquests of Ivan IV). Even in many places where defection was not deliberate or disruptive (throughout Siberia, for instance), church and state authorities became increasingly aware of a sort of passive apostasy, or simply nonparticipation in and ignorance of Orthodox practice.

The preferred solution to apostasy was to abandon superficial methods of recruitment and conversion and increasingly to use cultural knowledge to "penetrate into the secret inner world" of the non-Orthodox so as to truly transform their beliefs and loyalties.[6] Catechism in prospective converts' native languages was the first widely recognized means to this end. The initiative taken by the Russian Bible Society (under the tutelage of

[4] See Michael Khodarkovsky's essay in this volume.

[5] E. Smirnoff, *A Short Account of the Historical Development and Present Position of Russian Orthodox Missions* (London, 1903), 14.

[6] Ibid., 10.

the British and Foreign Bible Society) toward the publication of Christian writings in the myriad tongues of the Russian empire reflected the influence of European Romanticism and Protestantism in Russian society during the reign of Alexander I. Officially, however, these projects were abandoned when Alexander shut down the Bible Society in 1824.

The first sustained and successful manifestation of the new approach to missions in Russia was the Altai mission of Siberia, founded in 1830 by Archimandrite Makarii Glukharev (1792–1847). Makarii learned the languages of the Altai region and worked out translations of scripture into several of them. The greater efficacy of his mission than of previous efforts was further exemplified by his belief that conversion only begins with baptism. Also, Makarii insisted that the goals of his mission among Altai animists depended on the proper education of Russian settlers in the region. Though he was able to carry out his plans locally, Makarii's philosophies collided with the conservatism of the central church hierarchy, and were not applied elsewhere until later.[7]

The use of native languages was studied intensively in the 1850s by the lay orientalist Nikolai I. Il'minskii (1822–1891). Il'minskii was a professor at the Kazan Theological Academy, which, after reopening in 1842 in order to address the problem of apostasy, had rapidly become the center of eastern language studies and missionary training for all of the empire. In the late 1850s Il'minskii decided on a comprehensive strategy for missionary work in non-Russian convert communities to stave off possible defection from the church. Such efforts would focus primarily on offering an Orthodox school curriculum to children. Classroom instruction and church services would be conducted in the pupils' native languages, and schoolbooks consisting of translated scriptures would be published in these languages. In order to separate the cultural world of the Christian children from that of the unconverted in their midst (primarily Muslims), languages would be written using the Cyrillic alphabet. When possible, native speakers of the minority languages were to be appointed as clergy and teachers in these communities. As head of the Kazan Teachers Seminary (founded 1872), where both Russians and non-Russians were

---

[7] T. A. Dogurevich, *Svet Azii: Rasprostranenie khristianstva v Sibiri* (St. Petersburg, 1897), 84–92; P. P. Liubimov, "Religii i veroispovednyi sostav naseleniia Aziatskoi Rossii," in Glinka, *Aziatskaia Rossiia*, 1:215–16; Smirnoff, *Short Account*, 18; J. Glazik, *Die russisch-orthodoxe Heidenmission seit Peter dem Grossen* (Münster, 1954), 122. For more on the Altai mission, see David N. Collins, "Colonialism and Siberian Development: A Case-Study of the Orthodox Mission to the Altay, 1830–1913," in *The Development of Siberia: People and Resources*, ed. Alan Wood and R. A. French (London, 1989), 50–71. Makarii's long treatise, "Mysli o sposobakh k uspeshneishemu rasprostraneniiu khristianskoi very mezhdu evreiami, magometanami, i iazychinikami v Rossiiskoi Derzhave" (Thoughts on the means toward the most successful propagation of Christian faith among the Jews, Muslims, and pagans in the Russian domain), written no later than 1839, was first published in full in 1893–1894 in *PB*.

trained for this work, Il'minskii directed the proliferation of a large network of schools and parishes using his methods. Concentrated primarily in the Volga and Urals region, this network eventually extended into Siberia as well.[8]

In the Kazan Theological Academy, where Il'minskii had conceived his project, opinions were divided between adherents of his program and those of a theologically oriented, polemical strategy toward converting Muslims to Orthodoxy. The primary exponent of the latter school was Professor Evfimii A. Malov (1835–1918), another renowned orientalist and also an ordained priest. On the basis of extensive knowledge of the Quran and other Islamic texts, Malov constructed elaborate critiques designed to convince well-educated Muslims of the superiority of Christianity to Islam. Throughout his long career Malov spent several hours per week practicing these polemics in face-to-face meetings with Muslim students in Kazan, as well as publishing the arguments in book form.[9] Malov's ideas, though fundamentally different from Il'minskii's and Makarii's, were also considered a step toward the improvement of Russian missions.

The ideas of Makarii, Il'minskii, and Malov also informed a new semiofficial lay organization, the Imperial Orthodox Missionary Society, founded in 1869. The society had no administrative control over missions, yet aimed to raise broad public support, both moral and financial, for churches, schools, and other institutions serving converts from non-Christian religions. "It is desirable that every son of the Orthodox Church be a member of the Missionary Society," read a typical editorial of the society's bi-weekly *Pravoslavnyi blagovestnik,* "because the obligation of preaching Christ rests not on priests alone, but on every Christian.... If each person cannot drop everything and go to the Siberian tundras, he can [at least] help the missionaries in the fulfillment of their difficult task ... "[10] From the early 1890s to its dissolution in 1917, the society's membership ranged from fourteen to sixteen thousand.[11] The society established diocesan committees in the major cities of the empire, and solicited contributions on annual feast days established by the Holy Synod specifically for the Russian missions.[12]

The missionary practices pioneered by the three reformers were consonant with the doctrine of Official Nationality, which largely defined the organization of the Russian empire from the 1830s to 1917. Orthodox

[8] See Robert Geraci, *Window on the East: National and Imperial Identities in Late Tsarist Russia* (forthcoming, Ithaca, N.Y., 2001), chaps. 2, 4.

[9] Ibid., chap. 3.

[10] Arkhimandrit Lavrentii, "Pouchenie v den' prazdnovaniia 25–letnego iubileia Missionerskogo Obshchestva," *PB*, no. 2 (1895): 66.

[11] Glazik, *Die Heidenmission,* 234.

[12] Ibid., 235.

Christianity was the primary pillar of this ideology (followed by autocracy and nationality), though decisively not the end point. It was a defining feature of Russian identity (and hence a key component of assimilation into the Russian empire), yet would ultimately serve the spread of a more broadly conceived (that is, in political and cultural as well as religious terms) Russianness throughout the empire. If the doctrine prescribed a substantive, not just nominal, identity to all subjects of the empire, then it stood to reason that religious conversion should prepare its subjects for all facets of this identity. The missionaries' task in the nineteenth century was to promote the transformation of erstwhile foreigners into Russians in every way possible. By conceiving of religious conversion as a deeply psychological rather than merely mechanical process, reform-minded representatives of the Russian church committed themselves to a slower and much more labor-intensive process than previous missionary work. And they had to enlist the support and cooperation of the Russian people themselves. A chronicler of the Russian missions in Siberia claimed in 1897 that although "the missionary work of the new era" could hardly compete with its forebears in the quantity of convert baptisms, those conversions it did achieve were far superior in their quality and, presumably, durability.[13] Missionaries, for the most part, accepted the new demands of their work; they no longer expected mass conversions and indeed grew suspicious of them.

Missions to Muslims: A Checkered History

In the context of the early, unreformed missions, the original religious practices of potential converts to Orthodoxy did not need to be taken into account. In the new era, however, missionaries were expected truly to convince converts that Christianity (Orthodoxy) was better than their previous belief system. This was the chief idea behind the Malov school of polemical missions to Muslims.

In theory, however, such tactics were considered necessary only as an accelerating factor, for cultural Russification was viewed as the inevitable, manifest destiny of all peoples in the Russian empire. On the basis of nineteenth-century popular historiography and its portrayal of Russia's eastward expansion, one historian has argued that "educated Russians of the nineteenth century, both within the regime and without, perceived the state of which they were subjects not at all as a multinational empire consisting of a metropolis and various colonial dependencies, but rather as a nation-state in the process of formation, following a course marked

---

[13] Dogurevich, *Svet Azii*, 101.

out by countries like England and France centuries earlier" (and *not* comparable to these countries' overseas imperial expansion in the nineteenth century). Russians thought that their country's expansion would be accompanied, and facilitated, by the gradual assimilation of all border peoples into the Russian national culture. Indeed, Russian expansion was thought to have always had this cultural (as opposed to purely administrative) meaning, though before the nineteenth century it had been unplanned and unconscious.[14]

Since the late eighteenth century, many clerics and state officials had thought that the followers of other monotheistic religions, such as Islam, would be quicker to convert to Christianity than would polytheists or animists. Catherine II, who upon coming to power halted the action of Orthodox missions in the Russian empire, used an earlier, Enlightenment-era version of this logic in promoting the spread of Islam by Volga Tatar merchants southward into the region now known as Kazakhstan, much of which was under Russian protectorate status since the middle of the eighteenth century.[15] "Civilization" (and hence Russian control), Catherine thought, would take hold more readily in the presence of Islam than of the traditional religions of the steppe.[16] In the 1830s, when Makarii suggested extending his mission southward from the Altai peoples to their by then partially Islamicized Kazakh neighbors, the Holy Synod refused permission on the grounds that it would be premature, as there were too many "pagan" vestiges in Kazakh religion for a Christian mission to be effective.[17]

A few decades and thousands of apostasies later, predominant views of Islam had changed. Islam now seemed to present a *greater* challenge than the animistic religions of Siberia. Whereas those religions worked against Christianity only through spiritual inertia, clerics and scholars thought, Islam's high level of organization, well-developed theology, and cultural heritage created obstacles of exclusiveness and intolerance. The presence of Sunni Islam was now anchored in the Kazakh areas by an extensive network of mullahs, schools, and mosques. When a mission to the Kazakhs was again proposed, many in the Russian church claimed that it was now too late, as Islam had progressed too far among the Kazakhs. Islam and

---

[14] Seymour Becker, "The Muslim East in Nineteenth-Century Russian Popular Historiography," *Central Asian Survey* 5, no. 3–4 (1986): 25–47 (quote, 25). See also idem, "Russia Between East and West: The Intelligentsia, Russian National Identity and the Asian Borderlands," ibid., 10, no. 4 (1991): 47–64.

[15] Andreas Kappeler, *Russland als Vielvölkerreich: Entstehung, Geschichte, Zerfall* (Munich, 1992), 156.

[16] Ibid., 159.

[17] Dogurevich, *Svet Azii*, 94.

Christianity were now seen as two divergent paths at a fork in the road of human development. Once a people had progressed a certain distance down one road or the other, there was no turning back.[18]

Missionaries now denied any positive or progressive influence of Islam on the Kazakhs and unanimously denounced Catherine's promotion of the religion in both European Russia and in Kazakhstan as misguided and disastrous.[19] Some even claimed that before Catherine's reign the Kazakhs had been more inclined toward Christianity than Islam.[20] Il'minskii's work in the Orenburg Border Commission in the 1850s with fellow orientalist V. V. Grigor'ev inspired him to pursue efforts toward the cultural autonomy of the Kazakhs, and the lessening of Tatar migrants' religious and cultural influence.[21] Yet he never proposed tampering with either Tatars' or Kazakhs' own Islamic religion. His schools and books for Tatars were designed only for those converted in earlier centuries (those then referred to as "Baptized Tatars" and now known as "Kriashens"), and Il'minskii very bluntly denied the efficacy of polemical or educational work among Muslim Tatars.[22] Only a few Russian missionaries—Malov and his entourage—harbored optimism for the conversion of Muslims, and they had little success in their learned polemicizing. They were unable to get permission to establish operations among the millions of Muslims who became imperial subjects in the 1860s and 1870s. Turkestan's first governor general, K. P. von Kaufman, chose a policy of tolerating Islam without actively protecting or promoting it, and barred all Orthodox missions from the region.[23]

The year 1881, after the assassination of Alexander II and the accession of his extraordinarily conservative son, brought a reaffirmation of imperial doctrines resembling Official Nationality and advocating the aggressive pursuit of cultural homogeneity in the empire. With the resurgence of the idea of inevitable Russification (whether because or in spite of it) came a greater willingness to put pressure on Muslims to assimilate. These administrative initiatives were not supposed to take the place of, but

---

[18] I. Sotnikov, "Neskol'ko slov o vozmozhnosti uchrezhdeniia missii mezhdu kirgizami srednei ordy," *Pravoslavnoe obozrenie*, May 1872, 771–90.

[19] S. Rybakov, "Otchet chlena-sotrudnika S. Rybakova o poezdke k kirgizam letom 1896 po porucheniiu Imperatorskogo Geograficheskogo Obshchestva," *Zhivaia starina* 7, no. 2 (1897): 209–10.

[20] N. Simurg, "Kul'turtregery kirgizskoi stepi," *PB*, no. 8 (1910): 351–58 (quote, 352).

[21] See Isabelle Kreindler, "Ibrahim Altynsarin, Nikolai Il'minskii and the Kazakh National Awakening," *Central Asian Survey* 2, no. 3 (1982): 99–116.

[22] Robert Geraci, "Window on the East: Ethnography, Orthodoxy, and Russian Nationality in Kazan, 1870–1914" (Ph. D. diss., University of California at Berkeley, 1995), 44.

[23] On von Kaufman, see Daniel Brower, "Islam and Ethnicity: Russian Colonial Policy in Turkestan," in *Russia's Orient: Imperial Borderlands and Peoples, 1700–1917*, ed. Daniel R. Brower and Edward J. Lazzerini, (Bloomington, Ind., 1997), 115–35.

rather to support and enhance, a process that was thought to be fueled at the popular level by Russian peasants.

In 1893 the popular magazine *Niva* celebrated the organic, grassroots ideal of Russian cultural expansion in an article entitled "Our Movement Eastward." "The swiftness of our movement eastward and the durability of our conquest," the article asserted, "have depended not so much on our military power, as on the particularities of our national character, which is distinguished by gentleness and tolerance, and the essence of which is the great assimilating strength of the Russian people, which has absorbed and taken up so many tribes and nations."[24] This brand of Russian imperial nationalism did not find unanimous support in the administrative circles of St. Petersburg, but it did have many adherents in the Orthodox Church. In the same year, a prominent Moscow theologian wrote in *Pravoslavnyi blagovestnik* that through the missions converts would "fuse organically with [the Russian people], noticeably multiplying its ranks, filling its family with new close relations, with members beneficial to the entire family."[25]

With regard to Muslims, Il'minskii's pessimism was still the norm for the remainder of the tsarist period. Yet the fortunes of Malov and the polemicists improved. The increase in church and state support for conversionary efforts was marked chiefly by the 1884 reinstatement of Malov's chair in anti-Islamic polemics in the Kazan Theological Academy, Synod provisions of 1889 for the appointment of diocesan anti-Islamic missionaries, and of course the establishment of missions in the Kazakh steppe. The approaches of Il'minskii and Malov were pursued side by side, the former among Christians (and sometimes animists) and the latter among Muslims.

The church's approach to the Kazakhs, actually, was a hybrid of the Il'minskii and Malov philosophies.[26] Besides capitalizing on confidence in the polemical method of missionizing and the still considerably widespread belief in the ultimate inevitability of Russification, the steppe missionaries and their supporters depended heavily on the view that the Kazakhs were not genuine Muslims, but rather had been only recently and superficially Islamicized. It was widely agreed (however erroneously) that the religion had been spread to the steppe by Tatars only since the time of Catherine, and therefore that Islam was weaker there than elsewhere in Turkestan, where it had been rooted only a few centuries after

[24] V. M., "Nashe dvizhenie na vostok (Po povodu 25–letiia vziatiia Samarkanda russkimi voiskami)," *Niva*, no. 19 (1893): 451.

[25] N. Eleonskii, "Znachenie russkogo veropropovednichestva dlia Pravoslavnoi tserkvi i russkogo naroda," *PB*, no. 2 (1893): 11.

[26] On Il'minskii's mixed feelings regarding the missions to the Kazakhs, see K. Kharlampovich, "N. I. Il'minskii i altaiskaia missiia," *Pravoslavnyi sobesednik*, June 1905, 243–75.

the foundation of Islam. Kazakh culture was known to retain significant animistic elements, and its Islamic religiosity was reportedly shallow.[27] The missions were justified, in other words, by the idea that the steppe belonged culturally to Siberia more than to Central Asia. Still, there was disagreement and discussion about the history and relative strength of Islam and traditional "pagan" religions among Kazakhs. In any event, the Kazakh missions were thought to be working against time; they must save these people before they would be spoiled by Islam.

The Great Migration

Russian colonization of the Kazakh steppe increased dramatically after the first missions were already in place. The earliest Russian settlements there had been Cossack military colonies founded in the sixteenth and seventeenth centuries. Cossack migration continued for centuries, and eventually the settlements consisted of three clusters, the Ural, Siberian, and Semirech'e hosts (*voiska*). (By 1900, there were 404 Cossack villages in the steppe, holding one-seventh of the region's land.)[28] Next came fugitive Old Believers seeking to escape persecution under the Petrine regime. Commercial relations with Russia had also developed; these traditionally were maintained by Volga Tatars, but by the middle of the nineteenth century Cossacks and Russians were now selling grain in the steppe too. By 1846, Russian domination had enveloped all the Kazakh lands and all of the region's native, non-Slavic inhabitants had been classified as *inorodtsy* under Speranskii's 1822 law for Siberian administration.[29]

After the conquest of Tashkent to the south in 1864, the steppe was divided among three administrative districts: the newly formed Turkestan, and the districts of Orenburg and Western Siberia. At the same time, peasants from the Russian heartland—pressured by land shortage—had begun to migrate freely to the east and elsewhere in the empire.[30] Thirty-five thousand settlers relocated from European Russian to the steppe between 1865 and 1895; the 1897 census reported that Slavs then constituted about 16 percent of the steppe's population.[31] Anticipating an

[27] Sotnikov, "Neskol'ko slov"; Dogurevich, *Svet Azii*, 65; Poddubnyi, "Naselenie Aziatskoi Rossii," 162–63. This view is supported by Martha Brill Olcott, *The Kazakhs* (Stanford, Calif., 1987), 18–19. See also F. Poiarkov, "Iz oblasti kirgizskikh verovanii," *Etnograficheskoe obozrenie*, October–December 1891, 21–43.

[28] George J. Demko, *The Russian Colonization of Kazakhstan, 1896–1916* (Bloomington, Ind., 1969), 42.

[29] See Mark Raeff, *Siberia and the Reforms of 1822* (Seattle, 1956).

[30] The chief sources on migration to the Kazakh steppe are Demko, *Russian Colonization,* and Barbara A. Anderson, *Internal Migration during Modernization in Late Nineteenth-Century Russia* (Princeton, N.J., 1980), chap. 5.

[31] Olcott, *The Kazakhs*, 90.

upsurge in settlement, the government in 1868 had claimed ownership of all lands in the steppe.[32] The 1889 Resettlement Act, the beginning of official encouragement of migration to Siberia, designated many Kazakh areas as destinations. State authorities (of the Ministry of the Interior's Resettlement Administration) promised a land grant of at least fifteen desiatinas (about forty acres) to each settler household. An 1895 expedition was charged with determining how much land in the steppe was needed by the nomads; land in excess of the Kazakhs' needs was to be seized and made available for settlement.[33] Because the majority of Russian migrants seem to have been unregistered, however, the state was unable to make accurate estimates of land needs and thus to prevent conflict and animosity between Slavs (Russians, Ukrainians, and Belorussians) and Kazakhs over land.[34]

In 1896, the new Trans-Siberian Railroad became available for the transport of settlers, and the numbers skyrocketed. Of the total number of migrants to Asiatic Russia between 1896 and 1916 (6.5 million), roughly one-third (2 million) went to the Kazakh steppe.[35] In 1896 the densest Russian settlement was in the northern oblast of Akmolinsk, where 132 Russian villages had a combined population of over 99,000.[36] By 1916 nearly 42 percent of the population of the four northern steppe oblasts (Ural'sk, Turgai, Akmolinsk, and Semipalatinsk) was Slavic. However, after Syr Darya oblast was opened to settlement (1900), all restrictions on migration in the empire lifted (1904), and peasant land consolidation encouraged by the Stolypin reforms (1906–7), the greatest rate of inmigration was occurring in the southern steppe. By the time of World War I, the area of most rapid growth was Semirech'e, south of Semipalatinsk.

Migration of metropolitan subjects into the colonies by land, and on such a scale as occurred in late nineteenth-century and early twentieth-century Russia, made it impossible for the state to control effectively the extent of mixing between native and settler populations. Thus, the populistic ideology of Russian cultural expansion as applied to the Kazakh steppe was more than just a pan-historical abstraction. Missionaries could speak as eloquently as they liked about the benefits of natives becoming part of the Russian family, but Russian settlers had concrete ways in which to exercise their opinions on the matter. Potential converts, for their part,

[32] Ibid., 86–87.
[33] Ethnographers and state officials debated the question whether there was any actual excess of land in the Kazakhs' pastoral economy. A. A. Kaufman, the man in charge of the expedition, tended to give the Kazakhs the benefit of the doubt and provided in his recommendations for measures protecting Kazakh claims. Ibid., 88–90.
[34] Demko, *Russian Colonization*, 56.
[35] Ibid., 2.
[36] *Guide to the Great Siberian Railway* (St. Petersburg, 1900), 157.

could weigh the missionaries' words against their firsthand perceptions of who and what Russians were, and decide for themselves whether the club was worth joining. In addition to making them vulnerable to judgment, the resettlement of Russians into the new and unfamiliar environment of the steppe also exposed them to new and powerful cultural influences.[37] As a consequence of migration, by the time the Kazakh missions were established the cultural ground underneath them was already shifting.

The writings of missionaries are an excellent source on the social and cultural history of the steppe borderland during the period of intensive Russian settlement. Missionaries maintained close and constant contact with a wide range of the local Russian and native populations, and had as one of their chief concerns the relations between various groups in the areas of rapid colonization. Russian attitudes and ways of life in the steppe region were such that the missionaries, in addition to their official work of spreading Russian religion and culture to the Kazakhs, took on the task of keeping tabs on the Russians and setting them on the proper path. There was no easy way to divide the two roles, and therefore it was impossible, the missionaries found, to "go abroad" into Kazakh nomad communities for converts without simultaneously evangelizing among the Russians, and thus forging the Russian culture that in theory already existed. They were to be sorely disappointed and frustrated by the burden of this dual task.

Establishment of the Kazakh Missions

In 1881 the Missionary Society succeeded in having the Holy Synod approve plans for missions in the Kazakh steppe. The first missionary was sent out in 1883 into the eastern part of the steppe from the Altai mission in Tomsk diocese; soon a post was set up in the steppe itself, in the Cossack town of Bukon. Kazakh missions were also established to the west in Tobol'sk diocese in 1894. In 1895, the nine posts administered by Tomsk and Tobol'sk were transferred to the jurisdiction of the new Omsk diocese. They were now given a common administration in the town of Shul'ba under Archimandrite Sergii (the missionary quoted in the introduction to this essay); two years later the headquarters moved to Semi-

---

[37] Peter Holquist, for instance, has studied the effects of migration and settlement on Russian culture with particular regard to differences between Old Believers and mainstream Orthodox. See "The Transformation of Peasant Identities: Changing Attitudes among Orthodox and Old Believers in Western Siberia, 1875–1900" (M.A. thesis, Columbia University, 1989); and idem, "The Shifting Boundary: Regional and Religious Identity Among Old Believer and Orthodox Peasants of Western Siberia" (unpublished paper, 1991). I thank the author for sharing these papers with me.

palatinsk.[38] Other, smaller missions to Kazakhs opened in Orenburg diocese (1891) and in Astrakhan diocese (1898), both in the far western part of the steppe. Alongside these, new missions to Muslim peoples (among them Kazakhs) opened in Tobol'sk diocese in 1900 and in the new Turkestan diocese in 1913.[39]

The Omsk mission was the largest of all, and most of the sources consulted in this study are from there. For most of its existence, this mission consisted of eight or nine different posts (stany), each served by a designated missionary (as often from the monastic or black clergy as from the parish or white), usually assisted by one or two other clerical or nonclerical personnel (a sacristan or deacon, a schoolteacher or translator, or some combination thereof). Some but not all locations had a school and a hospice (priiut) for prospective converts; these institutions might receive funding directly from private individuals or from the Orthodox Missionary Society as well as from the diocesan mission itself. A head missionary coordinated all the posts from a central location. In 1900, at its height, the Omsk mission had a total of thirty personnel.[40]

A great number of the missionaries working in the steppe between 1881 and 1917 were from the Volga region and had been trained in one of the special institutions for missionaries in Kazan—the Kazan Theological Academy, the Kazan Teachers Seminary (founded by Il'minskii), and the two-year missionary courses attached to the Theological Academy late in the century to accommodate a less elite group than the regular academy students. All three programs, especially the last two, had significant numbers of non-Russian (in the language of the day, inorodets) students and graduates. Some had converted to Orthodoxy themselves; others' families had converted generations earlier, but most continued to identify themselves as something other than Russian—Kriashen (Christianized Tatar), Chuvash, Udmurt (Votiak), and so on. Il'minskii and his colleagues were emphatic in using minority languages in schooling and liturgy, and therefore encouraged all teachers and missionaries to retain affiliations with and loyalty to their native communities. Elsewhere I have described the controversies that arose over the issue of non-Russian

---

[38] Serafim, Pervyi v Rossii po vneshnei missii Kazanskii Missionerskii S''ezd, 3 vols. (Nizhnii Novgorod, 1911–12), 1:127; I. Zosima, "Neskol'ko slov o Kirgizskoi missii," PB, no. 19 (1900): 114–15.

[39] E. Eliseev, "Uchrezhdenie protivomusul'manskoi missii v Turkestanskoi eparkhii," PB, no.21 (1913): 602–11; no. 22 (1913): 647–58; no. 23 (1913): 679–87.

[40] "Otchet o sostoianii Kirgizskoi Dukhovnoi Missii Omskoi Eparkhii za 1900-i god," PB (1902): appendix, 40. Omsk diocese was exceptional in having a large number of personnel devoted specifically to the Kazakh mission. In 1899, for instance, the Omsk mission employed twenty-eight people spread among nine stations; each station was headed by a cleric with the title of "missionary." "Otchet o sostoianii Kirigizskoi Missii za 1899 god," ibid. (1900): appendix, 232. In the Orenburg mission, on the other hand, most personnel, in addition to working with the mission, had duties as parish clergy.

clergy, and the ways in which such clergy were sometimes torn by multiple and competing identities.[41]

Unfortunately, available biographical data on most of the missionaries in the Kazakh steppe are quite limited. Reports, memoirs, and the occasional obituary sometimes do mention, however, that a particular person was of non-Russian (usually Tatar) background; in those cases that information is of some use in interpreting the missionary's writings. It appears likely, though, that many more than these were from minority groups. One clue is that quite frequently the missionaries are identified in print as graduates of one or another of the Kazan institutions, which were known to have trained a great number of *inorodtsy*.[42] By the end of the nineteenth century as many non-Russians as Russians (if not more) were completing missionary training in Kazan. Another clue to non-Russian background is the implication in many reports that a given missionary already could more or less speak Kazakh by the time he came to the steppe. This would have been no great challenge for Volga inhabitants who already were fluent in one Turkic language (and indeed, the language skill did much to recommend such individuals for appointments in the steppe), whereas the number of Russians (even in the missionary training institutions) who mastered these languages was very small.[43] In this essay, therefore, we will speculate that non-Russian backgrounds frequently played a role in how the missionaries responded to the challenges and frustrations of their work.

Recruitment and Baptism

The several scores of Orthodox missionary personnel in the steppe, if they were really to anchor Christianity there, had a staggering task. In

[41] See Robert Geraci, "The Il'minskii System and the Controversy over Non-Russian Teachers and Priests in the Middle Volga," in *Kazan, Moscow, St. Petersburg: Multiple Faces of the Russian Empire*, ed. Catherine Evtuhov, Boris Gasparov, Alexander Ospovat and Mark von Hagen (Moscow, 1997), 325–48; and idem, *Window on the East*, esp. chap. 7.

[42] On Il'minskii's involvement in staffing the Kazakh missions in the 1880s with graduates of his schools, see Kharlampovich, "N. I. Il'minskii i altaiskaia missiia."

[43] Consistent self-identification by *inorodets* clergy as such seems to have been somewhat less common in the steppe than it was in European Russia. Most of the missionaries were not working with their "own" peoples, and they might have thought it prudent, given the borderland location, to identify themselves simply as Russians. One of the missionaries in the Orenburg diocesan mission explained his decision to do so when asked by a Muslim about his personal background and where he had learned to speak Kazakh. "I thought that if I revealed to him my Old Convert Tatar ancestry I would alienate him, as had happened with my predecessor, the teacher Grammakov. Therefore I just said that where I come from, in Kazan province, almost all of the Russians know how to speak Tatar, and I learned Kazakh during the time I was teaching in the Troitsk district [in the steppe, presumably]." V. Anisimov, "Iz dnevnika uchitelia Aleksandrovskoi missionerskoi shkoly v Turgaiskoi oblasti za 1898–1899 uchebnyi god," *PB*, no. 20 (1904): 166.

1895 the Kazakhs numbered over three million, constituting over 30 percent of the empire's Muslim population.[44] To complicate matters, the Kazakhs were widely dispersed and geographically elusive. Most were pastoral nomads: while roaming in search of grazing land for their large herds of sheep, cattle, and horses, they lived in tents (yurts) grouped into small mobile villages, or *auls.*

Nonetheless, by the late nineteenth century considerable numbers of Kazakhs in certain areas were beginning to settle.[45] In the northern parts of the steppe close to the Ural and Irtysh rivers, many had taken up agriculture seasonally as a way to raise feed for their livestock to supplement grazing (allowing them to increase the size of their herds). The settling movement was intensified (though probably not originally caused) by the onset of Russian domination.[46] In the 1860s, the Russian state encouraged Kazakh agriculture for reasons of political stabilization; the land pressure that later came with increased Russian settlement merely reinforced this policy.

During the winter, the missions concentrated their efforts on the already half-settled Kazakhs living close to or in Russian settlements. Come spring, when the land dried and the lowering of water levels removed obstacles to travel, the missionaries headed into the steppe to follow those Kazakhs who were roaming with their herds. Although the missionaries often stressed the voluntary and tolerant nature of their enterprise, by no means did they wait for the Kazakhs to come to them. Many of the missionaries' reports mentioned the number of versts they traveled in a given year, and oftentimes the numbers reached several thousand.

Following the Il'minskii system, the missionaries used the Kazakh language to whatever extent their skills allowed; the translation of the Gospels into Kazakh during the 1890s was meant to facilitate this. Otherwise, they employed Kriashens or other non-Russians as translators. But converts were expected eventually to learn the Russian language. For those potential converts who did not know Russian, language instruction was likely to begin as soon as they expressed an intention to be baptized. It was common for a baptism ceremony to be conducted in Kazakh and to include Kazakh music.

Upon the announcement of his or her intention to be baptized, the Kazakh would receive a Russian name. Normally, one had to wait forty days between this time and the baptism itself, in order to receive the proper spiritual training, which included memorizing Orthodox prayers. But in urgent situations—as when the life of the convert was under threat by either Kazakh kin, Tatar foes, or Russian chauvinists—the term might

---

[44] See *Entsiklopedicheskii slovar'* (1895), s.v. "Kirgizy," "Islam."

[45] According to Demko, 13 percent of the area's land was occupied by sedentary Kazakhs by 1901. Demko, *Russian Colonization,* 46. See also Rybakov, "Otchet," 171–72.

[46] Rybakov, "Otchet," 171–74; Olcott, *The Kazakhs,* 83–86.

An Orthodox missionary preaching in a Kazakh *aul* in the 1890s. E. Eliseev, *Zapiski mission-era bukonskogo stana Kirgizskoi missii za 1892–1899 gg.* (St. Petersburg, 1900).

be shortened or waived. Potential converts might already have had some spiritual training from their Russian employers before they were brought to the mission to declare their intention officially. Not infrequently such converts were Kazakh men or adolescents who had been working and living with Russian families since childhood.

The missionaries' tactical and rhetorical approach to the Kazakhs oscillated between two styles, which corresponded to their uncertain views on the strength of Islam in the steppe. The first and more prevalent characterization showed the Kazakhs as noble savages, essentially "pagan" and primitive, and only superficially "tainted" by Islam. Emphasis on positive character traits—hospitality, curiosity, love of work, and an ability to listen—suggested that the Kazakhs were deserving and capable of becoming Orthodox and Russian. Thus the missionaries' efforts would seem a charitable, winning cause that would be only a good influence on Orthodoxy. The missionaries eagerly sought any sign that Kazakhs were ignorant of Islamic prayers and rituals, and highlighted anything that would suggest an inclination toward Christianity, such as occasional similarities between spirits worshiped by Kazakhs and certain Russian saints.[47] They might also

[47] S. P——v, "Moi pervye shagi na missionerskom poprishche sredi Kirgizov," *PB*, no. 21 (1893): 37.

emphasize physical and behavioral traits of the Kazakhs that made them different from Tatars and more like Russians.[48]

But such a state of affairs was usually recognized as unstable. "We must hurry," wrote Father I. Nikol'skii, "to sow the word of God, to plant Russian education and take measures against the plundering of the faith of those who are still infants by rapacious wolves."[49] The wolves were the Tatars, and occasionally Muslim peoples from Central Asia, who generally bore the blame for any negative trait or disposition in the Kazakhs. At some times, the missionaries pessimistically emphasized the strength that the Islamic religion had gained among the Kazakhs, and warned that Russian well-being in the region was threatened by ever-increasing fanaticism and hostility. The missionaries frequently claimed that the Kazakhs respected an alleged Islamic law promising heavenly rewards for killing Christians, though no incident was ever reported.

Commentators outside the missions also pointed to Muslim propaganda as a great obstacle to the missions.[50] Armies of Tatar "fanatics" were said to be circulating rumors that the missions were planning to baptize coercively, that converts would have to do military service, or that the tsar had outlawed the missions. Not infrequently, the opposition manifested itself in disputes within Kazakh families, and kidnappings or murders of converts or intended converts.[51]

To the extent that Islam was recognized as a strong influence on the Kazakhs, the missionaries employed polemical arguments against that religion. In their writings, some missionaries dwelled almost exclusively on recounting the theological discussions they pursued in Kazakh yurts; they characteristically attributed all problems in the steppe to the force of Islam and were only peripherally concerned with social, economic, or cultural conditions.[52] Most recognized, however, that theology was only the tip of the iceberg when it came to accounting for and confronting the position of Islam. The Kriashen missionary Efrem Eliseev, for instance, had studied with Malov at the Kazan Theological Academy and was known for his own considerable published oeuvre in the polemical genre.[53] Yet his

---

[48] Sergii, "Zapiski Shul'binskogo missionera," ibid., no. 2 (1894): 56; no. 3 (1894): 104–5; idem, "Znachenie Kirgizskoi Missii v riadu drugikh pravoslavnykh Sibirskikh missii," ibid., no. 2 (1895): 91. See also N. Seifullin, "Paskha v stepi," ibid., no. 6 (1904): 265.

[49] I. Nikol'skii, "Prepiatstviia dlia deiatel'nosti Kirgizskoi missii i mery k ikh ustraneniiu," ibid., no. 5 (1896): 211.

[50] Dogurevich, Svet Azii, 96–97.

[51] For examples, see "Otchet o sostoianii Kirgizskoi Missii . . . 1899," 235, 250–51.

[52] See, for instance, the writings of G. Krashenninikov in PB, 1902–1908. A possible explanation for such an approach might be that it prevailed in parts of the steppe where there were few Russians. This is the impression created by such writings, though we do not know whether this is the cause or effect of approaches such as Krashenninikov's.

[53] See the list of Eliseev's works in Serafim, Pervyi v Rossii . . . S''ezd, 3:141–42.

diaries and reports in the ecclesiastical press show his awareness of a host of other factors influencing his work.

Depending on the resources of a particular community, the missionary might also pursue the schooling of Kazakhs using their native language. Muslims as well as converts attended the schools, in which case they were not expected to attend the religious lessons. Gaining the trust of Muslims might initially be difficult, yet several missionaries reported eventual progress in recruiting pupils. School attendance was no guarantee of future baptism or even of long-term interaction with the Russian community, however; as a result, some missionaries believed their pupils would soon forget what they had learned.[54]

Though the missionaries sometimes delighted in isolated achievements, neither they nor other commentators considered the missions among the Kazakhs highly successful.[55] During the last years of the century, the Kazakh missions in Omsk diocese baptized about fifty or sixty Kazakhs per year from Islam, plus occasional Jews, Buddhists, "pagans" (*iazychniki*), and sectarians. The numbers fell off to twenty-two in 1905, and fewer in 1906.[56] Significantly, the mission tended to be most successful among the settled elements of the Kazakh population—in particular the landless, laboring population of settled and half-settled Kazakhs who had become economically dependent on other groups.[57] Known as *dzhataks*, these Kazakhs were extremely poor, no longer having enough livestock to maintain a pastoral way of life year-round. *Dzhataks* were generally employed as laborers by Cossacks, Tatars, and Russian settlers. Even the poorest Russians employed them, paying them only a few kopecks per day. Though they paid Russian taxes, *dzhataks* were exempt from tsarist military service, and kept many of their own institutions, including *aul* schools and elected judges. Typically, *dzhataks* were already somewhat Russified before baptism.[58] Their predominance in the ranks of converts suggests that missionaries' polemical efforts were not their most important asset.

Indeed, some observers of the missions claimed that the conversion of *dzhataks* was not to be particularly valued. As the traveller N. Simurg indicated, *dzhatak* converts were not likely to be motivated by genuine faith but rather tended to imitate in superficial ways whomever exercised the greatest power over them, Russians or Tatars. Along with Christianity,

[54] Anisimov, "Iz dnevnika," *PB*, no. 22 (1904): 264–72; I. Khokhlov, "Moe znakomstvo s kirgizami," ibid., no. 15 (1900): 316–18.

[55] Dogurevich, *Svet Azii,* 94–95.

[56] Smirnoff, *Short Account,* 60; Serafim, *Pervyi v Rossii . . . S''ezd,* 1:127–28.

[57] Dogurevich, *Svet Azii,* 95.

[58] "Otchet o sostoianii . . . 1900," 69; Dogurevich, *Svet Azii,* 95. For some ethnographic discussion of the *dzhataks,* see A. Ivanovskii, "Kirgizskii narodnyi poet-pevets Nogaibai," *Etnograficheskoe obozrenie,* October–December 1889, 92–101, esp. 96–98.

these "pariahs of the steppe" too often acquired the worst habits of the Russian settlers, including heavy drinking and gambling. Before long, he said, they were likely to "fall away" (*otpadat'*) to Islam once again. In light of this, "for Christianity it would be better to convert one sober and principled person than a hundred worthless drunks who are ready to defect at the first convenient moment."[59] The *dzhataks* did not represent the sort of Russification the church had in mind.

Ideally, converts were expected after baptism to learn the Russian language, wear Russian clothing, and quit Muslim schools to go to Russian mission schools. If a convert was single and of sufficient age, marriage to a Russian was to be expected before long. One of the most important aspects of Russification was the settling of nomads into a sedentary agricultural life and Russian-style houses. In the worldview of the missionaries, agriculture was associated with hard work, nomadism or pastoralism with laziness. The Russian house often appeared as a symbol of the Russian civilizing influence. In contrast to the portable Kazakh yurt made of felt with an opening at the top for ventilation—or worse, the dugouts in which Kazakhs lived in the winter—missionaries idealized the permanent, roofed brick or stone Russian dwelling, often with a fenced-in yard and garden.[60] According to an ethnographic description of Kazakh life in the popular magazine *Niva*, "in the yurt of a nonnomadic Kazakh or *dzhatak*, filthiness, cold and disease reign constantly, so that the yurt is completely inappropriate for sedentary life."[61] In 1891 the monthly religious magazine *Strannik* (The Pilgrim) said of the converts' colonies around the Altai missions:

> The unaccustomed person who has seen only the [Russian] peasant settlements will be struck by the homeliness, disorder, and untidiness of the dwellings in the convert settlements. Crooked streets, or sometimes a lack of [streets] . . . a little house without steps, a little house without a roof, a house without a fence, without any kind of outhouse, in general the absence of everything the Russian person is accustomed to seeing in his village. All this, to the uninitiated, seems un-Russian, strange, miserable and clumsy.

Nevertheless, the author said, this was still an improvement over the former barrenness of the area, "the beginning of our own Russian life, which wasn't here before."[62] Father Sergii wrote in a similar vein to the Missionary Society, "It is pleasant . . . to enter the house of a new convert. The house is poor, made of raw brick, but nonetheless is not a tent [*iurta*] but

---

[59] Simurg, "Kul'turtregery," 357, 355.

[60] S. Rybakov, "Missiia v Turgaiskoi oblasti," *Pribavleniia k Tserkovnym vedomostiiam*, no. 2 (1897): 49.

[61] "K risunkam: Kirgizy,"*Niva*, no. 33 (1884): 788.

[62] "Khronika eparkhial'noi zhizni," *Strannik*, February 1891, 550.

a house [*dom*], decorated with holy icons."[63] These statements show that although even the purely technical requirements of the process were quite particular, the missionaries were optimistic about some converts' capability of becoming true Russians.

The Land Question

Converts were no longer allowed by the Russian government (nor by their own people) to inhabit the Kazakh lands. Since they were legally no longer considered Kazakhs, they had to acquire land and enroll in a Russian village. But usually even those who had already been settled were expected to live with their Russian sponsors for a while after baptism before establishing themselves independently, to assure that their religious education progressed as necessary. Besides, land was scarce at this time of heavy resettlement from the central Russian provinces.

Once land was found and the convert was ready, the mission offered direct assistance in settling. Sometimes a missionary would register the converts into a certain village; beginning in 1891 he could do this legally even without the permission of the village, though it might lead to conflict. An 1897 law guaranteed each convert one hundred rubles from the government. The missionaries often gave free initial stores of grain and seed to the converts, as well as training in farming (though ideally, Russian peasants were expected to set the example). The missionary Efrem Eliseev spent much of his time helping one family learn to grow wheat, and when the yield turned out poorly, he bought them a supply of flour. He expressed concern, however, that these kinds of favors might be construed as official payment for conversion rather than as Christian charity.[64]

Most of the missionaries favored arrangements in which a state land grant would provide a new home for a large number of converts in one place. The converts would be more easily kept track of when living together (since the number of missionaries was so limited), simplifying the missionary's oversight and protecting converts from abduction or harrassment by their Muslim kinfolk. Such an arrangement would also avoid the complications and conflicts involved in apportioning land for converts within already existing Russian villages. Formal registration into a Russian village also carried with it new tax burdens for converts, which could lead to dependence on Russians for employment to make ends meet. The poverty and dependence of converts, the missions worried, would give the

---

[63] Letter of Father Sergii, "Izvestiia iz Altaiskoi i Kirgizskoi missii," *PB*, no. 18 (1893): 40.

[64] Efrem Eliseev, *Zapiski missionera Bukonskogo stana Kirgizskoi missii za 1892–1899 gg.* (St. Petersburg, 1900), 44–45, 112–13. This book is a compilation of many of Eliseev's writings on the mission from *PB*.

missions a bad reputation. Muslim Kazakhs might see the economic plight of converts as punishment for betraying their families and communities.[65] In the worst case, converts might lose their land and be tempted to return to nomadism or pastoralism—and eventually, Islam.

The missionaries lobbied vigorously (and often successfully) for special treatment for the newly baptized, in the form of state grants and tax exemptions. Yet for many years the sole successful example of the convert community idealized by missionaries was Preobrazhenskoe ("Transfiguration," appropriately), built on two thousand desiatinas of high-quality land adjacent to the Bukon mission of Omsk diocese in 1898. The missionaries generally gave positive reports of the religious and agricultural progress of the converts in the settlement, and told them they were fortunate to be there.[66] Missionaries in Omsk diocese frequently stated the need for more such communities, and eventually two more were established, though the results varied with the quality of the land.[67]

But the Russian government was slow to solve the land shortage. This was oftentimes less a matter of principle than of finding available and appropriate land for each particular mission (though it would be incorrect to assume that the missions were of high priority to the state). Missionaries complained of being made to wait a decade or more for a response to their requests for land; in one case the Omsk mission waited six years only to receive a plot located sixty-five versts (about forty miles) from the location it had requested.[68] It had to be ascertained that local funds were available to irrigate the land, build a village on it, and so forth. In the meantime, the mission staff would be continually hounded by baptized Kazakhs impatient for land. The missions passed the buck to the government, pleading that conversion could be an economic (and therefore spiritual) disaster for the Kazakhs if they were not given material help immediately in the form of free land. In 1903 a representative of Omsk diocese complained, "The most burning question is the land question. There is no land that belongs to the newly baptized, so therefore there is nowhere for them to live. They have to wander from place to place, and hire themselves out as laborers not only to the Russians, but even to the Kazakhs."[69]

After the April 1905 toleration edict, the peasant revolts of 1905 and 1906 in European Russia, and Stolypin's announcement of his "wager on

[65] "Otchet o sostoianii . . . 1899," 244.

[66] See for instance "Otchet o deiatel'nosti Kirgizskoi Dukhovnoi Missii v 1903 g.," *PB* (1905): appendix, 64–66.

[67] "Otchet o sostoianii . . . 1899," 242; "Otchet o sostoianii . . . 1900," 54.

[68] "Otchet o sostoianii . . . 1899," 247–248.

[69] "O sostoianii Kirgizskoi missii v Omskoi eparkhii v 1902 godu," *Pribavleniia k tserkovnym vedomostiiam*, no. 28 (1903): 1057. For similar statements, see also A. M. "Iz pis'ma Kirgizskogo missionera," *PB*, no. 17 (1900): 38; and "Otchet o deiatel'nosti kirgizskoi dukhovnoi missii v 1903 godu," *PB* (1905); appendix, 103, 106.

the strong," the government was under greater pressure to give steppe lands to settlers and less attentive to the missions' pleas to set aside land for Kazakh convert communities.[70] In 1906, three of the nine posts in the Omsk diocese mission were closed, as annual funding from the Orthodox Missionary Society fell from twenty thousand rubles to eleven thousand.[71] Even the existence of Preobrazhenskoe was threatened when district re-settlement officials expressed a desire to take part of the settlement away from converts and offer it to Russian settlers.[72] Most disappointing to mis-sionaries (though perhaps not surprising after the 1905 religious tolera-tion law) was that many officials even put the Muslim Kazakhs' interests ahead of that of the converts, refusing to seize any more Kazakh pasture-land than was needed by Russians.[73]

The Russians as Role Models

In theory, Russians were supposed to complement the missions' work by setting proper examples of Christian, civilized, and Russian national values, and by participating directly in baptized Kazakhs' acculturation on a day-to-day basis. In reality, however, such expectations often led to dis-appointment. First, Russians themselves seemed to need missionaries to ensure their own proper religiosity, for the Orthodox Church did not adapt immediately to the migration to Siberia. For generations Russian communities, in their own opinion and in those of church leaders, were inadequately served by churches.[74] In the 1890s, though one of the chief tasks of the Siberian Railroad Committee in its capacity as the coordinator of settlement was to organize the proper funding of church construction in the borderland, the state's efforts did not keep pace with the influx of migrants.[75] As late as 1909, the head of the Kazakh missions in Orenburg diocese characterized Russian settlers as "very pitiful Christians in terms

---

[70] Olcott, *The Kazakhs*, 89. According to Olcott, Muslim Kazakhs' frustration over the issue of land was a significant factor in the 1916 uprising. Ibid., 104, 123–24.

[71] Serafim, *Pervyi v Rossii . . . S''ezd*, 1:127.

[72] "Otchet o sostoianii Kirgizskoi missii Omskoi eparkhii za 1906 god," *PB* (1908): appen-dix, 12–13.

[73] Ibid., 10–11.

[74] N. Griniakin, "Tserkovnaia Sibir' i ee nuzhdy," *Missionerskoe obozrenie*, March 1911, 734–42. See also isolated remarks such as those in F. Almet'ev, "Semiozernyi missionerskii prikhod Kustanaiskogo uezda, Turgaiskoi oblasti," *PB*, no. 5 (1905): 215; and I. Sirotov, "Poselok Kazanka vo vnutrennei Kirgizskoi orde," ibid., no. 2 (1903): 79.

[75] This issue is discussed in A. A. Kaufman, *Pereselenie i kolonizatsiia* (St. Petersburg, 1905), 121–23. Kaufman indicated that the committee's role was mainly to organize private fund-ing of churches, with the state providing free materials and settlers working ostensibly as vol-unteers (though Kaufman described the settler labor as forced). By 1903, he reported, 218 churches had been funded with the assistance of the committee, and 146 of these had al-ready opened. Ibid., 111.

of their religious life. Many of them, out of poverty, have no opportunity especially in winter to attend the nearest church. . . . These people, going for long times without seeing or hearing anything instructive, religious, or moral from Christian life, first feel a sort of ennui and emptiness in their spiritual lives, then even a cooling toward their faith."[76] By then the church was well aware of the problem, and had tried to take measures to speed the construction of parishes, churches and schools, yet complaints continued.[77]

The missionaries took up much of the slack. Having come to the steppe ostensibly to tend to non-Russian Siberians, they often became preoccupied with the welfare of Russian settlers.[78] Russian pioneer life, in the missionaries' eyes, could be a spiritually dangerous existence, for churches and clergy were often hard to find and the Orthodox were surrounded by non-Christians.[79] One isolated settler wrote to the nearest mission, pleading that a church be built for his community: "It will be hard for an Orthodox Christian to live without a church. From the constant contact with the Muslim Kazakhs even the most passionate Christian will forget God's commandments and the faith of his fathers. The enemy of Christianity will waste no time in planting weeds in injudicious souls."[80] A missionary surveying Turgai oblast at Christmas in 1891 (in preparation for setting up a new post) was shocked to learn that Russian settlers there were not celebrating the holiday. Many were employed by Kazakhs and, until the priest enlightened them, had even planned to work on Christmas Day. To the missionary's horror, some of the settlers were partially "Kazakhified" and had adapted to life in dugouts. According to a writer for the Holy Synod, this physical setting was perhaps even responsible for the waning religious consciousness of such Russians. "[T]here, in the far-off Kazakh steppe," he wrote, "in the dugouts, where the people take shelter, it is dark, dejected and damp, and almost nothing marks the Orthodox holiday."[81] Oftentimes it was as if the Russians themselves needed to be Christianized, or re-Christianized. In 1903 the Kriashen missionary N. Seifullin, having made a treacherous journey in the wettest weather of the

[76] "Otchet Orenburgskogo Eparkhial'nogo Komiteta Pravoslavnogo Missionerskogo Obshchestva za 1909 god," *PB* (1910): appendix 6, 201–2.

[77] Liubimov, "Religii i veroispovednyi sostav," 238–39.

[78] Peter Holquist argues similarly that in the case of missions to Old Believers in Western Siberia during the same period, oftentimes "the proselytizing activities of missionaries were inseparable from their activities on behalf of the settlers; they in practice became surrogate resettlement officials." "The Transformation of Peasant Identities," 129.

[79] The Orthodox were usually vastly outnumbered. In 1896, for example, the Missionary Society reported that Akmolinsk oblast was populated by 366,879 Kazakhs and only 24,024 Orthodox Cossacks and 5,661 Russian peasants. [Sergii], "Kirgizskaia missiia i vazhneishiia v nei sobytiia v 1895 godu," *PB*, no. 9 (1896): 22n.

[80] Quoted in E. Eliseev, "Pereselentsy v Kirgizskoi stepi," ibid., no. 1 (1897): 31.

[81] Rybakov, "Missiia v Turgaiskoi oblasti," 50.

year in order to visit some Russian settlers who had asked him to celebrate Easter Sunday with them, remembered his own baptism at age sixteen in his home village on the Kama river.

> Those were the moments of my life that I recalled, surrounded by the water overflowing the steppe, preparing to declare the good news of Christ's resurrection to these Orthodox folk, far from their home, in alien territory and surrounded by Muslim *auls*. What a confluence of circumstances! Then I, a Muslim, was enlightened by the joy of the resurrection among Russian villagers, and here Russian people, surrounded by a Muslim horde, are expecting from me the joyful hymn of Christ's victory, "Christ has risen!"[82]

If unattended, settlers might fall prey to Kazakh religious persuasion or even aggression. An 1893 article in *Pravoslavnyi blagovestnik*, for instance, told of a twelve-year-old girl sold to a mullah by a Russian peasant. The mullah "dressed her as a Kazakh [*po svoemu*], made her speak Kazakh, and she became an involuntary traitor to the Orthodox faith! She lived with him for more than a year. A peasant finally managed to free her from the Muslim yoke."[83] A similar notice circulated in 1898 reported that "a woman in Kazakh clothing presented herself to the local authorities and claimed that she is Orthodox, the daughter of an Orenburg Cossack, abducted fourteen years earlier" by some Kazakhs. She traveled with the nomads and had no way of being reunited with her people. Eventually she married a Kazakh, who eight years later decided to move his dwelling to a place closer to a Russian colony, and the woman was able to escape. (Though it is nowhere stated in the story that the woman either voluntarily or involuntarily gave up her Orthodox faith, the editors of one magazine that reprinted the story wrote, "we can assume that, perhaps, more such incidents will be found of Russian children kidnapped by Kazakhs and turned to Islam.")[84] In still another instance, a Russian family sent its son to study the Kazakh language with a mullah, but the mullah succeeded in teaching him much more. "The son studied with him two or three months and afterward had absolutely no desire to read the Gospel nor the Psalms, which before this he had always read well and willingly."[85]

---

[82] Seifullin, "Paskha v stepi," 266.

[83] Letter of I. Nikol'skii, in "Izvestiia iz Altaiskoi i Kirgizskoi Missii," *PB*, no. 20 (1893): 50. Note the use of the word "yoke" (*igo*) to invoke the historical memory of Muslim domination over Russia.

[84] The original notice appeared in *Turkestanskie vedomosti* (date unreported), and was reprinted in *Pribavleniia k tserkovnym vedomostiiam*, no. 11 (1898): 68, as well as in *PB*.

[85] Rybakov, "Missiia v Turgaiskoi oblasti," 50. Fears of Russians' conversion to Islam appear throughout the literature, and intensified after the 1905 toleration law. See Efrem Eliseev, "K voprosu o perekhode prirodnykh pravoslavnykh russkikh liudei v islam," *PB*, nos. 23–24 (1913): 688–703. By the time he wrote this, Eliseev's fears may have been heightened by his transfer southward to Turkestan diocese.

Kazakhs, according to the church press, were actively recruiting new Muslim converts, but Russians themselves were also to blame for the moral shortcomings that made them likely candidates for apostasy. Frequently the Russians' religious ignorance embarrassed the missionaries and stalled their work. Even if local peasants were favorably disposed toward teaching the Kazakhs about their language and culture, they might be incapable of it. For example, one Kazakh had to ask a missionary the meaning of "Amen," because the Russians he had asked did not know.[86] It was obvious that such Russians would be a handicap to the missions. S. Rybakov, a sympathizer of the missions who made ethnographic observations in the Kazakh settlements of Orenburg diocese in 1896, was disappointed by the condition of the Russian settlers there. Comparing his impressions of a Russian woman and a Kazakh woman, he wrote:

> It saddened me to think of the Russian woman, a representative of that dominant nation that wishes to bring enlightenment to the *inorodtsy*. Although she acknowledged "the Lord Jesus Christ" and belonged to a higher religion . . . , there was hardly any noticeable difference between the two with regard to intellectual and moral condition: both were equally ignorant and helpless.
>
> The thought came to mind: can this dominant nation bring enlightenment to the *inorodtsy* when they themselves are so ignorant and impoverished in their development? And do they deserve the prestige they enjoy? They themselves need to be educated and to educate themselves.[87]

Similarly, the ethnographer and missionary N. P. Ostroumov asked whether educators of the Kazakhs were not putting the cart before the horse: "Is it really conceivable to give a systematic education to all the Asian nomads when our native population of the empire still does not enjoy the blessings of universal education?"[88]

Missionaries hoped that neighboring Russians would not only actively cooperate with and participate in the evangelization of Kazakhs, "serving as a model and an example for the converts," but would also benefit from it.[89] Decisions regarding the location and administration of the missions might be made with specific attention to the needs of Russians. For example, a new suburb of the city Semipalatinsk was chosen as the future headquarters of the Omsk mission in 1895 because it would provide a place of worship for the Russian settlers who had moved there from the

---

[86] P——v, "Moi pervye shagi," 36.

[87] Rybakov, "Otchet," 216–17.

[88] N. P. Ostroumov, "Sposobny li kochevye narody Azii k usvoeniiu khristianskoi very i khristianskoi kul'tury?" *PB*, no. 22 (1895): 239–46; no. 23 (1895): 285–95.

[89] "Otchet o sostoianii . . . 1899," 234.

city itself for better living conditions.[90] Some missionaries expected local Orthodox religious life to be bolstered not only by the new presence of a church and clergy, but also by the inspiring sight of Kazakh conversions. In Shul'ba, Sergii described the first baptism he performed there as a rite of renewal for the Orthodox community as well as for the convert:

> At that time, I had been instructing the residents of Shul'ba in ensemble church singing, and the matter was progressing with great difficulty; they sang as if unwilling or shy. But now everyone sang loudly, with enthusiasm, and prayed sincerely. . . . At the end of the baptism (already eleven o'clock at night), many gave money to the newly-baptized Dmitrii, not knowing how else to express to him their gladness that he had become a Christian.[91]

The missionaries were sometimes pleased by the behavior of the local Orthodox in favor of the missionary efforts. Oftentimes it was Russian peasants representing Kazakh neighbors or employees who approached the missionaries asking that a Kazakh be baptized. Baptisms of Kazakhs sometimes attracted huge crowds of Russian settlers to the Orthodox Churches. It was common for Russian members of a congregation to donate clothing to intended converts so that they could begin to dress as Russians as soon as possible, as well as to protect them from abduction or assault by angry family members. Russian godparents also had to be found, and these were often merchants, government officials and their wives. Baptized Kazakh children were usually adopted by the godparents. Russian villages accepting converts might agree not to collect taxes from the newcomers for the first several years.[92]

Prominent local personalities frequently donated money to the missions, and were duly recognized by the church. One landowner offered a place to build a village for Kazakh converts near the steppe because he believed that the baptized Kazakhs should not remain economically dependent on Russians.[93] If the local community consisted predominantly of poor peasants, money might be raised from outside. This was the case with a new village near the Bukon missionary station that wanted to build a church. In 1898, Eliseev upgraded plans for the new church in Preobrazhenskoe by appealing to Orthodox donors throughout the empire by means of letters and advertisements; he raised fifteen thousand rubles.[94]

But at least as often as they experienced such support, the missionaries

[90] Eliseev, "Iz Kirgizskoi missii," *Pribavleniia k tserkovnym vedomostiiam*, no. 21 (1899): 838.
[91] Sergii, "Zapiski Shul'binskogo missionera," 55.
[92] "Otchet o deiatel'nosti . . . 1903," 86.
[93] "Predlozhenie ob ustroistve poselka iz novokreshchennykh Kirgizov," *PB*, no. 10 (1895): 82–87.
[94] Eliseev, "Iz Kirgizskoi missii," *Pribavleniia k tserkovnym vedomostiiam*, no. 25 (1899): 988.

were disappointed and ashamed by the failure of local Russians either to support the missions actively or to further their spirit by setting positive examples of Orthodox practice and Russian life. They accused some Russians of abetting the enemy by voluntarily compromising their culture to Asian influences. Father Nikol'skii railed against a local Russian official who dressed as a Kazakh and encouraged the natives to observe Islamic ablutions and prayers, "which they almost never practice even at home, since they're still not fully Islamicized. And so, a Russian *Orthodox* man, with a peaceful conscience, decides to teach the Kazakhs the correct fulfillment of religious, *Muslim* laws!"[95] Eliseev also wrote of his outrage at seeing a colonial official who imitated Kazakhs in dress. "He looked to me like a collegiate assessor, but his outfit: his smock . . . [and] underclothing . . . this was all Muslim. He was even wearing a Turkish fez." Eliseev charged him with cultural treason:

> "The government is concerned not only with the material well-being of its people," I said, "but also with their spiritual well-being. In opening a mission, the government wants its subjects to be enlightened by the light of Christian faith. Every Russian person, invested with the trust of the authorities, must serve this holy task by his example, and must not be a temptation, like you." I later heard that the district administration removed this smock- and turban-wearing assessor from service.[96]

In another instance, the missionary Georgii Golovkov of the Atbasar missionary post complained that a high-placed Russian official saw no reason for Kazakhs to convert to Christianity: "One shouldn't tamper with people's beliefs," the official said, "and on some issues Muhammedism is even better than Christianity." In his report, Golovkov added bitterly, "There is nothing Christian in this bureaucrat; he doesn't go to church, and there are no icons in his home."[97]

The missionary press often expressed alarm regarding the possibility of conjugal relations between Muslims and Christians and identified them as a source of apostasy. In most scenarios, the man was Kazakh and the woman Russian or Slavic. In one semifictional short story, "Without Faith," a Cossack woman has married a Kazakh man, moved to his *aul*, and borne

---

[95] Letter of I. Nikol'skii, in "Iz Semipalatinska," *PB*, no. 17 (1894): 48.

[96] Eliseev, "Zapiski missionera Bukonskogo stana Kirgizskoi missii Sviashchennika Efrema Eliseeva za 1893-i god," ibid., no. 5 (1894): 200. For more examples of such behavior on the part of Russians in the borderlands, see Willard Sunderland, "Russians Into Iakuts? 'Going Native' and Problems of Russian National Identity in the Siberian North, 1870s–1914," *Slavic Review* 55, no. 4 (winter 1996): 806–25. For contemporary discussion of Russians and cultural assimilation in the 1890s, see N. Kharuzin, "K voprosu ob assimiliatsionnoi sposobnosti russkogo naroda," *Etnograficheskoe obozrenie*, October–December 1894, 43–78.

[97] "Otchet o sostoianii . . . 1900," 62.

three children of mixed identity. The story is an exposé on the plight of these children, who are growing up in ignorance of the Orthodox religion. Though the husband has been promising for fourteen years to build a cottage for his Russian wife and children (not merely a separate yurt), he procrastinates, and the Russians must live in one yurt with the father's two other wives and mother, and with no icons.

The narrator, seeking refuge from a snowstorm, enters the yurt of the mixed couple. The two boys and one girl living there do not look to him like typical Kazakh or Muslim children. As the storm rages, the narrator crosses himself for protection, and discovers that the children do not know what this gesture means. They know little of either the Orthodox or the Muslim religion. By questioning their mother, the narrator learns that the children had been taught Orthodox prayers and gestures at an early age, but their grandfather, whom they visited regularly in the Cossack settlement, had taken most responsibility for their religious education. After their parents had a falling-out with the grandfather and stopped visiting, the children forgot these habits and assimilated many aspects of Kazakh culture. "What kind of Orthodox are they," the narrator asks, "if they were born and raised here in the *aul,* speak Kazakh, don't know how to cross themselves, and walk around in Kazakh clothing? The only thing Orthodox about them is that they're baptized."[98] According to the editors of *Pravoslavnyi blagovestnik,* which printed the story, a whole generation of children was then being raised by Russian Orthodox women and Kazakh-Muslim men under such illicit conditions.

When asked by the narrator whether she loves her husband, the Cossack mother answers that he is a kind man who has never uttered a stern word to his wife. On this score he is preferable to a Cossack husband, she explains, and it is not at all rare for women from her town to marry Kazakh men. "There were some Cossack men who used to look at me. But a Cossack is rarely kind to his wife. He's the type who isn't around much, he'll go anywhere to be with his gang and get drunk: gluttonizing, shouting, and boasting. He comes home, continues to curse, and wants to fight."[99]

The story blamed the Orthodox culture as much as that of the Muslims. But the author's choice of identifying the Orthodox settlers as Cossacks (as opposed to just "Russian") is well worth noting. Missionaries used Cossacks simultaneously as representatives of Russians in the steppe (so that stories such as the one above would serve as a warning to Russians) and as particular scapegoats for the missions' problems. They had been in the

---

[98] E. N. Matrosov, "Bez very," *PB*, no. 23 (1893): 49.
[99] Ibid., 48.

steppe much longer than other Russians, and had had greater exposure to the Kazakhs and to Islam. They may have played a role in introducing agriculture to some Kazakhs, but they also faced resentment because they owned so much land that Russian settlers (as well as Kazakhs) often had to rent from them.[100] *Pravoslavnyi blagovestnik* in 1896 reported on the efforts of Cossacks in some missionary areas to dissuade Kazakhs from being baptized. In explaining such hostility to the missionary efforts, the editors attributed it to a loss of national identity on the part of the Cossacks. They drew a distinction between the Cossacks and other Russians living in Siberia: "[t]he Russian Siberian [*sibiriak*] has always remained, at least, a Russian, living among Russians, hearing Russian speech, keeping Russian customs, in a word living in the Russian way [*zhivia po russki*]; the Cossack on the other hand has borrowed many traits from the non-Russians who surround him, has *become Muslim* [*obasurmanilsia*]. Here the so-called influence of the environment has made itself evident."[101] The phenomenon was explained as follows:

> The Cossacks enter into relations with [the Kazakhs]; because of the great supply of extremely cheap labor, the Kazakh is hired out as a worker, or a shepherd, or plows the field. He becomes a necessary member of the Cossack's family. Constantly hearing Kazakh speech, the master himself learns to speak Kazakh, and his children from an early age assimilate Kazakh speech better than their native Russian. From the constant habit of speaking Kazakh, the Cossack even begins to speak with his Russian brother in Kazakh. . . . Then unnoticeably he picks up other traits, which make the Cossack resemble a Kazakh: he cuts his hair short, tucks up his mustache, puts on comfortable Kazakh clothing, and begins to eat horsemeat.[102]

Many missionaries in the steppe were less concerned with historical or environmental explanations of the Cossacks' behavior than with simply steering clear of them. They referred casually to the Cossacks as lazy, irreligious, and depraved, and therefore unable or unwilling to serve as role models for Kazakh converts.[103] One report, explaining a preference for placing convert settlements close to Russian communities (rather than far off "in the bowels of the steppes"), asserted that "the proximity and cooperation of Russians—*but real Russian Christians, not Cossacks*—are absolutely necessary for converts."[104] Some missionaries insisted that the Cossacks needed the inspiration and religious guidance of these "real

---

[100] Demko, *Russian Colonization*, 45–48.

[101] [Sergii], "Kirgizskaia missiia i vazhneishiia v nei sobytiia," 68–69.

[102] Ibid. See also the remarks on Cossacks' tendency to lose their Russian national traits in Kharuzin, "K voprosu."

[103] "Otchet o sostoianii . . . 1899," 241, 245–46; "Otchet o sostoianii . . . 1900," 59.

[104] Ibid., 61 (emphasis added).

Russians" as much as the Kazakhs did.[105] Nevertheless, in some parts of the steppe Cossacks seem to have been the closest thing to "Russians" to be found, as one report suggested in 1903: "The Cossacks are very far from the correct teaching of the church and faith; therefore attention must first of all be paid to them, people who must serve as an example of Christianity for the Kazakhs. After all, it is primarily they who can facilitate the spread of Orthodoxy."[106]

Besides the Cossacks, the missionaries' scapegoats included Old Believers and sectarians. As far as Russian settlers were concerned, the missionaries saw the threat of these "domestic" heresies as more formidable than that of Islam.[107] Sectarians, of course, precluded the existence of a unified model of Orthodoxy for converts.[108] Implicit in many missionaries' accusations of misbehavior by these people is the awareness that Kazakhs were not likely to distinguish between mainstream Orthodox and members of the various sects. Eliseev, who claimed that sectarians had moved to the steppe to avoid taxes and conscription, reported that those in his region "insult the Kazakhs harshly and behave cruelly with them," and that "they chased away with bullets some Kazakhs who had settled near them."

> The Kazakhs called [the sectarians'] villages ... the "ugly villages," and the residents themselves ... the "ugly Russians." And the Kazakhs are completely right, from their point of view. The Kazakhs are very hospitable. If there is a piece of bread in the yurt, the Kazakh shares it with all present, and refuses no passerby shelter in his yurt. But these sectarians never receive anyone, neither Kazakhs nor Russians. If it happens that Russians do visit them, they scorn them and won't sit at the same table with them."[109]

In this last example, Eliseev took special care not to denounce the Russians themselves. He acknowledged that Orthodox Russians had a bad reputation among the Kazakhs but blamed the situation on the sectarians; indeed, the "regular" Russians too were witnesses to the sectarians' misbehavior. In explanations of their failure to recruit droves of Kazakh converts, however, not all of the missionaries were so delicate and indirect in blaming the Russian people.

---

[105] Eliseev, "Pereselentsy," 32.

[106] "Otchet o deiatel'nosti," 83.

[107] See, for instance, the continuation of the letter cited in note 80. "It will be hard for an Orthodox Christian to live without a church. ... The predatory wolf will come—the sectarian, the heretic, the schismatic, the unbeliever, who will lure the children of Orthodoxy to godlessness, to schism, to falling away from the Christian faith, the disturbance of God's temples, the abuse of the priesthood, and then it's farewell to our faith!" Eliseev, "Pereselentsy," 31.

[108] Eliseev, "Zapiski missionera ... 1893," 201.

[109] Ibid., 201–2.

The Kriashen missionary Efrem Eliseev on horseback in front of Kazakh yurts. E. Eliseev, *Zapiski missionera bukonskogo stana Kirgizskoi missii za 1892–1899 gg.* (St. Petersburg, 1900).

"Ugly Russians," Ugly Converts

Some missionaries accused Russians not only of ignorance and indifference, but of active, malevolent obstruction of the recruitment and conversion of Kazakhs. On the official level, Russian nationalism of the late tsarist period leaned more often to extreme inclusivity than exclusivity; it is rare to find racial prejudice used as an argument against exploiting opportunities for Russification. Among peasant folk, however (whose views are often less conspicuous in available sources) there was considerable resistance to the ideal of the unlimited assimilation of outsiders. For every Russian who aided the missions by showing the presumed superiority of Russian ways and teaching them to the Kazakhs, there were others who abused the Kazakhs, insisted they could never become true Christians, and talked them out of plans to be baptized. Father Sergii met a baptized Kazakh man who had been fired by his Russian employer after his conversion. "Now that you're baptized," this employer had complained, "it will be impossible to make you work on holidays. What kind of a worker will you be after this? Then you'll have to eat at the same table as us, and just as you were a dog, you're still a dog."[110] Other Russian or Cossack em-

[110] Sergii, "Iz zapisok Shul'binskogo missionera Ieromonakha Sergiia za 1894 god," *PB*, no. 7 (1895): 364–65.

ployers, according to missionaries, opposed the conversion of their workers because it could scare off Kazakh employees who were unwilling to convert; employers thus stood to lose their lowest-paid group of laborers.[111] In some cases, Russian hostility to the conversions was nearly as strong as Kazakh and Tatar opposition, so that the missionaries had to keep their work almost entirely secret.

An anonymous letter addressed to one of the Kazakh missionaries and printed in *Pravoslavnyi blagovestnik* was primarily concerned with the problem that many local Kazakh leaders were insufficiently familiar with the Russian language. This ignorance, the writer supposed, was due to the bad example set by Russian officials, and the nature of the problem was not primarily linguistic. "The *volost'* clerk is a sensitive spot in the steppe. Generally he is an individual of not a very high moral level, who deceives the Kazakhs at every step, takes bribes from them, and in every convenient instance gets drunk or commits outrages." The author argued that the prejudice against such clerks on the part of the Kazakhs "[is] fully deserved by these representatives of the Russian nationality, the only people seen by the real steppe dweller, who lives far from the cities and transportation lines of the Russian (Cossack) population." In conclusion the writer noted that the image of Russian culture in the steppe greatly affects the work of the mission, "which at the present time is meeting obstacles at every turn, and not only from the Kazakhs and Tatars, but even perhaps from Orthodox Russians. . . ."[112]

Such complaints make it hardly surprising that the missionaries sometimes tried to separate their spheres of action from the Russian communities. In 1896 Mikhail Putintsev became convinced that missions would be better off in villages than in cities. In the cities were not only many Tatar merchants, mosques, and mullahs, but also Russians who "have a seductive and depraving influence on the newly baptized Kazakhs,"[113] while the morals and faith of Russians in villages were sure to be more beneficial. His efforts resulted in the relocation of three missions away from the cities of Akmolinsk, Karkaralinsk, and Atbasar.

Even Russian villages, however, were not always considered safe for converts. Ironically, the model convert settlement, Preobrazhenskoe, was composed wholly of baptized Kazakhs, and very deliberately so. In theory, the new Orthodox would be "transfigured" into Russians through the example and the tutelage of Russian people themselves. Aside from the economic reasons for favoring the concentration of converts, however, some missionaries felt that separation was morally preferable as well.

---

[111] "Otchet o sostoianii . . . 1899," 247. See also "Otchet o deiatel'nosti . . . 1903," 63–64.

[112] "Golos svetskogo litsa o pravoslavnoi missii sredi kirgizov," *PB*, no. 6 (1894): 265–67. See also Olcott, *The Kazakhs*, 109–10.

[113] M. Putintsev, "Iz Kirgizskoi missii," *PB*, no. 1 (1896): 36.

The strongest and most direct indictments of the Russian people were made by the missionary Stefan Borisov, a converted native of the Altai region who served in the Bol'shenarymsk missionary station (Omsk diocese) in the mid-1890s. Borisov's descriptions of Russians in the steppe make it difficult to believe that he saw Russification as a desirable outcome of conversion. In 1894 he visited the Zyrianovsk mine, a place of employment for many Kazakh men. The director of the mine, Borisov reported, "very sympathetic to the tasks of the mission and appreciating the position of the needy, has always been happy to give work to the newly baptized [Kazakhs]—sometimes even in preference to Russians, because Kazakhs are more diligent in their work than Russian laborers, who often lose several days in carousing after they receive their pay, which the converts don't do."[114] Speaking of another region, around Bukhtarminsk, Borisov said, "The savagery and coarseness of morals, drunkenness, debauchery, licentiousness in all respects, are equally characteristic of the Orthodox and the schismatics."[115] He told of incidents such as Russians shooting at Kazakhs for fun, a government clerk encouraging Orthodox Russians to leave the church, and priests' homes being set on fire or their windows smashed by rocks.

> If such impudence and cheekiness from the local peasants are experienced by people whose position more or less guarantees them from insults, what is there to say of the "Asians," the common name for which in the mouths of the peasants is no more than "dog"? What haven't they endured, what haven't they seen! . . . It isn't surprising, after what's been said, if the suggestion of a missionary to become Orthodox is taken by many of the Kazakhs as a joke. As is well known, to a non-Russian, to be "Orthodox" is the same as to be "Russian."[116]

Like his colleagues, however, Borisov retained at least an abstract faith in an ideal brand of Russian settler more worthy of the missionary task. Perhaps the pure type still existed in central Russia. Missionaries' work would be greatly eased, he claimed, by the settling of "a larger number of the religiously healthy element—exclusively Orthodox peasants from the inner provinces. . . . Russian [*rossiiskie*] peasants, through their love of work and skill at tilling fields, could be a good example for both Siberians [Russians] and the newly baptized [Kazakhs]."[117]

[114] S. Borisov, "Zapiski missionera Bol'shenarymskogo stana Kirgizskoi missii, sviashchennika Stefana Borisova, za 1894 god," ibid., no. 13 (1895): 241.

[115] Ibid., no. 14 (1895): 280.

[116] Ibid., 283. For a similar litany of complaints about Russians' behavior, see Eliseev, "Zapiski missionera Bukonskogo stana Kirgizskoi missii za 1900 god," ibid., no. 17 (1901): 27–31.

[117] Borisov, "Zapiski," ibid., no. 16 (1895): 392–93.

Borisov directed blame for the difficulty of missionary work in the Bukhtarminsk region not only at the Russian peasant settlers, but also at the nonmissionary parish clergy in the steppe. In his view, the conversion of non-Russians was the job of all clergy, yet the parish clergy were complacent in leaving the task entirely to the missionaries. "If the pastors of the Church begin to be divided into those *obligated* and *not obligated* to preach the Holy Gospel—i.e., into missionaries and nonmissionaries," he wrote, "they will begin to limit strictly the circle and sphere of their influence. Just such a division will lead them . . . to internal disjuncture, weakness and, consequently, impotence."[118] If all the clergy could share the responsibility of missionary work, he suggested, the Orthodox population of the borderlands would cease to be a negative and oppressive influence on the non-Russians.[119]

There was likely an ethnic dimension to Borisov's unhappiness with the parish clergy. Though precise data are lacking, it appears that parish clergy in the steppe were usually Russian, whereas the missionaries posted there (whether black or white clergy) were more likely to be of minority background, either from the Turkestan-Siberia region (like Borisov), or more frequently from the middle Volga. Significantly, Borisov noted that in the Irtysh and Bukhtarminsk regions none of the local clergy knew the Kazakh language. To his consternation, a few local priests he had spoken with (including one he had suggested learn the Kazakh language "even if only to give himself something to do") were actually hostile to the missions' work among the Kazakhs. One parish priest, for example, was concerned about the social ramifications of the mission. "You missionaries baptize *exclusively* the dregs of non-Russian society: manual laborers, street cleaners, coachmen, unconscientious people. Isn't it true that this is the view of your mission held by the majority of thinking people?" Borisov had to agree that this opinion was widespread, but reminded the critical pastor that Christianity had originally been a movement from the bottom of society.[120]

Before the advent of the missions, Borisov charged, the local clergy made no attempt whatsoever to convert Kazakhs; the only baptisms of non-Russians were those requested specifically by those wishing to convert. In some communities, most of these converts had become "neo-sectarians" under the bad influence of local Russian dissenters.

That no attention at all was paid to the baptized Kazakhs [before the missions] is shown by the fact that the majority of the Kazakhs baptized at various

---

[118] Ibid., 393–94.

[119] At the time, religious circles also debated the responsibilities of parish clergy in proselytizing among Old Believers and sectarians, which was a large part of the church's missionary work. See, for example, "Vnutrennee tserkovnoe obozrenie," *Strannik*, January 1898, 745–60.

[120] Borisov, "Zapiski," 396.

times by the priests of the Bukhtarminsk region . . . have turned to the schism and have had so much time to be Russified and settled that now only by their facial features can one recognize that they were at one time not Russians.[121]

Unlike some of the other missionaries, Borisov was not surprised by the relationship between Russification and Old Belief or sectarianism. In fact, religious heresy seemed to Borisov a logical result of effective, grass-roots Russification—indeed, too effective and too exclusively grassroots. Continuing, Borisov wrote: "The old Russian cap with the tall four-pointed top, which is called in jest by present-day Orthodox 'the four calamities, the fifth is ruin,' is too out of harmony with the Asian physiognomy of the Byk residents, which, added to the gloomy, coldly fanatical, typical sectarian facial expression, becomes positively distorted and even repulsive."[122]

This flicker of racial essentialism was a rare occurrence in the missionaries' writings; it so boldly contradicted the goals of conversion and Russification that it is surprising that Borisov chose to publish the passage. The ugly appearance of the Russian cap on the Kazakh was a metaphor for a fundamental incommensurability the missionary saw between the two cultures. This incommensurability was rooted in race: while the Russian sectarians clash with the Russian character in their facial expression ("gloomy, coldly fanatical"), the Kazakhs (whether sectarian or not, so it seems here) do so in their faces themselves. Borisov's frustration, evidently, had brought him to a point 180 degrees opposite to the goals and assumptions with which he had presumably begun his work. When cultural transformation went the wrong way, when those converted to Orthodoxy took a detour into religious dissent, a latent racism could emerge in Borisov (despite his own Asian background, remarkably) to explain the flaws in the converts' Orthodox consciousness. Disappointed with Russians' indifference to the missions, he nevertheless did not attribute the difficulties solely to the shortcomings in local Russians' behavior and attitudes. As a result, he went so far as to question his good will toward the Kazakhs as well; perhaps they were innately incapable of assimilating with the Russian people.

The extent to which the ethnic identity of many of the missionaries may have colored their attempts to spread Russian nationality to the Kazakhs in the presence of an often unflattering and unsympathetic Russian settler community was revealed perhaps unwittingly by Efrem Eliseev (who had several years earlier quit Omsk diocese and moved to Tobol'sk to head the new anti-Islamic missions there) in a report to the Missionary

[121] Ibid., 395.
[122] Ibid.

Congress held in Kazan in 1910.[123] Arguing that Tobolsk diocese should appoint only ordained priests as missionaries to the Kazakhs, Eliseev used an odd analogy:

> If a secular missionary speaks persuasively about the priesthood, and does not himself wish to take this sacrament and cannot baptize anyone himself, then in the eyes of an *inorodets* such a person is not persuasive. This would be equivalent to a Jew talking about salvation through Christianity, or a Russian subject speaking of the superiority of being a citizen of the Chinese empire, while rejecting that citizenship himself.[124]

Probably inadvertently, Eliseev likened the difference between Orthodox clergy and laity to differences between religions and nationalities. While it is believable that clergy, particularly those with an academic education, could generally have experienced such a degree of alienation from the mass of Russian society, it is tempting to suppose that what Eliseev experienced was compounded by the fact that he (and many of his fellow missionaries) literally came from a different ethnic or national culture from that of the Russians.[125]

Conclusion

The failure of the Kazakh missions was surely overdetermined, and cannot be attributed solely to any one of the factors we have discussed here. The underdevelopment of church institutions in the steppe, reigning approaches to missions, competition for land, climatic hardships, the Tatar presence, and the complexity of Kazakhs' religious status all played roles. Yet certain features of the missions seem especially important, particularly those that made Russian missions nearly unique among those of European powers during the period. The comparison is important not only for historiographical purposes, but because the Russian church frequently lamented the relative failure of its missions compared with those of the Catholic and Protestant churches. When these other missionaries purveyed their faiths abroad on other continents, in relative isolation from a colonial metropolis, they were less concerned with the discipline of Europeans themselves or their effect on the missions. In the Russian borderlands, the tasks of empire and nation building often blurred together.

[123] Generally, reports at the 1910 Missionary Congress underlined the disillusionment of missionaries in the steppe. See Serafim, *Pervyi v Rossii . . . S''ezd*, 1:127–40, 180–210; and Frank T. McCarthy, "The Kazan' Missionary Congress," *Cahiers du monde russe et soviétique* 14 (1973): 308–32, esp. 327–29.

[124] Serafim, *Pervyi v Rossii . . . S''ezd*, 1:138.

[125] For more on this issue, see Geraci, "The Il'minskii System."

The mission was not only an explicitly nationalist one—this may have been true of other missions such as the French, after all—but more importantly, it was pursued at a time of massive demographic confrontation of peoples.

In this milieu, the Russian common folk had the task of not only inspiring but aiding directly in the development of Kazakh converts, and thus were the repository of missionaries' hopes. As the missionaries learned, though ordinary Russian settlers might indeed play a role in the transformation of converts, as often as not these were the "wrong" roles or even the "wrong" Russians. As a result, the missionaries often resented cultural mixing and assimilation as much as they endorsed it. They discovered that these processes could backfire and work directly against their goals. One could also say, however, that given the many other obstacles the missions faced, these groups were useful as scapegoats for the missions' failures. The concept of a unitary "Russian people" was an ideal, not a reality. Without specific knowledge about individual missionaries, one might assume that they as a group represented an overbearing and homogenizing "Great Russian Orthodox" ethnicity hostile to cultural diversity. Yet many of these agents of Russification were themselves at the margins as *inorodtsy*, or had been at one time. It may have been their imperfect (far from excessive) identification with the Russian label that accounted for their discomfort with the cultural configurations of the steppe. Did the *inorodets* missionaries see and experience things in their work that Russians alone would not have? Quite probably, though we make no claim that this alone can explain the overall inefficacy of the Kazakh mission. Our aim, after all, has not been to identify a single causal trajectory or to employ a single criterion for evaluating the mission, but to illuminate some key dynamics in the complex interethnic relations in the Russian empire's southeastern borderlands, and to demonstrate the problems, even dysfunctions, inherent in the Russian national-imperial project.

Chapter Twelve

Conversion to the New Faith: Marxism-Leninism and Muslims in the Soviet Empire

Shoshana Keller

Many scholars have referred to Marxism-Leninism in religious terms, although to do so is perilous from the outset. Marxism-Leninism was clearly not a religion in the plain sense that it rejected any notions of the sacred or supernatural. Yet it behaved as a religion in so many ways, and filled so many of the same societal roles as religions do, that the comparison is very fruitful. This quasi-religion also formed the cornerstone of a new identity, that of Marxist-Leninist proletarian, which Bolshevik leaders hoped would unite the many peoples who lived in the Soviet Union. Soviet agitation and propaganda workers, educators, and writers spread out across the country promulgating Marxist ideals with a missionary zeal, bent on persuading Orthodox believers, Armenian and Ukrainian Catholics, Jews, Buddhists, and Muslims that their traditional beliefs were not only incorrect, but part of a fraudulent scheme concocted by the former ruling class.

Several researchers have explored the religious aspects of Marxism-Leninism. Nina Tumarkin extensively analyzed the cult of Lenin as a conscious effort on the part of the Bolshevik leadership to use familiar religious forms to legitimate the government in the eyes of its subjects, and to

Research for this article was supported in part by a grant from the International Research and Exchanges Board (IREX), with funds provided by the National Endowment for the Humanities, the United States Information Agency, and the U.S. Department of State, which administers the Russian, Eurasian, and East European Research Program (Title VIII); a Dissertation Grant Award from the National Endowment for the Humanities: and a Short-Term Grant from the Kennan Institute for Advanced Russian Studies of the Woodrow Wilson Center.

give the mass of people an inspiring role model for their own lives.[1] Christel Lane discussed "Soviet Marxism-Leninism as political religion," meaning the attachment of sacred significance to a political ideology, creating something that is neither wholly religious nor wholly secular. She also explored the ways in which Soviet leaders developed and used ritual to enhance loyalty to the regime and its goals.[2] James Thrower applied Robert Bellah's model of civil religion, defined as "a myth of origin and legitimation, together with a myth of historic destiny," to a broader overview of Soviet ideology and scientific atheism.[3] All of these approaches grasp a significant aspect of Soviet governing philosophy and daily life. Religious or quasi-religious rituals, language, and imagery pervaded Soviet society, from the "Octoberings" (a Communist version of baptisms) and other life cycle rituals popular among Russian workers in the 1920s to the songs and slogans generated from Party propaganda offices.[4]

Convincing people that their beliefs were false was only part of the task, however. The ultimate goal of the Bolshevik "missionaries" was to make their audience embrace an entirely new way of living and thinking, which meant abandoning traditions of dress, family life, and calendrical observances, as well as a host of other customs undergirded by religion. They simultaneously promised the non-Russian peoples of the old empire autonomy and the freedom to develop their own cultures, and insisted that they join the (hoped for) international Communist revolution. The fundamental contradictions of these promises doomed the Soviet "conversion" campaign from the beginning. By the later 1920s efforts at persuasion had yielded to blunt force, and even force could not accomplish the ultimate goal. Marxist-Leninist theorists simply never anticipated what might happen if the masses did not agree that they could give up their religion while preserving their national or ethnic identity.

This chapter will provide a brief look at the quasi-religious nature of Marxism-Leninism and how it was presented to Muslims by propagandist-missionaries. I will discuss the motives and tactics of Soviet propagandists in the 1920s and 1930s, when missionizing efforts were at their most intense. Geographically and culturally, the Muslim areas of the Soviet Union were vast and cannot be dealt with equally in a short piece. My research has focused on Soviet Uzbekistan, which encompassed the most conservative Muslim areas of the Russian/Soviet empire, but I will try to draw in relevant

[1] Nina Tumarkin, *Lenin Lives! The Lenin Cult in Soviet Russia* (Cambridge, Mass., 1983).
[2] Christel Lane, *The Rites of Rulers: Ritual in Industrial Society—the Soviet Case* (Cambridge, 1981), 35–36.
[3] James Thrower, *Marxism-Leninism as Civil Religion: God's Commissar* (Lewiston, N.Y., 1992) 169.
[4] On Octoberings, see Richard Stites, *Revolutionary Dreams: Utopian Vision and Experimental Life in the Russian Revolution* (New York, 1989), 111–12.

material from other Muslim regions as well. I will differentiate between "Marxism" (pre- or non-Leninist writings by followers of Marx) and "Marxism-Leninism" (created by Lenin and all who claimed to follow him), and will apply the latter term to the ideology, forms, and rituals that the Soviet government established as the dominant form of discourse in society, regardless of how that form did or did not correspond to Soviet realities.

Marxism-Leninism as a Religious Ideology

In their attitudes toward religion, early Russian Marxists fell into two main camps: the strict materialists, who believed in nothing that could not be seen and measured, and the idealists, or Godbuilders (*bogostroiteli*). For the Godbuilders, led by Anatolii Lunacharskii, Alexander Bogdanov, and Maxim Gorky, pure materialism was too barren to inspire joyous enthusiasm and moral rigor among the masses. In his 1908 essay "Ateist" (The Atheist), Lunacharskii characterized pure materialism as a fatally passive pessimism, which could not lead to building anything better. He insisted on the importance of delight (*naslazhdenie*), and proposed a godless religion, centered on collective humanity and its future perfectibility.[5] In his larger work *Religiia i sotsializm* (Religion and Socialism), Lunacharskii summarized his concept of socialist religion in this way:

> God-killing is the most developed labor. But it is also the creator of a new religion, for it prepares for victory over nature, elimination of evil, the triumph of reason over spontaneity, eternally growing power, continuous perfection of the species, i.e., the fulfillment of the primordial desires of humanity. . . . The new religion demands still more self-sacrifice, but only [given] freely. It wants grace, and not victims, it wants loving devotion. Who, if not the proletariat . . . can become the carrier of the new religion?[6]

While Lunacharskii proclaimed a powerful vision of humanity's future, rooted firmly in nineteenth-century faith in eternal progress, he sharply rejected anything that smacked of mysticism and magic. But he did not hesitate to call himself a religious man, who believed that socialism must encompass a spiritual as well as material revolution.[7] Lunacharskii was always a "soft" Bolshevik, never approving of the violent antireligious tactics

---

[5] A. Lunacharskii, "Ateist," in *Ocherki po filosofii marksizma* (St. Petersburg, 1908), 107–16.

[6] Lunacharskii, unidentified excerpt from *Religiia i sotsializm*, reprinted in G. A. Gurev, *Antireligioznaia khrestomatiia* (Gomel', 1925), 341. Ironically, Lunacharskii's excerpt is printed in a section labeled "Against Godbuilding"!

[7] Lunacharskii, "Ateist," 156–61. See also A. Bogdanov, "Otkrytoe pis'mo Plekhanovu," *Vestnik Zhizni*, no. 7(1907), and Lunacharskii, *Religiia i sotsializm*, 2 vols. (St. Petersburg, 1908–11). For more detailed analyses of Lunacharskii's philosophy, see Thrower, *Marxism-*

developed by the Communist Youth League (Komsomol) and the Union of Militant Godless in the 1920s. Instead he advocated a hands-off approach toward Russian Orthodoxy and other traditional religions, arguing that they would naturally die out under socialist development.[8]

The Godbuilders' writings provoked a wrathful response from both Plekhanov and Lenin. The two men prided themselves on being militant materialists who heaped scorn on any contrary notions. In a series of scathing letters and articles against the Godbuilders, Plekhanov and Lenin systematically attacked their idealism and the roots of idealist philosophy, beginning with the eighteenth-century writings of Bishop Berkeley and Immanuel Kant. Plekhanov directed three open letters to Bogdanov, castigating him in relentlessly sarcastic terms for transforming "advanced people" into "knights of reaction," with the foul weapons of mysticism and superstition, and for being so un-Marxist that it was not even possible to banish him from the ranks, since he was not present there in the first place.[9]

Lenin used an identical approach in his 1908 book *Religiia i empiriokritika* (Religion and Empiriocriticism, the latter being one term for the theory of knowledge Lunacharskii and Bogdanov were pursuing), although he wrote at considerably more length and with even more venom. Lenin also wrote a series of letters to Maxim Gorky on Gorky's involvement with the Godbuilders, where he summarized his feelings in a more concise form:

> [Your theory of God] is patently incorrect and patently reactionary. Like the Christian socialists . . . you use a device that (in spite of your best intentions) repeats the hocus-pocus of the priests [*popovshchina*]: it cleanses the idea of God of the historical and commonplace (filth, superstition, sanctified darkness and degradation on the one hand, serfdom and monarchy on the other), while instead of the historical and commonplace reality the nice petty bourgeois phrase (God = "concepts of future organized social feelings") is inserted into the idea of God.[10]

Leninism as Civil Religion, 34–38; Tumarkin, *Lenin Lives!* 20–23, and Stites, *Revolutionary Dreams*, 102–3.

[8] Larry E. Holmes, "Fear No Evil: Schools and Religion in Soviet Russia," in *Religious Policy in the Soviet Union*, ed. Sabrina Ramet (Cambridge, Mass., 1993), 125–31.

[9] G. V. Plekhanov, *Materialismus Militans* (Moscow, 1973), 8, 119. The letters were originally published in the Menshevik journal *Golos sotsial-demokrata*, in the May and September 1908 issues, and in Plekhanov's essay collection *Ot oborony k napadeniiu* (Moscow, 1910). Related writings of Plekhanov may be found in G. V. *Plekhanov ob ateizme i religii v istorii obshchestva i kul'tury* (Moscow, 1977).

[10] Letter to Gorky, late November 1913, in V. I. *Lenin ob ateizme, religii i tserkvi* (Moscow, 1969), 274. See also Aileen Kelly's essay on empiriocriticism, "A Bolshevik Philosophy?" in *Toward Another Shore: Russian Thinkers between Necessity and Chance* (New Haven, Conn., 1998).

In spite of Lenin's intolerance of spiritual yearnings among his fellow members of the intelligentsia, he (and others in the Bolshevik leadership) apparently recognized the value of ritual as a way to legitimize the new government and society in the eyes of the masses of workers and peasants. In 1918, after a ribbon-cutting ceremony for the first outdoor statue of Marx, Lenin proposed that the scissors he used should be put in a museum, as though they were sacred objects of the Revolution. He also freely drew on the Russian radical tradition of publicly revering antitsarist martyrs to provide heroes for the people to emulate. Trotsky noted with approval that workers were spontaneously creating Bolshevik rituals, and argued along with Union of Militant Godless founder Emelian Iaroslavskii that this was a form of healthy competition with the church.[11]

Robert C. Tucker has argued that Bolshevism had a distinct millenarian character in the sense that Lenin strove to create a new society based on the yearnings of the oppressed. This observation could of course be made of Marxism as well, but Tucker points out that Lenin, as the charismatic leader/prophet of the only party that could free the masses from tsarist tyranny ("Nulla salus extra ecclesiam," in Tucker's formulation), unconsciously gave Bolshevism a character not unlike that of early Christianity.[12] Certainly the Godbuilders were also inspired by this millenial element in Marxism. Underlying millenialism combined with a widespread need of ritual allowed elements of the Godbuilders' visions and other quasi-religious ideas to begin creeping into the Bolshevik government's representation of itself even during Lenin's lifetime.

Beginning with Lenin's funeral, the religious imagery and ritual that Bolshevik leaders used to legitimate their regime began to overwhelm the sober materialism on which Marxism-Leninism was based. A number of factors played into this evolution, particularly the failure of the Bolsheviks to spark a worldwide revolution, and the realization that socialism would have to find a way to exist in only one country or not at all. The large influx of peasants into the Communist Party after the 1924 "Lenin levy" (a rapid induction of new members to shore up the party's proletarian character) was also an important factor, as it contributed to a deep social change within the Party.[13] The cult of Lenin, which peaked during the decade after Lenin's death and was then supplanted by the cult of the living Stalin, was only one aspect of the shift. A strong belief in the perfect society of the future sustained and inspired many during the grueling

[11] Tumarkin, *Lenin Lives!* 67–68; Richard Stites, "Bolshevik Ritual Building in the 1920's," in *Russia in the Era of NEP: Explorations in Soviet Society and Culture*, ed. Sheila Fitzpatrick, Alexander Rabinowitch, and Richard Stites (Bloomington, Ind., 1991), 297.

[12] Robert C. Tucker, "Lenin's Bolshevism as a Culture in the Making," in *Bolshevik Culture: Experiment and Order in the Russian Revolution*, ed. Abbott Gleason, Peter Kenez, and Richard Stites (Bloomington, Ind., 1985), 25–27.

[13] Moshe Lewin, *The Making of the Soviet System* (New York, 1985), 24, 39–40.

years of the first two Five Year Plans, while the vicious struggle against "enemies of the people" provided not only scapegoats, but a negative incentive to vigilance for the Soviet faith, equivalent to the Christian battle against Satan's forces. Soviet rituals often took the same form as those of Russian Orthodoxy, from carrying icons in solemn procession (in the Soviet case, large portraits of Lenin and Marx) to quoting Lenin's writings as scriptural proof texts.[14] Stalin's own noted habit of speaking and writing in the repetitious style of church liturgy made the ecclesiastical analogy even more pronounced. Even after Lenin's official cult had waned and disillusion with Soviet socialism had begun to set in, people claimed to encounter Lenin and receive his fatherly advice in their dreams, claims that would certainly have revolted the living Lenin had he heard them.[15]

It is interesting to note that outside of the Russian cultural context, sophisticated European intellectuals were also ready to embrace Marxism-Leninism with quasi-religious fervor. Marx's and Lenin's insistence that they had uncovered the scientific and immutable laws of history gave their writings a certainty and assurance of infallibility that mirrored the tone of religious texts. Many intellectuals could find comfort in that certainty without the embarassment of an association with traditional religion. Arthur Koestler unambiguously described his 1931 discovery of Communism as a conversion experience:

> To say that one had "seen the light" is a poor description of the mental rapture which only the convert knows. . . . the whole universe falls into a pattern like the stray pieces of a jigsaw puzzle assembled by magic at one stroke. There is now an answer to every question, doubts and conflicts were a matter of the tortured past—a past already remote, when one lived in the tasteless, colorless world of those who *don't know*. Nothing henceforth can disturb the convert's inner peace and serenity—except the occasional fear of losing faith again, and thereby losing what alone makes life worth living, and falling back into the outer darkness, where there is wailing and gnashing of teeth.[16]

Many Europeans of the time would have recognized Koestler's deep emotional response to Marxism-Leninism.[17] But Lenin and his successors

---

[14] The clearest depictions of these processions are in Soviet documentary films, such as those collected for the *Red Empire* series produced by Gwyneth Hughes. See "Revolutionaries" (episode 1) (Van Nuys, Calif: Vestron Video, 1990). See also Dziga Vertov's *Entuziasm* (1930) and *Tri pesni o Lenine* (1934).

[15] Tumarkin, *Lenin Lives!*, 252, relates a woman's statement made during the Twenty-second Congress of the CPSU that she had "tak[en] council with Lenin in [her] heart." Professor Devin Deweese has told me a more recent story of a young Tatar woman who was anxious about a difficult exam, but received reassurances from Lenin in a dream and passed the exam the next day.

[16] Richard Crossman, ed., *The God that Failed* (1949; reprint ed., New York, 1964), 18–19.

[17] See the other accounts ibid., 87–88.

had to convince not only Westernized Russians and Ukrainians of the truth of their philosophy, but Caucasians, Central Asians, Siberians, and many others as well. While Lenin spent a great deal of time pondering nationality issues after 1917, there is little if any material to indicate that he ever thought about how to turn Muslims, Buddhists, Bahais, and others into genuine Marxists. That formidable task was left to his successors.

Muslims into Atheists

Marxist-Leninists used constructive and destructive methods for making converts. The constructive method used images of the perfection of scientific socialist society and the new Muslim who inhabited it, however that perfection was defined at the time. The destructive method consisted of antireligious propaganda, which focused on destroying people's beliefs in their own traditions.

The first Communist to publish a lengthy piece on how to turn Muslims away from Islam to Communism was a former Muslim himself, the Tatar theorist Mirsaid Sultan Galiev. In a sense, Sultan Galiev belonged to the same school of thought as did members of the Jewish Socialist Bund: both believed that the greatest obstacle to their peoples' progress and happiness, outside of capitalism itself, was traditional religion. Both worked assiduously against Islam or Judaism, believing that they were acting in the best interests of their peoples. The Bolsheviks were quite happy to take advantage of their services, and made a point of using only Jewish propagandists against Judaism, and Muslim propagandists against Islam whenever possible (since Muslim antireligious activists were in much shorter supply than Jewish ones). It was not very long before Sultan Galiev's Tatar partisanship got him in trouble with his Communist Party superiors, however, and he was arrested in 1923.[18]

In his 1921 article "Methods of Antireligious Propaganda among the Muslims," Sultan Galiev argued that the largest impediment to conversion was not the impenetrability of Muslim belief (as missionaries had often claimed), but the historical legacy of Russian imperialism combined with Russian ignorance of Islamic religion and culture. He feared that Russian antireligious activists would not or could not take history into account when dealing with Muslims who had struggled against Russian Orthodox missionaries. He reminded his readers that for the past hundred years the entire Muslim world had been the object of economic and political exploitation by Western European powers, and that from the point of view

---

[18] Azade-Ayse Rorlich, *The Volga Tatars: A Profile in National Resilience* (Stanford, Calif., 1987), chap. 11.

of most Muslims, this exploitation was just another side of the Christian crusade against Islam. In view of this history, Marxist-Leninist propagandists needed to be particularly cautious in their approach to Muslims, in order to avoid being perceived as yet another "swarm" of Russian missionaries.[19]

A related worry for Sultan Galiev was that ignorance of religious differences would lead Russian propagandists to treat Islam as though it were just like Orthodoxy. He explained: "For us [Communists] religion is all the same, and thus the problem is completely clear and does not demand analysis. The question is merely one of which methods one needs to use in order to come correctly and painlessly to a resolution and implementation in real life."[20] But for Sultan Galiev this view was gravely mistaken. Islam was much more closely intertwined with its society than was Orthodoxy, and Muslims did not differentiate between sacred and secular as educated European Christians did. He feared that using the same propaganda methods against Islam that had been developed against Orthodoxy would backfire badly, be perceived as a Christian imperialist attack, and serve only to arouse Muslim hostility.

How then to avoid these risks? Sultan Galiev urged that destructive, anti-Islamic propaganda be eschewed in favor of a very cautious constructive atheist propaganda, saying:

> Once and for all we must knock from the hands of our opponents those weapons with which they can beat us on this issue: we need to say openly, to whom it is appropriate, that we are in no way fighting against any religion, we are only conducting propaganda for our atheist convictions, exercising our natural right to do so. Only this way of formulating the issue can give us a firm guarantee that they will not laugh at us and tar us with the same brush as the Black Hundreds Russian missionaries.[21]

Furthermore, this propaganda must be conducted in a very skillful and lively manner, not merely done in the form of distributing "little brochures on this theme . . . with hysterical titles (which no one will ever read). . . ." Here Sultan Galiev echoed Lenin's current preference for atheist propaganda written with the sharp wit of a Voltaire over the thunderously dull material the Party was turning out.[22]

---

[19] Mirsaid Sultan Galiev, "Metody antireligioznoi propagandy sredi musul'man," in *Stat'i, vystupleniia, dokumenty* (Kazan, 1992), 134–35. Originally published in *Zhizn' natsional'nostei* nos. 29 and 30 (14 and 30 December 1921).

[20] Sultan Galiev, "Metody antireligioznoi propagandy," 131.

[21] Ibid., 136. The Black Hundreds were reactionary mobs in the late nineteenth and early twentieth centuries, usually made up of Russian peasants, which carried out vicious pogroms against Jews and other peoples they deemed enemies of the true Russian people.

[22] Ibid., 136. V. I. Lenin, 'O znachenii voinstvuiushchego materializma" (1922), in *Polnoe sobranie sochinenii*, 33:26–27.

Sultan Galiev's solution to the problem of empty pamphleteering was to introduce Muslims to genuine Muslim atheist workers living in their midst, people who did not look like devils, who were quite ordinary in most ways, but who were "more positive, more developed, tougher and more energetic" than believers were. He felt that the presence of such workers in Muslim villages would produce many more atheists than any amount of lecturing.[23]

Sultan Galiev's most radical proposal for turning Muslims into Marxist-Leninists stemmed from his insistence on giving non-Russians full and equal rights within the young Soviet state. He believed that Muslims were culturally backward because of tsarist oppression, and still refrained from participating in the party and government because they distrusted its Russian base. Only demonstrating to Muslims their new status as equal partners in the state, in deeds as well as words, would convince them of the correctness of Marxism-Leninism. Without that equality, no amount of antireligious propaganda would produce the desired results.[24]

Unfortunately for Sultan Galiev, Lenin's delicately balanced nationality policy, and the less delicate feelings of rank-and-file Russian Communists, combined to bar most Muslims from equal access to political and economic power. Lenin supported the idea of national self-determination only to the extent that it promoted international working-class unity. His theory was that giving the non-Russian peoples of the empire the right to secede would also motivate them to choose freely to join the Soviet workers' state. He believed that under socialist conditions national chauvinism would disappear, and that only the bourgeois classes could possibly support national independence. Following this logic, the only non-Russian movements Lenin accepted as genuinely representing the interests of the workers were those that did not want to exercise the right of secession or question the validity of Russian authority within the USSR.[25] On a less theoretical level, the forces of both non-Russian self-determination and Great Russian chauvinism proved to be stronger than the Bolsheviks had expected. After the revolution there were numerous instances of bigotry and hostility between Russian and non-Russian, creating anger and mistrust instead of proletarian unity.[26]

Partly in response to this bigotry and partly from his own more realistic assessment of the nationalities issue in the Soviet Union, Sultan Galiev developed a version of Marxism that posited a revolution of colonized peo-

[23] Sultan Galiev, "Metody antireligioznoi propagandy," 137.

[24] Ibid., 138–39.

[25] Hélène Carrère d'Encausse, *The Great Challenge: Nationalities and the Bolshevik State 1917–1930* (New York, 1992), 40–43; Gerhard Simon, *Nationalism and Policy Toward the Nationalities in the Soviet Union: From Totalitarian Dictatorship to Post-Stalinist Society* (Boulder, Colo., 1991,) 71–72.

[26] Simon, *Nationalism and Policy toward the Nationalities*, 75–77.

ples against all colonizers, including Russian Marxists. His theories were at odds with those of Lenin, and clearly posed a danger to the unity of the new state. Sultan Galiev's active criticism of Soviet nationality policy led Stalin to order his arrest in 1923. The Bolsheviks condemned his theories under the general rubric of "Sultangalievism," a crime punishable by lengthy imprisonment.[27] His recommended methods for turning Muslims into Marxist-Leninists were buried or, if used, were not credited to him.

In April 1923 the Twelfth Party Congress of the All-Union Communist Party (bolshevik) (VKP[b]) seriously considered the issue of antireligious propaganda for the first time, possibly in response to the antireligious "carnivals" that the Communist Youth League, or Komsomol, had begun staging in December 1922. These carnivals featured parodies (often obscene) of Christian and Jewish clergy, beliefs, and deities, and provoked outrage across Russia.[28] The congress passed a resolution that emphasized a patient, educational form of propaganda, one that should "avoid all insult to the feelings of believers . . ." At the same time, the propaganda that the congress recommended was entirely negative in character, aimed at "clearly and convincingly revealing to each worker and peasant the lie(s) and contradiction(s) to his interests of any religion . . ." The congress's resolution focused on measures against the Orthodox Church, but also included a short section on Islam, which emphasized the "counterrevolutionary nature" of Islam and the need to tailor anti-Islamic propaganda to accommodate regional particularities. It did not discuss Judaism, Buddhism, or other religions within the USSR.[29]

Shortly after the Twelfth Congress met, anti-Islamic propagandists began appearing in Tashkent and other major Muslim cities. These early efforts were poorly organized, and some of them violated every principle laid down by the congress. One such propagandist, author Neimat Hakim, spoke on the topic of "Was Muhammed Really a Prophet Sent by Allah, or Simply a Brilliant Man?" He reportedly tried to convince audi-

[27] Alexandre Bennigsen and Chantal Lemercier-Quelquejay, *Islam in the Soviet Union* (New York, 1967), 109–17, 155.

[28] Stites, "Bolshevik Ritual Building in the 1920's," 297–98. While Stites credits the idea for the carnivals to economist I. I. Skvortsov-Stepanov, the Party seems to have paid little attention to what the Komsomol was doing until the degree of public anger became impossible to ignore. In the early years of the antireligious campaign Komsomol leaders advocated a more aggressive program than did most of their elders. See Daniel Peris, "The 1929 Congress of the Godless," *Soviet Studies* 43, no. 4 (1991): 715. In Andijan in 1928, Union of Militant Godless and Komsomol cells organized a "carnival" against the *Qurbon Bayram* religious festival, which they claimed attracted five thousand people to demonstrations and question-and-answer sessions designed to mock the clergy. "Andijon hayitga qarshi qattiq qozghaldi" {Hard struggle against the Andijan ritual renewed}, *Khudasizlar*, no. 4 (1928): 40–41. Given the overwhelming evidence that Andijan was a clerical stronghold, the high crowd estimate seems extremely doubtful.

[29] "O postanovke antireligioznoi agitatsii i propagandy," in *Dvenadtsatyi s''ezd RKP(b): Stenograficheskii otchet* (Moscow, 1968), 716.

ences that Muhammed suffered from hallucinations and had 999 wives. Hakim was followed by other antireligious speakers in the Old City of Tashkent, but they met with such strong resistance, even from native Communists, that they quickly halted their efforts.[30]

In Uzbekistan, efforts at anti-Islamic propaganda were desultory until April 1926, when a delegation of officials from Uzbekistan attended a series of workshops in Moscow for Communist Party personnel on general goals and methods of antireligious propaganda. Uzbek branches of the Union of Godless appeared shortly afterward.[31]

The all-Union and local branches of the Union of Godless used every outlet available to them to spread propaganda, including newspapers and journals, movies, public demonstrations, radio broadcasts, and posters. Their propaganda expressed three essential themes, two destructive and one constructive: first, mullahs, *ishans* (Sufi spiritual leaders), and other "cult servants" worked for the oppressing classes to help exploit workers and peasants; second, Islam brutally oppressed and exploited women; third, religion had developed as a way for primitive man to understand and control the incomprehensible forces of nature, and therefore, the "cure" for it was basic scientific knowledge. These themes were developed by Iaroslavskii, Trotsky, and others early in the 1920s. They faded in and out of prominence as the prevailing political winds from Moscow altered the focus of anti-Islamic propaganda, but remained essentially unchanged until after World War II.[32]

Party directives always stipulated that propaganda developed in Russia had to be tailored to fit local and non-Russian situations, although they

[30] N. Tiuriakulov, "K voprosu ob antireligioznoi propagande na Vostoke," *Kommunisticheskaia revoliutsiia*, no. 20 (October 1925), 74; Mannan Ramzi, *Khayoldan haqiqatga* [From illusion to the truth] (Tashkent, 1928), 31–32; James Critchlow, "Religious-Nationalist Dissent in the Turkestan Communist Party: An Old Document Surfaces," *Report on the USSR* 2, no. 3 (January 19, 1990): 20. Unfortunately none of these sources discusses where the propagandists came from.

[31] Russian State Archive of Social and Political History, Moscow, f. 62, op. 2, d. 739, ll. 1–17 (hereafter RGASPI). In August 1924 a circle of people around Iaroslavskii formed the Society of Friends of the Newspaper *Bezbozhnik* (The Godless). Cells of this group quickly sprang up around the country, including in Central Asia. In 1925 the group changed its name to the Union of Godless, adding the word "Militant" in 1929. The Union of Militant Godless was disbanded in 1942.

[32] *Dvenadtsatyi s"ezd RKP(b)*, 716; L. Trotsky, "Znachenie i puti anti-religioznoi propagandy," in Gurev, *Antireligioznaia khrestomatiia*, 17–20. The theme of women's foolish adherence to religion may also be found in anti-Islamic propaganda (See Lunacharskii, "Religioznyi ateizm ili vera bez boga," ibid., 339–41); but it is not as frequent as the oppression of women theme. Iaroslavskii's basic ideas were confirmed and slightly elaborated at the special Party Conference on Antireligious Propaganda of 27–30 April 1926, and again in late 1927 at a Party conference on "Party Enlightenment in the Eastern National Regions and Republics." "Zadachi i metody antireligioznoi propagandy," *Kommunisticheskaia revoliutsiia*, no. 12 (June 1926): 43–54; "Materialy soveshchaniia po postanovke partiinogo prosveshcheniia v vostochnykh natsional'nykh oblastiakh i respublikakh," ibid., no. 2 (January 1928): 86–94.

were never precise on how this was to be done.[33] The task of working out the details was assigned to native antireligious propagandists, who presumably knew best how to convince their compatriots of the truth of atheism. In Uzbekistan, it fell to the chairman of the Commissariat of Enlightenment, Mannan Ramzi, to take directives from Moscow and craft them into a set of practical instructions for atheist missionaries.

Ramzi's program for conducting anti-Islamic propaganda was first presented at a large party-sponsored conference, held in Tashkent in November, 1927. His instructions were later printed in an Uzbek-language pamphlet, although he had spoken to the conference in Russian.[34] Ramzi's pamphlet indicated his underlying assumptions in its very title: *Khayoldan haqiqatga* (From illusion to the truth). He envisioned anti-Islamic propaganda not as an end in itself, but as a tool for bringing about a greater revolution: "Communism takes people away from all kinds of darkness and oppression to a free life. It frees people from being captive to the forces of nature and society."[35] This statement echoed the utopian visions of the Godbuilders.

The cornerstone of Ramzi's plan for freeing people from their captivity was scientific, materialist education. The foundation of religion was ignorance and fear of natural forces, which were then used by the ruling class to exploit the masses.[36] Therefore, the most effective atheist agitators, especially in rural areas, were doctors, agronomists, and party members who could explain basic scientific principles to the peasants. Ramzi cautioned against blunt declarations of the nonexistence of God, in line with some of the tactics that had been favored by Sultan Galiev.[37] At the same time, he did not avoid crude anti-Islamic propaganda, advocating the use of radio broadcasts and movies to defame Muslim clergy. In addition, he was not above ridiculing peasant superstitions.[38]

Soviet schools were a logical place for impressing antireligious propaganda and Marxism-Leninism upon a captive audience, and the Union of

[33] "Ob antireligioznoi propagande sredi natsional'nostei SSSR," *Kommunisticheskaia revoliutsiia*, no. 12 (June 1926): 62–68.

[34] Ramzi, *Khayoldan haqiqatga.* The Russian stenogram of Ramzi's presentation is in the Party archive of the Central Soviet of the People's Democratic Party of Uzbekistan, Tashkent, f. 58, op. 3, d. 1168, ll. 45–59 (hereafter PATsS-NDPUz). Of course, Ramzi did not develop his program independently. His major proposals were perfectly congruent with those of the Twelfth Party Congress, which had in turn been developed further at the Thirteenth Plenum of the Central Asian Bureau of the Central Committee of the All-Union Communist Party, held in Tashkent 28–30 May 1927. Ramzi's work was a more detailed explication of his superiors' broad policies, and was undoubtedly written under their supervision.

[35] Ramzi, *Khayoldan haqiqatga,* 15.

[36] Ibid., 7–8.

[37] Ibid., 64–65.

[38] Ibid., 44, 58–59, 66. For a more detailed analysis of Ramzi's pamphlet, see Shoshana Keller, "Islam in Soviet Central Asia, 1917–1930: Soviet Policy and the Struggle for Control," *Central Asian Survey* 11, no. 1 (March 1992): 25–50.

Militant Godless attempted to use them as much as possible, although with limited success. I could find surprisingly little material, in or out of the archives, on atheist education before 1941. One of the few references I found dated from the 1929 campaign against the *Qurbon Bayram* holiday (Feast of the Sacrifice, in Arabic *'Id al-adha*), a festival marking the end of the pilgrimage season and Abraham's near-sacrifice of his son Isaac—in the Muslim tradition Ishmael. This was a circular letter from the head of the Tashkent District Union of Militant Godless organization, detailing a list of suggestions and plans for how schools were to observe the holiday. The author asked teachers to hold at least four "conversations" with their students on the themes of the class essence of Islam, revolutionary holidays (such as May Day), who celebrated *Qurbon Bayram* and why, and the lives of children in capitalist countries. She also asked them to hold similar talks with parents after school hours. Young atheists and school-based Godless cells were encouraged to set up "antireligious corners" in their classrooms, decorate their schools with slogans and banners, and put out a special antireligious newspaper for the holiday.[39]

However, there is no indication that these plans were ever put into action. In 1929 many school teachers in Central Asia were active or former clergy. There were probably very few people available who would have been willing or able to carry out the district organizer's instructions. Even by the later 1930s, when the Soviet school system had grown tremendously, many teachers balked at conducting antireligious propaganda in schools. In 1934 Uzbek Union of Militant Godless chair K. M. Makarov bitterly complained that in a discussion about new textbooks not one word had been said about antireligious texts, and in 1936 there were NKVD complaints that teachers were still openly observing Ramadan.[40] This lack of active atheism in the schools did not make Uzbekistan unusual; atheism was given very low priority in school curricula across the USSR.[41]

Party policy in the late 1920s regarding religious holidays was inconsistent. In the spring of 1927 the Uzbek Commissariat of Labor (Narkomtrud) passed a resolution declaring Christmas, Easter, the beginning of Ramadan and *Qurbon Bayram* to be "special days of rest."[42] In 1928–29 Narkomtrud and the Central Executive Committee of Uzbekistan af-

[39] Circular letter to district-level educational and political enlightenment organizations, 30 April 1929, Central State Archive of Uzbekistan, Tashkent, f. 94, op. 5, d. 28, ll. 17–18 (hereafter TsGA Uz).

[40] UMG protocol on the preparation of antireligious teachers in Uzbekistan, TsGA Uz, f. 94, op. 5, d. 1423, l. 15; Spetszapiska No. 3, 14 January 1936, signed by NKVD Deputy Leonov and Deputy Head of SPO UGB NKVD Zelentsov, PATsS-NDPUz, f. 58, op. 12, d. 638, l. 10.

[41] Holmes, "Fear No Evil," 125–26.

[42] TsGA Uz, f. 86, op. 1, d. 5820, l. 282, 16 February 1927.

firmed this resolution, giving workers two days off each for Ramadan and *Qurbon Bayram* and one day for Christmas (on 25 December, although the Orthodox Church still observed the old calendar date of 6 January) and Easter. At the same time they announced a series of "revolutionary holidays," such as Lenin's death (22 January), Paris Commune Day (22 March) and Constitution Day (the first Friday of July), which were probably ultimately intended to replace the traditional ones.[43] The published decisions gave no reason for continuing to observe the old holidays, but most likely it was a compromise measure to keep the peace.

Nevertheless, Muslim holidays were always occasions for an outpouring of propaganda from the Union of Militant Godless. In fact, about the only time the Tashkent district group conducted anti-Islamic propaganda was during Ramadan (*Uraza* in Uzbek) and on the *Qurbon Bayram* holiday. What is perhaps most interesting about the campaigns against these holidays is that they generally took an economic, rather than a militant atheist, tack.

During the years of the first Five Year Plan Ramadan and *Qurbon Bayram* fell in early spring, which threatened to interfere substantially with the state's agricultural plans. Muslims who were fasting during daylight hours worked less, but the Soviet government was trying to establish "cotton independence" (freedom from having to import cotton from capitalist countries) by plan deadlines, and had a very strong interest in pushing work tempos.[44] In addition, the observance of *Qurbon Bayram* involved slaughtering livestock for a ritual feast. In the face of the mass killings of farm animals that were occurring in response to collectivization and the forced sedentarization of Central Asian nomads, the state was determined not to lose more animals to a religious festival.[45] That meant that observance of the holidays had to be eliminated, and the Union of Militant Godless was charged with a large part of the task.

The propaganda campaigns against Ramadan and *Qurbon Bayram* had three broad goals: unmasking the counterrevolutionary essence of religion and national chauvinism, increasing membership in the Godless organizations, and fulfilling cotton sowing plans and protecting cattle from slaughter. Of those goals, meeting the agricultural quotas and increasing Union of Militant Godless membership were the top priorities. Making Muslims into Marxist-Leninists was not mentioned at all.

Anti-Islamic propagandists emphasized above all the evils of shirking

---

[43] *Uzbekistanskaia pravda*, no. 13 (8 March 1929): 4. The original decisions were announced by TsIK Uzbekistan 20 October 1928, and by Narkomtrud 18 February 1929.

[44] Ian Murray Matley, "Agricultural Development," in *Central Asia: 120 Years of Russian Rule*, ed. Edward Allworth (Durham, N.C., 1989), 289–91.

[45] In Kazakhstan alone approximately seven million horses and sheep were killed during the first Five Year Plan. Zh. B. Abylkhozhin et. al., "Kazakhstanskaia tragediia," *Voprosy istorii*, no. 7 (1989): 53–71; Martha Brill Olcott, *The Kazakhs* (Stanford, Calif., 1987), 183.

farm work and slaughtering cattle. The Ramadan/*Uraza* fast would take labor away from industry and agriculture and lead to failure to fulfill plans. Observing *Qurbon Bayram* would wreck the economy of the country, affecting not only agricultural plans, but those for industry, collectivization, and the liquidation of kulaks as well. Union of Militant Godless activists enlisted the help of the Commissariats of Health and Agriculture in impressing the "wrecking" aspects of fasting and feasting upon the populace. They organized special cadres on the collective farms to do local propaganda against the holidays. In the cities they held antireligious demonstrations in public and broadcast atheist lectures on the radio, pushing for a "100 percent worker refusal" to aid the clergy in any way.[46]

While Union of Militant Godless officials did not describe these campaigns as missions for Marxism-Leninism, their propaganda created positive images of a new kind of Muslim that emerged amid the negative exhortation. This new Muslim was a hard-headed skeptic, free from superstition and no longer beholden to the clergy, but at the same time fiercely loyal to the Soviet state and ready to give it instant obedience. Political posters gave striking illustrations of this new Muslim: one showed evil-looking caricatures of *ishans* and *bays* (Central Asian kulaks) attempting to block elections to the soviets (local councils), only to be shooed out by well-muscled, good-looking peasants. By implication, physical strength and beauty were part of Marxist belief. Another poster from the same period depicted a bold, unveiled woman pointing the way toward the voting places, against a background of veiled, almost inhuman female figures.[47]

These images reflected an increased emphasis in the later 1920s on attacking the Islamic religion, but taking great care not to attack the national identity of Muslims. This paradoxical position reflected earlier concerns of Sultan Galiev and Iaroslavskii that Muslims would see antireligious propaganda as merely a new face on old Christian persecution, but it was more immediately related to the priorities of Party policy toward the nationalities. This policy had three phases in its official version: first, the "flowering" (*rastsvet*) of non-Russian cultures, which included the policy of *korenizatsiia*, or "rooting," that is, filling the cadres with the highest possible percentage of titular nationalities in a given region. This was accompanied by a highly visible campaign against all mani-

---

[46] Circular letter from Moscow to "all soviets" of the Godless, 30 March 1930, and "Theses" on Ramadan, 17 January 1930, State Archive of the Russian Federation, Moscow, f. 5407, op. 1, d. 17, ll. 36, 58b-60. Godless officials instructed that these theses were to be translated into local languages and broadcast on the radio, supplemented with accounts of counterrevolutionary activities by the clergy and figures for the liquidation of kulaks according to the Five Year Plan of the local district.

[47] P. Zaitsev, "Provedenie izbiratel'noi kampanii v Uzbekistane," *Vlast' sovetov*, no. 9 (1927): 10, 11, 13.

festations of "Great Russian chauvinism," and the encouragement of many non-Russian cultural expressions. The flowering and *korenizatsiia* phase lasted until around 1933, when it was replaced by the "rapprochement" (*sblizhenie*) phase, which signaled the end of efforts at *korenizatsiia*, establishment of stronger central control, and the beginning of intensive Russification. Neither the rapprochement, nor its successor phase, "merger" (*sliianie*), had terribly well-defined temporal boundaries.

The first years of systematic anti-Islamic propaganda coincided with the Party's promises that non-Russian cultures should flower, making it very important that antireligious workers find some way to show that one could be a good Marxist-Leninist and still enjoy nonreligious national customs and pride. The fact that this was an impossible assignment in Muslim areas, where the tradition did not distinguish between sacred and secular, much less between "religious" and "national," did not seem to occur to anyone. Nonetheless, Union of Militant Godless officials and others tried to fulfill instructions.[48]

Muslim women unveiling themselves provided a powerful image for the purposes of attacking Islam while affirming Muslim women as equal human beings. In 1934 Russian film director Dziga Vertov made a remarkable documentary, *Three Songs About Lenin,* which not only contributed to the Lenin cult but gave Soviet Muslims a direct role in it. The film is divided into three segments, the first of which is called "My Face Was in a Dark Prison." It opens with shots of Muslim men praying in a mosque as a blind man walks down the road, and then cuts to scenes of veiled women walking under heavy burdens.[49] The traditional veil in Central Asia was a full-length, black horsehair *paranji*, similar to the *chador* of modern Iranian women. The general impression made in Westernized eyes by these figures, walking along with only their hands visible, is one of almost complete dehumanization.

Vertov's point is that Lenin is freeing Muslim women from their prison. He shows a young girl (unveiled) walking into a former mosque that has been converted into a reading room. There she sits and studies the works of Lenin while a man plays the *dutar*, a traditional two-stringed plucked instrument. Next, Vertov shows us scenes of women flinging off their veils and smiling broadly. Aside from the veil itself, they retain their traditional dress. We see them cultivating gardens, and driving tractors and even a car. At the end of the segment, they listen with tremendous sorrow as funeral orations for Lenin are broadcast over the radio. Their friend, father and leader, the man who freed them, has died. This segues fairly seam-

[48] M. Kobetskii, "Antireligioznoe vospitanie v sovetskoi shkole natsional'nykh raionov," *Kommunisticheskaia revoliutsiia*, no. 6 (March 1928): 61–62.

[49] This segment appears to have been filmed in Turkmenistan, with opening scenes possibly shot in Samarkand.

lessly into the second segment of *Three Songs*, which is devoted to Lenin's funeral and depicts it in terms just short of outright worship.[50]

Vertov's film was a paean to Lenin, not part of any effort to undermine Islam but a product of Vertov's perceptions of that effort. The great campaign beginning in 1927 to force Central Asian women to unveil by administrative fiat was a part of the whole anti-Islamic drive, and was aimed at pushing women and Central Asian family structure rapidly out of the traditional mold and into the Soviet one. Unlike the depiction in Vertov's film, however, the actual campaign was a disaster, not least for the women it purported to help.[51] *Three Songs About Lenin* is a very interesting, if unintentional, example of the use of Muslim or Turkic traditional images or figures in the cause of promoting Marxism-Leninism.

Much of the effort to show Muslims that it was possible to be a Marxist-Leninist and retain one's national identity and pride did not fully develop until after World War II, but it is worth mentioning some examples here at least in passing. One of the most visible ways in which the combination of Soviet and national pride was demonstrated was through the development of "national" or "folk" dance troops and musical groups. Of more direct interest is the use of Mulla Nasreddin Hoja, a trickster figure in Turkic folklore, to demonstrate a long history of free thought among Muslims who became part of the Soviet empire.

Nasreddin Hoja (also called Afandi, Mulla Nasreddin, or simply the Hoja, an honorific name) has been the subject of humorous anecdotes among Turkic- and Persian-speaking peoples for centuries. The earliest known Afandi stories date back to the Crusades. In these anecdotes Mulla Nasreddin pokes fun at pretentious fools among the lowly and the powerful, even the fourteenth-century conqueror Timur Lang (Tamerlane). Often he is the butt of the joke himself, but the point is always to illuminate some larger human folly.

The first printed collection of Afandi stories was published in Istanbul in 1837, and circulated in Turkestan. Translations of this collection into other Turkic languages appeared within thirty years.[52] The Soviets produced their own collections of anecdotes, in Russian and various Turkic languages, that showed Afandi as an early sympathizer with the poor and the workers, and a great skeptic when it came to the clergy. In one tale Afandi comes upon a group of mullahs in Samarkand discoursing learnedly on the miraculous lives of various saints, and innocently asks,

---

[50] Dziga Vertov, *Tri pesni o Lenine* (Moscow: Mosfilm, 1934).

[51] Gregory Massell, *The Surrogate Proletariat: Moslem Women and Revolutionary Strategies in Soviet Central Asia, 1919–1929* (Princeton, N.J., 1974); Shoshana Keller, "Trapped Between State and Society: Women's Liberation and Islam in Soviet Uzbekistan, 1926–1941," *Journal of Women's History* 10, no. 1 (spring 1998): 20–44.

[52] *Ozbek Sovet Entsiklopediiasi,* vol. 1 (Tashkent, 1971), 560.

"So, the most honorable saints of whom you speak, whenever did they eat?" He is saying, were they not human too?[53]

Numerous stories concern Afandi and his donkey. The donkey is so clever that in some tales it becomes a *qadi*, a Muslim judge, with no one seeing anything amiss. In other stories *qadis* and donkeys are compared directly, and unfavorably for the *qadis*. There is a statue in Samarkand that illustrates yet another Afandi-and-donkey tale, showing Afandi teaching the Quran to the animal. This statue neatly encapsulates the strategy of using venerated Turkic images to convey a message deeply offensive to believing Muslims.[54] As the 1971 *Ozbek Sovet Entsiklopediiasi* explained, under socialist conditions Afandi anecdotes served to attack "ulcers" in society that were incompatible with Soviet morality.

It is instructive to compare these collections of anecdotes with non-Soviet collections. While many of the stories do overlap, in the Turkish or Persian stories Nasreddin Hoja often prays or complains to God (and gets answered!). He mocks corrupt clergy, but never attacks the institution as a whole, much less the Quran itself.[55]

Atheist activists enlisted Islamic religious language itself in the cause of showing the compatibility of national identity with Marxism-Leninism. In 1928 Ipatkhojaev, an Uzbek member of the Tashkent District Bureau of the Union of Militant Godless, suggested translating the Quran into Uzbek, on the intriguing theory that greater knowlege of what the Quran actually said would be helpful for antireligious propaganda. However, the bureau decided that it did not have the funds to pursue this project.[56] A more successful attempt in this direction involved the concept of the *umma*, the community of the faithful. In the Quran Muhammed calls his followers *umma*, the community of all Muslims, regardless of other tribal, ethnic, or racial affiliations, and as such the word has some very powerful resonances. The Soviets co-opted the equivalent Uzbek word, *omma*, and altered its meaning to "masses," as in the phrase *mehnatkash omma*, "the working masses."[57]

---

[53] *Anekdoty o Nasreddine Afandi* (Tashkent, 1989), 12.

[54] Ibid., 4; *Afandi latifalari* [Anecdotes of the Afandi] (Tashkent, 1989), 190. The tale illustrated by the statue, "Eshak-mulla" (The donkey-mullah), is on p. 201 of the latter collection. Another example of Soviet attempts to demonstrate a history of atheism among the Turkic peoples is a book by A. S. Mamedov, *Svobodomyslie prosvetitelei Azerbaidjana* (Baku, 1987), which discusses nineteenth-century "freethinkers" in Azerbaijan.

[55] Idries Shah, *The Subtleties of the Inimitable Mulla Nasrudin* (London, 1983) (largely a collection of recent stories, wherein Afandi must deal with airplanes and British bureaucrats); Mehdi Nakostan, *Mulla's Donkey and Other Friends* (Boulder, Colo., 1974); Turgay Yagan, ed., *Stories of the Hodja* (Istanbul: n.d.).

[56] Protocol No. 6, February 11, 1928, RGASPI, f. 62, op. 2, d. 1196, l. 107.

[57] Ramzi used the phrase in 1927, but he was undoubtedly not the first (Ramzi, *Khayoldan haqiqatga*, 11). It continued to be used throughout the Soviet period (*Afandi latifalari*, 6).

Mulla Nasreddin Hoja teaching his donkey to read the Quran. This statue in Samarkand illustrates Soviet use of folklore to uproot Islamic piety. Photograph by Anvar Zaitov, courtesy Shoshana Keller.

The Failure of Atheist Propaganda

Despite the best efforts of speakers, writers, filmmakers, and other atheist activists, the majority of Muslims in the USSR never became loyal Marxist-Leninists. This is not to say that the campaign had no impact; rather, the impact it made was much more restricted in scope than the original propagandists had hoped.

The Bolsheviks trapped themselves in contradictory promises regarding freedom of national expression and safety within the international proletarian union, and in their naive attempts to attack Islam while leaving national identity sacrosanct. The only way they found out of that trap was through the use of force, but force served only to harden the opposition against their campaign.[58]

The Party and atheist activists ignored abundant early warnings that Muslims would not accept Russian-engineered separation of religion and national identity, issued most articulately by Sultan Galiev. Uzbek Communists angrily rejected proposals in 1923 for atheist propaganda in a Tashkent Party organization. Four years later Ramzi sharply criticized party members for adhering to religion, and emphasized that "there is no place in our party for religious communists." He lamented the fact that "communists and workers" were attending circumcision ceremonies and other such events, and demanded that these "sick people" cease their activities.[59] From the standpoint of Party doctrine, substituting Communism for Islam was not as dangerous as combining the two, as did the many Muslim Communists for whom Marxism-Leninism could never supplant their traditional rituals and beliefs. These Muslim Communists learned to be quite adept at repeating the appropriate condemnations of religious belief, and even calling themselves "Muslim atheists," while continuing to celebrate their sons' circumcisions and making sure there was always a mullah present at their funerals. It was this breed of Muslim Communist

[58] There were many levels of coercion or force in the anti-Islamic campaign, from quiet threats to public humiliation to arrest and murder. Massell, *The Surrogate Proletariat*, 317. "Doklad k TsIK UzSSR i rukovoditel'iam nashei Respubliki. Iz Trudiashchikhsia grazhdan-musul'man, very-imamov i vsego naroda goroda Tashkenta i Tashkentskoi Oblasti UzSSR . . . v period s 1922 do nachala 1926 gg., osobenno v 1924–25gg," TsGA Uz, f. 904, op. 1, d. 32, ll. 33–38; "Prakticheskie zadachi, vytekaiushchie iz otsenki polozheniia sostoiat v sleduiushchem," RGASPI, f. 62, op. 1, d. 554, l. 312; RGASPI, f. 62, op. 2, d. 1593, ll. 17, 19; 8 January 1927 OGPU report on Muslim clergy, RGASPI, f. 62, op. 2, d. 1145, l. 8.

[59] Ramzi, *Khayoldan haqiqatga*, 55–57. In February 1928 the Central Control Commission of the Communist Party of Uzbekistan (TsKK KP[b]Uz), which was the party's internal ideological watchdog, circulated a memo emphasizing the need for struggle against "alcoholism, religious belief, and trust in alien elements," within the Uzbek party. "Po otchetu TsKK KP(b)Uz," 4 or 14 February 1928 (signed by A. Karimov), RGASPI, f. 62, op. 3, d. 205, ll. 22–24.

who survived not only the anti-Islamic persecutions of Stalin's time, but the Soviet Union itself.[60]

By the time Ramzi presented his guide for anti-Islamic propagandists in November 1927, Party officials had realized that propaganda alone was not going to help them achieve their goals, particularly not under the conditions and in the amount of time Stalin's planners were allowing them. The Party, primarily through the secret police agencies, turned from anti-Islamic propaganda to anti-Islamic violence, all the while continually denying that it had done so. As early as March 1927 the Central Committee of the Uzbek Communist Party advocated deliberately stirring up hostility among Muslim clerical factions and arresting clerics outright.[61] A 1929 or 1930 telegram from the area of Andijan cryptically stated that as part of the collectivization drive 1,038 "functionaries of the clergy have been cut down [*urezano*]." "Cut down" here seems to be in the sense of "their numbers were cut down by . . . ," which could mean that they were simply driven out of business, but possibly also arrested, exiled, and killed.[62] In the Old City of Bukhara in June 1929, to the horror of Uzbek Party officials, a unit of the OGPU converted the three-hundred-year-old Khudoiar-Otolik mosque into a stable for the use of its horses.[63] The Uzbek officials were horrified because they knew that this blatantly illegal action would stir up popular hostility against them, but also because the incident had occurred in June and they did not find out about it until August. It was a very clear illustration of the Party's lack of control over many peripheral areas.

Even so, the Party continued to approve of violence against clerics, mosques, and believers. Between 1927 and 1939, the decline in the clerical population of Uzbekistan was steep: by 72 to 80 percent in Ferghana oblast, by 79 percent in Andijan district, and by 68 to 73 percent in Uzbekistan overall. One may conservatively estimate, based on incomplete data, that at least ten thousand Muslim clergy were arrested and/or killed during this period.[64] Mosques suffered a similar fate: roughly 69 percent of the mosques in Uzbekistan were closed between 1917 and late

[60] Chantal Lemercier-Quelquejay, "From Tribe to *Umma*," *Central Asian Survey* 3, no. 3 (1984): 21–22.

[61] "K voprosu ob usilenii bor'by s dukhovenstvom (stenograficheskaia zapis' osnovnykh polozhenii)" (resolution of the Fifth Plenum of the TsK KP[b]Uz), PATsS-NDPUz, f. 58, op. 3, d. 152, ll. 5b–6.

[62] 'Vozvrashchat' Khoziaistva Chinovnikam-Dukhovenstvu Osnovnom Iavliaiushchikhsia Trudovymi" (the date is difficult to ascertain), RGASPI, f. 62, op. 1, d. 554, ll. 333–34.

[63] "O zakrytii mecheti 'Atalyk' v Bukhare i peredache ee pod koniushniu" (8 August 1929 session of I/B TsK KP[b]Uz), PATsS-NDPUz, f. 58, op. 5, d. 85, ll. 1–12.

[64] These estimates are put together from a variety of imperfect sources: PATsS-NDPUz, f. 58, op. 2, d. 955, l. 62; RGASPI, f. 62, op. 2, d. 1593, ll. 1–36; Rakhim(a) Aiubov, "Dokladnaia zapiska, 'O rabote Uzbekskogo Dukhovenstva,' " 13 February 1929, PATsS-NDPUz, f. 58, op. 5, 613, l. 11; "Svodka o nalichii i pol'zovanii molitvennykh domov razlichnykh reli-

1935, with a second wave of closings occurring between 1936 and 1938.[65] The number of ordinary believers who were beaten, arrested, or killed during this period, which includes the thousands of women who died as a result of the unveiling campaign, is impossible to estimate.[66]

While the tide of violence did a great deal of damage to Islam, especially in that it eliminated several generations of teachers and leaders, violence did not destroy religious belief, and it certainly convinced no one of the truth of Marxism-Leninism. What it did instead was to foster duplicity. The mass of rural believers learned to hide their rituals and customs under a variety of ruses, such as raising pigs as a show of their Communist faith.[67] In many cases the believers did not even have to hide their practices very well, since collective farm chairmen and other local officials, often Muslim themselves, tended to cooperate much more readily with believers than with atheists. In 1928 the OGPU complained that a prominent village Party member refused to unveil his wife and observed all traditional Muslim customs. When challenged, he reportedly replied: "I keep *Uraza*, perform my prayers, and if this is not suitable then expel me from the party—I will become a merchant."[68] This man had been a Party member since 1920, but had apparently missed many of the implications of Communist doctrine. On a more serious level, agents who tried to arrest underground clergy in the mid-1930s were harassed and physically attacked, while women on many collective farms continued to wear the veil long after it had been banned.[69]

gioznykh techenii po raionam i gorodam Uzbekskoi Respubliki" (signed by Deputy Chair TsIK Sovetov Manzhara and Director of the Special Section Gudkin), TsGA Uz, f. 86, op. 10, d. 770, l. 1; Comrade Zaiko, "Spravka: Net tochnogo ucheta sluzhitel'ei kul'tov," TsGA Uz, f. 837, op. 32, d. 1359, l. 99; UzSovnarkom "brigade members" Usievich, Mikhailenko, and Basharin, "Dokladnaia zapiska o sluzhiteliakh kul'ta po Bukharskoi Oblasti," TsGA Uz, f. 837, op. 32, d. 1269, l. 129; TsGA Uz, f. 837, op. 32, d. 1269, l. 147, 1 September 1939.

[65] TsGA Uz, f. 86, op. 10, d. 770, l. 1. This *opis'* also holds many records from the TsIK UzSSR Commission on Cults and its companion group the Commission for the Investigation of Petitions on Closing Mosques, Houses of Prayer, etc., which reported to the Presidium of the Central Executive Committee of Soviets (TsIK Sovetov). These two commissions oversaw the "legal" mosque closings during the second half of the 1930s, although they did not keep organized statistics.

[66] Women who unveiled were assaulted and/or killed, often by male members of their own families who were protecting family and religious honor. Because secret police documentation of these deaths was hugely inadequate by their own estimates, one can only make educated guesses as to the actual death toll. See Keller, "Trapped between State and Society," and Marianne Kemp, "Unveiling Uzbek Women: Liberation, Representation, and Discourse, 1906–1929" (Ph.D. diss., University of Chicago, 1998), 297–307.

[67] F. N. Oleshchuk, *XVII S''ezd VKP(b) i zadachi antireligioznoi raboty* (Moscow, 1934), 15.

[68] RGASPI, f. 62, op. 2, d. 1593, l. 13. In 1929 Commissariat of Justice officials also complained of local judges who could not work because they were fasting. TsGA Uz, f. 904, op. 1, d. 64, ll. 186–87. See also M. Mitrofanov, "Partiinoe i obshchestvennoe stroitel'stvo v kishlake," *Revoliutsionnyi vostok*, no. 7 (1929): 299.

[69] "O zaselenni dukhovenstva v kolkhoze 'Kommuna' Leninskogo raiona UzSSR: Po materialam na 25/III-1936 g.," PATsS-NDPUz, f. 58, op. 12, d. 638, l. 52; TsGA Uz, f. 837, op. 32,

Rural Muslims found underground ways to spread knowledge and observance. According to the émigré scholar Baymirza Hayit, the clergy organized a religious network in 1934–35, sending small groups of people, often from Sufi orders, to recite the Quran and preach in villages and cities: "The groups plunged into the crowd riding on hobby-horses [*Steckpferden*] and dressed in motley turbans. They were generally known in Turkestan as the 'Horseback *Ishans*.' At meeting places the people recited the Quran and performed after the pattern of the dervishes the rhythmic movements of the *zikr* [prayer ritual]."[70]

The NKVD began to crack down on these horseback *ishans* in the fall of 1935, condemning thirty-two of them to be shot in Kokand in October. The *ishans* were accused of promulgating the slogan, "The Komsomol for this world, the *murid* [Sufi follower] for the next," meaning that Communists should remain Muslims to ensure their well-being after death as well as in life. Apparently they, too, were trying to find ways to be both Muslim and Communist, according to their own notions.[71] The horseback *ishans* were only one of many groups of underground clergy who continued to function under the harsh conditions of Soviet rule.

Members of the urban educated elite, who benefited from Communism and the Western modernity it brought to Muslim areas, tended to retain at least a residual attachment to Islam. These people became the political leaders, the professional class, and the intelligentsia, who pronounced the right slogans at the right times but also were instrumental in helping their republics or national areas to break away from the tottering Soviet Union in 1989–91. They may have paid lip service to Marxism-Leninism, but they were no more true converts than the rural masses.[72]

The Bolsheviks, during the period discussed here, failed to replace Islam with Marxism-Leninism in Central Asia for many reasons. They put themselves in an impossible position by assuming that religion could be separated from other components of identity, and they failed to take into account the lasting power of ancient customs and rituals. They failed to heed the warnings of Sultan Galiev, who was correct in predicting that Muslims would never trust a system run by Russians that did not give them

---

d. 1359, ll. 99–100; Report on counterrevolutionary clergy, 10 April 1936, PATsS-NDPUz, f. 58, op. 12, d. 638, l. 93; E. M. Iaroslavskii, "Ob ocherednykh zadachakh antireligioznoi propagandy sredi natsional'nostei," *Antireligioznik*, no. 8–9 (1938): 23–26, noted the strength of the customs of bride price and the veil.

[70] Baymirza Hayit, *Turkestan im XX. Jahrhundert* (Darmstadt, 1956), 309. Hayit does not document this account.

[71] Ibid., 309–10.

[72] There are many new studies emerging that focus on Central Asian Muslim identity in the 1980s and later. See Nazif Shahrani, "Central Asia and the Challenge of the Soviet Legacy," *Central Asian Survey* 12, no. 2 (1993): 123–35; Jo-Ann Gross, ed., *Muslims in Central Asia: Expressions of Identity and Change* (Durham, N.C., 1992).

equal power in the government. Finally, when propaganda and education did not have their predicted effects the Soviets resorted to using violence to destroy Islam, a tactic that also completely obliterated any hopes of making Muslims into atheists.

The forces that ultimately had the biggest impact on Muslim society were not ideological but those that transformed everyday life. The radical changes wrought by the Soviets in the economic, social, educational and political spheres gave young Muslims a host of new opportunities, if they were willing to obey the Party's rules. Those rules included at least public lip-service paid to atheism, success in the educational system (which meant acceptance of the Russophilic, atheist values enforced there), and learning to say what superiors wanted to hear. However, the new Soviet structures and the pupils they produced did not begin to exert significant power until the late 1930s (with the generation that took power after the Terror) and did not take deep root until after World War II. Even then the Soviet system made its most profound impact on the small stratum of the urban elite; the vast majority of rural Muslims were less affected by the enforcement of Communist values.

Conclusion

The essays in this volume offer a variety of perspectives on the central theme of religion and empire in Russian history. Taken as a whole, they underscore the general point that religion was far from a hermetic, bounded realm of personal or even communal spirituality. It transcended the distinctions between public-private and spiritual-secular. It permeated personal subjectivity, intersecting and overlapping with numerous other dimensions of identity: nation, region, language, estate, race, occupation, class, gender, and political beliefs. It was important in the Russian empire's ideological underpinnings and was used as a tool in its day-to-day and year-to-year administration. It was no less central to the ways in which imperial subjects interpreted and negotiated their status and experiences.

This conclusion, and indeed the volume as a whole, cannot hope to encapsulate all of the various functions and meanings of religion in Russia. Instead, it focuses on the issues of missions, conversion, and toleration. In these essays, one can discern patterns in official preferences for different degrees of homogeneity in the empire, depending on the nature of different religions and the circumstances surrounding their practice. We can also make a number of generalizations regarding the methods used to pursue conversion, the success or failure of such efforts, and reactions to them among various groups. By way of such comparisons, we will attempt to specify where minority religions stood on a continuum between toleration and persecution in tsarist Russia.

The Russian state and church conceptualized the challenges presented by the different religions in the empire as a set of concentric zones or orbits extending outward from an Orthodox center. This scheme was not described explicitly except for a broad distinction sometimes made by the church between its "internal" and "external" mission, that is, its proselytizing activites to the nominally Orthodox and to the non-Orthodox. (Occasionally the church also used the terms "internal" and "external" to designate conversion efforts within the empire and outside the empire respectively.) Closest to the center were Old Belief and the various deviations from mainstream Orthodoxy known as the sects and the heresies. Further out were the other Christian religions: the Uniate, Catholic, Gregorian (Armenian), and various Protestant churches. Finally the non-Christian religions—Buddhism (Lamaism), Judaism, Islam, and a variety of tribal, polytheistic religions—were considered furthest from Orthodoxy.

Both Russian state and church authorities were most zealous with regard to pulling the religions thought of as within the Orthodox fold into the center where they would collapse into mainstream Orthodoxy. The reining in of such groups was usually not even thought of as "conversion." Because these groups posed the most direct challenges to the state church, they enjoyed the least tolerance of all. Before the manifesto on religious toleration of 17 April 1905, most had no legitimizing legal category, and it was illegal for anyone to practice them. (The Old Believers gained formal toleration in 1883, but it is not clear that this measure was honored in practice.) The priority given to eliminating this sphere was fairly constant during the imperial period, but it was pursued through a combination of missionary efforts and persecution that varied over time. Georg Michels and Eugene Clay both suggest that such efforts be compared with the Counter-Reformation campaign to rationalize and institutionalize Catholicism, not only to bring Protestants back into the church but also to educate the faithful so as to prevent further apostasy. Whether there was any clear historical demarcation between a purely confessional logic and the emergence of more nationalistic motives in the "internal" missions is hard to say, since Orthodoxy in Russia had always had its own "national" church. The integration of this innermost confessional zone into Orthodoxy was seen not only as more justifiable and more necessary, but also as easier to achieve than that of the others. It was not handicapped by significant linguistic or cultural differences.

Of course, the problem of achieving conformity and discipline within the ranks of the Orthodox was the sort of problem any church or state might face, even without a multiethnic empire. Yet in Russia the issues of forging an Orthodox religious community and the cultural construction of an empire could not easily be separated. Russians often saw the spread of their culture to the minorities of the empire simply as the nation-building process writ large. Because of new cultural influences and the sparseness of state institutions, Orthodox communities of Slavs who migrated into conquered borderlands required continual shoring up both for their own sake and for that of the new subjects the state wished to acculturate. Not accidentally, officials were stricter in the labeling and pursuit of so-called Orthodox heretics when these groups were active in politically sensitive borderlands of the empire, as were the Podgornites in the Ukraine.

Not all of the groups considered to be within the "internal" Orthodox fold, however, were Russian or Slavic. There were always non-Russian converts and descendants of converts who continued to practice other religions. Their formal, nominal membership in the church was enough to compel church and state to pursue their full integration. The most notable examples were Tatars, Bashkirs, Chuvash and other residents of the Volga-Urals region who had converted from Islam or indigenous religions after the Russian conquest but remained linguistically, socially, and religiously distinct from the Slavs. Authorities usually deemed retaining these people in the Orthodox Church to be crucial for the integrity of the political order. Because of cultural obstacles and the need to overcome the influence of the competing religion, efforts to return these groups to the fold were sometimes thought of as part of the "external" mission.

Moving outward to the next zone, one finds that the differences between Orthodoxy and other Christian denominations were not considered by Russian officialdom to be as threatening as deviations within Orthodoxy. Because most non-Orthodox Christians in the empire were categorized as Europeans, they were not subject to the same "civilizing mission" mentality that Russians felt toward non-Christian peoples. Therefore, few actual attempts were made to change the religious affiliation of Christian groups en masse. Frequently, however, constraints were placed on Christian churches, their clergy, and their schools to limit the spread of these faiths beyond a particular ethno-national constituency. Left entirely to their own devices, the state feared, other denominations might supplant Orthodoxy among Russians and destabilize the political and social order of multiethnic regions. Some Christian denominations such as Lutheranism were generally left alone, particularly when they were practiced by elites loyal and useful to the state; in fact, it is likely that occasionally the very policies being discussed here were initiated in part by Baltic Lutheran advisers to the tsars. Yet during the reactionary last decades of the nineteenth century, even some of these denominations experienced official assaults on their power and autonomy.

In the case examined by Theodore Weeks, one Christian denomination, the Uniates, saw official policy turn overnight from toleration to extreme persecution. In the background was the Polish question. Restraints were placed upon the practice of Catholicism in Russia because of its potential affiliation with Polish separatism, not because of some desire to Russify the Poles (let alone to "civilize" them). Those receiving the harshest treatment were the Uniates, who were thought of as half Orthodox and thus as within the church's fold. According to official opinion, the Uniate Church was a ruse for the cultural and political Polonization of Orthodox Russians. Particularly striking in the forced conversion of the Uniates was the considerable historiographical effort applied by Russian officials toward elaborating a particular version of the past. Even so, Weeks argues that the abruptness and recklessness of the measures taken in 1839 and 1875 came not from St. Petersburg officials (who tended to favor a more gradual, cautious approach to the process) but from regional authorities such as archbishops and provincial governors.

When one turns to the non-Christian religions of the empire, one also turns from West to East, or from Europe to Asia, in officials' classifications of the peoples in the Russian empire. The conversion of non-Christians to Orthodoxy underpinned the political theology of the Russian state and was an important tool of imperial expansion. But the actual process of conversion was least of all spiritual, and usually relied on a mixture of material incentives, intimidation, force, and official discrimination against those refusing to convert. Hundreds and even thousands of people were baptized at one time. Though there is evidence that church and state authorities made periodic, ritual pleas for missionaries to eschew heavy-handed approaches and focus on spiritual matters (for instance in the 1720s), these instructions were often half-hearted and were rarely heeded for long. Even though such conversions were ineffectual in the long run from the standpoint of subjective identities (usually resulting in only nominal changes in identity), they might appeal to secular authorities for administrative or economic reasons: for example, since conversion was in many cases accompanied by reclassification to serf or state peasant status, it often helped to reduce labor shortages. To the extent that conversion amounted to coercion, one can speak of religious intolerance in the most literal sense. And when coercion was countenanced by the state, such intolerance can be called official policy.

To be sure, throughout the tsarist period many secular and ecclesiastical officials held to a utopian vision of universal conversion to Orthodoxy by the empire's diverse subjects. But this vision usually fell victim to more practical, realistic considerations prevailing at particular moments. Implicitly, many essays in this volume stress the disincentives and obstacles to ambitious proselytizing and conversion. In some cases, priority was placed on the establishment of conformity among subjects closer to the Orthodox fold. In Kholmogory in the late 1600s and early 1700s, Bishop Afanasii may have reasoned that the church would be in no position to extend its influence over non-Christians without first establishing itself firmly among Russians in the region. Analogous conditions existed at various times in the Kalmyk and Kazakh steppe, where the respective missions to Buddhists and Muslims were limited by the presence of Old Believers or other Orthodox dissenters.

In many cases military or diplomatic concerns led authorities to tolerate non-Christian religions rather than to pursue homogeneity. Such matters were particularly important in the southern frontier regions, where the minority peoples had coreligionists living within the territorial boundaries of the Persian, Ottoman, and Chinese empires. The Russian government tried to avoid explicit pressure for conversion out of concern that the religious interests of people on the Russian side of the border could be used as a pretext for foreign intervention or expansion—which was exactly Russia's strategy with regard to the Ottoman empire and its Christian subjects. The eastern Caucasus was a particularly problematic area, with Muslim communities under strong influence of popular leaders in the bordering empires. No direct attempts to convert Muslims were advisable. The war fought by the muridists and Shamil against Russia in the second quarter of the nineteenth century forced a halt to all missionary work even in the parts of the Caucasus that had earlier been under Byzantine influence.

Even the Jews, the ethnic minority most often subject to persecution in Russia, were rarely the target of attempts at full-scale religious conversion. As John Klier shows, the most thorough and sustained effort to Christianize them took place in the second quarter of the nineteenth century through the military canton system, in which Jewish boy-conscripts as young as twelve years of age were forced to become Christians with no apparent regard for their own wishes or religious feelings. Yet the practice was abandoned after the reign of Nicholas I when Russian officialdom experienced a "loss of faith in the ethics of agressive conversion." Indeed after 1881, the state (if not the church, which was still occasionally training missionaries to proselytize among Jews) more or less stopped encouraging conversion altogether and redefined laws and quotas as pertaining to all persons "of Jewish origin." Klier argues that this was not because Jews were viewed from a racialist standpoint, but because the government simply did not want a deluge of insincere or duplicitous converts. Evidently, the aggressive conversion of Jews had been challenged on the basis not only of its ethics but also of its practicality.

Rather than replace hopes of conversion with an entirely laissez-faire stance toward religion, however, administrators usually chose a middle path of establishing special imperial administrations and hierarchies to domesticate and co-opt, in effect, the largest minority religions. This administrative approach seems to have originated in the eighteenth century under Catherine II, and might be thought of as the "modern" alternative to converting minority peoples outright. From different points in the eighteenth and nineteenth centuries, Islam, Buddhism, and Judaism were all subject to such imperial administration, along with some Christian churches. Such bodies were composed mostly of clergy of the religion in question, with a cleric at the top appointed by the tsar. On one hand, they represented formal approval of and even facilitation of the practice of these religions. On the other hand, by placing restrictions on religious institutions—maximum numbers and mandatory qualifications for clergy, approval processes for constructing places of worship, curricular requirements for confessional schools, limitations on religious contacts abroad, and special censorship of religious books—they would allow the state to control the overall influence of minority religions even while observing a principle of formal tolerance. They might also provide an indirect and relatively inconspicuous means of state intervention in favor of social groups more friendly to Russian rule. For example, the promotion of a particular official *ulema* (clergy) in the eastern Caucasus was hoped (in vain, as it turned out) to weaken the power of Sufi muridism during the guerrilla war.

Conversion was not abandoned in the nineteenth century, but a new attitude toward such work gradually developed. Blatant religious persecution had ebbed during the reign of Catherine II. In the era of romanticism that followed, national belonging was seen as a matter of inner essence, not simply external conformity. Moreover, most European churches were carrying out missionary efforts without the backing of coercive state force, and the Russians did not want to be a conspicuous exception. State and church, therefore, began to insist that religious conformity and conversion were mostly spiritual matters not to be tainted by more instrumental motives or external pressures. Missionary work came to be seen as rational persuasion requiring specific theological, cultural, and sometimes linguistic training in addition to exceptional personal qualities. The theological seminaries and academies devised special tracks for missionary education—for both "internal" and "external" missions. Eventually, the state followed by providing funding for special missionary posts. (These new "professional" missionaries are discussed by Clay with regard to missions against sectarianism and Orthodox heresy, and by Geraci with regard to missions against Islam.) Until the end of the tsarist period, the church had small numbers of personnel pursuing ostensibly voluntary conversions from all of the principal non-Christian religions on a small scale. The only fields in which proselytizing was really expected to yield large numbers of converts were those of the animist or polytheistic peoples and non-Russian apostates. In both these cases, the church's continued determination came not only from the moral condemnation of these subjects' religious status, but also from the fear that if these people were not won for Orthodoxy, they would join one of the competing world religions such as Islam or Lamaism. The resulting imbalance, it was thought, might weaken the Russian state or even jeopardize Russian culture. This was an abrupt reversal of the Catherinian policies which illustrates the displacement of the ideology of civilization by that of nationalism.

Sergei Kan describes the missionary bishop Ivan Veniaminov as an exemplar of the new, more tolerant and gradualist, approach to evangelization. An advocate of the notion that "civilization" corrupts as much as it enlightens, Veniaminov stressed religious education without also expecting the Europeanization his predecessors had demanded, such as Russian literacy, changes in residency and subsistence, or even the complete eradication of traditional beliefs and rites. Kan argues that the greater success of Veniaminov's Christianizing among the Alaskan Tlingits (which he compares with less successful Orthodox missions in Siberia) was in part due to Veniaminov's policy of separating religious conversion from secular governance, and suggests that this new approach to missions was correlated with the church's assertion of its own independent sphere in Alaska. Though the "spiritualization" of missions was manifest in many parts of the empire in the nineteenth century, it may have had a head start in Alaska because that region was not governed directly by the Russian state but by a private monopoly, the Russian American Company. The effectiveness of this approach became most evident, in fact, after Russia sold Alaska to the United States and the mission became wholly "external" to Russia proper. The Alaskan mission, therefore, was of all Russian conversion efforts the one most resembling those undertaken by the churches of Western Europe in colonies overseas.

Among the Buriats and the Kalmyks, according to Dittmar Schorkowitz, the "enlightened" method never seemed to take hold. In the Baikal region, which was administered more directly, the missions were under much firmer state control, with the Holy Synod cooperating with the Ministries of Internal Affairs and State Domains. Their methods were also cruder, with spectacular (and purely formal) mass baptisms of shamanists and Lamaists being performed up until the end of the nineteenth century. The Kalmyk steppe was administered separately by the Ministry of State Domains and was thus less subject to pressures from other government bodies. As a result, the ministry was able to stall the introduction of missions into the steppe in order to avoid the abuse of converts that had occurred in Siberia. In the last third of the century, other ministries encouraged mass conversion efforts among the Kalmyks, but the campaign never became as extensive or as violent as the Buriat campaign.

The failure of " enlightened" approaches to Orthodox conversion in the Volga region in the late nineteenth century figures prominently in the essays by Paul Werth and Agnès Kefeli. Many participants in the Mari ethnic-religious revival were defectors from Orthodoxy, as were many Kriashens who were closer to the resilient Muslim Tatar culture of the region than to Russian Orthodox culture. Werth and Kefeli are both concerned with the nature of local alternatives to Orthodoxy, and both suggest that the rejection of Orthodoxy had perhaps more to do with feelings about community than with religious doctrine. The adherents of Kugu Sorta in fact adopted much of the worldview they had been exposed to by the Orthodox, but were intent on remaining separate from the Russians and their church. To some extent, Russian missionaries had undermined their own attempt to decouple Orthodoxy and Russian identity; they were largely responsible for the spread of native literacy and ethnic consciousness among the Mari. Russian missionaries also attempted to bolster the separate identity of the Kriashens (the descendants of Tatars and others converted to Orthodoxy in the sixteenth through eighteenth centuries), but in this case they were too late. Instead of remaining with the Orthodox Church or asserting their own distinctive religion and identity, most Kriashens eventually were drawn to the Muslim Tatars. Culturally and economically they had always been more dependent on Tatars than on Russians, for they spoke Tatar. Before the 1860s, Islamic education and Arabic literacy (even for girls) were much more readily available than Russian schooling. Moreover, Kefeli suggests, the Orthodox missionaries made a serious error in regarding Tatar and Kriashen women as passive victims of Islam. In fact, women played an important role in the spread of Islamic teachings, and their activities largely escaped the attention of church and state authorities.

In many cases where conversion was still pursued it was packaged so as to appear more justified, more realistic, and less manipulative than before. Just as the term "reunion" (*vozsoedinenie*) was used to describe the conversion of the Uniates, the name of the Society for the Resurrection of Christianity in the Caucasus invoked the return of Muslims to a similar historical norm or destiny. For the Kazakhs, the argument was not that they had once been Christian but that they had been converted to Islam only recently and superficially. In both cases, the retention of some animist practices was used as supposed evidence that these peoples' conversion to Christianity was not such a lost cause as among other Muslims.

Another strategy for sweetening the pill of pressure to convert to Orthodoxy was the use of non-Russian personnel. In the Caucasus, eighteenth-century conversion campaigns were carried out in part by Georgian priests. Similarly, Weeks notes, after the 1863 Polish uprising the state called in not Russian but Austrian clergy to promote the "Russifying" measure of purging the Uniate churches and rites of Polish-Catholic elements. In the Kazakh steppe, the missions hired non-Russian personnel trained under the Il'minskii system for the sake of providing subject communities with teachers and clergy more familiar with their languages, more culturally accessible, and less chauvinistic than Russians. Such measures may indicate not only a desire to mask the Russifying aspects of conversion but also considerable difficulty in finding Russian personnel capable and willing to engage in missions.

Officially, then, the trend during the last century and a half of tsarist rule was toward considerable formal "tolerance" and protection of minority religions, both Christian and non-Christian. Yet this was counterbalanced by a high degree of special state protection of official Orthodoxy, and a clear understanding that the non-Orthodox were second-class citizens. In effect, religious categories were demarcated and regulated by the autocracy much as estate (*soslovie*) categories were. Religious diversity was "tolerated" only in a particular configuration established by the state in accordance with perceived historical and ethno-national conditions. For most of the tsarist era, and for some groups during its entirety, formal religious affiliation could not be chosen freely, and to practice a religion without formal affiliation was a crime. To be sure, this state of affairs did not restrict religious practice or provoke unrest as much as forced universal membership in the Orthodox Church would have, but still it did not amount to real freedom of worship and did not always hold back unrest. The Muslim spiritual administration established for the Caucasus in 1869 under the Ministry of the Interior, Mostashari tells us, failed to garner the respect of the Muslim people. In the Volga region, the regulation of Muslim clerical qualifications and confessional schools through the muftiate and the Ministry of Education was a continual source of public disorder. Although the religions themselves were tolerated in a spiritual sense, then, were so many "domesticating" restrictions piled up on the minority faiths through their "self"-administrations (usually far beyond the regulations imposed on the Orthodox religion or even other Christian churches) that the situation came to resemble persecution more than tolerance? And although conversion was supposed to be pursued only by peaceful and tactful means, did coercive behavior on the part of church and state officials in the borderlands make official "tolerance" appear hypocritical?

Judging from the circumstances around and responses to the toleration law of 17 April 1905, the answer to these questions is yes. The law, vaguely labeled "On the Strengthening of the Foundations of Religious Toleration," effected an actual change from intolerance to toleration only for Old Believers and Orthodox sects, whose religions were now accepted as legitimate. Conversion from Orthodoxy to Christian denominations outside of the Orthodox orbit was now legalized as well: previously, all besides the Uniates had already been "tolerated" yet not allowed to spread freely. In a sense, conversion from Orthodoxy to non-Christian religions was legalized, but the law stipulated that one could return formally only to a faith one had actually never stopped practicing. In other words, it remained illegal to leave Orthodox practice to embrace one of these religions, but became legal to nullify Orthodox status that had been only nominal (though the church and state had sometimes granted this before 1905 in any event). The large exodus from Orthodoxy to other religions occurring in the aftermath of this decree (noted in many of these essays), was in part legally sanctioned and officially processed, and in part unregulated and illegal. This development spoke eloquently of the huge failure and very limited success of centuries of tsarist efforts at the cultural integration of the empire. Many church and state personnel were so outraged and alarmed by it that they sought to counteract it by any means possible. This explains the paradox of simultaneous "blossoming and persecution," in Dittmar Schorkowitz's words, not only of Lamaism but indeed of many minority religions after 1905.

The last essay in the volume, that of Shoshana Keller on the Soviet anti-Islamic campaign, helps us to place the tsarist system in perspective. Much of the discussion pertains to Soviet antireligious campaigns in general, not only those against Islam. The essay highlights the analogies between tsarist attempts to supplant particular religions with Orthodoxy and Soviet attempts to replace all religions with secular thinking and Marxist-Leninist doctrine.

The Bolsheviks did not agonize over the question whether to erase religious worldviews from the Soviet population and "convert" them to socialism. The scientific basis claimed by their ideology seemed to allow no compromise. As to how to achieve the desired changes in mentality and identity, though, they faced quandaries not unlike those of the tsarist administrators: how to counteract and overcome the communal tenacity of a religion as well as its doctrinal persuasion, whether to favor gradual and piecemeal change or "shock therapy," how to uproot religious forms of identity while preserving others such as nationality, and so on. For a decade, the Communists attempted to take an "enlightened" approach: exhibiting sensitivity to particular religions and cultures, focusing on persuasive and peaceful means, and trying not to antagonize and alienate their subjects. In light of the tsarist experience, it is hardly a surprise that Stalin and the Bolsheviks quickly lost patience with such means and resorted to intimidation and violence. Nor is it surprising that even this method did not always produce the desired result, as Keller shows, often simply driving religious worship underground or creating strange syncretic identities as in the case of the "Muslim Communists."

The religious diversity of the Russian empire has until recently been a relatively neglected issue in the historiography of Russia. Within a short time, however, interest in it has exploded as a result of the collapse of the Soviet Union and of Communist rule all over Eastern Europe. Interethnic and interconfessional warfare and the continuing potential for communal conflict in this part of the world should convince skeptics that studying the interplay between religious, ethnic, and national identities in culturally diverse societies and empires is more than a purely academic pursuit.

Notes on Contributors

J. EUGENE CLAY is an associate professor in the Department of Religious Studies at Arizona State University. He has published several articles on the history of Christian dissent in Russia from the seventeenth century to the present. He is currently writing a historical survey of Russian sectarianism.

ROBERT P. GERACI is an assistant professor of history at the University of Virginia and the author of *Window on the East: National and Imperial Identities in Late Tsarist Russia* (forthcoming with Cornell University Press, 2001). He is currently researching the relationship between nationality and capitalist entrepreneurship in imperial Russia.

SERGEI KAN is a professor of anthropology and Native American studies at Dartmouth College. He has been conducting ethnographic and archival research in southeastern Alaska since 1979, and is the author of *Symbolic Immortality: The Tlingit Potlatch of the Nineteenth Century* (Smithsonian Institution Press, 1989) and *Memory Eternal: Tlingit Culture and Russian Orthodox Christianity through Two Centuries* (University of Washington Press, 1999). He has edited a forthcoming collection of essays, *Strangers to Relatives: the Adoption and Naming of Anthropologists in Native North America* (University of Nebraska Press, 2001), and is writing a biography of the Russian anthropologist Lev Shternberg.

AGNÈS KEFELI is an instructor of Tatar language at the Critical Languages Institute of Arizona State University and a Ph.D. candidate in the Department of History at the same university. She is completing her dissertation,

"Kriashen Apostasy: Popular Religion, Education, and the Contest over Tatar Identity (1854–1917)." She also holds graduate degrees from the University of Paris and the Ecole des Hautes Etudes en Sciences Sociales.

SHOSHANA KELLER is an assistant professor of Russian and Eurasian history at Hamilton College. Her book *To Moscow, Not Mecca: The Soviet Campaign Against Islam in Central Asia, 1917–1943* is forthcoming with Praeger Publishers.

MICHAEL KHODARKOVSKY is an associate professor of history at Loyola University Chicago. He is the author of *Where Two Worlds Met: The Russian State and the Kalmyk Nomads, 1600–1771* (Cornell University Press, 1992) and *From Steppe Frontier to Russian Empire: Colonial Encounters in the Southern Borderlands, 1500–1800* (forthcoming with Indiana University Press, 2001).

JOHN D. KLIER is Corob Professor of Modern Jewish History and head of the Department of Hebrew and Jewish Studies at University College London. He has published widely on Russian-Jewish relations, most recently *Imperial Russia's Jewish Question, 1855–1881* (Cambridge University Press, 1995) and *Rossiia sobiraet svoikh evreev* (Moscow and Jerusalem: Most Kul'tury/Gersharim, 2000).

GEORG MICHELS in an associate professor of history at the University of California, Riverside. He is the author of *At War With the Church : Religious Dissent in Seventeenth-Century Russia* (Stanford University Press, 2000).

FIROUZEH MOSTASHARI is an assistant professor of history at Regis College in Weston, Massachusetts. She has published articles on Russo-Azerbaijani relations and is currently preparing a book on Russian colonialism.

DITTMAR SCHORKOWITZ is an anthropologist and historian of Russia's non-Slavic nationalities. He is the author of *Die soziale und politische Organisation bei den Kalmücken (Oiraten) und Prozesse der Akkulturation vom 17. Jahrhundert bis zur Mitte des 19. Jahrhunderts: Ethnohistorische Untersuchungen über die mongolischen Völkerschaften* (Frankfurt: Peter Lang, 1992) and most recently of *Staat und Nationalitäten in Russland: Der Integrationsprozess von Burjaten und Kalmücken, 1822–1925* (Stuttgart: Franz Steiner, 2001). He is also interested in problems of violence in the Caucasus and the Balkans. He is a lecturer at the East European Institute, Free University of Berlin, and editor in chief of the series *Gesellschaften und Staaten im Epochenwandel.*

THEODORE R. WEEKS is an associate professor of history at Southern Illinois University in Carbondale. He is the author of *Nation and State in Late*

Imperial Russia: Nationalism and Russification on the Western Frontier, 1863–1917 (Northern Illinois University Press, 1996) and articles on nationality in the Russian empire's western borderlands. He is presently working on a book-length study of Polish-Jewish relations and the beginnings of modern Polish antisemitism during 1855–1914.

PAUL W. WERTH is an assistant professor in the History Department at the University of Nevada, Las Vegas. He is currently completing a study entitled *At the Margins of Orthodoxy: Mission, Governance, and Confessional Politics in Russia's Volga-Kama Region, 1827–1905* (forthcoming with Cornell University Press). He is also working on a study of religious toleration in the Russian Empire from the late eighteenth to the early twentieth century.

Index